POLS

POLS

Great Writers on
American Politicians
from Bryan to Reagan

EDITED BY

Jack Beatty

PUBLICAFFAIRS
New York

Published in the United States by PublicAffairs™,
a member of the Perseus Books Group.

Book design by Jane Raese
Text set in Granjon

Library of Congress Cataloging-in-Publication Data
Pols : great writers on American politicians from Bryan to Reagan / edited by Jack Beatty.
p. cm.
ISBN 1-58648-015-4
1. Politicians—United States—Anecdotes. 2. United States—Politics and government—
20th century—Anecdotes. I. Beatty, Jack.
E747.P65 2004
973'.09'9—dc22
2004050591

FIRST EDITION

10 9 8 7 6 5 4 3 2 1

CONTENTS

INTRODUCTION

Pols collects some of the best biographical and historical writing I know of. The writers need no selling from me. I chose them for their quality and for the variety of approaches taken to their subjects. Conrad Black defines FDR's greatness; Richard Hofstadter draws an intellectual portrait of Herbert Hoover. Lou Cannon discusses a source of Ronald Reagan's success—his humor; and William E. Leuchtenburg lights up FDR's shadow on LBJ's successes and failures. Vachel Lindsay panegyrizes William Jennings Bryan, Philip Roth satirizes Richard Nixon. C. Vann Woodward depicts the tragedy of a politician ahead of his time—the populist leader Tom Watson; and Norman Mailer, in his account of the 1960 Democratic National Convention, treats John F. Kennedy as a cynosure of the latent energies of a decade he would not survive. David McCullough takes us aboard the *Ferdinand Magellan* for Harry Truman's 1948 whistle-stop campaign. Fred Greenstein revises the reputation of President Dwight D. Eisenhower; Arthur M. Schlesinger, Jr., revises Ike revisionism. Ronald Reagan vs. Tip O'Neill: The clash of titans frames John Aloysius Farrell's essay. In "ER, Political Boss," Blanche Wiesen Cook chronicles Eleanor Roosevelt's coming-of-age in the 1920s; in an excerpt from *Boss,* Mike Royko gives us a day in the life of Chicago mayor Richard J. Daley. John Dos Passos captures TR in a prose poem; Robert A. Caro narrates the life of Sam Rayburn in the grand manner. Garry Wills explores the themes of rejection and respect in Jesse Jackson's life and politics, while Richard Ben Cramer dramatizes the moment when George H. W. Bush decided to risk the respect that was his birthright to defeat Michael S. Dukakis.

Thanks to the people at PublicAffairs behind *Pols*: Peter Osnos, publisher, who came up with the idea and title of the book; David

Patterson, Melanie Peirson Johnstone, and Katherine Miller, who guided it skillfully across a course of hurdles faced uniquely by anthologies, and William Whitworth, to whom it fell to edit book chapters into stand-alone essays, a feat made the more difficult by his—and my—reluctance to part with a single word of them. Bill counseled me for and against selections, and I was smart enough to take his advice. Having worked with him for nearly twenty years at *The Atlantic Monthly*, I knew its value. In the line of *Atlantic* editorships that starts with James Russell Lowell's in 1857 and extends to Cullen Murphy's today, William Whitworth's will be remembered for his qualities: intellectual, aesthetic, and moral integrity; clarity of thought and expression; curiosity about every aspect of human experience; reasoned engagement in American politics and the issues of public life; and a commitment to making things—the family, the school, the country, the world—better. I dedicate this book to him for his achievement, his example, and his friendship.

Special thanks to my agent, Rafe Sagalyn, who makes it possible for me to earn my living; and my wife Lois, who makes it possible for me to live.

POLS

Tom Watson

REBEL OF A LOST CAUSE

"The tradition of all the dead generations weighs like a nightmare on the brains of the living."
— KARL MARX

The rise and fall of Tom Watson is the saddest story in American political history. Watson (1856–1922) was a lawyer of jury-swaying eloquence who became a power in Georgia politics by leading the Populist revolt of the 1890s in which white and black farmers found common ground in common grievance. When that revolt was crushed, Watson lost his way—fell back on a paranoid politics fed by morbid vulnerability to loss. Arbitrary punishment and emotional abuse in childhood, he once wrote his wife, left a "scar" on his heart: "The better part of me is poisoned. A mistaken train-ing leaves a trace from which there is no escape . . . had I not been abused, ridiculed, mocked and scorned there would be sunshine where now is shadow . . ." These formative injuries made him liable to fantasies of persecution: "I have imagined enemies where there were none; been tortured by indignities which were crea-tures of my own fancy, and have magnified the gloom of every reverse." Watson became a prisoner of these tendencies after 1896 and led many of his followers into his lurid world. "A frustrated man and a frustrated class," C. Vann Woodward writes in *Tom Watson, Agrarian Rebel* (1938), "found that their desires and needs were complimentary."

Watson started out blaming the "interests" for the Populist defeat, which was fair enough. But his anger needed people. So, in increasingly symptomatic projections, he imagined new enemies of the southern farmer—blacks, Catholics, and Jews—and in *Watson's Jeffersonian Magazine* and other publications he wrote things that have got men killed. The politician who had championed class unity over racial division now defended lynching. The race card played against him by his political enemies, he brooded, kept him from becoming the William Jennings Bryan of Populism, so he supported Jim Crow laws that removed blacks from politics. His attacks on Catholics and Jews were bait to Bible Belt prejudice, pornographic essays in negative solidarity.

"What is the matter with thomas e. watson?" a Georgia newspaper asked in a front page headline. An accompanying editorial called Watson "the basest, most depraved, most poisonous man in Georgia today." On his death a liberal journal held Watson responsible for the "sinister forces of intolerance . . . , prejudice, religious jingoism, and mobbism" that had revived the Ku Klux Klan in the South. But Watson, Woodward writes, "did not produce those forces; he was produced by them." Watson's story "is in many ways the tragedy of a class, and more especially the tragedy of a section."

The last cabinet meeting of the Confederate States of America took place near Tom Watson's home in Washington, Georgia. The war was over; the slave-based economy of the Old South was no more. The New South began in a kind of economic Fall from which its leading sector, agriculture, never recovered. A pattern of adverse change worked against the southern farmer. Cotton, his one cash crop, brought $1 a pound just after the war, but barely nine cents a pound by the '90s. Populist rhetoric blamed the railroad "tyrants" who overcharged farmers and "the grasp of the gigantic, cold-blooded money trust" that starved them for credit. But the proximate cause of the farmer's fall was the central institution of the postwar southern economy, the lien system of financing agricultural production.

"Emancipation had erased the slave system's massive investment in human capital," Lawrence Goodwyn explains in *The Populist Moment*, "and surrender had not merely invalidated all

Confederate currency, it had also engendered a wave of Southern bank failures." In many southern counties the only creditor was the "furnishing merchant," the proprietor of the town store. To obtain the supplies needed to begin planting, the farmer borrowed from the merchant against the collateral of next season's crops at interest rates often exceeding 100 percent. With ever-falling prices for those crops, the farmer could rarely settle his loan. So, year on year, he borrowed to retire a debt that cruelly receded before him. The merchant required him to grow only cotton, and to buy everything from his fertilizer to his clothing only from the merchant's store—and at prices marked up 20 to 50 percent. "At the same time he signed away his right to buy in the cheapest market," Woodward writes, "the farmer pledged himself to sell in the lowest market . . . Such was the strait-jacket in which from eighty to ninety percent of the cotton growers, proprietors and tenants, black and white, normally found themselves."

This cycle of futility wore out Tom Watson's father, and cost him his farm. As a lawyer Tom defended people caught in similar predicaments, good men driven to thievery, even violence, by despair. With homespun jokes, with lachrymose appeals to fellow feeling garnished by quotations from literature and the Bible, he played off the class resentments of juries, making a name for himself as a "tribune of the people." Instead of liberalism, the South has personal-injury lawsuits, the journalist Nicholas Lemman observed in a recent *New Yorker* profile of Senator John Edwards (D., N.C.), who made a fortune as a trial lawyer off damages awarded his clients. But *class* injustice cannot be ameliorated at the trial bar. Remedy must be sought through politics. The sentiments Tom Watson mined in court made fallow ground for Populism.

Populism rose up from the southern farm. It had scattered roots—in Texas, Arkansas, Alabama—among groups of farmers resisting railroad rate increases and seeking an alternative to lien-slavery. These groups merged in the Farmer's Alliance, which, "in one of the most amazing feats of organization in American history, attained a membership of three millions in the South alone by 1890." The Alliance platform called for unprecedented state intervention in the economy, including state ownership of railroads and the establishment of a "sub-treasury" to replace the lien system. The federal government would open warehouses, or "subtreasuries," in which farmers could store their crops while waiting for prices to rise and using the crops as collateral for low-interest federal loans.

This program of democratic radicalism appealed to Watson, who had been feeling his way toward it while serving in the Georgia state legislature, where he attacked the nexus between state government and the railroads. He first served the Alliance as a lawyer taking on the "jute bagging trust," which had doubled the price of the bagging used to cover cotton bales. In a well-circulated speech to an audience of Alliance men Watson attacked the bagging trust as "a symbol of the wrong they put upon us . . . "—and "they," we feel, is a wider category than "jute baggers" could ever fill. The jute baggers capitulated, the Alliance took heart, and later that year (1889) Watson ran for Congress. The Alliance vote, black and white, put him over. He went to Washington as a Democrat, but broke with the party over its truckling to big business, and returned to Georgia in 1892 as a candidate for reelection of a newborn third party. The Alliance began as a self-help organization, forming purchasing cooperatives and other instruments of economic autonomy. But corporate power in league with southern state governments frustrated these efforts. So the Alliance, as the People's Party, entered politics to wrest control of government from its enemies.

Since the end of Reconstruction the South had known only one-party rule. To defeat a Democrat a candidate had to capture black, nominally Republican, votes. Blacks were not yet completely disfranchised; they had made the difference for Watson in 1890. But he had run as a Democrat then. The Democrats were the white man's party, and they branded defectors to the People's Party as traitors to their race. Watson, trying to change the subject of southern politics from race to class, was ahead not only of his time but of ours. The momentum of the same past that defeated him is still unspent. In the 2002 elections a sitting governor of Georgia was turned out by white rural voters angry over his decision to reduce the size of the Confederate emblem on the state flag. In the following selection Woodward evokes the passion and violence aroused by the Populists' bi-racial appeal.

RACE, CLASS, AND PARTY
C. Vann Woodward

Speculating upon the approaching struggle for reelection, Watson wondered whether the people understood the nature of the conflict before them. It was, he believed, the same struggle that in the past had been fought "upon the field of battle, behind barricades, in the streets of cities, about the scaffold and guillotine ... but never at the ballot box, as it will next October and November." It was, in his terms, the struggle between "Democracy and Plutocracy":

> We wonder if the people generally understand the full significance of this fact? Do our friends understand it? Do our enemies appreciate its meaning? If so, then the coming contest will be sharp indeed. There will be neither asking nor giving of quarter, for upon both sides there will be the consciousness that the contending forces are not unequally matched, and that as they represent totally different and opposing ideas and theories, there can be but one settlement of the matter at issue, and that it must come through the utter overthrow of the one or the other of the parties to the contest.

Before proceeding further it might be well to arrive at some understanding of the nature of these combatants who had such "totally different and opposing ideas and theories." Who were the Populists?

Aside from the new factory proletariat of a few cities (themselves of recent rural origin), the Populists were agricultural and rural. But so were the great mass of people of the state and of the South, and that mass was divided by class and race lines. Were they exploiters or the exploited?

In answering such questions the Populists themselves were confusing. In resolving themselves into the People's Party, the Oglethorpe County Alliance referred to its members as "the peasantry of America." On the other hand, a Populist of Douglas County said, "Some of our people were once rich, and most all were well to do . . . and it is no fault of theirs that they are reduced to such straights [*sic*]." Tom Watson struck nearer the truth when he said, "You stand for the yearning, upward tendency of the middle and lower classes." Therefore, they were "the sworn foes of monopoly—not monopoly in the narrow sense of the word—but monopoly of power, of place, of privilege, of wealth, of progress." Individualist and middle-class in tradition and aspiration, they accepted the basic capitalistic system. Watson summed up their objectives: "Keep the avenues of honor free. Close no entrance to the poorest, the weakest, the humblest. Say to ambition everywhere, 'the field is clear, the contest fair; come, and win your share if you can!'"

In general, the southern Populists were mainly the agrarian masses, including tenant, small landowner, and a surprising number of large landowners, together with the industrial proletariat. They were united by their resentment of the crushing oppression of capitalist finance and industrialism. Watson himself recognized the complexity of his ranks. "There is a gradation in servitude," he said. The laborer was the first to feel the lash, the cropper next, the tenant next, and the landlord next—in Watson's hierarchy of serfdom. "But," he added, "the livery of the serf is there all the same." This livery, he believed, would become the uniform of the army that he led against its oppressors.

Tom Watson was himself one of the largest landowners in the state, with more tenants on his land than his grandfather had slaves. There were other large landowners high in the party ranks, who fought side by side with small farmers and tenants. In this regard a remark of Charles A. Beard upon the battles of Jefferson's day might be recalled: "It is a curious freak of fortune that gives to the slave owning aristocracy the leadership in a democracy of small farmers, but the cause is not far to seek. In a conflict with capitalism, the agrarians rallied around that agrarian class which had the cultural equipment for dominant direction." There is room for doubt whether there was an "aristocracy" of the tidewater sort in Georgia. At any rate, the former slave-owners were divided in the 'nineties. While some became Populists, many of the larger owners became merchants, bankers, and small capitalists, and fought the Populists as bitterly as did the businessmen of the towns.

It is undoubtedly true that the Populist ideology was dominantly that of the landowning farmer, who was, in many cases, the exploiter of landless tenant labor. But about half of the farms in the state at that time were operated by owners, dirt farmers, and the rank and file of the Populists were of this poverty-ridden small farmer class. They were surely more exploited than exploiting, and the Populist contention that the tenant was in the same boat as the owner had much truth in it. The southern urban proletariat was yet an embryonic class, largely of immediate agrarian background. They were not yet class-conscious, and thought more as farmers than as industrial workers. Obviously the Populist attack did not strike at the whole system of capitalist exploitation, as did socialism, but in its time and section the Populist Party formed the vanguard against the advancing capitalist plutocracy, and its fate was of vital consequence to the future.

That class contradiction was not magically resolved in the Populist-agrarian potpourri is indicated by various signs. Once the Colored Farmers' Alliance proposed to call a general strike of Negro cotton pickers. The *Progressive Farmer,* paper of Colonel L. L. Polk, president of the National Alliance (white), did "not hesitate to advise our farmers to leave their cotton in the field rather than pay more than 50 cents per hundred to have it picked." The Negro brethren were attempting "to better their condition at the expense of their white brethren. Reforms should not be in the interest of one portion of our farmers at the expense of another."

The Populist struggle in the South, moreover, was fought under such peculiar circumstances as to set it apart from the history of the national movement, and to call for special treatment. "Political campaigns in the North," wrote a veteran of Alabama Populism, "even at their highest pitch of contention and strife, were as placid as pink teas in comparison with those years of political combat in the South."

Taking into comparative account the violence of the passions un-loosed by the conflict, the actual bloodshed and physical strife, one is prepared to give assent to that judgment.

What explained the bitterness and violence that characterized the Populist struggle in the South? To answer in a word—"race." And that is much too simple an answer. But if to race be added the com-plexities of the class economy growing out of race, the heritage of manumitted slave psychology, and the demagogic uses to which the politician was able to put race prejudice—then "race" may be said to be the core of the explanation.

In later life Watson once wrote a retrospective (and quite candid) comparison of his own career with that of William Jennings Bryan. In it he said: "Consider the advantage of position that Bryan had over me. His field of work was the plastic, restless, and growing West: mine was the hide-bound, rock-ribbed Bourbon South. Besides, Bryan had *no everlasting and overshadowing Negro Question to hamper and handicap his progress:* I HAD." There is no doubt that Watson thought of the Negro problem as the nemesis of his career. He fled it all his days, and in flight sought every refuge—in attitudes as com-pletely contradictory and extreme as possible. At this stage, however, he faced his problem courageously, honestly, and intelligently. As the official leader of the new party in the House, and its only Southern member in Congress, Watson was the logical man to formulate the Populist policy toward the Negro. This he did in a number of speeches and articles.

The Populist program called for a united front between Negro and white farmers. Watson framed his appeal this way:

> Now the People's Party says to these two men, "You are kept apart that you may be separately fleeced of your earnings. You are made to hate each other because upon that hatred is rested the keystone of the arch of financial despotism which enslaves you both. You are deceived and blinded that you may not see how this race antagonism perpetu-ates a monetary system which beggars both."

This bold program called for a reversal of deeply rooted racial prejudices and firmly fixed traditions as old as Southern history. In place of race hatred, political proscription, lynch law, and terrorism it was necessary to foster tolerance, friendly cooperation, justice, and political rights for the Negro. This was no small task; yet Watson met each issue squarely.

It should be the object of the Populist Party, he said, to "make lynch law odious to the people." Georgia at that time led the world in lynchings. Watson nominated a Negro to a place on the state executive committee of his party, "as a man worthy to be on the executive committee of this or any other party. Tell me the use of educating these people as citizens if they are never to exercise the rights of citizens." He spoke repeatedly from the same platform with Negro speakers to mixed audiences of Negro and white farmers. He did not advocate "social equality" and said so emphatically, since that was "a thing each citizen decides for himself." But he insisted upon "political equality," holding that "the accident of color can make no difference in the interests of farmers, croppers, and laborers." In the same spirit of racial tolerance he was continually finding accomplishments of the Negro race at home and abroad to praise in articles and speeches.

Tom Watson was perhaps the first native white southern leader of importance to treat the Negro's aspirations with the seriousness that human strivings deserve. For the first time in his political history the Negro was regarded neither as the incompetent ward of White Supremacy, nor as the ward of military intervention, but as an integral part of southern society with a place in its economy. The Negro was in the South to stay, insisted Watson, just as much so as the white man. "Why is not the colored tenant open to the conviction that he is in the same boat as the white tenant; the colored laborer with the white laborer?" he asked. With a third party it was now possible for the Negro to escape the dilemma of selling his vote to the Democrats or pledging it blindly to the Republican bosses. Under Watson's tutelage the southern white masses were beginning to learn to regard the Negro as a political ally bound to them by economic ties and a common destiny, rather than as a slender prop to injured self-esteem in the shape of "White Supremacy." Here was a foundation of political realism upon which some more enduring structure of economic democracy might be constructed. Never before or since have the two races in the South come so close together as they did during the Populist struggles.

No one was more keenly aware of the overwhelming odds against his social program than Tom Watson. In an article in the *Arena* he wrote:

> You might beseech a Southern white tenant to listen to you upon questions of finance, taxation, and transportation; you might demonstrate with mathematical precision that herein lay his way out of poverty into comfort; you might have him "almost persuaded" to the truth, but if the merchant who furnished his farm supplies (at tremendous usury) or the town politician (who never spoke to him excepting at election times) came along and cried "Negro rule!" the entire fabric of reason and common sense which you had patiently constructed would fall, and the poor tenant would joyously hug the chains of an actual wretchedness rather than do any experimenting on a question of mere sentiment. . . . The Negro has been as valuable a portion of the stock in trade of a Democrat as he was of a Republican.

. . .

A westerner, the most eminent student of Populism, has remarked, "Perhaps only a Southerner can realize how keenly these converts to Populism [in the South] must have felt their grievances." A southerner might add, "only a southerner of that period"—which followed close upon Reconstruction. The motives of the most sincere Populists were not above the basest construction by Democrats, many of whom were perfectly honest in their suspicions. It was widely believed that they were in secret alliance with the Republicans, and therefore not only traitors to their section, but to their race as well—enemies of white civilization. The worst slander, however, was the product of editors and politicians who believed that any means was justified by the end they had in view. When a responsible editor wrote that "The South and especially the tenth district is threatened with anarchy and communism" because of "the direful teachings of Thomas E. Watson," there were thousands who believed him literally. Populists were subjected to every type of epithet, scurrility, and insult Democrats could devise. There is record of Populists' being turned out of church, driven from their homes, and refused credit because of their beliefs. Families were split and venomous feuds started. As already noted, one of Tom Watson's brothers was secretary of the mass meeting that pronounced him a traitor; a second brother, a merchant, remained a Democrat, and a third became a Populist. A southern Populist leader told a western writer, "The feeling of the Democracy against us is one of murderous hate. I have been shot at many times. Grand juries will not indict our assailants. Courts give us no protection."

To overcome the harsh penalties attached to revolt—the compulsions of tradition as well as economic pressure making for conformity—there must have been tremendous forces at work upon the southern masses. It is furthest from the intention of this work to suggest that adequate cause can be discovered in the eloquence of Thomas E. Watson, or the eloquence of anybody else. More eloquent than any orator in the cause of revolt were the hard times of 1891–1892 that opened the "heart-breaking 'nineties."

After a two weeks' tour of observation in the cotton belt of Georgia in December 1891, the editor of the *Southern Alliance Farmer* wrote that "the farmer has about reached the end of his row." The crop was selling at "the lowest price that cotton has reached in a third of a century," and "hundreds of men will be turned out of house and home, or forced to become hirelings and tenants in fields that they once owned. . . . The doors of every courthouse in Georgia are placarded with the announcements of such [sheriffs'] sales. Hundreds of farmers will be turned adrift, and thousands of acres of our best land allowed to grow up in weeds through lack of necessary capital to work them. . . . The roads are full of negroes begging homes." There was a veritable "epidemic of distress and foreclosures of mortgages now sweeping over our state." The president of the Burke County Alliance wrote Watson: "Our county is in a terrible, terrible condition. Out of fifteen hundred customers at one store only fourteen paid out; five hundred paid less than 50 cents on the dollar." Mrs. W. H. Felton wrote, "We sold our cotton crop in 1892 for a little over four cents the pound, and it did not pay taxes, guano, and farm supplies."

In the factory slums of the New South, where tenement houses had hardly weathered gray yet, hunger and destitution prevailed. The

Atlanta *Journal* reported that just outside Atlanta in the workers' district of the Exposition Mills—the mills that occupied the same buildings in which Henry Grady hailed the birth of the New South just ten years before—"famine and pestilence are to-day making worse ravages than among the serfs of Russia." The millworkers are paid "the magnificent sum of 36 cents a day for their labor, and . . . the average wage fund in the factory district is 9 cents a head divided among the members of the family." The bodies of their dead remain unburied. One may see "rooms wherein eight and ten members of one family are stricken down, where pneumonia and fever and measles are attacking their emaciated bodies; where there is no sanitation, no help or protection from the city, no medicine, no food, no fire, no nurses— nothing but torturing hunger and death."

"There is a song in the fields where the plowshare gleams," wrote one editor, "a song of hope for the harvest ahead, and the man at the plow-handles seems happier than he has been, as the furrows are formed at his feet." "Yes," answered Tom Watson, "'there is a song in the field'—and it begins, 'Good-by, old party, Good-by,' and ends with a cheer for the St. Louis platform [of the People's (Populist) Party]." Patrick Walsh was more forthright in his appeal: "We know the farmers of the South are impoverished and discontented," but "Better, a thousand times better, suffer the ills of the present, suffer poverty, rather than . . . division and separation from the Democratic party."

The farmers felt differently about poverty and the Democratic Party. In Watson's district "as well as all over the State . . . the People's party element have been meeting twice a month, on Saturday afternoon, in schoolhouses, for two years, and signal fires are on every hilltop. They are imbued with the spirit of turning things upside down."

The Democratic campaign against Watson's reelection, and against Populism in general, had no beginning. It was simply continuous with the battle of 1890. The bitter former head of the Alliance in Georgia, L. F. Livingston, spent a good part of the spring of 1892 on a speaking campaign throughout Georgia against Watson and Populism. At his home town, however, the local Alliance met before he spoke and endorsed the People's Party and the St. Louis platform. The same action was taken in other places where he spoke. At Douglasville the revolt was dramatized by circumstances. A mixed throng was waiting at the courthouse yard to hear Livingston meet a Populist champion in debate, when the president of the county Alliance mounted the steps, announced that the Democratic speaker would not abide by the terms of the debate agreement, and called upon all who counted themselves Populists to adjourn to the Alliance warehouse across the railroad. "Cross over the railroad bridge so everybody can see," yelled someone. "With cheer upon cheer the great crowd swayed and broke—the great majority of those composing it turned their steps toward the warehouse," crossing over the high, arched footbridge into the rebel ranks.

The Democratic State Central Committee met and issued an appeal to the people of the Tenth District. "The chief of the Third Party in Georgia [C. C. Post] is a Republican and an infidel," they proclaimed. "He believes neither in Democracy nor in our God." Populism is the work of "selfish and designing men" who preferred, "like Satan, to rule in hell [rather] than serve in Heaven. . . . Come back, brethren, to the good old Democratic ship. . . . Come back, brethren, come back." An eminent Methodist divine informed the people that a Populist victory would result in "negro supremacy," "mongrelism," and the "destruction of the Saxon womanhood of our wives and daughters." It was reported that merchants were refusing credit to all farmers who did not disavow the intention of voting the Populist ticket.

The old party was shrewd in its selection of a candidate to oppose Watson in his race for reelection. Major James Conquest Cross Black, an Augusta lawyer, was the very blossom of middle-class respectability and conservatism. He was a deacon in the Baptist Church and for years had conducted an adult Sunday school class. Born in Kentucky in 1842, he had served as a private in the Confederate Army. His title of "Major" was honorary, after the southern manner.

In 1890 Black had publicly denounced the Farmers' Alliance. He summed up his political ideology by saying, "He was a Democrat because he was a Georgian." His eloquence was mentioned in terms of awe. It was reported that "an Augusta lawyer actually and seriously asked for a new trial in a case when a jury had assessed heavy damage" on the ground that Major Black's eloquence "had swept the jury beyond bounds of propriety and practicability." The Superior Court, however, held that "nobody but God Almighty could fix the bounds or limit the influence of human eloquence."

Not content to rely upon Black's God-given eloquence, however, his party rushed its heaviest oratorical artillery to Watson's district. A special election to fill the insignificant office of county ordinary in Glascock brought Senator John B. Gordon, Governor William J. Northen, Patrick Walsh, and Major Black down upon the citizens' heads. Governor Northen informed the voters that C. C. Post was an "infidel," an "anarchist," and, on top of that, "an infamous cur." His wife was "an atheist herself," who "makes $1,000 a month selling her damnable heresy." It was no breach of the code of southern chivalry to attack Mrs. Post because "she has unsexed [sic] herself." When Mrs. Post denied the charge and Mr. Post resented it, the Democratic press advocated "a sound caning and notice to leave the state," for having "cast the lie in the face of Georgia's chief executive." Mobbing was too good for "the atheistic, anarchistic, communistic editor of the *People's Party Paper.*"

A month later the governor renewed the attack, "setting the crowd wild" when he asked, "Shall they strike down Gordon and uphold Post, the foulest of God's creatures?" At this, it was reported, "Every drop of blood seemed to boil in the veins of the patriotic audience." The governor then read what he alleged was Jerry Simpson's charge, "that our men sold their honor and our women their virtue." General Gordon interrupted to say, "My God! Hear that, Third Party men. Hear that!" It was said that "A look of solemn thought that could not be mistaken spread over the faces of the Third Party division of the audience." General Gordon, who introduced himself as "a farmer and nothing but a farmer," also spoke in an informing manner of "this preacher of atheism, this sympathizer with bloody-handed anarchy, this shameless defamer of our spotless, pure and peerless Southern womanhood. (Cries of Never, Never, Never.)" Major Black, said the general, "illustrates that lofty and chivalric manhood, which next to the South's peerless womanhood, is her most flawless crown of im-mortality." In discussing Watson's candidacy, he pointed out that he was "base," "false," "cowardly," and a "self-important little fly." In answer to Watson's searching article on Gordon's fantastic political and business career, the General reviewed his own record in the Con-federate Army.

"Senators left the halls of Congress," wrote Watson from Washing-ton, "and swooped down to the attack; Governors left the State House and flopped down to the attack; chairmen of executive com-mittees, editors" joined them in the strife, and with what result? The Populist candidate for county ordinary was quietly elected by more than a two to one majority. It was the first Populist victory over the Democrats at the polls in Georgia.

.   .   .

Georgia Democrats were thoroughly alarmed by the prospects, but, because this was a presidential election year, they could not—as they did in 1890—make sweeping pledges of radical reform. Bound to their reactionary capitalist allies of the East, they obediently chose electors at their state convention pledged to Grover Cleveland. Wat-son described this meeting: "Protectionists like Pat Walsh and Evan Howell, sweetly smiled as they swallowed the pill on the Tariff Ques-tion. And the Cleveland men like Hoke Smith tried to look pretty as they voted for Free Silver, which Cleveland repudiated. And the 'Al-liance Democrats' strove to appear happy in a convention which scornfully spat upon their demands." After the national convention nominated Cleveland, Watson rejoiced: "The Harrison and Cleve-land wings of Plutocracy have been driven in upon each other, and are open to an aggressive movement. The atmosphere has cleared wonderfully and the battle is now on."

At the national convention of the People's Party in Omaha, Wat-son's lieutenants, Post, Ellington, and Branch, played prominent roles. The third party, particularly in the solidarity of the southern states, suffered an irreparable injury in the death of Colonel L. L. Polk a few weeks before the convention. His nomination for the presidency was practically agreed upon. Being a southerner of wide popularity, he would have provided a powerful opponent of Cleveland in the South. The nomination of General James B. Weaver, a western veteran of many reform battles, was thought unfortunate by some, particularly in the South. C. C. Post, in changing Georgia's vote to Weaver, said his state had been one of the strongest opponents of the nominee. Watson, along with other southerners, had been mentioned as a possible nominee for vice president, but the nomination went to General James G. Field of Virginia to balance the Union general on the ticket.

The first state convention of the Populists in Georgia appears to have been a model of harmony. The delegates met unpledged, and nominated candidates (none of whom had spoken in their own behalf) by acclamation, "and without resort to ballot." The main purpose of the delegates, observed a Democratic paper, seemed to have been "to glorify Watson, and they did it elaborately and with unction." Enthusiasm and confidence were boundless.

Through all these events Watson had remained in Washington. The news that he was returning to take personal command in Georgia was greeted by newspaper-men with cheers. "It means that whatever the rest of the earth may do, the good old tenth district will furnish its full proportion of news . . . there may be no news at all, but the night editor sitting at his desk may feel no fear; the tenth district will be astir. From one end to the other its political fires will be ablaze and plenty of choice, entertaining news will come in every night. . . . The Colonel [Watson] has in him those picturesque elements that appeal to the newspaper mind. He is not prosaic. He is individual. He illuminates his public career with the brilliance of imagination."

Before the train reached the border of his district it was met at every station by cheering crowds of Populists and boarded by a delegation who accompanied him home. At Thomson between four and five thousand "yeomen" met him, carried him on their shoulders to a gaily decorated carriage, and drew him to a stand erected for his speech. "Proud Caesar," said the *Chronicle,* "never entered the gates of imperial Rome with more pomp and éclat than did Mr. Watson enter Thomson today." He addressed them for two hours and a half, giving a detailed account of his "stewardship," arraigning the Democratic Party, and making a plea to "wipe out the color line, and put every man on his citizenship irrespective of color."

It was observed by several that he looked "pale and emaciated" upon his return. At the end of his speech he was seized with a violent fit of vomiting. His greatly increased burden was apparently telling on his strength. C. C. Post had managed party affairs during Watson's absence, but not long after Governor Northen's vicious attack upon him and his wife, a mob at Quitman attacked Peek, the Populist candidate for governor, and Post, striking Post with a rock. Whether because he believed his life endangered or for some other reason, it was immediately after this—on the day Watson arrived from Washington—that Post announced that he was leaving for Michigan.

Stranded in the midst of a seething battle without an official leader, the party now leaned for leadership upon Watson. On his shoulders also fell the editorship of the *People's Party Paper.* To these burdens was added the handicap the Democrats had devised in 1891 by gerrymandering his district so as to exclude two old counties and add two new ones, Hancock and Wilkinson. The new counties, observed Watson in his private journal, "had not belonged to my District when I was elected and therefore did not understand the issues upon which I had defeated Hon. Geo. T. Barnes." This meant additional campaigning and organization. Watson's victory in Burke County, which was now removed, had been "considered by politicians as the most important victory of his campaign" in 1890.

Along with these discouragements and handicaps there were a few happier experiences. On his return he was greeted with the first number of *The Revolution,* a new Populist paper published in Augusta, bearing under its title the quotation, "'Not a Revolt; It's a Revolution'—Thomas E. Watson." This along with *The Wool Hat* of Gracewood provided a genuine, if crude, expression of the feelings of the radical farmer element. His own paper reported twenty-two Populist papers published in Georgia in September 1892. The throngs of cheering rebels that gathered at county seat and crossroads to hear their hero carried silken banners thirty and forty feet long inscribed with Populist slogans and pictures of Watson. To the tune of "The Bonny Blue Flag" they sang "The Young Wife's Song," written by Watson:

My husband came from town last night
As sad as man could be;
His wagon empty—cotton gone—
And not a dime had he.
He sat down there before the fire,
His eyes were full of tears;
Great God! how debt is crushing down
This strong man—young in years!

Huzza! Huzza! It's queer I do declare!
We make the food for all the world,
Yet live on scanty fare.

Although Major Black accepted Watson's formal challenge, and several meetings occurred between them, the three months' campaign that followed was far from resembling a formal debate. It was a bitter struggle that raged back and forth across the state, its most intense battles centering in the Tenth District. The "debates" were seldom more than party rallies, where rival generals reviewed their troops and made a show of force.

At Thomson, Black repeated some of the usual charges against C. C. Post. C. H. Ellington, president of the State Alliance, leaped up to defend Post. "And we are not ashamed of him!" he shouted. The next moment "pistols and knives were drawn and the adherents of the two parties stood before one another at bay. . . . Bloodshed and wholesale riot was only narrowly averted." One fight broke out after the meeting, and the following day Ellington and a Democrat fought in the streets of Thomson.

In providing special trains to the rallies, the railroads were obliged to set apart separate cars for the two parties. Even then strife was not prevented. As a train pulled out of Thomson, a passenger yelled out, "Hurrah for Col. Black! Watson is a deserter from the Democratic Party and sold out!" "You are a God damned liar," asserted Watson. The unfortunate Democrat had not reckoned with the vigilance of his man. Over two passengers Watson leaped, laying his defamer low in the aisles and bruising him considerably before they were separated. When the conductor remonstrated, the congressman would brook "no truckling to petty officials of the Southern Railroad."

The audience at Sparta was predominantly Negro, and on the platform with Watson sat a Negro speaker. On the outskirts of the crowd a brass band from the Democratic barbecue, in progress down in the grove, kept up a din. During Watson's speech a man on horseback pushed his way into the crowd shouting, "A free dinner for everybody; you are all invited down to the barbecue—white and colored." "You may have the trees," shouted Watson, "but we have got the men; and these men are not going to be enticed away from free, fair discussion of these great public questions by any amount of barbecued beef!" The dusky ranks held firm though dinnerless—even remaining to escort the speaker to his boarding house.

Major Black's constantly reiterated theme was that "it is un-American and un-Christian, arraigning one class against another," that he was "a friend of all classes," and that the farmer's distress was "exaggerated." Watson's repeated answer was that there was "an irrepressible conflict between the farming interests and Democracy . . . between the laboring classes and the old party." As for exaggeration of the farmer's distress: "when I am addressing people who bend over the cotton rows to pick out six-cent cotton which costs them eight cents, there is no need to dwell on the topic."

For forty-five minutes after Black finished his speech at their joint meeting in Augusta, Watson was unable to make himself heard. He finally had to give up the attempt. At the capitol in Atlanta the following week he was howled down again by an organized band who kept up the cry of "communism," a charge recently made by Governor Northen.

The following morning at eight o'clock General Weaver, his wife, and their party arrived in Atlanta to fill a speaking engagement. The Populist candidate for president had received a respectful hearing on his southern tour until he reached Georgia. There the Democratic press whipped up fury against him by charges of "cruelty and oppression" practiced on the people of Tennessee by Weaver during the war. The day before he arrived in Atlanta a gang of Democrats at Macon had rotten-egged General Weaver while he spoke, striking Mrs.

Weaver on the head. When he learned of the treatment dealt Watson at the capitol, Weaver canceled all engagements and abandoned his campaign in Georgia. Explaining to the state chairman of the People's party, he wrote:

> I find the spirit of organized rowdyism at some of the points visited within the state so great as to render it unadvisable for me to attempt to fill the engagements at points not already reached. Personal indignity was threatened at Waycross . . . at Albany we were met by a howling mob which refused to accord us a respectful hearing . . . at Macon . . . rotten eggs were thrown prior to the introduction of the speakers, one of which struck Mrs. Weaver upon the head.

Watson's reply to these Democratic tactics was stinging. "Remember," he wrote, "that for the first time in the history of the Republic a Presidential candidate has been driven from the hustings, and his wife found no protection in her sex from the brutal attacks of 'Southern chivalry' as represented by Bourbon Democracy! They call us the ragtag scum of creation. Thank God, we have never yet dreamed we could win our way to public favor by insulting women, and striking them in the face with eggs." State chairman Irwin, in a letter "To the Voters of Georgia," proclaimed that "The scenes that have been enacted in Georgia during the month of September are only repetitions of Revolutionary France before the crisis came. . . . It is generally believed that plans are being perfected to defraud the People's Party of its vote. Vehement rage prevails wherever People's Party speakers obtain a hearing. . . . The times are ominous. They resemble the days that preceded secession and civil war. There will be bloodshed and death unless there is a change."

To the plea made to Governor Northen by the Populist candidate for governor, that the governor assist him in obtaining a fair division of election managers, Northen, after considerable delay, replied that he could "see no reason now to believe that the proper authorities desire or intend fraud at the coming state election." To the Populists, however, it seemed plain enough that the Democratic machine was bent on employing every device of terror and fraud it had learned and perfected in Reconstruction fights—together with a few new ones.

From Washington, Georgia, was issued a circular addressed "To the Democratic Farmers and Employers of Labor of Wilkes County," and signed by the Democratic chairman of that county. It warned of the impending peril of a Populist victory and advised:

> This danger however can be overcome by the absolute control which you yet exercise over your property. It is absolutely necessary that you should bring to bear the power which your situation gives over tenants, laborers and croppers.... The success [of the Populists] ...means regulation of control of rents, wages of labor, regulation of hours of work, and at certain seasons of the year strikes....
>
> The peace, prosperity, and happiness of yourselves and your friends depend on your prompt, vigorous and determined efforts to control those who are to such a large extent dependent upon you.

Other Democratic handbills and circulars flooded Watson's district: one to prove that he had defeated "a Worthy Colored Man's Claim in Congress"; another on Watson's opposition to a colored contestant's claim upon a seat in the Georgia Legislature in 1882; another to prove him in the pay of Republican bosses.

As the day of the state election approached threats became coercion and coercion turned into bloodshed and open battle. The *Chronicle* reported three homicides in Augusta in a few days preceding the election, which, according to the editor, were "the natural results of paternal, socialistic and communistic utterances of reckless third party leaders." On election day, Dan Bowles, Democrat, was "marching a line of 50 negro voters to the polls" six miles out of Augusta when he encountered a group of Populists. Isaac Horton, a Negro Populist, sought to disengage one Negro from the line, and a general fight ensued. Bowles shot Horton through the heart. Verdict, "justifiable homicide." On the same day, in Augusta, Henry Head, a Democratic deputy sheriff, was shot through the stomach while attempting to arrest Arthur Glover, secretary of the Populist Campaign Club in the Fifth Ward, a workers' district. Glover escaped to the South Carolina woods, a posse after him.

At Rukersville, Elbert County, a white man, a Populist this time, was on his way to the polls with "a squad of negroes and white men," when encountered by B. H. Head and other Democrats. Head recognized in the Populist "squad" some Negroes "who had once lived with him and who bore the name of Head." Becoming infuriated, Head picked up a wagon standard and struck an old Negro. The Negro's son then struck Head, after which the latter ran across the street to his home, returned with a double-barrelled shotgun, and "deliberately shot down two Negroes," one of whom died. Another white Democrat drew a pistol and shot three Negroes, after which the Populists were driven from the polls. One estimate had it that fifteen Negroes were killed by Democrats in Georgia during the state election. "If the law cannot protect us," warned a correspondent of Tom Watson, "we will protect ourselves with Winchesters."

Watson professed to be encouraged by the results of the state election. The Populist candidate for governor was defeated by a two-to-one vote. "But three months have passed," Watson reminded the Democrats, "between the organization of the People's Party and the election, and in the rock-ribbed state of Georgia more than one-third of the hosts assembled at the polls adhered to the People's banner."

With the state election out of the way, the Democratic machine could now concentrate its full attention upon the fight on Watson. "So intense is the interest and concern felt in the campaign," said the *Constitution,* "that even here in Atlanta . . . nothing is talked of except the race between Black and Watson. Men declared at the democratic headquarters yesterday that they would much prefer to see Black elected than Cleveland. They viewed it as the supremest issue in Georgia to beat Watson, for they declare that he will endanger the peace and prosperity of the South if his incendiary speeches are not hushed."

The election in the Tenth stirred interest in a wider circle. "The first question asked by everyone when the probabilities of the South are considered is, 'What are Watson's chances?'" "Mr. Watson is now a national character and there is not a single congressional contest going on in the nation that is being looked upon with as much interest as the one in his district." President Cleveland was reported to have

remarked to a group of Georgians after the election that "he was almost as much interested in Major Black's campaign in the Tenth district of Georgia as he was in his own election."

Others in the North made more practical manifestations of their
interest in the defeat of Tom Watson. Augusta businessmen made
personal appeals to their financial connections, "especially those in
New York City," for campaign funds. They argued that Watson was
"a sworn enemy of capital, and that his defeat was a matter of importance to every investor in the country." The New York *Tribune* reported that "Insurance and railroad companies responded liberally, so
that $40,000 was in hand for use, in addition to the local funds."

After his experience with his opponents' methods in the state election, Watson could not face the congressional election without misgivings. "They have intimidated the voter, assaulted the voter,
murdered the voter," he wrote. "They have bought votes, forced
votes, and stolen votes. They have incited lawless men to a pitch of
frenzy which threatens anarchy." To his private journal he confided:
"It was almost a miracle I was not killed in the campaign of 1892.
Threats against my life were frequent and there were scores of men
who would have done the deed and thousands who would have sanc-
tioned it. Fear of the retaliation which my friends would inflict prevented my assassination—nothing else." Governor Northen was
heard to say that "Watson ought to be killed and that it ought to have
been done long ago."

"There is no wiping out the fact that this is a revolution," observed
a Populist paper, "and it depends upon the enemy whether it shall be
a peaceful or a bloody one. To be candid about the matter we believe
it will be the latter."

One of the most zealous and effective workers for Watson's cause
was H. S. Doyle, a young Negro preacher. In the face of repeated
threats upon his life, Doyle made sixty-three speeches during the
campaign in behalf of Watson's candidacy. Toward the close of the
campaign Doyle met with a threat of lynching (called "imaginary" by
the Democratic press) at Thomson, and fled to Watson for protection.
Watson installed him on his private grounds and sent out riders on
horseback for assistance. All night armed farmers roared into the village. The next morning the streets were "lined with buggies and

horses foaming and tired with travel." All that day and the next night they continued to pour in until "fully two thousand" Populists crowded the village—arms stacked on Watson's veranda. Prominent among them was the Populist sheriff of McDuffie County. They marched to the courthouse under arms, where they were addressed by Doyle and Watson. "We are determined," said the latter, "in this free country that the humblest white or black man that wants to talk our doctrine shall do it, and the man doesn't live who shall touch a hair of his head, without fighting every man in the people's party." The farmers remained on guard for two nights.

"After that," testified Doyle, "Mr. Watson was held almost as a savior by the Negroes. The poor ignorant men and women, who so long had been oppressed, were anxious even to touch Mr. Watson's hand, and were often a source of inconvenience to him in their anxiety to see him and shake hands with him, and even to touch him."

The spectacle of white farmers riding all night to save a Negro from lynchers was rather rare in Georgia. So shocking was the incident to the Democratic press, so clearly subversive of order and tradition, that their indignation knew no bounds. "Watson has gone mad," announced the *Chronicle,* and the *Constitution* gravely agreed. The whole South was "threatened with anarchy and communism" because of "the direful teachings of Thomas E. Watson."

That the danger to Doyle was not imaginary seems indicated by the fact that the following week, when he was speaking at Louisville, a shot intended for the speaker struck a white man in the back and killed him. Two days later when Watson and Doyle spoke at Davisboro they were accompanied by a guard of forty men carrying rifles. The following week another Negro was shot and killed by a white Democrat in the county where the previous murder occurred. At Dalton a Negro man who had spoken for Populism was murdered at his home by unknown men.

From Watson's town came the report that "nearly all the ladies whose husbands are Democrats have left Thomson, and many Democratic families have moved away, as they feared their lives were in danger." The mayor of the city appealed to Governor Northen for "six or eight hundred soldiers" on election day, for fear "the third party people would burn the town and massacre the Democrats." A battalion in Atlanta and three companies in Augusta received "orders to march to Thomson at a moment's notice."

A careful scholar's characterization of the Georgia election of 1892 as a "solemn farce" admits of possible error only in the choice of the adjective. That it was a farce is clear enough. Reconstruction practices of terror, fraud, corruption, and trickery were all revived. Democrats found little difficulty in identifying the "cause" of 1892 with the "cause" of 1872, and justified any means by calling the end holy. Populists retaliated in kind to some extent, but they were not nearly so skillful or successful.

Federal supervisors under the direction of United States marshals were in attendance at the polling in Augusta, but against the Democratic local police they were powerless to prevent wholesale repeating, bribery, ballot-box stuffing, voting of minors, and intimidation. Negro plantation hands and laborers were hauled to town in wagon loads, marched to the polls in squads, and voted repeatedly. Negroes were hauled across the Savannah River from South Carolina in four-horse wagonloads and voted in Augusta. Whiskey was dispensed by the barrel in Augusta wagon yards, and cash payment made to voters.

By such methods as these Watson was defeated. At that, he carried by ample majorities all counties within his district before it was gerrymandered, with the exception of Richmond. Of the two new counties, Wilkinson's vote was nearly a tie, and scores of Populist votes were "not allowed," while the irregularities in Hancock were notorious. Most flagrant were the abuses in Richmond County, where Black received 10,776 of the total of 17,772 votes he received in the whole district. The total vote in Augusta was about double the number of legal voters.

The attitude of many Democrats in Georgia was much the same as that expressed by those of Alabama over the same election: "Yes, we counted you out. What are you going to do about it?" It even crept into unguarded paragraphs of Democratic editorials. At Augusta the victors celebrated by an elaborate funeral ceremony, in which "Watson was laid out in great state."

"Who believes it?" asked Watson of the result. "Not the Democratic bosses who stole the ballots. Not the managers who threw out returns. Not the newspapers who have to 'cook' their news with such care. Not even the candidates who received the stolen goods. Nobody believes it. Least of all do we of the People's party." In one month, between the state and the national election, the Democratic majority dwindled from 71,000 to 31,000. "So we decided not to die. We unanimously decided to postpone the funeral."

He proclaimed himself undismayed at the result. Considering the fact that not a single daily paper in the state was friendly to the Populists, that "all the machinery was against us; all the power of the 'ins'; all the force of old habit and old thought; all the unseen but terrible cohorts of ignorance and prejudice and sectionalism," as well as "all the money . . . all the concentrated hatred of capital, special privilege," he refused to take too tragic a view of the election returns. The national poll of the third party was truly phenomenal, but its greatest hope—the breakup of the Solid South—was disappointed. Watson's work was still before him.

With spontaneous impulse the defeated hordes of Populists marched on Thomson from all over the district to voice their feelings against the fraudulent election and commiserate with their leader. "Four thousand then," announced Watson. "Six thousand today, and growing stronger and stronger as Democratic methods and frauds become more apparent." At ten in the morning the firing of a small cannon, which they brought with them, announced the arrival of the delegation from Richmond. It had marched from Augusta to Watson's doorstep—a distance of thirty-seven miles! With much heat and enthusiasm resolutions condemning the election methods were adopted, and $877.95 was raised (much of it in small coin) to finance a contest of Black's election before the House.

Before he returned to Washington for the second term, Watson announced that he would "in all possible and proper ways carry on the third party fight. I am determined never to give it up as long as I live."

Excerpted from C. Vann Woodward, *Tom Watson, Agrarian Rebel* (New York: Oxford University Press, 1963), pgs. 186–209.

William Jennings Bryan

GIGANTIC TROUBADOUR

William Jennings Bryan (1860–1925) has had a bad Hollywood.
Frederic March's portrayal of him as a Bible-thumping reactionary defending ignorance in the Scopes "monkey trial" in
Inherit the Wind (1957) made Bryan ridiculous to later generations,
who knew naught else of him. He died ridiculous to the urban
sensibility of his own generation, just days after testifying in the
trial that man was *not* a mammal.* "Bryan lived too long, and
descended too deeply in the mud," H.L Mencken wrote in his
obituary, "to be taken seriously hereafter by fully literate men,
even of the kind who write schoolbooks." The mud included
defending the Ku Klux Klan.

"A man can be born again; the springs of life can be cleansed
instantly," Bryan once wrote. But his reputation has yet to be resurrected, and the paradoxical role of faith in his career suggests
why. The evangelical Christianity that led him to condemn evolution also lent conviction to his social progressivism—he championed women's suffrage, the income tax, and the direct election of
senators, among other reforms—and his peace activism.

How could the same man who espoused enlightened causes
believe that a real Jonah sojourned in the belly of a real whale and
that the moral well-being of a modern society could depend on

---

*"[L]ike every other man of intelligence and education I do believe in organic
evolution," Woodrow Wilson said in 1912. "It surprises me that at this late date
such questions should be raised." Campaigning for president in 2000, George
W. Bush said, "[O]n the issue of evolution, the verdict is still out."

taking Biblical fish stories literally? Our reactionaries tend to be all of a piece, from the mud up. Bryan eludes us, breaks our categories, as faith does. But call faith "principle" to take the Jesus out of it, and Bryan emerges as among the most principled politicians in American history—on the strength of one act.

As a new book on the sinking of the *Lusitania* reminds us, Bryan resigned as secretary of state in the Wilson administration to protest the President's bellicose note to Germany, which Bryan feared could drag the U.S. into the European slaughter. Bryan had seen the end of the war in its beginning. "It is not likely that either side can win so complete a victory," he presciently wrote in a 1914 letter to Wilson, "as to dictate terms, and if either side does win such a victory it will probably mean preparations for another war." Among Bryan's losing crusades—"He had rather be wrong than president," Speaker Thomas Reed once quipped—was his call for the creation of international machinery to settle disputes between nations short of war. In his conception the United States should lead this effort by acting as the world's peace broker. He saw the Great War as the New World's opportunity to save the Old, and repeatedly urged Wilson to mediate between the Powers: "As the greatest Christian nation, we should act." But Wilson put him off, while the American ambassador to Britain, Walter Hines Paige, schemed with the Foreign Office to work around Bryan, end U.S. neutrality, and bring America into the war on the Allied side.

Wilson owed his nomination to Bryan's support, and their break hurt both men and embarrassed the administration. At Bryan's last cabinet meeting, a colleague urged him to reconsider. Over 100 American lives had been lost on the *Lusitania,* a British passenger liner—carrying, Bryan pointed out to Wilson, war supplies to Britain—and public feeling against Germany ran high. Don't, his colleague warned, "destroy yourself." Bryan replied: "I believe you are right. I think this will destroy me. But whether it does or not, I must do my duty by my conscience."

Maledictions rained down upon him.

"Unspeakable treachery"—the *New York World.* "Stabs—yes, let it be said—stabs the United States in the back"—the *Philadel-*

phia Inquirer. "Men have been shot and beheaded, even hanged, drawn and quartered, for treason less heinous"—the *Louisville Courier Journal.* The publicity, including salutes from western newspapers, made Bryan the leading voice of the American peace movement. "If others desire that our flag be feared," he told audiences across the country, "let us [resolve] that it shall be loved."

Bryan's Biblical faith was risible—and the source of his moral strength. In 1915 his vision of America as "the Nazerene's" instrument for world peace motivated as brave an act as ever taken by an American statesman. If only Robert S. McNamara or Colin Powell had shown such courage.

Vachel Lindsay's "Bryan, Bryan, Bryan, Bryan" evokes another of Bryan's victory-in-defeats, casting the "Great Commoner" as David of the agrarian West battling the Goliath of eastern capital in the presidential election of 1896. That clash of Americas pitted Bryan, a thirty-six-year-old Nebraska congressman who had captured the nomination of a divided Democratic Party with his stirring "Cross of Gold" speech at their Chicago convention, against former Ohio governor and congressman William McKinley. McKinley was the creature of Mark Hanna, a mining and traction magnate. From businessmen frightened by Bryan's "radicalism," Hanna collected $16,000,000 in campaign funds to spend against Bryan's $600,000. And yet Bryan, a tireless campaigner with a pharyngeal miracle of a voice, gave Hanna and his millions a race.

Those who heard it—and they included Clarence Darrow, his nemesis at the Scopes trial—never forgot the Cross of Gold speech. "Having behind us the producing masses of this nation and the world," Bryan perorated, "supported by the commercial interests, the laboring interests, and the toilers everywhere, we will answer their demand for a gold standard by saying to them: You shall not press down upon the brow of labor this crown of thorns, you shall not crucify mankind upon a cross of gold." It was a depression year, and they were Democrats. "They roared their lungs out," John Dos Passos wrote in USA, "(crown of thorns and cross of gold) carried him round the hall on their shoulders, hugged him, loved him, named their children after him, nominated him for president, boy orator of the Platte, silver tongue of the plain people."

As economics Bryan's silver cure was strictly voodoo. But the cross of gold evoked more than the composition of the currency. Millions of farmers who had fallen from economic independence to peonage since the Civil War, industrial workers who had seen their right to strike suppressed by court injunctions—for them, America had turned into a cross. And they knew who had put them on it: the railroads, the industrial corporations, the big banks, Wall Street, the Rothschilds (alas)—"the Money Power," which had run away with the country since the end of the Civil War. This was the era when Henry Lloyd Demarest could write that Standard Oil did everything to the Pennsylvania legislature "except refine it." When senators did not represent states so much as interests—the "Senator from Sugar," the "Senator from Textiles," the "Senator from Shoes," even the "Senator from Jute." In the name of its victims Bryan arraigned the money power for hijacking democracy. It struck back through its bagman, Mark Hanna, who voiced a vigilante sentiment shared in many boardrooms when, asked what the Republicans would do if Bryan won, he burst out, "Do you think we'd let that damn lunatic get into the White House? Never!"

While McKinley sipped lemonade on his front porch, receiving delegations that spoke to him in North-Korea style laudations, while Hanna circulated cash to city machines to pay repeaters $5 a vote, while factory owners threatened to fire workers who voted for Bryan, Bryan went to the people, traveled 18,000 miles by train to address them, sometimes giving thirty-six speeches a day. Seventy thousand heard him in Louisville, fifty thousand in Columbus, thirty thousand in Toledo, and ten thousand in Springfield, Illinois, among them young Vachel Lindsay. Twenty-five years later, he wrote an epic poem expressing what Bryan meant to the millions who, for one ecstatic fall, believed him when he said, "The humblest citizen of all the land, when clad in the armor of a righteous cause, is stronger than all the hosts of error."

BRYAN, BRYAN, BRYAN, BRYAN
The Campaign of Eighteen Ninety-Six, as Viewed at the Time by a Sixteen-Year-Old, etc.
Vachel Lindsay

I

In a nation of one hundred fine, mob-hearted, lynching, relenting,
    repenting millions,
There are plenty of sweeping, swinging, stinging, gorgeous things
    to shout about,
And knock your old blue devils out.

I brag and chant of Bryan, Bryan, Bryan,
Candidate for president who sketched a silver Zion,
The one American Poet who could sing outdoors,
He brought in tides of wonder, of unprecedented splendor,
Wild roses from the plains, that made hearts tender,
All the funny circus silks
Of politics unfurled,
Bartlett pears of romance that were honey at the cores,
And torchlights down the street, to the end of the world.

There were truths eternal in the gab and tittle-tattle.
There were real heads broken in the fustian and the rattle.
There were real lines drawn:
Not the silver and the gold,
But Nebraska's cry went eastward against the dour and old,
The mean and cold.

It was eighteen ninety-six, and I was just sixteen
And Altgeld ruled in Springfield, Illinois,
When there came from the sunset Nebraska's shout of joy:
In a coat like a deacon, in a black Stetson hat
He scourged the elephant plutocrats

With barbed wire from the Platte.
The scales dropped from their mighty eyes.
They saw that summer's noon
A tribe of wonders coming
To a marching tune.

Oh, the longhorns from Texas,
The jay hawks from Kansas,
The plop-eyed bungaroo and giant giassicus,
The varmint, chipmunk, bugaboo,
The horned-toad, prairie-dog and ballyhoo,
From all the newborn states arow,
Bidding the eagles of the west fly on,
Bidding the eagles of the west fly on.
The fawn, prodactyl and thing-a-ma-jig,
The rakaboor, the hellangone,
The whangdoodle, batfowl and pig,
The coyote, wild-cat and grizzly in a glow,
In a miracle of health and speed, the whole breed abreast,
They leaped the Mississippi, blue border of the West,
From the Gulf to Canada, two thousand miles long:—
Against the towns of Tubal Cain,
Ah,—sharp was their song.
Against the ways of Tubal Cain, too cunning for the young,
The longhorn calf, the buffalo and wampus gave tongue.

These creatures were defending things Mark Hanna never
    dreamed:
The moods of airy childhood that in desert dews gleamed,
The gossamers and whimsies,
The monkeyshines and didoes
Rank and strange
Of the canyons and the range,
The ultimate fantastics
Of the far western slope,
And of prairie schooner children

Born beneath the stars,
Beneath falling snows,
Of the babies born at midnight
In the sod huts of lost hope,
With no physician there,
Except a Kansas prayer,
With the Indian raid a howling through the air.

And all these in their helpless days
By the dour East oppressed,
Mean paternalism
Making their mistakes for them,
Crucifying half the West,
Till the whole Atlantic coast
Seemed a giant spiders' nest.

And these children and their sons
At last rode through the cactus,
A cliff of mighty cowboys
On the lope,
With gun and rope.
And all the way to frightened Maine the old East heard them call,
And saw our Bryan by a mile lead the wall
Of men and whirling flowers and beasts,
The bard and the prophet of them all.
Prairie avenger, mountain lion,
Bryan, Bryan, Bryan, Bryan,
Gigantic troubadour, speaking like a siege gun,
Smashing Plymouth Rock with his boulders from the West,
And just a hundred miles behind, tornadoes piled across the sky,
Blotting out sun and moon,
A sign on high.

Headlong, dazed and blinking in the weird green light,
The scalawags made moan,
Afraid to fight.

II

When Bryan came to Springfield, and Altgeld gave him greeting,
Rochester was deserted, Divernon was deserted,
Mechanicsburg, Riverton, Chickenbristle, Cotton Hill,
Empty: for all Sangamon drove to the meeting—
In silver-decked racing cart,
Buggy, buckboard, carryall,
Carriage, phaeton, whatever would haul,
And silver-decked farm-wagons gritted, banged and rolled,
With the new tale of Bryan by the iron tires told.

The State House loomed afar,
A speck, a hive, a football,
A captive balloon!
And the town was all one spreading wing of bunting, plumes, and
    sunshine,
Every rag and flag, and Bryan picture sold,
When the rigs in many a dusty line
Jammed our streets at noon,
And joined the wild parade against the power of gold.

We roamed, we boys from High School,
With mankind,
While Springfield gleamed,
Silk-lined.
Oh, Tom Dines, and Art Fitzgerald,
And the gangs that they could get!
I can hear them yelling yet.
Helping the incantation,
Defying aristocracy,
With every bridle gone,
Ridding the world of the low down mean,
Bidding the eagles of the West fly on,
Bidding the eagles of the West fly on,
We were bully, wild and woolly,
Never yet curried below the knees.
We saw flowers in the air,

Fair as the Pleiades, bright as Orion,
—Hopes of all mankind,
Made rare, resistless, thrice refined.
Oh, we bucks from every Springfield ward!
Colts of democracy—
Yet time-winds out of Chaos from the star-fields of the Lord.

The long parade rolled on. I stood by my best girl.
She was a cool young citizen, with wise and laughing eyes.
With my necktie by my ear, I was stepping on my dear,
But she kept like a pattern, without a shaken curl.

She wore in her hair a brave prairie rose.
Her gold chums cut her, for that was not the pose.
No Gibson Girl would wear it in that fresh way.
But we were fairy Democrats, and this was our day.

The earth rocked like the ocean, the sidewalk was a deck.
The houses for the moment were lost in the wide wreck.
And the bands played strange and stranger music as they trailed
    along.
Against the ways of Tubal Cain,
Ah, sharp was their song!
The demons in the bricks, the demons in the grass,
The demons in the bank-vaults peered out to see us pass,
And the angels in the trees, the angels in the grass,
The angels in the flags, peered out to see us pass.
And the sidewalk was our chariot, and the flowers bloomed
    higher,
And the street turned to silver and the grass turned to fire,
And then it was but grass, and the town was there again,
A place for women and men.

III
Then we stood where we could see
Every band,
And the speaker's stand.

And Bryan took the platform.
And he was introduced.
And he lifted his hand
And cast a new spell.
Progressive silence fell
In Springfield,
In Illinois,
Around the world.
Then we heard these glacial boulders across the prairie rolled:
"The people have a right to make their own mistakes. . . .
You shall not crucify mankind
Upon a cross of gold."

And everybody heard him—
In the streets and State House yard.
And everybody heard him
In Springfield,
In Illinois,
Around and around and around the world,
That danced upon its axis
And like a darling broncho whirled.

IV
July, August, suspense.
Wall Street lost to sense.
August, September, October,
More suspense,
And the whole East down like a wind-smashed fence.

Then Hanna to the rescue,
Hanna of Ohio,
Rallying the roller-tops,
Rallying the bucket-shops.
Threatening drouth and death,
Promising manna,
Rallying the trusts against the bawling flannelmouth;

Invading misers' cellars,
Tin-cans, socks,
Melting down the rocks,
Pouring out the long green to a million workers,
Spondulix by the mountain-load, to stop each new tornado,
And beat the cheapskate, blatherskite,
Ropulistic, anarchistic,
Deacon—desperado.

V
Election night at midnight:
Boy Bryan's defeat.
Defeat of western silver.
Defeat of the wheat.
Victory of letterfiles
And plutocrats in miles
With dollar signs upon their coats,
Diamond watchchains on their vests
And spats on their feet.
Victory of custodians,
Plymouth Rock.
And all that inbred landlord stock.
Victory of the neat.
Defeat of the aspen groves of Colorado valleys,
The blue bells of the Rockies,
And blue bonnets of old Texas,
By the Pittsburg alleys.
Defeat of alfalfa and the Mariposa lily.
Defeat of the Pacific and the long Mississippi.
Defeat of the young by the old and silly.
Defeat of tornadoes by the poison vats supreme.
Defeat of my boyhood, defeat of my dream.

VI
Where is McKinley, that respectable McKinley,
The man without an angle or a tangle,

Who soothed down the city man and soothed down the farmer,
The German, the Irish, the Southerner, the Northerner,
Who climbed every greasy pole, and slipped through every crack;
Who soothed down the gambling hall, the bar-room, the church,
The devil vote, the angel vote, the neutral vote,
The desperately wicked, and their victims on the rack,
The gold vote, the silver vote, the brass vote, the lead vote,
Every vote? . . .

Where is McKinley, Mark Hanna's McKinley,
His slave, his echo, his suit of clothes?
Gone to join the shadows, with the pomps of that time,
And the flame of that summer's prairie rose.

Where is Cleveland whom the Democratic platform
Read from the party in a glorious hour,
Gone to join the shadows with pitchfork Tillman,
And sledge-hammer Altgeld who wrecked his power.

Where is Hanna, bulldog Hanna.
Low-browed Hanna, who said: "Stand pat"?
Gone to his place with old Pierpont Morgan.
Gone somewhere . . . with lean rat Platt.

Where is Roosevelt, the young dude cowboy,
Who hated Bryan, then aped his way?
Gone to join the shadows with mighty Cromwell
And tall King Saul, till the Judgment day.

Where is Altgeld, brave as the truth,
Whose name the few still say with tears?
Gone to join the ironies with Old John Brown,
Whose fame rings loud for a thousand years.

Where is that boy, that Heaven-born Bryan,
That Homer Bryan, who sang from the West?

Gone to join the shadows with Altgeld the Eagle,
Where the kings and the slaves and the troubadours rest.

Excerpted from Vachel Lindsay, *Collected Poems* (New York: Macmillan, 1925), pgs. 97–105.

Theodore Roosevelt

LEGEND

Edmund Morris has written over 1,500 pages on the life of Theodore Roosevelt and Teddy has yet to shoot an elephant or turn into a Bull Moose. These developments await Morris's third volume. John Dos Passos offers us essence of Teddy in this prose poem from *USA*.

THE HAPPY WARRIOR
John Dos Passos

The Roosevelts had lived for seven righteous generations on Manhattan Island; they owned a big brick house on 20th Street, an estate up at Dobbs Ferry, lots in the city, a pew in the Dutch Reformed Church, interests, stocks, and bonds, they felt Manhattan was theirs, they felt America was theirs. Their son,

Theodore,

was a sickly youngster, suffered from asthma, was very nearsighted; his hands and feet were so small it was hard for him to learn to box; his arms were very short;

his father was something of a humanitarian, gave Christmas dinners to newsboys, deplored conditions, slums, the East Side, Hell's Kitchen.

Young Theodore had ponies, was encouraged to walk in the woods, to go camping, was instructed in boxing and fencing (an American gentleman should know how to defend himself), taught Bible Class, did mission work (an American gentleman should do his best to up-lift those not so fortunately situated);

righteousness was his by birth;

he had a passion for nature study, for reading about birds and wild animals, for going hunting; he got to be a good shot in spite of his glasses, a good walker in spite of his tiny feet and short legs, a fair horseman, an aggressive scrapper in spite of his short reach, a crack politician in spite of being the son of one of the owning Dutch fami-lies of New York.

In 1876 he went up to Cambridge to study at Harvard, a wealthy talkative erratic young man with sidewhiskers and definite ideas about everything under the sun;

at Harvard he drove around in a dogcart, collected stuffed birds, mounted specimens he'd shot on his trips in the Adirondacks; in spite of not drinking and being somewhat of a christer, having odd ideas about reform and remedying abuses, he made Porcellian and the Dickey and the clubs that were his right as the son of one of the own-ing Dutch families of New York.

He told his friends he was going to devote his life to social service: *I wish to preach not the doctrine of ignoble ease, but the doctrine of the strenuous life, the life of toil and effort, of labor and strife.*

From the time he was eleven years old he wrote copiously, filled di-aries, notebooks, loose leaves with a big impulsive scrawl about every-thing he did and thought and said;

naturally he studied law.

He married young and went to Switzerland to climb the Matter-horn; his first wife's early death broke him all up. He went out to the badlands of western Dakota to become a rancher on the Little Mis-souri River;

when he came back to Manhattan he was Teddy, the straight shooter from the west, the elkhunter, the man in the Stetson hat, who'd roped steers, fought a grizzly hand to hand, acted as Deputy Sheriff,

(a Roosevelt has a duty to his country; the duty of a Roosevelt is to uplift those not so fortunately situated, those who have come more re-cently to our shores) in the west, Deputy Sheriff Roosevelt felt the white man's burden, helped to arrest malefactors, bad men; service was bully.

All this time he'd been writing, filling the magazines with stories of his hunts and adventures, filling political meetings with his opinions, his denunciations, his pat phrases: Strenuous Life, Realizable Ideals, Just Government, *when men fear work or fear righteous war, when women fear motherhood, they tremble on the brink of doom, and well it is that they should vanish from the earth, where they are fit subjects for the scorn of all men and women who are themselves strong and brave and highminded.*

T.R. married a wealthy woman and righteously raised a family at Sagamore Hill.

He served a term in the New York Legislature, was appointed by Grover Cleveland to the unremunerative job of Commissioner for Civil Service Reform,

was Reform Police Commissioner of New York, pursued malefactors, stoutly maintained that white was white and black was black,

wrote the Naval History of the War of 1812,

was appointed Assistant Secretary of the Navy,

and when the *Maine* blew up resigned to lead the Rough Riders, Lieutenant-Colonel.

This was the Rúbicon, the Fight, the Old Glory, the Just Cause. The American public was not kept in ignorance of the Colonel's bravery when the bullets sang, how he charged without his men up San Juan Hill and had to go back to fetch them, how he shot a running Spaniard in the tail.

It was too bad that the regulars had gotten up San Juan Hill first from the other side, that there was no need to get up San Juan Hill at all. Santiago was surrendered. It was a successful campaign. T.R. charged up San Juan Hill into the governorship of the Empire State;

but after the fighting, volunteers warcorrespondents magazinewriters began to want to go home;

it wasn't bully huddling under puptents in the tropical rain or scorching in the morning sun of the seared Cuban hills with malaria mowing them down and dysentery and always yellowjack to be afraid of.

T.R. got up a round robin to the president and asked for the amateur warriors to be sent home and leave the dirtywork to the regulars

who were digging trenches and shovelling crap and fighting malaria and dysentery and yellowjack

to make Cuba cosy for the Sugar Trust

and the National City Bank.

When he landed at home, one of his first interviews was with Lemuel Quigg, emissary of Boss Platt who had the votes of upstate New York sewed into the lining of his vest;

he saw Boss Platt too, but he forgot about that afterwards. Things were bully. He wrote a life of Oliver Cromwell whom people said he resembled. As Governor he doublecrossed the Platt machine (a righteous man may have a short memory); Boss Platt thought he'd shelved him by nominating him for the Vice-Presidency in 1900;

Czolgocz made him president.

T.R. drove like a fiend in a buckboard over the muddy roads through the driving rain from Mt. Marcy in the Adirondacks to catch the train to Buffalo where McKinley was dying.

As President

he moved Sagamore Hill, the healthy happy normal American home, to the White House, took foreign diplomats and fat army /officers out walking in Rock Creek Park where he led them a terrible dance through brambles, hopping across the creek on steppingstones, wading the fords, scrambling up the shaly banks,

and shook the Big Stick at malefactors of great wealth.

Things were bully.

He engineered the Panama revolution under the shadow of which took place the famous hocuspocus of juggling the old and new canal companies by which forty million dollars vanished into the pockets of the international bankers,

but Old Glory floated over the Canal Zone

and the canal was cut through.

He busted a few trusts,

had Booker Washington to lunch at the White House,

and urged the conservation of wild life.

He got the Nobel Peace Prize for patching up the Peace of Portsmouth that ended the Russo-Japanese war,

and sent the Atlantic Fleet around the world for everybody to see that America was a firstclass power. He left the presidency to Taft after his second term leaving to that elephantine lawyer the congenial task of pouring judicial oil on the hurt feelings of the money-masters

and went to Africa to hunt big game.

Big game hunting was bully.

Every time a lion or an elephant went crashing down into the jungle underbrush, under the impact of a wellplaced mushroom bullet,

the papers lit up with headlines;

when he talked with the Kaiser on horseback

the world was not ignorant of what he said, or when he lectured the Nationalists at Cairo, telling them that this was a white man's world.

He went to Brazil where he travelled through the Matto Grosso in a dugout over waters infested with the tiny man-eating fish, the piranha,

shot tapirs,

jaguars,

specimens of the whitelipped peccary.

He ran the rapids of the River of Doubt

down to the Amazon frontiers where he arrived sick, an infected abscess in his leg, stretched out under an awning in a dugout with a tame trumpeterbird beside him.

Back in the States he fought his last fight when he came out for the republican nomination in 1912 a progressive, champion of the Square Deal, crusader for the Plain People; the Bull Moose bolted out from under the Taft steamroller and formed the Progressive Party for righteousness' sake at the Chicago Colosseum while the delegates who were going to restore democratic government rocked with tears in their eyes as they sang

On ward Christian so old gers
March ing as to war

Perhaps the River of Doubt had been too much for a man of his age; perhaps things weren't so bully any more; T.R. lost his voice during the triangular campaign. In Duluth a maniac shot him in the chest; his life was saved only by the thick bundle of manuscript of the speech he was going to deliver. T.R. delivered the speech with the bullet still in him, heard the scared applause, felt the plain people praying for his recovery but the spell was broken somehow.

The Democrats swept in, the world war drowned out the righteous voice of the Happy Warrior in the roar of exploding lyddite.

Wilson wouldn't let T.R. lead a division, this was no amateur's war (perhaps the regulars remembered the round robin at Santiago). All he could do was write magazine articles against the Huns, send his sons; Quentin was killed.

It wasn't the bully amateur's world any more. Nobody knew that on armistice day, Theodore Roosevelt, happy amateur warrior with the grinning teeth, the shaking forefinger, naturalist, explorer, magazine-writer, Sunday school teacher, cowpuncher, moralist, politician, righteous orator with a short memory, fond of denouncing liars (the Ananias Club) and having pillowfights with his children, was taken to the Roosevelt hospital gravely ill with inflammatory rheumatism.

Things weren't bully any more;

T.R. had grit;

he bore the pain, the obscurity, the sense of being forgotten as he had borne the grilling portages when he was exploring the River of Doubt, the heat, the fetid jungle mud, the infected abscess in his leg,

and died quietly in his sleep

at Sagamore Hill on January 6, 1919,

and left on the shoulders of his sons

the white man's burden.

Excerpted from John Dos Passos, *U. S. A,* Volume 1 (New York: Random House, 1937), pgs. 142–148.

James Michael Curley

SCANDAL'S MAYOR

From his election to the Boston Common Council in 1898 to his defeat in the mayoral primary of 1955, James Michael Curley (1874–1958) dominated Boston politics. Mayor in four different decades—the 1910s, 1920s, 1930s, and 1940s; also an alderman, a state representative, four-term U.S. congressman, governor of Massachusetts, and a Democratic candidate for the U.S. Senate, Curley, no stranger to delusion, broadcast his availability to run for president in 1940. Few picked up the signal. Outside Boston, he was damaged goods.

If he is not the only politician in American history to be reelected while in jail, he can't have much company. He gave his salary away in $100 tips, living, in a twenty-room house, on contractor kickbacks. "Never use a checkbook, don't ask me why," he told one of his sons. "Just never write a check." To inoculate himself against the politics of resentment, which fueled his career, he had shamrocks carved into the green shutters of his mansion. The Proper Bostonians, as Cleveland Amory denominated the Cabots and the Lowells, treated the Irish badly from the time they staggered down the gangways of the famine ships in the 1840s to well into the 1920s, when NO IRISH NEED APPLY headers still appeared over ads for domestic help in the *Boston Evening Transcript*. Curley, the son of poor Irish immigrants, made sure the Boston Irish never forgot, playing the ethnic card against Yankee Protestant politicians, institutions, and accusations, especially when he faced charges of corruption—that is, incessantly.

In 1913 Curley, then in his second term as a congressman, made his first run for mayor. His opponent, the incumbent mayor, John F. "Honey Fitz" Fitzgerald, the grandfather of John F. Kennedy, looked too formidable to defeat at the polls. So Curley drove him from the race by sexual blackmail. Fitzgerald had been in the compromising arms of Elizabeth "Toodles" Ryan, a cigarette girl at a suburban roadhouse and, at twenty-three, the same age as his daughter, Rose. Curley sent a black-bordered letter to Fitzgerald's wife, Josephine, threatening to make her husband's lubricity public if he did not withdraw from the race. Plump, smiling, John Fitzgerald opened the door of his Dorchester home that evening to find Josephine and Rose waiting for him in the hallway. He later told friends it was the worst moment of his life. Josephine insisted that he comply with the letter's demands. But he dithered. So Curley made good on his threat by announcing that he would deliver a series of public lectures on such themes as "Great Lovers in History: From Cleopatra to Toodles" and "Libertines in History from Henry the Eighth to the Present Day." Pleading ill health—he had fallen down a flight of stairs while inspecting the charred hulk of a rooming house—Fitzgerald withdrew.

Curley made short work of Thomas Kenny, the candidate the city's reformers quickly put in the race to save Boston from Curley, whose years as the president of the Tammany Club and ward boss of immigrant Roxbury had made him terrible to respectability. Curley was "absolutely unscrupulous as a public servant," Kenny charged. How unscrupulous he couldn't begin to imagine. Even as Kenny spoke, Curley's "poison gas squad" was calling the wives of Kenny's campaign operatives, asking, Did you know that your husband was *not* out campaigning, but keeping tryst with a woman at a "notorious" South End boarding house? The wives would be given the address; and some of them, going to investigate, showed photographs of their husbands to the building custodian, who, as he had been paid to do, would identify the men as frequent visitors to the building. The day after the election the front page of the Yankee *Boston Herald* showed a snarling Tammany Tiger emerging from its den, its awful eye trained on a pile of neatly stacked bags labeled CITY TREASURY. Above the cartoon was the prophetic headline, "THE LOOT AND THE TIGER." In his inaugural address, Curley talked like a reformer, promising that in his administration "the policy of discharging political debts through the mediumship of the city treasury shall cease," and the *Herald* registered surprise: Could we have been wrong about Curley?

THE RASCAL KING
Jack Beatty

Curley was "a man of wonderful force, but without scruple," one city councilor remarked, in a comment typical of the way Curley's fierce will-to-do impressed even hostile observers. Right after his election the papers were full of accounts of the mayor-elect's aggressive lobbying of Assistant Secretary Franklin Roosevelt to have the Navy Department award a contract for a new supply ship to the Boston Naval Shipyard. Shortly after their meeting, the navy yard got the contract. Next, Curley lobbied Treasury Secretary William Gibbs McAdoo to locate a new bank of the just-created Federal Reserve system in Boston. An announcement soon followed that Boston would get the bank. The man got things done.

In his inaugural he called for the creation of a fund to which substantial private citizens would subscribe to "boom Boston"—that is, to attract new businesses through publicity. When a leading banker refused to contribute, Curley threatened to withdraw the city's deposits from his bank. Like many of his efforts to run over people, this one backfired, but it put the city on notice that its new mayor would use irregular means to achieve his ends. When James J. Storrow, the city councilor from Beacon Hill, held up a measure of Curley's, the mayor told a reporter that he "very much feared" the lights might go out along Beacon Street, the garbage go uncollected, and the sewers plug up, backing so much water into Storrow's basement that he would need a canoe to navigate it—unless, of course, the councilor saw things Curley's way. "We do not expect tyrants of the Russian or Asiatic type in our American cities," one newspaper observed, while noting that Boston appeared to have the makings of one in Mayor Curley.

He began his workday a well-advertised hour before John Fitzgerald had begun his, and, to sustain his energy through the afternoon, frequently dipped into a box of choice candies he kept in his rolltop mahogany desk. Though he was home for dinner every evening, he often took a secretary, a chief clerk, and sometimes a stenographer along with him, turning the Mount Pleasant Avenue house into a virtual annex of City Hall at night. Whether exhausting a photographer walking with him from Mount Pleasant to City Hall with the breathless mayoral gait, or leading officials on an 11 P.M. to 2 A.M. tour of the city's most sordid lodging houses, or taking part in a raid on a Chinatown gambling den, or winning a horse race at Franklin Field, or dispatching two toughs who had set upon an old man on Boston Common, or snuffing out the flame of a match with a single pistol shot while taking some target practice in his office, or leaping onto the field during a Braves-Giants game to demand that the umpire eject a Giant who had thumbed his nose at the fans—Mayor Curley seemed to be everywhere, doing everything. Two years of this pace was enough for his chauffeur; having put over 125,000 miles on the mayor's imposing black machine, Tammany Tess, he quit to spend more time with his family.

You can't get people excited about a sewer, Fiorello La Guardia once said, capturing a problem of municipal politics (and politicians) in a quip. The problem is the meager claim the stuff of city government makes on the imagination. People don't get excited about street repairs or subway extensions, and fire trucks leave them cold. Nor does city government engage ideological passion. There is no "liberal" or "conservative" way to pick up the trash. Mayors have to find some other way to make what they do interesting.

Curley made his government interesting by acting out the impulses of his core constituency. He knew that each one of those thousands of fans wanted personally to tell the umpire to eject that contumelious Giant, so he did it for them. Similarly, he knew his constituents wanted to voice their clotted resentments against Boston's Protestant elite, and with an appetite for the work, he did it for them.

One of Curley's favorite tactics in this culture war was to insist that there was an Irishman at the bottom of everything American. He made himself something of a one-eyed expert on colonial America, and what that eye saw was the hitherto hidden contribution that the Irish had made to that history. Myles Standish, in Curley's telling, was really an Irish soldier of fortune "whom the Pilgrim fathers secured to do their fighting for them." The Boston Tea Party was really a beer party: Sam Adams's Indians had fortified themselves against the night air by getting a snout full of ale at a waterfront saloon run by an Irishman. The "shot heard 'round the world" was not fired at the North Bridge in Concord after all. The American Revolution had really begun months earlier, when a raiding party captured British munitions stored at Fort William in Portsmouth, New Hampshire. The raiding party was led by—who else?—an Irishman.

Curley's historical contributions, tossed off in speeches or offered as ruminations to reporters, elicited countercontributions from members of the Protestant elite, who resented Curley's attempts to adulterate their roots. One South End pastor, trumping Curley in audacity, went so far as to claim that St. Patrick was really a Scot.

Much of this revisionism was offered in good spirits. But there was something permanently bitter in the ethnic cup, and Curley was the man to stir it to the top. In January 1916, at a particularly low point in his administration, the Lord delivered John Farwell Moors into his hands.

Moors was a banker, a member of the Finance Committee, an Anglo-Saxon Protestant grandee, and one of the charter members of the Immigration Restriction League—in short, an ideal foil for Curley. One afternoon, speaking to the New England Woman's Department of the National Civic Federation gathered at the Back Bay home of Mrs. Frederick L. Ames, Moors made what he thought were some anodyne remarks about the failure in recent years of the "highly educated portions" of the Boston community—code for its Anglo-Saxon Protestant members—to run for public office. "Not a rich man's son under forty years of age today is taking an important part in the political life of this city." He urged them to do so. And then he turned to the community that was politically ascendant. The passage is worth quoting in full because it prompted a gorgeously purple burst from Curley. "Boston," Moors told the women gathered in Mrs. Ames's parlor,

> became a city nearly two hundred years ago. . . . A generation later the potato famine in Ireland drove hither for a refuge thousands of suffering people, mostly peasants. The third generation of famine-stricken people is now dominant in the city.
>
> Their ancestors were united by English oppression and absentee landlordism into a compact mass of antagonism to all things Anglo-Saxon. We Anglo-Saxons gave them a refuge here, but . . . the welcome was not of a kind to break the mass into individual units. When they became numerically supreme, as in time they did, they became also politically supreme, to our exclusion.
>
> The one great need for years has been this, that the different races which make up our cosmopolitan city, should not remain distinct and antagonistic, but should work together, as, in truth, fellow citizens. . . .

Not a warm passage, certainly. Its bland face does not hide the speaker's resentment at being politically displaced, like the youthful Henry Cabot Lodge from the hills of the Common, by the Irish horde. And that plea for ethnic harmony at the end has the look of a sop. Still, the passage would not seem to supply much tinder for offense.

The mayor was attending a dinner at the Boston City Club in honor of the eighty-seven-year-old former mayor of Boston Thomas N. Hart when he was asked his reaction to Moors's speech. Earlier in the evening he had shaken the hand of John F. Fitzgerald, and in that singular gesture exhausted his quota of charitable feeling. "I shall spend two hours getting the facts together," he said. "A thing like that merits two hours spent in preparation."

He prepared a written reply. Assailing Moors as "a pathetic figure of a perishing people who seek by dollars and denunciations to evade the inexorable and inevitable law of the survival of the fittest," he called for his resignation from the Finance Committee. In saying that the Famine had forced the Irish to come to America, Curley implied,

Moors had committed an ethnic slur—though in truth if Moors had said that the Irish had come for the waters Curley would have found some other equally gossamer pretext on which to hang his attack. For he was after bigger game than Moors.

"A strange and stupid race, the Anglo-Saxon," he went on. "Beaten in a fair, stand-up fight, he seeks by political chicanery and hypocrisy to gain the ends he lost in battle, and this temperamental peculiarity he calls fair play." He heaped sarcasm on Moors's political theory. "'And,' adds Mr. Moors, sadly, 'When the Irish became numerically supreme they became politically dominant'! How absurdly American this was, the majority daring to rule the minority; but that is one of the peculiarities of the American system, so different from the Anglo-Saxon system of the man doffing his hat and pulling his forelock to his masters and betters." And he launched into his patented recital on the perfidious colonial past, "the halcyon days when the traders in rum, salt cod and slaves were . . . engaged with the New England Genealogical Society in fabricating family histories." Quoting Cardinal O'Connell's very words of nine years before, he concluded, "The Puritan is passed; the Anglo-Saxon is a joke; a newer and better America is here. . . . No country is ever ruined by a virile, intelligent, God-fearing, patriotic people like the Irish, and no land was ever saved by clubs of female faddists, old gentlemen with disordered livers, or pessimists croaking over imaginary good old days and ignoring the sunlit present. . . . What we need in this part of the world is men and mothers of men, not gabbing spinsters and dog-raising matrons in federation assembled"—a hit at the ladies in Moors's audience.

Moors replied that he did not recognize "either what I said or the spirit in which I said it" in Curley's jeremiad. He was partially right there, and right all through that the mayor's aim was "to stir up ill will on the part of the citizenship of Boston." The attack was an arrant piece of demagogy. But only those insensible to the charm of invective will wholly regret it.

The following Sunday Curley was denounced by some of Boston's leading Protestant ministers. From the pulpit of the Warren Avenue Baptist Church, the Reverend Frederick E. Heath put to a missing Curley a series of rhetorical questions. "Mr. Curley, did you ever hear of Charles Sumner? Mr. Curley, did you ever hear of a man named Webster? Was he a 'clod'? Were Lloyd Garrison, Channing, Longfellow, scores of others all 'clods'? Were the Puritans all clods? Who founded Massachusetts? The Celtic people, I suppose you say." If the mayor could traffic in personalities, so could the minister. "Where did he go on one occasion?" he asked the audience, which laughed at this tickle of the jail issue. "I'll not say it. You have fully answered for me."

From the pulpit of the Clarendon Street Church, the Reverend Madison C. Peters retailed a ranker brand of bigotry. In whatever cities in whatever states the Irish had achieved political dominance, he said, they had been "a hiss and a byword, violating every law of God and man, increasing taxes, depreciating property and disgracing the city."

The controversy simmered for weeks, providing newspaper readers with comic relief from the ghastly news of the European war. And yet the diversion was dearly bought. In a pluralist society there is always plenty of intergroup tension to go around. When politicians exploit that tension or inflame it they poison the common well. Who knows how many relationships between Irish and Yankee Bostonians were strained, how many intimacies choked off, how much spontaneous feeling curdled by Curley's tirade and the polarization of opinion it created? Blacks and whites in New York City must have gone through something similar during the mayoralty of Ed Koch, with many whites cheering his blunt comments about black leaders and issues, while most blacks winced at them. BRING US TOGETHER: so read the famous sign Richard Nixon glimpsed in Ohio during the 1968 presidential campaign. That is what people say they want from politicians, but they so rarely get it and so rarely punish the politicians who don't give it to them that it may be a mere piety, something they say to throw pollsters off the scent of their resentments.

As mayor of Boston, Curley had broad powers to regulate public entertainment. No reader who has gotten this far will be surprised to learn that he was not shy about exercising them. He had pronounced views about cultural matters: cross those of Cotton Mather with those of Cardinal O'Connell and you have them. Reinforcing his views was the politics of his views. He knew where the votes lay, and in Catholic Boston they were not on the side of those favoring free artistic expression.

While still mayor-elect, Curley stated that he considered public morals "perhaps the most important problem of all." He promised that he would be guided in his "course of action by recognized authority on moral questions, [subscribing] to the views so timely and ably expressed by His Eminence, Cardinal O'Connell." Since the cardinal, by all reports, considered the mayor an embarassment to the Catholic faith, Curley's pledge of fealty must have scalded him. And in equal degree it must have disturbed those who feared that Curley would extend Irish majoritarianism from politics to culture. Would the arch baiter of the Puritan theocracy sponsor a Catholic version of what he condemned?

Indeed he would. The phrase "banned in Boston," that infallible booster of sales for theatrical producer and publisher alike, entered the language in the Curley years. As he suffered his texts' "bitch" and "bastard" genteeled to "dame" and "buzzard," the playwright Ben Hecht would wash his hands of Boston. Even as late as 1939, *Life with Father,* in which New Yorkers could hear "Oh, God," was considered too daring for Bostonians, whose ears would be offended by anything stronger than "Oh, Gad." In 1927, during a Curley interregnum, Boston banned sixty-eight books, including works by H. G. Wells, Ernest Hemingway, John Dos Passos, Sinclair Lewis, and Sherwood Anderson.

Even without Curley, Boston would not have been a center of cultural modernism. "I say that Boston commits the scholastic error and tries to remember too much," wrote H. G. Wells after a visit in 1905, "and has refined and studied and collected herself into a state of hopeless intellectual and aesthetic repletion. . . . The capacity of Boston, it would seem, was just sufficient but no more than sufficient, to comprehend the whole achievement of the human intellect up, let us say, to the year 1875 A.D. Then an equilibrium was established. At or about that year Boston filled up." Boston's impermeable self-content echoes in the old joke about the Beacon Hill lady who, chided for never traveling, replies, "Why should I travel when I am already here?"

Nor was Curley a pioneer in local censorship. Since 1878 Boston's morals had been monitored by the Watch and Ward Society, which described itself as a "quasi-governmental law enforcement agency" dedicated to "the protection of family life in New England." It had succeeded in banning *Leaves of Grass* in the year of its founding, and through the influence of the Lowells, Peabodys, and Cabots who were its officers, this WASP bastion, to quote Cleveland Amory, "maintained a militant inhospitality to sex stimula of all sorts" right up to 1945, when it banned Kathleen Winsor's *Forever Amber* into bestsellerdom. Curley's Puritanism, in short, was as much in the Boston tradition as bad restaurants serving inedible sticky buns.

What Curley did was to apply this tradition with his characteristic sweep—sometimes giving it a twist of ethnic politics. Thus early in his term he sought to ban the late-night dances held at the Copley-Plaza Hotel by S. Hooper Hooper, the leader of the Boston cotillion. Curley's case was both moral* and political. If sailors and marines could not cavort all night in the dance halls of Charlestown, he argued, why should Back Bay debutantes be granted the privilege? Hooper, who prided himself on running irreproachable dances—he had kept the Bunny Hug and the Turkey Trot on a year's probation in Boston when they were all the rage across the country—fought back, telling the mayor there was no question of the dances' legality. When Curley's corporation counsel, John Sullivan, ruled that the dances were strictly private affairs—it would have been a bold sailor who dared to crash one—Curley had to relent.

He could and did ban the tango at Franklin Park, however. Somehow it ran afoul of the moral code he drew up under which bare feet, suggestive jokes, impersonations of effeminate persons, depictions of drug fiends, disrobing scenes, Salome dances, and plays teaching les-

---

*"There have been more young girls ruined in Boston through the medium of all-night dancing," he declared, "than by any other force in the community."

sons in immorality were banned in Boston. Perhaps the tango dancers were shoeless.

Isadora Duncan wore shoes, but Curley banned her interpretive Grecian dances anyway because she showed her bare legs. He had similar scrapes with Pavlova and Ruth St. Denis. Mary Curley had him pull down the curtain in the middle of Mary Garden's performance of *Thaïs,* according to Francis Curley. As Garden peeled off the fourth veil in her Salome dance, Mary, sitting up front next to her husband, grew agitated. "James"—a mark of her displeasure; in good weather he was "Father"—"I want this show stopped. It's nothing but burley." He objected. She persisted. He complied.

Curley shut down the war drama *Across the Border* because it contained "curses and oaths." When the theater management urged the realism of such language, Curley was unmoved; maybe that was how soldiers died on the western front, but more was expected of them in Boston. The play reopened, minus the oaths. David Belasco's play *Marie O'Dile* may have run for a year in New York, Chicago, and Philadelphia, but the Knights of Columbus had condemned it, and that was all Curley needed to warn it away from Boston. Eugène Brieux may have been a member of the French Academy, but his *Maternity* touched on the subject of abortion, making it impossible for the play to be presented in Boston. On receiving the report of John Casey, his "morality censor"—a man described by a contemporary newspaper as the "brigadier general of the municipalities' purity brigade"—Curley stopped the Boston run of *The Hypocrites,* a film in which a nymph representing the allegorical figure of Truth flitted across the screen "wearing so few garments that Venus by comparison looked like a little woman in a big fur coat."

Given the mayor's zeal to ban even bare feet in public, Bostonians were shocked to discover, in September 1916, that Curley not only allowed a movie condemned by the American Federation of Catholic Societies to open in Boston, but he had also lobbied a leading Pennsylvania politician to get the film past the Philadelphia censors, one of whom had characterized it as "unspeakably vile." *Where Are My Children?* was promoted in ad copy like this: "Do you believe in birth control? There are realistic reasons pictured for and against it in that daring photoplay 'Where Are My Children?' . . . Why do not the censors stop this film?" The answer to that question, in Boston at any rate, was simple; the mayor seemed to have a financial interest in it. "I merely helped a friend, who had money invested in the project. I did it for a friend . . . ," the mayor said, repairing to a tested locution, when reporters asked him why he had gone to Washington to lobby Senator Boise Penrose, the Republican boss of Pennsylvania, to get the film shown in his state. But even as he was giving that interview in his second-floor office, the shouts of newsboys flogging the evening editions on the narrow street outside could be heard in the room: "Curley exposed! Curley exposed! Read all about it! Just out!" For Penrose, in an interview quoted in those editions, was saying that Curley had told him that he did have a financial interest in the film.

The situation was irresistibly ironic. "Mayor James M. Curley, the man who saw a menace to our morals in the twinkling toes of Pavlova," the *Boston Journal* noted, "a demoralizing danger in the dreamy dances of the diaphanous Duncan, and a calamity in the bare-legged prancing of the brown-stained St. Denis, has lobbied in Washington on behalf of a movie based on birth-control." And "birth-control" was a euphemism: *Where Are My Children?* is about young women who receive abortions without, to quote someone who has seen it, "undergoing any dire consequences."

The episode exposes a hard truth about our subject: He would sometimes allow shameless vistas to open between his principles and his practices. Money, then and later, was the root of his hypocrisy.

★   ★   ★

James Curley took "honest graft." The oxymoron comes from George Washington Plunkitt, the sage of Tammany Hall, a New York State senator, and a fellow who would feel right at home in a world where taxes are "revenue enhancements" and liars "misspeak." In "A Series of Very Plain Talks on Very Practical Politics," published in 1905, Plunkitt explained to the journalist William R. Riordon how he had made politics pay. "There's all the difference in the world between the two," he said of honest versus dishonest graft. "Yes, many of our men have grown rich in politics. I have myself. I've made a big fortune out of the game, and I'm gettin' richer every day, but I've not gone in for dishonest graft—blackmailin', gamblers, saloon-keepers, disorderly people, etc.—and neither has any of the men who made big fortunes in politics. There's an honest graft and I'm an example of how it works. I might sum up the whole thing by sayin': 'I seen my opportunities and I took 'em.'" Senator Plunkitt's opportunities came in this form: when the city was about to buy a piece of land, he would get wind of it through friends at City Hall, buy up the land, and sell it to the city at profit. That was "honest" graft. Of course, only by comparison with the organized vice run by Tammany Hall did it merit the epithet.

Curley's opportunities were different from Plunkitt's, but he took them with the same unembarrassed grasp. Having grown up poor, he intended to live rich.

On March 17, 1915, St. Patrick's Day, construction began on a house that would symbolize Curley and "Curleyism" to generations of Bostonians. The house sat on a two-acre rise of land facing a park in the "green necklace" that Frederick Law Olmsted, a poet in landscape, had planted across Boston twenty years before. Between the park and the house was a twisting motor parkway; past the park, visible through its trees, lay a prim pond. Beyond, nestled among the hills of Brookline, were the estates and "farms" of some of the oldest and wealthiest families in Massachusetts. Altogether, the district was as far in ambience as one could go from Roxbury and still be within the city limits. "It has a pleasing, picturesque, garden-like air," George William Curtis wrote in 1859. "It is the same smooth and comfortable and respectable landscape that strikes the American eye in England." It was, as a recent historian of the area has written, a "gentleman's landscape." And James M. Curley, no gentleman, was building a fine brick house there.

"Where did Curley get it?" press and public alike began to ask almost as soon as the ground was broken. Where did a man with a salary of $10,000 a year and no declared savings get the money to build such a house? That question could not be answered without taking one over into illegality. The land alone cost that much. And just the year before, the mayor had bought a summer home in Hull, a resort town on the South Shore of Boston, worth $10,000. Moreover, as the house took shape over the spring and summer, people could see that there was nothing ordinary about it. Designed by the architect Joseph McGinniss, who did commissioned work for the city, it was a neo-Georgian mansion of twenty-one-plus rooms and over ten thousand square feet, with a thick tile roof, sculptural medallions on its brick cladding, a heated garage, and gracious landscaped grounds. Outside it was impressive enough; inside it was downright opulent. The twenty- by thirty-two-foot oval mahogany-paneled dining room with its crystal chandelier, the baronial forty- by sixty-foot first-floor hall, the twenty-eight carved mahogany doors, the five bathrooms (by now the Curleys had five children), the high ceilings, the Italian marble fireplaces, the gold-plated light fixtures, the massive two-story bronze chandelier in the front hall taken from the Austro-Hungarian embassy in Washington, and the breathtaking three-story spiral staircase that curled around it were the appurtenances of great wealth—in fact, many of them had come from the estate of an owner of Standard Oil. The only sign that a man of the people lived in this palazzo was the shamrocks cut into the thirty white shutters outside.

The house swallowed the Curley administration. It led to graft; graft led to scandal; scandal led to defeat. To pay for the land, Curley had to engage in one kind of graft. The labor took another; the interior Versailles yet another. Besides paying for the house, Curley had to find the money to live up to it, to afford the servants, gardeners, and cooks needed to run it. So the house cost him (to say nothing of the taxpayer) dear. Abandoning the old neighborhood cost him politically, too. In the 1915 state election the Tammany-backed candidate running for state representative in Ward 17 lost to a candidate who predicted that Curley "would lose his head with his sudden rise to power and forget the people who made him what he is politically" when he moved out to the shores of Jamaica Pond. Yet there was vision behind this mansion on a jut of land next to a busy highway where all eyes could see it—or so the years would prove.

To divert attention from the unanswerable question "Where did he get it?" Curley did one of the strangest things in his career. He quoted to the press portions of a letter that a Yankee neighbor of his, Dr. Edmund D. Spears, had sent him. The letter, which complained about the "abomination on the shutters"—the shamrock cutouts—caused a sensation; one didn't have to be the proverbial well-balanced Irishman—a fellow with chips on both shoulders—to take offense at this. But later, when reporters pressed him for a copy of Spears's letter, the mayor said that he had, well, misspoken. Dr. Spears's complaint had really been about the funerary urns set in the brickwork over the front entrance. Curley made no attempt to explain why he had distorted Spears's letter except to imply that it was all somehow a joke. To this day, people remember Curley's libel of Dr. Spears, the "rich Yankee neighbor" offended in his contemptibly narrow heart by the shamrock shutters. It is part of the Curley legend. It was also a lie told by a man trapped in lies about money.

Watergate did not stop the federal government in its lumbering tracks. The Nixon administration continued, with the president feigning unconcern about the "fifth-rate burglary" and its toxic ramifications. Yet the essential story of the Nixon administration can be written as the history of Watergate. In the same way the history of the first Curley administration can be read in the bricks and mortar and, more to the point, the stained glass and gold plate of Curley's house.

Curley got the fancy appointments from a Roxbury junk dealer and former treasurer of the Tammany Club named Marks Angell, who had purchased them from the Fairhaven, Massachusetts, estate of Henry H. Rogers. Marks Angell (né Max Angelovitz) had backed Curley early in his career and had long stood in the sun of Curley's favor. In 1908, while on the Board of Aldermen, Curley helped Angell secure a license to open a kosher slaughterhouse in Ward 17. At the time Thomas M. Joyce, a member of the Common Council who was often embroiled with Curley, charged him with being Angell's secret partner. That charge would be leveled again.

Under Mayor Curley, Angell's Roxbury Iron and Metal Company got a street (Hill Top Street in Dorchester) built solely for its convenience, to give its trucks easier passage; there had been no pressure from the neighborhood for a new street. The city generously paid Angell more in damages for the land-taking than it assessed him in betterments for the improvement. First Angell's son-in-law and then his brother-in-law also got special consideration from the mayor in the bidding to run the refreshment concession at Franklin Park. It took a protest from the Finance Commission to stop their too-high bid from winning the contract. Angell did submit a low bid to demolish the city-owned Probate Building—but alone among the bidders, only Angell knew that the city would not enforce the time limitation in the contract. Because he did not have to remove the debris within the stipulated twenty days, he could bid lower than the competition. Curley had suggested the twenty-day clause to the superintendent of the Buildings Department, as he had suggested to the Transit Commission that it let Angell's junk firm handle its refuse without the bother of bidding for the job. His "suggestions" were, of course, commands to city employees. Finally, Angell was a habitué of the mayor's office, using Curley's telephone and often posing as his special agent on visits to local corporations to solicit their junk business.

In incendiary testimony before the Finance Commission in late 1917, a former city treasurer threw light on why Angell got so much city business and enjoyed the run of City Hall. Curley, he told the startled commissioners, had once let slip in conversation that he had a half interest in the Roxbury Iron and Metal Company. In granting contracts to Angell, Curley was filling his own pocket. This was in direct violation of the City Charter, which prohibited any city official from having a financial interest in firms doing business with the city.

Having workmen perform labor on the mayor's private residence in exchange for city contracts was also a violation of the charter, yet that is how 350 the Jamaicaway got built. The contractors who worked on the house did so on the understanding that city contracts would come their way. Curley paid them either nothing or a fraction of their fees. When the Finance Commission was about to open an investigation of a contractor who had installed some flooring in City Hall after laying the floors at the house, Curley quickly paid his bill to the contractor, whose books carried the notation "NC"—"no charge"—opposite the entry for the Curley job. The whole house was "NC." "Governor, did you pay for that house?" John Henry Cutler, the ghostwriter of Curley's *I'd Do It Again,* asked Curley in 1956. "He had the largest brown eyes I've ever seen on a person," Cutler said, "and he gave me a wink as if to say of course he didn't pay."

There remained the land—the $10,000 question. The Finance Commission, in hearings held in the fall of 1917, finally got to the bottom of the land. On September 2, 1913, Francis L. Daly, the co-proprietor of the firm Sullivan & Daly, a plumbing supply house, bought out his partner, Daniel P. Sullivan, for $8,000. The money, he told the Finance Commission, was a gift from his uncle, who had since died, destitute, leaving no record of any bequest to his nephew. Daly wrote his check to Sullivan on August 28, the same day that his close friend Congressman James M. Curley, about to launch his campaign for mayor, had withdrawn $4,100 from one bank and taken a $3,900 loan from another. Testifying under oath before the Finance Commission, the mayor claimed he used this $8,000 to buy stock from a New York wool broker named Nathan Eisman, who, like Daly's uncle, had also since died—leaving no sign of ever having lived. From this stock deal, Curley said, he realized $12,500, a profit of 166 percent, and with that sum bought the land for what was by then the most notorious house in Massachusetts.

This was almost certainly perjury. During the mayoral campaign Curley had spoken openly of what he had done with the $8,000. "I am a partner in the Daly Plumbing Supply Company," he said in a speech on January 7, 1914, "from which concern I net a sufficient income to render me independent of political office." And in a signed article published in the *Boston Post* on December 13, 1915—which he later disavowed, disingenuously—he said he had bought the land for his house from the proceeds of his half interest in the Daly firm, which on becoming mayor he sold back to Daly. But this too was a lie; he never sold his interest in Daly Plumbing Supply. Daly himself, in headline-making testimony, denied that he had bought out Curley (which was why Curley had to invent Eisman).

At the Finance Commission hearing, Curley was questioned about the *Post* article saying he had bought his house on his share of the Daly business. "Didn't you think it was your duty to correct the impression?" one of the commissioners asked. Curley replied, with revealing scorn, "No, when you consider the kind of cattle it would interest." Asked how the writer of the article obtained the information in it, the mayor denied that he was the source. "It was merely a matter of current rumor evolved into a statement"—a truly Nixonian formulation in the way it dispensed with human agency.

If the $10,000 did not come from Daly and if Eisman was a phantom, where *did* Curley get it?

In all probability the $10,000 came from two contractors, George M. Stevens, the general manager of "Diamond" Jim Timilty's Central Construction Company, and his brother-in-law, William J. Clark, an officer of another construction firm. Daly met them over lunch. He knew they wanted to do business with the city. They knew he was a close friend of the mayor's. When he suggested they might want to invest $10,000 in a real estate venture of a suspiciously vague character, they agreed. Ostensibly they were buying fifty shares in the Oakmont Land Company, the municipal equivalent of one of those CIA fronts with names like Southern Trading Company. Run by Daly's brother-in-law, Edwin Fitzgerald, Oakmont was supposed to use the money to buy some industrial land in Jamaica Plain. Investigation revealed, however, that Oakmont had already secured funds for that purchase from a bank. Daly gave Fitzgerald the $10,000, but he returned it to Daly, who testified that he was not sure what he had done with it. To quote Gertrude Stein, this was interesting if true.

The following train of conjecture cannot be far short of the facts: Clark and Stevens, and their firms, wanted contracts from the city, and they paid for them. Daly either passed along their $10,000 to Curley, who used it to pay off his note on the land, or kept it to satisfy a loan for the land that he had made earlier to Curley. For its part, Central Construction got its bribe back, with interest. It received a steady flow of no-bid jobs, magnanimously charging the city $2.26 a square yard of paving for work that cost $1.66 a square yard in New York. The paving contract, wrote the *Boston Journal,* "is as crooked as a snake in a hurry."

For *his* pains Daly got fat on city contracts. The month before Curley's inaugural speech ("Special privilege in any form is objectionable and the removal of this cancer from the body politic must be undertaken at once"), Daly's father-in-law, Peter Fitzgerald, to quote the arch language of the Finance Commission report, "was engaged in selling from a cart butter, cheese, and eggs." But six weeks later he and his son Edwin were in the insurance and bonding business. As exclusive agents for the National Surety Company, the Fitzgeralds got 80 percent of the city's employee bonding business, which totaled $784,000, in 1914 and 94 percent, totaling $965,000, in 1915. They also captured 76 percent of the bonds the city required of contractors, which, in 1915, came to $1,149,000; a large share of the city's automobile insurance business; and half its policies covering elevators and boilers.

In addition, the Finance Commission found suggestive irregularities in the Fitzgeralds' accounting practices. "Loans" made to Francis L. Daly were not paid back. A phantom New York stockbroker named John J. Cassidy, whom Peter Fitzgerald claimed lived at the Hotel Knickerbocker (which had never heard of him), got $4,000. Only the terminally credulous could doubt the real destination of this money. In his testimony before the Finance Commission, John Sullivan removed even their doubts when he said that Curley had spoken several times of his half-interest in the Daly firm. The corporation counsel had warned Curley either to sell out or to declare his interest, as the law required. Curley fired him before he could resign.

Confronted with clear evidence of multiple violations of the City Charter and of perjury, the Finance Commission instructed its special counsel, Henry F. Hurlburt, to present its case against Curley to the district attorney of Suffolk County, Joseph C. Pelletier, for possible prosecution. Unimpressed by Hurlburt's case, Pelletier refused to prosecute. Curley had dodged another bullet, one that would have ended the career of most politicians, though reversals seemed rather to propel Curley. According to Martin Lomasney, "Curley went in to Pelletier, got down almost on his knees, talked of his wife and family, and begged him to stay the execution of the law. 'Hold on, Joe, for God's sake, give me a chance. Think of my wife and family. Think of our party. Think of our people.'" But Curley did not have to beg.

The mayor and the district attorney were firm political friends. Years before, when Curley was on the City Council, Pelletier had refused to prosecute Curley on another set of charges. When Pelletier tried to take the gubernatorial nomination away from the incumbent governor, Eugene Victor Foss, in the 1912 Democratic primary, a grateful Curley delivered his ward for Pelletier—one of only three Boston wards he won.

"I am a candidate for reelection," Curley announced to the Tammany Club in a ninety-minute speech on New Year's Eve 1916, "and I have not the slightest fear of the outcome." His campaign got a power of help from history. James M. Curley was a war mayor in 1917. He warmed to the cause slowly—as late as June, two months after war was declared, he denounced it in a speech in the North End as a "war for commerce," in the *Boston Journal*'s paraphrase, and played on "the ancient prejudices of his hearers by attacking Great Britain, now our ally in a war to the death for democracy." But soon he glimpsed the war's political uses. He did not visit any flag factories, but no parade, flag raising, or troop embarkation was safe from him. He embraced the war in its most Wilsonian aspect, as democracy's crusade against despotism. In his war proclamation to the city, he put it this way: "Truly, God hath said, 'I am tired of kings.'" As an Irish American, he cannot have liked joining an alliance led by a British government that had the blood of Irish patriots—the Dublin rising had been crushed the year before—still dripping from its hands. And President Wilson's failure to protest the hanging of Sir Roger Casement for running German guns to Ireland was a special trial. Even so, the president had carried 80 percent of the vote in Irish South Boston in the November presidential election, putting the lie to aspersions on Irish-American loyalty, while making it easier for Curley to praise Wilson and, with whatever reservations, to support his war.

Curley was a patriot, not a jingo. While he was mayor there were no outrages against German Americans in Boston (Dr. Karl Muck, the German-born director of the Boston Symphony Orchestra, would be arrested under Curley's successor for failing to play "The Star-spangled Banner") and no abridgments of the right to dissent.

The United States' entry into the war released what one historian calls a "brainless fury" against all things German. "Hamburger" and "sauerkraut" disappeared from restaurant menus to be replaced by "liberty sandwich" and "liberty cabbage." In San Rafael, California, a man suspected of disloyalty had his hair cut in the shape of a cross. In Pensacola, Florida, a committee of vigilantes flogged a German American, forced him to shout "To hell with the Kaiser; hurrah for Wilson," and ordered him to leave the state. In New Brunswick, New Jersey, Rutgers students stripped an antiwar protester, coated him with molasses and feathers, and paraded him through the streets as an object lesson for "pro-Germans." The governor of Iowa banned the speaking of German, even over the telephone. In Collinsville, Illinois, a mob of five hundred seized a young German American—who, ironically, had tried to enlist in the navy but had been turned down because he was blind in one eye—bound him in an American flag, dragged him through the streets, and hanged him. A jury acquitted the mob's leaders in twenty-five minutes. By contrast, a New Hampshire jury sentenced a man to prison for three years for calling the conflict "a [J. P.] Morgan war and not a war of the people."

Partly to sway the German-American vote in the 1916 city council election, Curley had allowed interned German sailors to give a band concert on the Common to mark the kaiser's birthday. Now, in wartime, while President Wilson repeatedly refused to speak out against attacks on German Americans, Curley insisted that the enemy was the German militarists, not the German people, whose liberation from the Prussian clique he spoke of as an Allied war aim. While Wilson was clapping Socialists and dissenters into jail for exercising their constitutional rights, Curley was defending the right of Socialists and peace demonstrators to meet on Boston Common. "The right of free speech is a very sacred one," he said. "In its defense, Mary Dyer, years ago, gave her life on Boston Common, near the very spot where these men will conduct their meeting. These men are asking for the same right—free speech."

Curley later said that the most moving experience of his life was listening to Madame Schumann-Heink, the great Austrian-born opera singer, give a performance on the Common for three thousand departing soldiers and their families. Hearing that she was in town staying with friends, he called to ask if, with only a day's notice, she could sing the boys off to war. He made a special request of a song: "Boy of Mine," an excusably saccharine ballad popular that grim year.

She agreed, and mastered the song in an hour. A naturalized American citizen, Madame Schumann-Heink, owing to her two German and one American marriages, had sons fighting in both the U.S. and German armies. Shortly before she was to go to the Parkman bandstand for the concert, she received a cable informing her that her son in the German army had been killed in action. She showed Curley the cable and, overcome with grief, said she could not go on with the show. "You do understand the meaning of the English words, don't you?" Curley gently pressed, meaning the words to "Boy of Mine." Madame Schumann-Heink squared her Wagnerian shoulders. "Ja, I think this is what they want, the mommas and the poppas." She would do it.

He introduced her to the audience as the woman who was famous for singing "Stille Nacht" on Christmas Eve. Families, some of them with their sons for the last time, waited on the grass as the big woman with the cablegram crumpled in her dress pocket made ready to sing. From the first note, tears streamed down her cheeks.

> Boy of mine
> Boy of mine
> Although my heart is breaking
> I seem to know you'd want to go,
> Pride in your manhood waking. . . .
>
> But I'll be here waiting, dear
> And at the glad dawn's waking
>
> I'm here to say I love you so
> Dear little boy of mine.
> Dear little boy of mine.

One by one the Allied nations sent missions to Boston. Parades, dinners, flowery toasts: Curley was in his element. Marshal Joseph Joffre's visit in May was the grandest of these occasions. In his welcoming speech, Curley predicted that the kaiser would "abdicate through fear" at the prospect of fighting the American soldier, an observation that must have given brittle amusement to the hero of the Marne. Half a million persons cheered the marshal (with the mayor beside him in an open touring car) as the parade in his honor wound through streets lined with schoolchildren waving the tricolor and shouting, "Vive la France!" Mrs. Curley, waiting on the reviewing stand in front of City Hall with Boston's veterans of the Civil War, waved two French flags as a signal for the crowd to pay tribute to Joffre—at which the wizened Grand Army of the Republic treasures beside her, grappling with their canes, stood and cheered with such unseasonal vim that the whole place, according to one observer, "went mad." Later, in a ceremony on the Common, nine-year-old Mary Curley, ducking to avoid being kissed by Joffre's great white furry mustachios, presented the marshal with a check for $175,000 for the war orphans of France. She made the presentation in French, and if this wasn't one of the proudest moments in her father's life, then one misreads the width of his smile in the news photographs.

Afterward, over and over in a darkened theater, Mary sat through the newsreel of the presentation. She stayed for just one more showing, and what a shame she did, for as the marshal bent down to buss her on the cheek a lady in the row in front of her remarked to her neighbor, "Who is that ugly little girl?"

The great danger to Curley had always been a simultaneous challenge from both an Irish candidate minus Fitzgerald's libidinous baggage and a Protestant "reform" candidate. While he and the other Irish candidate divided the Irish vote, the reform candidate could win merely by holding Kenny's 1914 vote. That danger now materialized.

The Irish candidate was first in the ring. Congressman James A. Gallivan was a native of South Boston, graduate of the Boston Latin School, the city's most prestigious public high school, and a star first baseman on the Harvard team of 1888. He had served two terms as state representative and two as state senator, and spent thirteen years on the Board of Street Commissioners before winning Curley's former congressional seat in 1914. "I'll tear the hide off him," he said of the mayor in announcing his candidacy.

The city's citadel of reform, the Good Government Association, one wit noted, "will endorse anybody who runs against Curley, even if it was a cockeyed, bowlegged Chinaman who wears pajamas to work and a kimono when he goes to a party." The association did not have to cast its net so far as that. In March, former congressman Andrew J. Peters resigned his post as Wilson's assistant secretary of the treasury and moved back to Boston. He seemed to be making himself available as a candidate for mayor, though as one association member's diaries reveal, in the end he had to be actively courted.

Like Curley, Peters lived in Jamaica Plain, but in the house where, in 1872, he had been born, and which had been in the Peters family—whose fortune was sturdily built on wholesale lumber and the China trade—since the late eighteenth century. Andrew went to St. Paul's School, Harvard College, and Harvard Law. The family summered in Maine, and Andrew grew to manhood among the improving props of spinnakers and spars. The house in Jamaica Plain, the "cottage" on Vinalhaven Island, the farm in Dover, a rustic Boston suburb—the life that he and his wife, Martha, heiress to the great Phillips estate in Boston, carved out for themselves was the stuff of an upper-class nineteenth-century idyll. After several terms representing Jamaica Plain in the state legislature, Peters won four terms in the House of Representatives from the Eleventh Congressional District, which included eight Boston wards, before Wilson appointed him to the Treasury Department. A member of the Tavern, the Tennis and Racket, the Somerset, the Exchange, the Eastern Yacht, and the New York Harvard clubs—and also of the Country Club, in Brookline—Andrew J. Peters was a man of reputation and standing.

"Yet beneath Peters' brownstone exterior," to quote the late Francis Russell, "lurked a perverse personality known only to a select few." Unfortunately for Curley, Peters's was one of the few perversions in Boston of which Curley's agents were unaware.

Sometime in 1917, perhaps as a result of the tensions of the campaign, Peters became morbidly attracted to an eleven-year-old girl who would become known by the plangent name of Starr Faithfull. Her father, a Beacon Hill wastrel, had abandoned Starr, her mother, and her sister. Peters, a distant cousin by marriage, agreed to act as temporary guardian to the girls, who soon became playmates of his five children. He began reading Starr choice bits of Havelock Ellis's *Studies in the Psychology of Sex*. He taught her to use ether. And one day, while she was in a stupor, he raped her. Thereafter, she knew no rest from his "anesthetic advances."

Starr looked much older than she was, and within a few years Peters was taking her with him on out-of-town trips. She kept a diary of their travels. "Spent night AJP Providence. Oh Horror, Horror, Horror!!!" reads one entry.

★   ★   ★

"Ripping," James Michael Curley replied when reporters asked him what he thought of Peters's candidacy. One reporter misunderstood; did the mayor say "Rip him"? Vexed, Curley corrected him. "Ripping. Don't you know the meaning of ripping? Haven't you heard the word 'bully'?"

The last candidate to enter the race, Congressman Peter F. Tague, was Martin Lomasney's cat's-paw. Lomasney, the West End boss, had resolved to drive Curley from office because Curley had done nothing to stop a City Council dominated by members of the Good Government Association from gerrymandering his ward. Lomasney, who finally endorsed Peters two days before the election, hoped Tague would drain Irish votes away from Curley in Charlestown and East Boston, which were both in Tague's congressional district. Like Gallivan, whom John Fitzgerald had persuaded to enter the race, Tague could keep his congressional seat while running for mayor. He had nothing to lose by playing the spoiler.

With Irish South Boston lost to Gallivan, Irish Charlestown seemingly lost to Tague, and Boston's thirty-five thousand registered Republicans sure to turn out heavily for Peters, "Mayor Curley as a potential political factor is gone," a leading Democrat predicted. Day after day now, a kite flew over City Hall with a sign on it saying, PETERS FOR MAYOR. "Many consider it an omen," wrote one reporter.

Curley had only one card left to play, a journalist observed: "That card is his own driving and magnetic personality on the stump." A month before the opening of the campaign in November, he had already made a staggering 678 public appearances in this red-white-and-blue year. Now, in the last weeks before the election on December 17, he seemed to be trying to surpass that record. He kept shirts of different collar sizes in the drawers of his big chiffonier, and as the sinews of his speaking parts swelled from delivering as many as ten non-acoustically assisted speeches a night, he would go up a collar size—16 1/2 at the beginning of the evening, 17 in the middle, and a turgid 18 inches at the end. He had become his voice, his "magnetic and mellifluent larynx," as the *Boston Journal* labeled it.

There were no arguments he could advance either for himself or against the other candidates that could stand a moment's scrutiny. Gallivan was asking audiences, "Who put the 'plum' in 'plumbing'?" and Curley could hardly pretend that if he were reelected the city would not get "eight years of Marks Angell and Frankie Daly." The most he could say against the "slacker congressmen" was that, in the hour of national crisis, they belonged in Washington, passing a bill to draft "alien slackers"—foreign nationals who happened to be in the United States when war broke out. In fact, Gallivan and Tague had come out for a bill that would do just that, but, citing the divisive effect it would have on inter-Allied relations, the State Department asked them to drop it. The most Curley could say against "the gentleman from Dover," as he tauntingly called Peters, was that the nation needed him at his former job, "for the first duty of every citizen is to serve his country in whatever capacity will best contribute to a speedy ending of the war. . . . More money is being handled by the Treasury than ever in the history of the country. If Peters wants to serve, the way to do it is to go back to his old job in the Treasury Department. . . ." As an "issue," this was almost contemporary in its vacuity.

With no case to make, Curley's rhetoric had to substitute for argument. He had to do it all with a phrase. Thus he called the newspapers, which were against him, "wells of information poisoned by subsidy." Thus he said of Peters's head that it "more nearly resembled a complete vacuum than ever before known in the history of Boston," warned of the real Peters campaign "being waged under the cloak of dignity," and unmasked Peters's supporters as "purchasable camp followers." Gallivan was "a desperado of American politics." John R. Murphy, the chairman of the Finance Commission, "had the brains of a caterpillar." Curley waxed biblical on "the floodgates of wrath, envy, malice, vituperation, corruption and debauchery" opened by his opponents, whom he referred to collectively as "this distinguished and motley array of plunderers." In a rally across the street from "that foul sheet," the *Boston Post,* he put all of his frustration and fury into a cascade of Homeric invective. "With the rotten *Post* against me, with the American against me, with the *Herald* against me, with the Romanoff of Ward 8 against me, with Peters and his millions, with Tague, with Gallivan and his egotism against me, with every corrupt boss and rotten newspaper against me—with all of these powers of rottenness and corruption against me, they can't beat Jim Curley."

He had two short films made: *Boston Doing Its Bit,* which showed him doing his bit to kill the kaiser with words, and *A Day in the Life of the Mayor of Boston,* which accompanied him, as one reviewer noted, "from the moment he sips his morning coffee until he tucks himself in under his bedclothes at night." And he put the owners of Boston's twenty-six theaters on notice that if they wanted their licenses renewed they had better show his films.

Through a surrogate, Curley raised the "race issue" against Peters, whom he often identified as "my only opponent," in hopes of polarizing the contest on ethnic grounds. In *The Hibernian,* edited by a political ally, there appeared a full-page political ad with a cutout of Curley:

RE-ELECT JAMES M. CURLEY, MAYOR.
Do not be deceived by false issues.
The Peters Issue Is—Down with the Irish.
The Good Government Issue Is—Down with the Irish.

The text of the ad continued: "We know that a quiet house-to-house canvass is being made among the Republicans in the interests of Peters, in which it is whispered that the Irish are fighting among themselves and now is the time to elect one of our own, meaning a Yankee." It was a stiff dose of the old poison.

On the Sunday before the election Curley made twenty-eight appearances across the city in eight hours. But such prodigies of energy would not help him now. People had ample doubts for whom he would use that energy—for them, or for Marks Angell; for Boston, or for Jim Curley.

On election day, hundreds of Peters voters in the South End fell victim to a Curley trick: They had been mailed cards bearing Peters's signature directing them to the wrong polling places. A Charlestown drunk was released from the Charles Street Jail after serving only a week of a thirty-day sentence on condition that he vote for Curley. There was a near-riot in Martin Lomasney's West End ward as city officials, challenging voters waiting in line, fought with city employees suspected of planning to vote against Curley. Two fistfights broke out in front of City Hall, where a Negro in a tall hat walked up and down all day carrying a sign that said, SHOP EARLY, KEEP TO THE RIGHT, RE-ELECT CURLEY.

At just before five the newsboys came running down School Street shouting "Peters Elected! Peters Elected!" And then, "Curley Out!" Led by a vagrant hope, perhaps, the mayor dropped by the old aldermanic chambers, where the city clerks were writing the returns up on blackboards. A glance at the numbers confirmed the worst. Peters, barely adding to Kenny's total in 1914, wound up with 39,924 votes; Gallivan, the real spoiler, got 19,415; Tague, a nonfactor, 1,694; a Socialist candidate, a few hundred; and Curley, 28,850. He had won only six of Boston's twenty-six wards—had carried only the poorest Irish districts, which then and later were "with Curley" despite Curley. He made a brief statement to the clerks—"I have served four years as Mayor with honor to myself and benefit to the city"—and when he finished there was no applause.

Directly, he left City Hall, passing through what one witness remembers as "a group of silent men" on his way out the rear door. Just as he emerged, a band carrying a PETERS FOR MAYOR banner rounded the corner. Spying Curley, the bandsmen struck up Chopin's "Funeral March." In the upper floors of the City Hall Annex, one of the mayor's supporters who did not want the solemnity of the moment disturbed—and who had never heard Curley say that the life of politics was a picket-fence existence—hurled a tin pot down on their heads.

Excerpted from Jack Beatty, *The Rascal King: The Life and Times of James Michael Curley, 1874–1958* (Cambridge, MA: Da Capo Press, 2000), pgs. 154–211.

Warren Harding

BLOVIATOR

Warren Gamiel Harding (1866–1924) could be terse: "I love you clothed but naked more," he wrote in a love letter. But in public he spoke fog. After H. L. Mencken made memorable sport of the style of his March 1921 inaugural address, Harding delegated his aide, the sainted Judson Welliver, to write most of his speeches.

GAMALIELESE
H. L. Mencken

On the question of the logical content of Dr. Harding's harangue of last Friday I do not presume to have views. The matter has been debated at great length by the editorial writers of the Republic, all of them experts in logic; moreover, I confess to being prejudiced. When a man arises publicly to argue that the United States entered the late war because of a "concern for preserved civilization," I can only snicker in a superior way and wonder why he isn't holding down the chair of history in some American university. When he says that the United States has "never sought territorial aggrandizement through force," the snicker arises to the virulence of a chuckle, and I turn to the first volume of General Grant's memoirs. And when, gaining momentum, he gravely informs the boobery that "ours is a constitutional freedom where the popular will is supreme, and minorities are sacredly protected," then I abandon myself to a mirth that transcends, perhaps, the seemly, and send picture postcards of A. Mitchell Palmer and the Atlanta Penitentiary to all of my enemies who happen to be Socialists.

But when it comes to the style of a great man's discourse, I can speak with a great deal less prejudice, and maybe with somewhat more competence, for I have earned most of my livelihood for twenty years past by translating the bad English of a multitude of authors into measurably better English. Thus qualified professionally, I rise to pay my small tribute to Dr. Harding. Setting aside a college professor or two and half a dozen dipsomaniacal newspaper reporters, he takes the first place in my Valhalla of literati. That is to say, he writes the worst English that I have ever encountered. It reminds me of a string of wet sponges; it reminds me of tattered washing on the line; it reminds me of stale bean-soup, of college yells, of dogs barking idiotically through endless nights. It is so bad that a sort of grandeur creeps into it. It drags itself out of the dark abysm (I was about to write abscess!) of pish, and crawls insanely up the topmost pinnacle of posh. It is rumble and bumble. It is flap and doodle. It is balder and dash.

But I grow lyrical. More scientifically, what is the matter with it? Why does it seem so flabby, so banal, so confused and childish, so stupidly at war with sense? If you first read the inaugural address and then heard it intoned, as I did (at least in part), then you will perhaps arrive at an answer. That answer is very simple. When Dr. Harding prepares a speech he does not think it out in terms of an educated reader locked up in jail, but in terms of a great horde of stoneheads gathered around a stand. That is to say, the thing is always a stump speech; it is conceived as a stump speech and written as a stump speech. More, it is a stump speech addressed primarily to the sort of audience that the speaker has been used to all his life, to wit, an audience of small town yokels, of low political serfs, or morons scarcely able to understand a word of more than two syllables, and wholly unable to pursue a logical idea for more than two centimeters.

Such imbeciles do not want ideas—that is, new ideas, ideas that are unfamiliar, ideas that challenge their attention. What they want is simply a gaudy series of platitudes, of sonorous nonsense driven home with gestures. As I say, they can't understand many words of more than two syllables, but that is not saying that they do not esteem such words. On the contrary, they like them and demand them. The roll of incomprehensible polysyllables enchants them. They like phrases which thunder like salvos of artillery. Let that thunder sound, and they take all the rest on trust. If a sentence begins furiously and then peters out into fatuity, they are still satisfied. If a phrase has a punch in it, they do not ask that it also have a meaning. If a word slides off the tongue like a ship going down the ways, they are content and applaud it and wait for the next.

Brought up amid such hinds, trained by long practice to engage and delight them, Dr. Harding carries over his stump manner into everything he writes. He is, perhaps, too old to learn a better way. He is, more likely, too discreet to experiment. The stump speech, put into cold type, maketh the judicious to grieve. But roared from an actual stump, with arms flying and eyes flashing and the old flag overhead, it is certainly and brilliantly effective. Read the inaugural address, and it will gag you. But hear it recited through a sound-magnifier, with grand gestures to ram home its periods, and you will begin to understand it.

Let us turn to a specific example. I exhume a sentence from the latter half of the eminent orator's discourse:

> I would like government to do all it can to mitigate, then, in understanding, in mutuality of interest, in concern for the common good, our tasks will be solved.

I assume that you have read it. I also assume that you set it down as idiotic—a series of words without sense. You are quite right; it is. But now imagine it intoned as it was designed to be intoned. Imagine the slow tempo of a public speech. Imagine the stately unrolling of the first clause, the delicate pause upon the word "then"—and then the

loud discharge of the phrase "in understanding," "in mutuality of interest," "in concern for the common good," each with its attendant
glare and roll of the eyes, each with its sublime heave, each with its
gesture of a blacksmith bringing down his sledge upon an egg—
imagine all this, and then ask yourself where you have got. You have
got, in brief, to a point where you don't know what it is all about. You
hear and applaud the phrases, but their connection has already escaped you. And so, when in violation of all sequence and logic, the final phrase, "our tasks will be solved," assaults you, you do not notice
its disharmony—all you notice is that, if this or that, already forgotten, is done, "our tasks will be solved." Whereupon, glad of the assurance and thrilled by the vast gestures that drive it home, you give a
cheer.

That is, if you are the sort of man who goes to political meetings,
which is to say, if you are the sort of man that Dr. Harding is used to
talking to, which is to say, if you are a jackass.

The whole inaugural address reeked with just such nonsense. The
thing started off with an error in English in its very first sentence—
the confusion of pronouns in the *one-he* combination, so beloved of
bad newspaper reporters. It bristled with words misused: *Civic* for
civil, luring for *alluring, womanhood* for *women, referendum* for *reference,* even *task* for *problem.* "The *task* is to be *solved*"—what could be
worse? Yet I find it twice. "The expressed views of world opinion"—
what irritating tautology! "The expressed conscience of progress"—
what on earth does it mean? "This is not selfishness, it is
sanctity"—what intelligible idea do you get out of that? "I know that
Congress and the administration will favor every wise government
policy to aid the resumption and encourage continued progress"—the
resumption of what? "Service is the supreme *commitment* of life"—
ach, du heiliger!

But is such bosh out of place in a stump speech? Obviously not. It is
precisely and thoroughly in place in a stump speech. A tight fabric of
ideas would weary and exasperate the audience; what it wants is simply a loud burble of words, a procession of phrases that roar, a series
of whoops. This is what it got in the inaugural address of the Hon.
Warren Gamaliel Harding. And this is what it will get for four long

years—unless God sends a miracle and the corruptible puts on incorruption. . . . Almost I long for the sweeter song, the rubber-stamps of more familiar design, the gentler and more seemly bosh of the late Woodrow.

Excerpted from H. L. Mencken, *The Baltimore Evening Sun*, March 7, 1912.

Herbert Hoover

OUR CONTEMPORARY

Hoover's name is synonymous not merely with failure but with unfeeling failure. Hoover fed his dog on the White House lawn while jobless Americans went hungry. He flung bromides at the Great Depression—"Prosperity is just around the corner"—but did nothing to end it or ameliorate the suffering it caused millions. In progressive historiography Hoover makes a villainizing contrast with Franklin D. Roosevelt, the one dour and ideologically rigid, the other buoyant and experimental. Yet, for all the policy innovations of the New Deal, FDR could not end the Depression. And Hoover did act. He began with exhortations, but the deepening crisis forced him to abandon laissez-faire. He intervened in the economy with emergency subsidies to railroads, banks, building-and-loans, and agriculture. To increase the supply of credit he rewrote the nation's banking laws. He even resorted to deficit spending. In 1932 Roosevelt ran against him partly from the right, attacking Hoover's un-Hooverian attachment "to the idea that we ought to centralize everything in Washington" and his fiscal profligacy. "[G]iven later developments," a Roosevelt economist wrote in his memoirs, "the campaign speeches often read like a giant misprint, in which Roosevelt and Hoover speak each other's lines."

Yet in American political culture they speak enduringly different lines. Hoover, and the conservative tradition before him and since, speaks of economic life as a "race," with the government as "the umpire of fairness in the race" and with the "winner . . . he who shows the most conscientious training, the greatest ability, and the greatest character." For conservatives, the emphasis on

79

character lends moral significance to economic adversity, and makes them reluctant to mitigate it lest initiative be undermined. Their resistance to "welfare," unemployment insurance, and the minimum wage also reflects market brutalism: people will work for less the worse off they are. FDR speaks of economic life as a quest for security from the vicissitudes of the market for which individuals cannot be held responsible and should not have to face on their own. As David M. Kennedy tells us in *Freedom From Fear: The American People in Depression and War, 1929–1945,* in a series of 1934 messages to congress Roosevelt spelled out "the ideology of modern liberalism." Changes in the economy and society require government to be more than an umpire, he said, preparing legislators for the introduction of Social Security in 1935: "[I]n the earlier days" security came from "the interdependence of members of families upon each other and of the families within a small community upon each other." But now: "The complexities of great communities and of organized industry make less real these simple means of security. Therefore, we are compelled to employ the active interest of the Nation as a whole through government in order to encourage a greater security for each individual who composes it." The Constitution calls for the federal government "to promote the general welfare," and it is its "plain duty to provide for that security upon which welfare depends."

That public philosophy prevailed up until the 1970s, when foreign competition began to undermine the job security of the American middle class. Our time has witnessed the return of Hooverian assumptions parallel with the return of what the *New York Times,* in a 1996 series titled "The Downsizing of America," called the "worst economic insecurity since the Great Depression." American workers can no longer afford "security," experts quoted in the series said. It fetters economic motivation. Risk is the virtue of the hour. Fear motivates now. "Just-in-time" production has spawned an increasingly "just-in-time" work force, hired for the length of the "project," then let go. In the "free-agent" economy, a lifetime career with one employer, a form of security taken for granted through the 1960s, cannot be expected.

Driving the new insecurity is a hydra of forces—globalization, automation, immigration, the rise of investor capitalism. Today in manufacturing, tomorrow in high tech and financial services, more and more Americans compete with Third World workers paid Third World wages. Capital and technology can move. You stay home. Technology can replace you. Your company can down-size you to give a perverse fillip to its stock price. Your defined-risk 401(k) pension rises and falls with the manipulated tides of speculation. And you've got to face these risks alone. Unions represent only 9 percent of the private-sector workers, down from 35 percent in the 1960s. Through free-trade agreements like NAFTA and immigration policies that force wages down, government exposes you to economic insecurity, not protects you from it.

Today, more young people believe that if they fail the fault is theirs and not that of economic and social circumstances than at any other time since the 1920s. "You're on your own"—according to David Frum, the commentator and former speechwriter for George W. Bush, that is conservatism's message to Americans. The grip of Hooverian assumptions about economic life reflects the Hooverian realties.

That individualism endures in a world swept by economic forces beyond not only individual but state control testifies to its centrality in our political culture. The communitarian vision of the New Deal looks like the aberration now. As the memory of why the New Deal was necessary faded in the postwar prosperity, many Americans came to regard federally centered "community" as "statism" and to fear it more than the market insecurity it tried to mitigate. Richard Hofstadter's essay describes a strain of the American character that, writing in the progressive afterglow of 1948, he thought Americans had outgrown. "Herbert Hoover and the Crisis of American Individualism" is thus a poignant document, a manifestation of the historical obsolescence it describes.

HERBERT HOOVER AND THE CRISIS OF AMERICAN INDIVIDUALISM

Richard Hofstadter

> The test of the rightfulness of our decisions must be whether we have
> sustained and advanced . . . prosperity.
> — HERBERT HOOVER

In the autumn of 1919 John Maynard Keynes, out of his disgust and bitterness with the terms of the Versailles Treaty, wrote a devastating book, *The Economic Consequences of the Peace.* Keynes's judgments of the peacemakers of World War I were severe, but concerning one, Herbert Hoover, he wrote:

Mr. Hoover was the only man who emerged from the ordeal of Paris with an enhanced reputation. This complex personality, with his habitual air of weary Titan (or, as others might put it, of exhausted prizefighter), his eyes steadily fixed on the true and essential facts of the European situation, imported into the Councils of Paris, when he took part in them, precisely that atmosphere of reality, knowledge, magnanimity, and disinterestedness which, if they had been found in other quarters also, would have given us the Good Peace.

Of the work that had been carried out during the first six months of that year by the American Relief Administration under Hoover's direction, Keynes said:

Never was a nobler work of disinterested goodwill carried through with more tenacity and sincerity and skill, and with less thanks either asked or given. The ungrateful Governments of Europe owe much more to the statesmanship and insight of Mr. Hoover and his band of American workers than they have yet appreciated or will ever acknowledge. The American Relief Commission, and they only, saw the European position during those months in its true perspective and felt towards it as men should. It was their efforts, their energy, and the American resources placed by the President at their disposal, often acting in the teeth of European obstruction, which not only saved an immense amount of human suffering, but averted a widespread breakdown of the European system.

These words did not seem extravagant in 1919; nor did they sound unfamiliar in either Europe or America. Hoover appeared a gigantic figure—"the biggest man," said the London *Nation,* "who has emerged on the Allied side during the war." He had risen to this international acclaim—second only to Wilson's and considerably more lasting—from a background as dramatic as it was obscure. The outbreak of the war had found Hoover living quietly in London, unknown to the general public of any nation, an international businessman and mining engineer of modest repute. At the age of forty he had accumulated a considerable fortune; this was not remarkable, but the global scope of his career was.

Between 1899 and 1911, in addition to a few engineering tasks undertaken in his native country, Hoover had dug mines, supervised a variety of enterprises, and acquired interests on four continents. Starting in Australia in 1897–8, he had spent part of 1899 in China, 1901 in Japan, 1902 in New Zealand, 1903 in India, 1904 in Rhodesia and the Transvaal, 1905 in Egypt, 1907 in Burma, the Malay States, and Ceylon, 1908 in Italy, 1909 in Russia, Korea, and Germany, 1910 in France, and 1911 again in Russia. He had offices in San Francisco, New York, London, Melbourne, Shanghai, and for periods in St. Petersburg and Mandalay. He had lived a large part of his mature life on ocean liners. He was associated with over a score of business concerns. In Russia he had managed various interests on an estate containing about seventy-five thousand tenants and laborers. In China he had witnessed the Boxer Rebellion and supervised the construction of barricades to defend Tientsin against siege. At Tomsk in Siberia he had felt reverberations of the 1905 Revolution. In Burma he had been down with tropical malaria. He had found time to publish two books: a textbook on *Principles of Mining,* and a translation with his wife's aid of Georgius Agricola's sixteenth-century metallurgical treatise, *De Re Metallica.*

Hoover's first war job had been to remove thousands of American tourists who were stranded in Europe when the war broke out. Then he accepted the chairmanship of the Commission for Relief in Belgium. For four years, in spite of terrible obstruction by both Germany and the Allies, Hoover's commission fed ten million people. The task was accomplished with astonishing efficiency, and when the commission's accounts were tallied at the close of operations its overhead was found to be only three eighths of one percent of total expenditures, and a surplus was bequeathed for the peacetime reconstruction of Belgium. In 1917, assuming the position of Food Administrator for the United States, Hoover conducted, with spectacular success and without power to employ rationing, a program of food supply and conservation that made his name a household word. As head of the economic restoration of Europe at the close of the war, he distributed twenty million tons of food to three hundred million people, ran a fleet of ships, directed the railroads and coal mines of central Europe, and restored crippled communications.

In a time of havoc and hatred the name Hoover came to mean food for the starving and medicine for the sick. From the ranks of his co-workers a fanatic body of admirers had gathered about him. In several European countries streets were named for him. After five years of war service without salary and without attention to his private affairs, his fortune had been somewhat scaled down, but he was rich in popularity.

Within little more than a decade the story of Hoover's wartime career was all but forgotten. The man who had fed Europe had become a symbol of hunger, the brilliant administrator a symbol of disaster. The *Hooverstrassen* of the Armistice period had given way to the dismal Hoovervilles of the Great Depression. And the great engineer left the White House under as dark a cloud of public disfavor as any president since John Quincy Adams, over a century before.

There was nothing mythical about Hoover's vaunted ability. The bare outlines of his career show that the admirers of the relief commissioner, the food administrator, and the cabinet secretary were not mistaken in thinking they had found a man of extraordinary energy, initiative, and efficiency. What ruined Hoover's public career was not a sudden failure of personal capacity but the collapse of the world that had produced him and shaped his philosophy.

The things Hoover believed in—efficiency, enterprise, opportunity, individualism, substantial laissez-faire, personal success, material welfare—were all in the dominant American tradition. The ideas he represented—ideas that to so many people made him seem hateful or ridiculous after 1929—were precisely the same ideas that in the remoter past of the nineteenth century and the more immediate past of the New Era had had an almost irresistible lure for the majority of Americans. In the language of Jefferson, Jackson, and Lincoln these ideas had been fresh and invigorating; in the language of Herbert Hoover they seemed stale and oppressive. It is a significant fact that in the crisis of the thirties the man who represented these conceptions found himself unable even to communicate himself and what he stood for. Almost overnight his essential beliefs had become outlandish and unintelligible. The victim of his faith in the power of capitalism to survive and prosper without gigantic governmental props, Hoover was the last presidential spokesman of the hallowed doctrines of laissez-faire liberalism, and his departure from Washington marked the decline of a great tradition.

Most striking about Hoover's social philosophy is the doggedness with which he holds to it and his willingness to endure opprobrium by acting upon it. Hoover's administration after the crash of 1929 is one protracted rite of hara-kiri. No president, not even Grover Cleveland, has ever been seduced by his convictions into blunter defiance of majority opinion. On this score Hoover can always be acquitted of the charge of revising his ideas to cater to mass sentiment.

Hoover's confidence in what he calls the American system owes a good deal to the circumstances of his early career. He is a self-made man out of ancient American mythology, whose early life story would have delighted Abraham Lincoln. Since Andrew Johnson, whose father was a porter and who began life as an illiterate tailor's apprentice, no occupant of the White House has arisen from circumstances more modest. Hoover's father was a blacksmith who ran a sales agency for agricultural machinery as a sideline; he was the descendant of perennially obscure pioneering stock dating from colonial times. During the nineteenth century the Hoover family had moved from North Carolina to Ohio and from Ohio to Iowa, where Hoover was born in 1874. Both parents were practicing Quakers.

Hoover's father died when the boy was six, his mother when he was not yet ten, leaving their savings of fifteen hundred dollars to three children. Young Hoover went west to Willamette, Oregon, in the care of his maternal uncle, Dr. John Minthorn, who soon made rich profits in the Northwestern land boom; Hoover entered his uncle's business as an office boy.

On the suggestion of a visiting engineer, the boy took qualifying examinations in 1891 for the newly opened Stanford University. Although his preparation was inadequate, the institution relaxed its standards to swell the freshman class. When a shrewd university examiner saw in Hoover a redeeming flair for mathematics, he was admitted under the modest handicap of being "conditioned" in English. For the rest of his life he struggled with his prose, which has always been suggestive of a light fog moving over a bleak landscape.

At Stanford Hoover studied under Professor John Branner, an eminent geologist. To support himself he not only took on a number of odd jobs, but, more important, worked during summers as Branner's assistant on geological surveys and during school terms as Branner's secretary. He also plunged into campus politics on the side of the antifraternity or "democratic" faction, organizing the poorest element of the student body, boys who lived in abandoned workmen's shacks on the edge of the campus. In such relatively extroverted roles Hoover partially overcame his shyness and quickly won respect. Will Irwin, a fellow undergraduate, recalls: "'Popularity' is not exactly the word for his reaction and influence on his fellows. A better word probably would be 'standing.'" In 1893 Hoover was elected treasurer of the student body, his sole experience in running for office until the presidential campaign of 1928. At Stanford he also met the daughter of a Monterey banker, Lou Henry, whom he married in 1899.

Stanford did a great deal for Hoover, and he later became a patron, a trustee, and the founder of its Hoover War Library. But when he took his engineering diploma in 1895 a depression was approaching its depths, and his prospects were not immediately promising. Unable to get a post as engineer, young Hoover took a common laborer's job in a mine near Nevada City, and the summer after his graduation found him working deep in the Sierras, pushing a hand-car and shoveling ore at two dollars and a half a day.

Hoover did not stay buried in the mines. In a few months he became office assistant to Louis Janin, a well-known San Francisco engineer, and graduated rapidly to more responsible positions. Then a call came to Janin from a large British mining firm for an American engineer who could direct new gold mines at Coolgardie in Australia. Not yet twenty-four, Hoover found himself on a steamer bound for a job in the Antipodes at a salary of $7,500, standing at the threshold of the fabulous business career that was to make him a millionaire before he was forty.

For one who was to advise at the Paris Peace Conference, Hoover's background was in some ways propitious. He came to the war with a Quaker heritage. Unlike the elder statesmen who were running the show, he had no political outlook and no worries over a constituency. He was more immune to the terrible passions the war had stirred, he had seen with his own eyes the falsity of Allied atrocity stories, and he knew that cruelty was not the exclusive quality of the Germans. His point of view was much like a nonbelligerent's, and, so far as possible, it was free of other than practical economic considerations. As he put it many years later in speaking of the Peace Conference: "I dealt with the gaunt realities which prowled about outside."

But Hoover's program for peace was not confined to the relief of hunger. With Wilson he shared the belief that Europe should be reconstructed on the principles of liberal capitalism. He was in favor of withdrawing from Europe "lock, stock, and barrel" unless the Allies would accept the Fourteen Points of Woodrow Wilson's plan for ending World War I, and he was relentlessly determined that the United States should keep a free hand in all economic matters. Wherever food relief was concerned, Hoover kept one eye on the market for American agricultural surpluses, which gave him a practical as well as a humanitarian reason for criticizing the blockade maintained against Germany between the Armistice and March 1919. When Allied economic collaboration was proposed in November 1918, Hoover cabled one of his Paris representatives to veto

> anything that even looks like inter-allied control of our economic resources after peace. . . . After peace over one half of the whole export food supplies of the world will come from the United States, and for the buyers of these supplies to sit in dictation to us as to prices and distribution is wholly inconceivable. The same applies to raw materials.

This businesslike reply settled all possibility of inter-Allied economic action.

On the whole, Hoover's letters and memoranda to Wilson were perspicacious. Because he was sure that it would be a hundred times more difficult to maintain capitalism and democracy in Europe if Germany were economically destroyed, he argued for a settlement without vengeance and opposed many of the worst features of the final treaty. It might be necessary to plunder Germany for the satisfaction of the Allies, but he knew there was a political and economic limit to it. Germany might even be stripped of her surplus for a generation, he wrote Wilson on June 5, 1919, but more than this was utterly impossible, for it would kill the chances of democracy in Germany and "she will turn either to Communism or Reaction, and will thereby become either militarily or politically on the offensive." The treaty would go far to destroy the seeds of democracy in Germany and would hamper the course of world recovery. As for the post-Armistice blockade, it was "absolutely immoral. . . . We do not kick a man in the stomach after we have licked him."

An important part of his work, which had the ardent support of the Allied Supreme Council, was Hoover's anti-Bolshevik policy. In addition to the "transcendent purpose" of American relief, which was to feed the starving, he later explained:

my job was to nurture the frail plants of democracy in Europe against
. . . anarchy or Communism. And Communism was the pit into which
all governments were in danger of falling when frantic peoples were
driven by the Horsemen of Famine and Pestilence.

"The whole of American policies during the liquidation of the
Armistice was to contribute everything it could to prevent Europe
from going Bolshevik or being overrun by their armies," he stated in
1921. To Wilson he suggested that during the post-war period food be
distributed in Russia only on condition that the Soviets cease military
operations.

When Hoover returned from Europe late in 1919 it was as a major
political figure whom both parties were eager to claim, but whose
politics were unknown. In March 1920 he described himself in a public statement as "an independent progressive" who objected "as much
to the reactionary group in the Republican Party as I do to the radical
group in the Democratic Party." First he denied that he was seeking
public office. Then he announced that he would accept the Republican nomination if the party would adopt "a forward-looking, liberal,
constructive platform on the treaty and on our economic issues." (He
was for the League of Nations with reservations.)

By thus announcing his affiliation, without receiving any party
commitments in return, Hoover lost one of his trump cards. Assured
that his towering popularity would not be available to the Democrats,
the Republican Party professionals, who had no use for the engineer,
felt free to nominate a party regular. Hoover had popular following
and plenty of funds and publicity; he was far better known than
Harding, far more appealing than Lowden or Wood. But the bosses
won and Harding became president. In any case it is unlikely that
Hoover could have captured the Republican nomination, but Wen-
dell Willkie's feat in 1940 suggests that it was within the bounds of
possibility. Had Hoover become president in 1920, it is easy to believe
that the country would have been spared the ghastly farce of the
Harding administration and that Hoover himself could have left office in 1929 after two terms, one of the most admired chief executives

in all American history! Instead Hoover qualified as one of Harding's "Best Minds" and entered the cabinet as secretary of commerce.

★   ★   ★

It was ironic, in view of his later attitudes, that when Hoover took over the Department of Commerce he became a great bureaucrat. Once considered the least of the cabinet posts, the secretaryship of commerce rose under Hoover to equal Andrew Mellon's Treasury Department in its importance to the big-business government that settled upon Washington in the twenties. Its functions grew rapidly: several subdivisions sprang up, others were taken from the Interior Department, plans were made for a huge new building, and activities were accelerated to a remarkable pitch. Many years later Hoover observed: "No one with a day's experience in government fails to realize that in all bureaucracies there are three implacable spirits—self-perpetuation, expansion, and an incessant demand for more power."

One common criticism of the bureaucrat—inefficiency—has never been made of Hoover's regime in the Commerce Department, for its results were far out of proportion to its increase in expenditures and personnel. Business trends were studied and reported as never before. One relatively minor division, the Office of Simplified Practice, rendered annual savings to business and the public which alone more than repaid the nation for the department's budget, and Simplified Practice was only a small part of a grand, well-publicized campaign waged by the ex-engineer against economic waste.

The secretaryship of commerce was a strategic spot from which to advance Hoover's presidential ambitions, and he launched a course of activity which brought him press attention that rivaled Coolidge's. During the honeymoon of the twenties it was not difficult to woo the public and big business at the same time. Hoover particularly ingratiated himself with public-utility interests by making several strong speeches opposing federal regulation of power and favoring state regulation, the effectuality of which had been sharply reduced by court decisions. These speeches were distributed in pamphlet lots of 25,000 to 500,000 by the National Electric Light Association, the propaganda agency of the utility companies.

Hoover also tried to promote business by encouraging foreign investments and fighting for optimum markets for American buyers. His championship of American trade warranted the boast of Assistant Secretary of State William R. Castle to an exporters' convention that "Mr. Hoover is your advance agent and Secretary of State Kellogg is your attorney." The expansion of foreign investments, however, proved to be an inflationary boomerang. Every dollar invested abroad called for returns. When the total overseas investment became so huge that the annual interest payments and other returns in a given period exceeded the new investment flowing out, the balance of international payments on these invisible items would swing back to the United States and some of our foreign markets would eventually be lost. It was impossible to sell to the world, lend to the world, and refuse to buy from the world without eventually courting disaster.

But few people worried over such things in the heyday of Republican prosperity, and Hoover's cabinet service maintained his popularity. His work in Mississippi flood relief in 1927 reminded the electorate of his earlier humanitarian career. In the public mind he was the fit and proper successor to Coolidge. Yet he was still distrusted by the professional politicians, and, curious as it may seem, Wall Street politicos were afraid of him, longing for the renomination of the reliable Coolidge or, failing that, the nomination of Andrew Mellon. William Allen White in his biography of Coolidge records Chief Justice William Howard Taft's wonderment and disgust as he watched the Wall Streeters line up against Hoover because they knew he had "grumbled at the market."

Hoover was generally reputed the "most liberal" of the Harding-Coolidge cabinet. He had sat quietly through the scandals of the Harding era. He had done nothing wrong, even though he had done nothing to stop those who did. There were murmurings of suspicion about him in some quarters, particularly among farmers who doubted that he had any solution for the ills of agriculture, but none of his failings loomed very large in 1928. Although he had given no support to the liberal proposals of the twenties, other than a child-labor amendment and unemployment insurance, he was looked upon with an indulgent suspension of judgment: Perhaps his progressivism was only in hiding; perhaps he would be a more liberal man when he was no longer in political fetters under Harding and Coolidge. "It may be fair to say," wrote a liberal economist, "that he has done as well in that *milieu* as anyone could be expected to do." Such was the state of opinion when he captured the Republican nomination.

Hoover had worked hard for the presidency and he wanted to make the office his crowning triumph. He must have dreamed of the image he would leave for historians—a success in business, a fabulous success in humanitarian undertakings, a magnificent success in presidential leadership. Hoover the engineer would be the symbol of the coming age of material fulfillment, as Jefferson had been of democracy and Lincoln of emancipation.

But as a politician Hoover proved a failure, in dealing both with other politicians and with the public. He was unaccustomed to running for office and changing in response to popular will. His background in business, where he was supremely persuasive in working with his peers, had not trained him in give-and-take with masses of men. A good part of his life had been spent giving orders to "Orientals" and what he confidently called the "lower races." A rough and speculative occupation like mining and mine promotion demands a considerable sacrifice in human values, and it failed to develop in Hoover such compensating graces as diplomacy or social flexibility. There is evidence that he had developed a vein of arrogance beneath his matter-of-fact exterior. Once in a communication to an English mining journal he had waved aside the misappropriation of investors' funds by corporation officials with the remark that capital is "often invested" by such insiders "to more reproductive purpose than if it had remained in the hands of the idiots who parted with it." Accustomed as he was to successes and popular esteem, to managing men and machines with remarkable effects, it is unlikely that he had ever felt helpless before the bigness and difficulty of the world. Hoover

was one of those bright and energetic businessmen who, precisely because of the ease with which success has been attained in their immediate experience, refuse to learn deeply from anything outside of it.

Psychologically, Hoover was ill-adapted to the peculiar requirements of political life. Still shy, still far from articulate, he was anything but a dynamic public figure; he detested politics and its
countless silly indignities, he was addicted to worry, and he was sensitive to criticism. Little gifted with the arts that make for facile human
relationships, he would have found his position uncomfortable even
in prosperous times. Small wonder that near the end of his term he
should have groaned: "This office is a compound hell."

Hoover's greatest handicap, however, lay not in his personal limitations but in his philosophy. He devoutly believed in the comparatively
unregulated profit system under which he had grown up. He would
not say that the system was invulnerable—it could, of course, be
thrown out of gear by wrong thinking and unwise practices; he knew
also that it was subject to cyclical fluctuations, which he felt could be
diminished. But its basic principles were thoroughly "sound." If it
were allowed to proceed with no more than a smack and a dab of
government regulation here and there to prevent "abuses," it could
not fail to minister more and more effectively to human welfare.
From the end of the 1893 depression, in fact, to the crash of 1929—a
stretch of about thirty-two years covering Hoover's entire maturity—
this system had suffered no major setback. To be sure, there had been
a "banker's panic" in 1907—very short-lived and easily ascribed, as its
name suggests, to unsound practices. There had been a downward
turn in business just before the World War—but that was inconclu-
sive. There had been a brief depression in the early twenties—but
that was an outcome of wartime dislocation, not a natural ingredient
of the "normal" economic situation. Plainly the system worked, and it
worked well.

But this was not all. Since his childhood Hoover had seen a marked
rise in American wages and standards of living. The productivity of
American workmanship and technology had been steadily growing.
Telephones, radios, automobiles, electric lights, refrigerators—all
these inventions had come into broad popular use. American ingenu-

ity and enterprise, Hoover believed, would continue to manufacture the goods of life more efficiently and cheaply. Prices would fall. Increased productivity and lower costs would enable industry to pay higher wages, and higher wages would provide an expanding sales outlet. Through skillful promotion of foreign markets, surpluses could be sold abroad. Thus the whole economy would spiral upward in a never ending cycle: more telephones, more radios, more automobiles, more schools, more opportunities for everybody. It was the dawn of a golden age. In his triumphant acceptance address of 1928 Hoover declared: "We in America today are nearer to the final triumph over poverty than ever before in the history of any land. . . . We shall soon with the help of God be in sight of the day when poverty will be banished from this nation." He had become a wild-eyed Utopian capitalist.

Hoover has always described his brand of economics as "true liberalism," which he contrasts with the false liberalism of his critics on the left, and in the sense that his liberalism is more akin to historic nineteenth-century economic doctrines he is correct. He had come out of an Iowa farm environment that was intensely Republican in politics and had migrated into the open economic atmosphere of the Far West. His international experiences in business and long residence abroad had done no more to modify the native cast of his thinking than to change his typical mid-American accent. Just as Jefferson's travels in Europe had confirmed his political prejudices, so Hoover's acquaintance with European economic life had intensified his opposition to statism and his confidence in the superiority of "American" ways of doing things. With Jefferson and the economic individualists he agreed, on the whole, that that government is best which governs least, a conviction that was confirmed by his successes with local and voluntary forms of action. Even as a bureaucrat in Washington he had made it his concern to prime the pump of private business initiative rather than play a paternalistic role. Although his government experience and his allegiance to progressivism—he had been a mild

Bull Mooser in 1912—qualified somewhat his allegiance to the abstract principle of laissez-faire, he was determined to keep centralized government activity at what he considered a reasonable minimum.

Hoover, moreover, was trained as an engineer, and his social philosophy was infected with a professional bias. Economy and efficiency became ends in themselves. To him it mattered dearly not only what goals were adopted but exactly *how* a job was done. This craftsmanlike concern for technique, a legitimate thing in itself, stood him in bad stead politically during the depression, when the people grew impatient for results regardless of method.

Hoover's postwar function as the defender of Western capitalism from the Bolsheviks also seems to have made its mark on his style of thought. One of his most persistent themes has been the unworkability of socialism, another his tendency to see Bolshevism in every measure of public ownership. In 1922 he declared that the failure of socialism in Russia, for all the misery that accompanied it, was not an unmitigated misfortune to humanity, because it was "necessary for the world to have this demonstration." Not only did he refuse to recognize the Soviet government; he also refused to recognize Soviet economics. Trade with Russia was impossible, he declared during the twenties, because the Soviets, under their economic system, could never "return to production," would never be able to export, and hence never able to buy.

Even the platform of the Raskob-financed Democrats in 1928 represented "state socialism" because it had liberal planks on power and agricultural relief. As Hoover later explained in *The Challenge to Liberty,* public ownership "of no matter how small a segment of an industry will be followed rapidly by other steps." Indignantly he vetoed Senator Norris's bill to establish a government plant at Muscle Shoals with authority to sell power and nitrates:

> I am firmly opposed to the Government entering into any business the major purpose of which is competition with our citizens.... The remedy for abuses in the conduct of that industry [power] lies in regulation.... I hesitate to contemplate the future of our institutions, of our Government, and of our country if the preoccupation of its officials is

no longer the promotion of justice and equal opportunity but is to be devoted to barter in the markets. That is not liberalism; it is degeneration. . . .

The real development of the resources and the industries of the Tennessee Valley can only be accomplished by the people in that valley themselves . . . solely for the benefit of their communities and not for purposes of pursuit of social theories or national politics. Any other course deprives them of liberty.

In 1922, disturbed by worldwide ferment, Hoover expounded his social philosophy in a little book entitled *American Individualism*. He admitted that individualism, untempered, would produce many injustices, but asserted that in the United States it had fortunately been qualified by the great principle of equality of opportunity:

Our individualism differs from all others because it embraces these great ideals: *that while we build our society upon the attainment of the individual, we shall safeguard to every individual an equality of opportunity to take that position in the community to which his intelligence, character, ability, and ambition entitle him; that we keep the social solution free from frozen strata of classes; that we shall stimulate effort of each individual to achievement; that through an enlarging sense of responsibility and understanding we shall assist him to this attainment; while he in turn must stand up to the emery wheel of competition.*

Americans have learned, Hoover went on, that the strong are not necessarily the most fit, that society runs more smoothly when they are restrained. But we also know that "the one source of human progress" is the opportunity of the individual to use his personal equipment as best he can. The idea that men are really equal "was part of the claptrap of the French revolution." The most the individual can expect from the government is "liberty, justice, intellectual welfare, equality of opportunity, and stimulation." As evidence that substantial equality of opportunity still existed in the United States, Hoover observed: "Of the twelve men comprising the President, Vice-President, and Cabinet, nine have earned their own way in life without economic inheritance, and eight of them started with manual labor." For a man who presided over one of the greatest statistical agencies in the world, Hoover's idea of an adequate statistical sample was pretty meager; but his choice of the Harding cabinet to illustrate the opportunities that awaited the self-made man showed a magnificently perverse intuition.

While campaigning against Al Smith, Hoover again stated that American individualism is no free-for-all, that it calls for "economic justice as well as political and social justice. It is no system of laissez faire."

> It is as if we set a race. We, through free and universal education provide the training of the runners; we give to them an equal start; we provide in the government the umpire of fairness in the race. The winner is he who shows the most conscientious training, the greatest ability, and the greatest character.

The conception that the banker's son and the sharecropper's son have equal chances in life because there is a free public-school system, and that the government provided by Harding, Coolidge, and Mellon was simply "the umpire of fairness" in the race, may seem an eccentric one, but it was not peculiar to Hoover. The entire generation of businessmen of which he was a part was under singular disadvantages in understanding the twentieth century. They had been brought up by the masterful post–Civil War generation of business magnates and had inherited their ideas. The success of the earlier generation had been impressive, and the prestige of its ideas, despite their inherent weaknesses, ran correspondingly high wherever the old promises of American individualism still warmed the spirits of men. That life is a race which goes to the swift was still plausible to many people in 1891 when Hoover entered Stanford, and classic spokesmen of the *status quo* like William Graham Sumner at Yale were still thundering at undergraduates the truth that millionaires are the bloom of a competitive civilization. Although the heated criticisms of the Progressive Era slightly tarnished these notions, they were refurbished and repolished in the New Era of the twenties. The terrible and sudden collapse of 1929 left the inheritors of the old tradition without a matured and intelligible body of ideas to draw upon and without the flexibility or morale to conceive new ones. Driven to reiterate with growing futility the outworn creed upon which they had been suckled, the very men who had made such a fetish of being up to date, pragmatic, and hardheaded in their business activities now displayed in politics the sort of archaic, impractical, and flighty minds that made the Liberty League possible.

Hoover, had he been challenged with the overpowering implausibility of his notion that economic life is a race that is won by the ablest runner, would have had a ready answer from his own biography: had he not started in life as a poor orphan and worked in the mines for a pittance, and had he not become first a millionaire and then president of the United States? There are times when nothing is more misleading than personal experience, and the man whose experience has embraced only success is likely to be a forlorn and alien figure when his whole world begins to fail.

In October 1929 Hoover ceased to be the philosopher of prosperity and turned to the unexpected and melancholy task of rationalizing failure. His interpretation of the depression was simply that the "American system," though fundamentally healthy, had been brought to grief temporarily by incidental and accidental influences, chiefly from abroad.

"The origins of this depression lie to some extent within our own borders through a speculative period," the president admitted in his December 1930 message to Congress; but, he continued, if overspeculation had been its only cause, the depression would have been easily conquered. It was a world depression, and its roots were in the Great War. "The major forces of depression," Hoover concluded, "now lie outside of the United States."

During the 1932 campaign he amplified his thesis. He reminded his Democratic opponents of the enormous cost of the war in lives and money, of huge government debts, of political instability that had "paralyzed confidence," of the growth of standing armies, of revolutions and agitations in China, India, and Russia, of overproduction of key products in the Indies, Cuba, Brazil, Ecuador, the Congo, Burma, Australia, and other parts of the world. Overproduction had "crashed into the immutable laws of supply and demand" and had "brought inevitable collapse in prices and . . . a train of bankruptcies and destruction of buying power for American goods." Panic-stricken countries had dumped their holdings of securities into the American market; gold had thus been withdrawn from the United States, and "the consequent fear that swept over our people" caused them to draw huge sums from the banks. How mistaken, then, to believe that the most serious causes of the depression could be located in the United States. "We," concluded Hoover reproachfully, "did not inaugurate the Great War or the panics in Europe." The final article in Hoover's version of the depression was that it had been beaten at last by his policies, only to be revived by the uncertainties of the 1932 election and Roosevelt's failure to reassure business.

If the American system (which, as Hoover said, "its enemies call capitalism") was basically sound, such psychological factors as loss of confidence might be playing an important part in deterring recovery. So earnestly did Hoover believe in the importance of confidence that he journeyed from Washington to Philadelphia in the gloomy fall of 1931 in part because he felt that his attendance at a World Series game would be a public demonstration of his own serenity. This desire to stimulate confidence was the cause of the absurdly optimistic statements by Hoover and others that flooded the press in the months following the crash. Shortly after the market break he made one of his most famous remarks: "The fundamental business of the country, that is, the production and distribution of commodities, is on a sound and prosperous basis." Other hopeful statements followed. On March 8, 1930, he assured the country that the crisis would be over in sixty days.

It has been widely assumed, because of this series of sanguine announcements from the White House, that Hoover had no conception how serious the situation was. A close study of his actions behind the scenes shows that this was not true. Privately he had a dark view of the nature and probable duration of the crisis. He had been warned almost at the outset by Federal Reserve officials that "the situation . . . is honeycombed with weak spots. . . . It will take perhaps months before readjustment is accomplished." The psychology of "confidence" economics, however, demanded that the public be given sweeping reassurances, and the president took the risk of sacrificing what was left of his reputation as a prophet. Unfortunately, he was saddled for the rest of his life with the "prosperity-is-around-the-corner" theme.

It was, in fact, not Hoover's initial estimate of the crisis, but his subsequent estimate of his own remedies that was really at fault. On November 21, 1929, he called a grand conference of business moguls and told them confidentially, according to a summary of his prepared notes:

> that he viewed the crisis more seriously than a mere stock market crash; that no one could measure the problem before us or the depth of the disaster; that the depression must last for some time; and that there were two or three millions unemployed by the sudden suspension of activities.

He continued that steps must be taken to prevent distress and "maintain social order and industrial peace." The burden must not be thrown immediately upon labor. Such a course would cut purchasing power and bring about "industrial strife, bitterness, disorder, and fear." Instead, wages should be "temporarily maintained" until intensified competition and the shrinkage in demand forced the price level down. Then later, when wages were reduced, they should not fall faster or further than the cost of living. Values could thus be "stepped down" gradually and without undue hardship. Both industry and labor promised to support this program, the former by maintaining production and wage rates, the latter by withdrawing some wage demands already made. Faithful adherence to his plan, Hoover believed, might reduce price levels sufficiently to lower costs of production to a point at which profits could again be made; inflated capital values would be reduced until they approached realities. Then the normal upward and onward course could be resumed. As Hoover told the people, "We have come out of each previous depression into a period of prosperity greater than ever before. We shall do so this time."

Hoover was asking the businessmen to forswear all their natural inclinations. The first impulse of industrialists was to reduce production and employment, cut wages, and so far as possible maintain prices. The most businesslike reaction in administration councils came from Andrew W. Mellon, who said in the fall of 1930: "Curtailment of output, without question, will correct the present condition within a short time," and who, in his own vast system of enterprises, was curtailing output with admirable zeal. But under Hoover's plan the industrialists were to continue to produce and pay prevailing wage rates, even though there was no market for their goods in sight. It is surprising, perhaps, that they agreed to follow his plan, and even more surprising that, so far as wage rates were concerned, they generally made an effort to comply. Not until the summer of 1931 did manufacturers generally reduce wage scales. Production, however, was another matter. They would not produce for a nonexistent market; the volume of output and the total wage bill shrank drastically; the depression deepened.

Had the fundamental business of the country actually been sound, one might perhaps have expected Hoover's program to work. In the teeth of the evidence he seems indeed to have believed that it was taking effect, and there soon began in his curiously stubborn mind a series of flights from reality which took him further and further into a private world in which things behaved as he expected. Because, on his postulates, his program should have been successful, he went on talking as though it were, and the less his ideas worked, the more defiantly he advocated them. A half-year after his November conference, when a group of manufacturers, bankers, and bishops came to urge more positive action against unemployment, he said: "Gentlemen, you have come six weeks too late." In the bitter summer of 1931, ignoring the shrinkage in employment and the fact that business was on the verge of a panic of wage-cutting, he boasted that his administration had "steadily urged the maintenance of wages and salaries."

Carried to its logical conclusion, a deflationary solution of the depression would have required, as it always had in the past, a considerable number of bankruptcies in foundering enterprises. In a time of falling prices this was the most important way in which a large part of the great debt burden could be liquidated and inflated capital claims reduced. But as the depression deepened, it became evident that such a procedure now involved the gigantic risk of toppling the entire so-cial-economic structure. A large part of the debt was held by savings banks and mortgage and life-insurance companies, in which the savings of millions were invested, and it would have been fatal to let them fail. To shore up the financial structures of such institutions with government credits, Hoover at last in December 1931 asked Congress to create the Reconstruction Finance Corporation. In this respect the hands-off policy had to be abandoned.

If Hoover's economics did not call for strong governmental action, it did require a great deal more initiative than any president had ever brought to bear to meet a depression. The historic policy in all previous major depressions had been almost complete laissez-faire, and Hoover was the first president in American history to bring any federal leadership to such an emergency. But like a timid beast he shied away from any federal compulsion over business, when compulsion was necessary even to his own modest program. Without legal power he could not ensure that business leaders would maintain production and wage rates, to say nothing of employment. And yet to one with his political philosophy such compulsion was unthinkable. The entrepreneur's right *not* to produce, his right to let factories remain idle, is, after all, one of those great traditional rights of private ownership that Hoover was so eager to defend. To destroy it would revolutionize inherited law and morals.

However, it was not merely his political scruples but his economic doctrines that held Hoover back. A refusal to look for domestic causes of the depression, and hence for positive domestic remedies, grew logically out of his theory that the depression was a foreign product. From the premise, which few cared to deny, that this was a world depression which had aggravated the internal depression of the United States, Hoover reasoned to the conclusion, which was thoroughly questionable, that there was no major flaw in America's domestic economy. One can search in vain among his public statements, with their dolorous allusions to revolutions in China and overproduction of cocoa in Ecuador, for an appreciation of the fact that there were vital domestic causes for depression that might have made themselves felt even if the Creditanstalt had never failed. More than ever in history the business boom of the twenties had been based upon expansion in consumers' goods, and more than any other it was dependent upon sustained consumption. The level of consumption in the United States was high, but it did not continue to grow in proportion to the vast productive capacity of American industry. There had been a persistent agricultural depression under the prosperous surface of the twenties. In industry unemployment had slightly increased, and the growth in real wages was small. Important factors upon which the boom had been built slackened before the stock-market crash of 1929. Investment in housing, for example, one of the vital sources of the boom, fell off after 1925 and declined drastically between 1928 and 1929; and in the last year of prosperity the decline spread from residential to industrial and commercial building. The rate of expansion in automobile-manufacturing and road-building flattened out before the crash came. Such things were reflected in the rate of investment in capital goods, which went into decline a year before the market crash. The country was overstocked with savings to be invested and goods to be sold, and the inability of savings to find good investment outlets in industries that were rapidly saturating their markets drove capital into speculative channels. This unhealthy speculation Hoover saw and disapproved, but he preferred to look abroad rather than to see what lay behind it.

During his career as secretary of commerce Hoover had answered the problem of America's tremendous productive capacity with the injunction: sell abroad; and the problem of its accumulated savings he had likewise answered: invest abroad. His thesis that the depression began in the rest of the world and spread to America, if true, was a boomerang. No one had been more active than he in increasing the equity of the United States in this floundering world economy. But the conception that America's economic salvation lay in overseas markets and investments, once again, rested upon a misconception of the domestic economy.

Never did Hoover acknowledge how feeble was the purchasing power of the American people in comparison with the forces of production they had created. It was quite in character when, in *The Challenge to Liberty* (1934), he airily denied that there was any serious maldistribution of wealth in the United States. Propagating this insidious idea, he declared, was a device "of those who are anxious to destroy liberty. A competent study will show that over 90 per cent of the national income goes to persons receiving less than $10,000 per annum income and over 97 per cent to persons receiving less than $50,000 annually." The income classes chosen for this illustration were so broad as to conceal the relevant facts about income distribution and purchasing power. The Brookings Institution study *America's Capacity to Consume,* which appeared in the same year as *The Challenge to Liberty,* showed that the nation's 631,000 richest families had a total income considerably larger than the total income of 16,000,000 families at the bottom of the economic scale. From the standpoint of purchasing power, these 16,000,000 families, the Brookings economists concluded, had incomes too small even to purchase "basic necessities." Such was the potential market at home during the years when Secretary Hoover had been working so hard to expand American markets abroad.

★   ★   ★

The inflexible state of mind that underlay Hoover's approach to the depression can be seen in two vital policies: his prescription for the ills of agriculture and his attitude toward relief. In the first of these he was trapped by an optimistic miscalculation; in the second by his loyalty to the American folklore of self-help.

The president's farm policy was embodied in the Agricultural Marketing Act of 1929, which established the Federal Farm Board. During periods of glut the Farm Board was to enter the market and buy the surpluses of "overproduced" crops, thus sustaining prices until the market returned to "normal." It was taken for granted—and this was typical of Hoover—that any overproduction that might occur would be occasional, not chronic; in short, that the fundamental position of American agriculture was sound. This supposition had no foundation in reality. American agriculture since the world war had completely outgrown the sum total of its domestic and foreign markets; partly, as Hoover was sometimes aware, because new competing areas had opened elsewhere in the world, partly because of the changed position of the United States from a debtor to a creditor nation, which made it difficult for other countries to buy our exports, partly because of changing consumer habits, and partly because of those same high tariffs which Hoover had insistently defended. The result of the Hoover policies was that the government became burdened with enormous and growing stores of unmarketable wheat and cotton. Each year's unsold surplus in government warehouses hung heavily over the next year's market, and prices plummeted downward to disastrous new lows. Finally in 1932 the Cotton Corporation began to beg farmers to plow up every third row in their fields. This coordinated scarcity, which Hoover's administration sought in vain through voluntary action, was achieved by the Roosevelt administration through heavy inducements and at times compulsion.

More than anything else it was his attitude toward relief that shaped the image of Hoover which still prevails in the popular mind. After successfully distributing relief on various occasions to over 150,000,000 people throughout the Western world, the president understandably thought himself an authority on the subject; here, as in other fields, his views could not be changed. When he discussed relief in public, it was generally as a question of political and moral theory, not of economics or human need. He earnestly believed that relief was a job for "the voluntary agencies of the country together with the local and state governments." His reasons for keeping relief a local concern he made clear in February 1931:

> The moment responsibilities of any community, particularly in economic and social questions, are shifted from any part of the nation to Washington, then that community has subjected itself to a remote bureaucracy.... It has lost a large part of its voice in the control of its own destiny.

No need to debate the merits of this as a statement of political theory. The depleted treasuries of local governments were simply inadequate to the relief burdens of the crisis. Hoover did pledge that if the time came—as he was sure it would not—when local agencies failed, he would "ask the aid of every resource of the Federal Government because I would no more see starvation amongst our countrymen than would any senator or congressman." But no direct federal relief was undertaken. "I am opposed," said the president firmly, "to any direct or indirect government dole. The breakdown and increased unemployment in Europe is due in part to such practices." Huge relief appropriations would also make impossible the balanced budget that he considered "indispensable to the restoration of confidence."

The peculiar economic theology that underlay Hoover's attitude toward relief was highlighted by the political aftermath of the 1930 drought. In December Hoover approved a Congressional appropriation of $45,000,000 to save the livestock of stricken Arkansas farmers, but opposed an additional $25,000,000 to feed the farmers and their families, insisting that the Red Cross could take care of them. Finally, when Congress did vote an additional twenty millions to feed the farmers, it was stipulated, to satisfy presidential scruples, that the money should go as a loan rather than a gift. Endorsing the loan, Hoover remarked that for the federal government to *give* money for relief "would have injured the spiritual responses of the American people. . . . We are dealing with the intangibles of life and ideals," he added. ". . . A voluntary deed is infinitely more precious to our national ideals and spirit than a thousandfold poured from the Treasury."

Even for a people brought up in the same folklore, it was becoming hard to understand the Hoover *mystique.* Hoover had never been so solicitous about the "spiritual responses" of the businessmen who had been beneficiaries of federal subsidies or of Secretary Mellon's handsome tax refunds. And the idea that money given by the federal government would demoralize reliefers, while money given by their neighbors or the Red Cross or local governments would not, seemed too fanciful to command respect. Resentment was aggravated by Hoover's political gaucheries. During these black, hungry days he allowed newsreel men to photograph him feeding his dog on the White House lawn.

★   ★   ★

No longer a Utopian, Hoover assumed in his post-presidential career the role of a hopeful Jeremiah. Now that affairs had fallen into the hands of reckless men, he seized every possible occasion to give warning. In his earnest book *The Challenge to Liberty* and in a series of speeches before Republican conventions he predicted that the managed economy foreshadowed in the New Deal would of necessity destroy economic freedom, the basis of all other freedoms, and that tampering with "Socialist methods" would only bring a middle-class reaction toward fascism.

When foreign affairs took the spotlight from the domestic transgressions of the New Dealers, Hoover at first threw himself on the side of isolationism, but after the outbreak of the war he retreated to a more equivocal position and after Pearl Harbor became a qualified internationalist.

In 1938 the ex-president went on a tour of ten European countries. Hitler gave him the rare privilege of a forty-minute interview, after which Hoover issued a press statement reaffirming his belief in freedom and popular government. Upon his return to the United States Hoover promptly launched a campaign against American intervention in Europe. The idea of collective security, whether through economic or military action, he asserted, was "dead." Besides, the aggressions of the Axis would be vented upon others than the United States: "The face of Germany is turned more east than toward Western Europe. The face of Japan is turned west into Asia." Even if the democracies should be aligned against the totalitarian states, the United States must stay out of a European war; otherwise ours would become "practically a fascist government."

"If the world is to keep the peace," Hoover advised, "then we must keep peace with dictatorships as well as with popular governments." Totalitarianism, he argued, is nothing new; it is very much like the personal autocracies of earlier times—and we have always "had to

live with such bedfellows." The people of the democracies "must reconcile themselves to the fact that nations of that sort are going to continue to exist." Even the people of dictator nations, after all, have a
right to pursue their destinies under whatever form of government
they please, however repugnant to Americans. Confident that fascism, like that other heresy, Marxian socialism, would "fail some
time," he urged Americans to hold fast to their traditional liberties
and "revitalize" democracy at home. Shortly after the Munich Conference he reaffirmed his belief that "there is more realistic hope of
military peace for the next few years than there has been for some
time."

Less than a year later Europe was at war. But Hoover was not discouraged. To publisher Roy Howard he predicted: "The Allies can
defend their empire. I do not see any possibility of their defeat. They
will control the seas and sit there until their enemies are exhausted."
In one of his first wartime statements he suggested that the United
States sell only defensive weapons to the Allies, excluding such things
as heavy bombers, which by involving the U.S. in offensive warfare
against civilians would incur lasting ill will.

Three days after the French surrender to Hitler, Hoover made his
quadrennial address to the Republican National Convention. Perhaps
to spike a current rumor that he wanted to lead a Hoover-Lindbergh
isolation ticket, he acknowledged that we could no longer be insu-
lated against great world wars. "There is no such thing as economic
isolation. . . . There is no such thing as moral isolation." But he repeated his warnings against entering a democratic world crusade.
"Whatever the outcome of this world cataclysm, whatever the solution of our domestic crisis," he advised gloomily, "the pattern of the
world will not again be the same. Dictatorships, totalitarian economics, and militarism will long continue over a large part of the earth."
America's proper task in this crisis was to arm itself for defense of the
Western Hemisphere. In the meantime we might give cautious help
to nations that were "fighting for their freedom."

Less than two months before Pearl Harbor, Hoover urged the nation to pursue neither an outright isolationist nor an interventionist
foreign policy. We should simply concentrate on war production,

send tools to Britain, and "await developments." With the help of our weapons England would be able to withstand a German invasion; we need not send men. By remaining at peace we could preserve our strength and "give real aid to reconstruction and stabilizing of peace when Hitler collapses of his own overreaching." Hoover made it clear that he expected a German collapse even if the Nazis should suffer no military defeat. In another statement he warned that if the United States joined Britain in the war and undertook an invasion of Europe, the preparations alone would take five years or more.

In 1942 Hoover collaborated with Hugh Gibson, a veteran American diplomat, in a book entitled *The Problems of Lasting Peace,* which set forth no less than fifty conclusions on how to make a lasting settlement. The Hoover-Gibson program was based upon a compromise between the extremes of isolation and American world dominion, and it accepted "the American idea of 1919 that peace should be built on fostering representative government." In general tone the proposals were strongly reminiscent of the position Hoover had taken at the close of the First World War. They called for a settlement that would nurture, and not strangle, the chances of representative government in the enemy nations, for a peace without plunder and revenge, for disarmament, and an international organization that would enforce peace by means of an international air force.

The key to the problem of peace, however, was in economics, and the postwar economic world envisioned by Hoover and Gibson was the same will-o'-the-wisp that Hoover had sought on the domestic front. A few of the fifty conclusions came strangely from one who had signed the Smoot-Hawley Tariff Act, particularly the suggestion that tariffs be no higher than will "preserve fair competition of imports with domestic production." The authors also favored international monetary stabilization, easy access to raw materials through equal prices and open markets, the disruption of monopolies and cartels, and the abolition of trade quotas and privileges.

Lasting peace [they declared] must include economic freedom regu-
lated to prevent abuse. . . . The long view should be to *restore international trade to free enterprise. . . .*

International economic freedom cannot function if there is to be a
degree of domestic managed economy which stifles free enterprise, for
then there would be no substantial force behind private trading, and
government must take over.

One cannot escape the feeling that the authors were prescribing a
peace for the wrong war. Were they not proposing again that an essentially Wilsonian settlement be made, but without Wilson's mistakes? Hoover had always had criticisms of Wilson, but they
concerned means, not ends. (Wilson, he declared in 1942, "made a
magnificent fight" for "the best ideals of America.") A few things that
were vital to Wilson were of small concern to Hoover—for example,
the independence of the smaller nations. But on the whole it was the
similarities, not the differences, that stood out. Freedom of the seas,
removal (in some measure) of economic barriers among nations, the
creation of some sort of League, open diplomacy, a "fair" adjustment
of colonial claims, disarmament, a sanely merciful settlement, no an-
nexations or indemnities—all these principles are shared by the historic Fourteen Points of 1918 and the fifty proposals of 1942.

Thus in world as in domestic affairs the keynote of Hoover's public
career remained the same—a return to the conditions, real or imagined, of the past. Free trade, free enterprise, competition, open markets, open opportunities—this was the logic of *American Individualism*
and *The Challenge to Liberty* projected on a larger scale. The future
would be just like the past, but more so; we would go back, back to
the rosier world of 1913—and even beyond that, for the men of 1913
themselves turned to the mid-nineteenth century for their governing
principles.

Speaking to his party in 1940, Hoover explained his 1938 trip to Europe by saying that he had gone abroad to find out what causes dictatorships. There were many complex factors involved, he admitted, but
he had had no difficulty in spotting the main source: it was *economic
planning.* "In every single case before the rise of the totalitarian governments there had been a period dominated by economic planners."

Here in all its rigidity was revealed Hoover's religious faith in the planless world of the free market. For a generation managed economies had been developing in all the industrialized nations of the world. This trend had been enormously spurred by the war. Hoover himself had said two years earlier that managed economies would "long continue over a large part of the earth." Could he have seriously believed that free enterprise might be restored to the postwar world? In all history no more heroic setting-back of the clock had ever been proposed. Since economic planning had become such a universal phenomenon, it might have been natural to ask: "If planning caused dictatorships, what caused planning? Was it, perhaps, the universal decline of the planless economy under the stewardship of the Hoovers?" That the New Deal might presage an American fascism, as Hoover insisted, was at least a possibility—one that conventional liberals generally refused to admit; but that Hooverism had brought a reaction toward the New Deal was a historical certainty. That there was anything natural, not to say inevitable, about this trend toward managed economies was a conclusion Hoover could never acknowledge without abandoning the premise upon which his public life had been built—that unmanaged capitalism was an economic system without a major flaw. No, it must be a series of unwise choices based on novel and fallacious thinking; things could easily have happened otherwise; *it was simply a strange coincidence, a curious universal mistake.* Perhaps, then, if we should gird ourselves for a new try, perhaps if we were Spartan enough and wise enough, if we would think a little straighter and work a little harder, we might leap out of the fading world of the twentieth century and land in the one that flourished so brightly in Hoover's mind.

But at times, it appears, even Hoover became tired of his own unheeded warnings, and at the Republican National Convention of 1944 he dropped a hint of his weariness. Recalling his speeches at the two previous conventions, he said:

Each time I knew even before I spoke that our people would not believe that the impairment of freedom could happen here. Yet each subsequent four years has shown those warnings to have been too reserved, too cautious.

How frustrating it was to find one's predictions so startlingly confirmed and yet discover again and again that one really had no audience! This very confession was made before a convention whose platform substantially capitulated to the Roosevelt domestic program. Could it be true that the great American tradition was nearing its end because the people had no ear for spokesmen of the old faith? Could it be true that a salvation so plainly in sight, so near to our grasp, would be blindly refused? If this should come to pass, Herbert Hoover at least had earned his absolution. He had tried to lead the nation out of the wilderness and back to the comforts and splendors of the old regime. He had given his warnings and they had been spurned. Perhaps, after all, it was the spirit of the people that was not fundamentally sound.

Excerpted from Richard Hofstadter, *The American Political Tradition and the Men Who Made It* (New York: Knopf, 1948), pgs. 279–310.

Huey P. Long

KINGFISH

The story seems too good to be true—but people who should know swear that it is true. The first time that Huey P. Long campaigned in rural, Latin, Catholic south Louisiana, the local boss who had him in charge said at the beginning of the tour: "Huey, you ought to remember one thing in your speeches today. You're from north Louisiana, but now you're in south Louisiana. And we got a lot of Catholic voters down here." "I know," Huey answered. And throughout the day in every small town Long would begin by saying: "When I was a boy, I would get up at six o'clock in the morning on Sunday, and I would hitch our old horse up to the buggy and I would take my Catholic grandparents to mass. I would bring them home, and at ten o'clock I would hitch the old horse up again, and I would take my Baptist grandparents to church." The effect of the anecdote on the audiences was obvious, and on the way back to Baton Rouge that night the local leader said admiringly: "Why, Huey, you've been holding out on us. I didn't know you had any Catholic grandparents." "Don't be a damn fool," replied Long. "We didn't even have a horse."

T. Harry Williams began his Pulitzer prize–winning biography *Huey Long* (1969) with this charm offensive on behalf of Huey Pierce Long (1893–1935), who needs it. As governor of Louisiana from 1928 to 1932 and as a United States senator from 1930 to 1935 who ruled the state through a figurehead governor—"Oscar, you sonofabitch, shut up!" Huey shouted at him one of the few times he dared to speak up—Long created "the nearest approach to a totalitarian state the American republic had ever seen," in Arthur

M. Schlesinger, Jr.'s judgment. Ramming bills through an intimidated legislature, throwing anti-Long mayors and parish officials
and judges out of office, wielding the state police and even the
National Guard as political cudgels, the "Kingfish," as he styled
himself, aimed to destroy his opponents in the manner not of a
democratic politician, who accepts that the other party will have its
day, but of a Bolshevik or Fascist leader who does not intend to
surrender power.

Buffoonery made Long seem more ridiculous than menacing.
He tried hard not to be taken seriously. He captured headlines, for
example, when he peed between the legs of a man standing at a
urinal in the men's room of a Sand's Point, Long Island, night
club, and missing. (Huey emerged from the men's room holding a
napkin on a cut above his eye.) With his white suits and pink ties,
his half-time pep talks to the LSU football team, his Tabasco
billingsgate—he labeled one flatulent politician "Whistle
Britches"—he gave "colorful" a bad name. Although first elected
before it, the Great Depression charged Long with situational
charisma—mass distress won him a national hearing for his
snake-oil remedies. Running on the slogan "Every Man a King,"
Long, the son of a prosperous farmer in a poor section of the state,
stoked the grievances of the aggrieved: the "folks at the forks of
the creek," the white poor of backwoods Louisiana to whom Long
brought schools and textbooks and roads—the "rednecks" and
"hillbillies" and "one-gallus men" kept in ignorance and isolation
by the Bourbon oligarchy ruling the state since Reconstruction.
Beyond Louisiana, Long shaped a program to appeal to the millions of Americans out of work and low on hope.

Long promised that by confiscating the fortunes of "Rockefeller, Morgan, and their crowd" and by raising taxes sharply on
the merely well-to-do, he could give every American family a
$6,000 "household estate," a guaranteed income of $2,500 a year
(almost double the median), education subsidies for the kids, and
pensions for the old folks. As economics, Share Our Wealth was
travesty. "Contemporary analysts estimated that even if all existing
wealth were in liquid form and could be cashed out and distributed," David M. Kennedy observes, "confiscating all fortunes

larger than a million dollars (more than Long called for) would produce not five thousand dollars per family but a mere four hundred." As politics, however, Long saw the scheme as his ticket to the White House.

"According to the testimony of intimates," Williams writes, "he intended to run some liberal Democrat as a third-party entry [in 1936] and so divide the liberal vote that the Republican candidate would win. The Republican would be incapable of dealing with the depression, the economic system would go to pieces, and by 1940 the country would be crying for a strong leader to save it. That savior could be only one man." In *My First Days in the White House,* a puckish exercise in egomania published just after his death in 1935, Long even named his cabinet, including, as secretary of the Navy, one "Franklin D. Roosevelt of New York."

Hodding Carter, a Pulitzer prize–winning editor, published an anti-Long newspaper in Hammond, Louisiana. His essay originally appeared in the *American Mercury,* in 1949. It was republished in *The Aspirin Age: 1919–1941,* edited by Isabel Leighton.

> *"A demagogue is a politician that don't keep his promises."*
> — HUEY LONG, *Born Funny*

> *"The supporters of Riley Joe Wilson, a candidate for Governor running against Long, boasted that their man had gone barefoot as a boy. Long's riposte became one of the most famous in Louisiana politics: "I can go Mr. Wilson one better; I was born barefoot."*
> — T. HARRY WILLIAMS, *Huey Long,* p. 250

HUEY LONG
American Dictator
Hodding Carter

The Louisiana of the eighteenth century was not the America of the Eastern seaboard. Its people were not Englishmen or the sons of

Englishmen, protesting because the privileges of free men at home were too skimpily granted to the colonial free.

Instead, the Louisianians were successively the vassals of two decadent and dying monarchies. The brothers Le Moyne had come in the name of the French king to colonize the lower Mississippi. To populate the colony there had followed an impotent conglomerate to be gutted by the elect: Canadian *coureurs de bois* and their Indian women; professional soldiers of short life expectancy; a few adventurous or disappointed members of the French aristocracy; and a pitiful succession of immigrants, peasants and artisans, sewer-scourings and exiled whores, having in common only poverty, hopelessness, and neglect.

Among such settlers there was scant thought of self-government. They were monstrously exploited. In 1763 France presented the vexatious colony to Spain; and a handful of rebels who plotted a free nation on the Mississippi discovered before a Spanish firing squad that political liberty was not for Louisianians. Not until a quarter of a century after the American colonies proclaimed themselves free did the Louisiana Purchase bring the promise of freedom. But even afterwards there was no democracy in Louisiana. From the first, government was directed by the entrenched few. Creole gentry and American merchant and planter perpetuated a basic agreement. Only gentlemen and politicians managed by gentlemen should direct the backwoodsmen who spilled over into the new territory and the descendants of the French and Spanish riffraff.

So, almost uninterruptedly, Louisiana politics from the Purchase until the Civil War was a story of genteel corruption, of steady political degeneration, of venality, of a studied neglect of civic advancement. Reconstruction further debilitated self-government; and where Reconstruction ended, rule under the gold-directed manipulation of the Louisiana Lottery began. At the beginning of the twentieth century, Louisianians could count on the fingers of one hand those major public servants who in all Louisiana history had been honest and progressive, active in behalf of the small people, and given to implementing campaign promises with administrative performance.

Throughout the years the same political pattern prevailed. The city dominated the state: New Orleans, the nation's mecca of the flesh-pots, smiling in not altogether Latin indifference at its moral deformities, and, like a cankered prostitute, covering those deformities with paint and lace and capitalizing upon them with a lewd beckoning to the stranger. Beyond New Orleans, in the south, French Louisiana, devoutly Catholic, easygoing, following complacently its backward-glancing patriarchs, suspicious of the Protestants to the north. And in central and northern Louisiana, the small farmers, principally Anglo-Saxon; bitter, fundamentalist Protestants, hating the city and all its evil works, leaderless in their disquiet and only vaguely aware that much of what they lacked was in some way coupled with the like-as-like office seekers whom they alternately voted into and out of public life.

Diversity was not so pronounced among the political leaders of these divided groups. They were, for the most part, conservative stereotypes; and even in New Orleans the machine politicians were guided in the things that mattered. They co-operated with the bankers, the large merchants, the oil and sugar and cotton interests, the affluent votaries of the status quo. A wise statesman didn't antagonize the railroads, the banks, the refiners, the lumbermen, the enterprising developers—or exploiters—of the great and noble State of Louisiana. A wise statesman dressed and acted like one. He orated, with elocutionary fire, about the glories of the past and the wonders of the future, about the dark days of Reconstruction, about white supremacy and black threats, God's mercy and the rightness of the established order. A wise statesman steered a safe course between the Scylla of Standard Oil and the Charybdis of the poor man's yearnings. He promised good roads and occasionally produced a few. He predicted the beautiful but tantalizingly distant day when Louisiana would come into its own. And among his own kind he made deals that kept his own kind in office.

Such was the political Louisiana in which Huey Pierce Long was born in 1893, in impoverished Winn Parish in north Louisiana, a breeding ground of economic and political dissenters. His background was tailormade for a politician. A log cabin, albeit a substantial one, was his birthplace. His father was a farmer of small means but with considerable ambition, who managed to send six of his nine children—but not Huey—to college.

Young Huey hated both farm work and conformity. In high school he discovered his talent for spell-binding oratory, and the power of a vocabulary enriched by Biblical allusion and directness, acquired naturally in a devout Baptist home. This gift was useful in school politics, and soon thereafter in the art of the traveling salesman, an occupation which he chose upon graduation because his father was not able to send him, the eighth child, to college.

The years between his graduation and his becoming a member of the Louisiana bar at twenty-one tested to the limit his extraordinary physical energy and driving mental discipline—the only discipline which he ever perfected in himself. He married before he reached the voting age, and supported himself and his wife by peddling Cottolene, a cooking compound, throughout north Louisiana, meeting thereby and making friends of many farm folk who were to become the core of his political organization. He attended Oklahoma University Law school for one tempestuous term. Then, incredibly, he completed the three-year law course at Tulane University in eight months and, securing a special examination from the Louisiana Supreme Court, became a lawyer at twenty-one. No other student at Tulane has ever matched this record.

As Huey Long put it in his autobiography, he "came out of that courtroom running for office."

He hung out his shingle in Winnfield, county seat of Winn Parish. And here he received his first lessons in an economic-social philosophy that would later burgeon into a gaudy, national movement. His first benefactor in Winnfield was a state senator named Harper, a prosperous man for the locality, but a "radical" who proposed a redistribution of national income as the only cure-all for the country's ills. During the First World War, Harper published a pamphlet calling for conscription of the nation's wealth as well as its manpower. A federal grand jury indicted him. He was defended by his young disciple,

Huey, who was deferred in the draft because he had a wife and child. (Huey also tried to gain exemption as a public official. He was a notary public.) Huey, through questionable strategy, won Harper's acquittal.

Most of his other early cases were minor ones, the only kind available to a beginner in a crowded profession. But at twenty-four Huey sought the one state office open to one of his age, a state railroad commissionership. The Railroad Commission was Louisiana's three-man utilities regulating body. He won. In the campaign he gained another ally, an older Winnfield man named O. K. Allen, who lent him five hundred dollars to help finance his campaign. Later, when Long was elected United States senator, he rewarded O. K. by making him his governor, stooge, and errand boy.

As railroad commissioner, Huey was something uncomfortably new and strange. Some regarded him as a radical menace; others saw only a coarse publicity-seeking clown, a thickening, comical-looking youngster with a face that was a puffy caricature of a cherub, with its dimpled chin, snub nose, and unruly, curling reddish hair. But among the masses there were multiplying thousands who saw a champion, a new Great Commoner. He damned and insulted Bigness in all its Louisiana manifestations: Standard Oil, the state's dominant and frequently domineering industry; the large corporations; the corporation lawyers. He clamored for a common carrier pipeline law—Standard had denied the use of its own to the independents, among them a company in which Huey owned stock—and for a higher severance tax on oil. He won a telephone rate reduction.

In 1920 he supported, for governor, John M. Parker, a one-time Bull Moose, because he believed the comparatively liberal Parker would deal strongly with Standard Oil. But Parker, to Huey's thinking, was too lenient after he became governor. Huey broke with him, was indicted and convicted of libeling the governor, and was fined a dollar and given a thirty-day suspended sentence. He refused to pay the fine, so the judge and opposing counsel made up the dollar themselves.

But he was winning friends and influencing voters. In 1924, at the height of the bitter Klan fight in Louisiana, Huey Long, now thirty, announced for governor. He tried to go down the middle on the Klan issue. He almost succeeded. Before election day he predicted that he would win if rain didn't keep the mud-farmers away from the polls. It rained. Yet, in a three-cornered race, he polled seventy-three thousand votes against eighty-four thousand and eighty-one thousand for the other two candidates. His day had not yet dawned. But already the uneasy feeling had arisen among his opponents that he would be unbeatable the next time.

★   ★   ★

From 1925 to 1928 Huey mended political fences, kept himself in the headlines, and built up a large and lucrative practice as attorney for some of the vested interests against which he ranted. He explained it in his autobiography this way: "When the millionaires and corporations fell out with each other, I was able to accept highly remunerative employment from one of the powerful to fight several others who were even more powerful. I made some big fees with which I built a modern house in the best residential section of Shreveport at a cost of forty thousand dollars." There were other and less charitable explanations of his affluence.

The 1928 campaign was more like a cyclonic disturbance than another three-way race for the governorship. Huey was probably the most indefatigable campaigner and best catch-as-catch-can stumper the demagogically fertile South has yet produced. He belabored and promised and defamed, speaking in the harsh, bitter language of the poor man, eighteen and twenty hours a day. His promises were bright ones, long overdue: good roads for the farmer, lower utility rates, free bridges, free school books. He mixed filthy imputations with rhapsodic pleading. Beneath the erroneously named Evangeline oak, he drove his program home to open-mouthed, whooping Cajuns:

And it is here that Evangeline waited for her lover Gabriel who never came. This oak is an immortal spot, made so by Longfellow's poem. But Evangeline is not the only one who has waited here in disappointment. Where are the schools that you have waited for your children to have that have never come? Where are the roads and the highways that you spent your money to build, that are no nearer now than ever before? Where are the institutions to care for the sick and disabled? Evangeline wept bitter tears in her disappointment. But they lasted through only one lifetime. Your tears in this country, around this oak, have lasted for generations. Give me the chance to dry the tears of those who still weep here.

No rain fell on election day this time. The evil city again rejected him, but Catholic and Protestant farmers united to give him a lead, though not a clear majority. His two opponents wouldn't join forces; and at thirty-five Huey Long sat in the governor's chair that he was to transform into a throne. Louisiana's poor whites had come into their own. "Every man a king, but no man wears a crown," Huey's campaign banners had proclaimed. No man, that is, but Huey himself. And already he was boasting, "I'm going to be president someday."

The campaign had been only a movie trailer, teasingly heralding what was to come. Long summarily discharged every state job holder under executive control who had not actively supported him. Loyal lads from the bayous and burnt stump lands began to replace the town and city slickers. Lacking a majority at the first session of the legislature, he swapped patronage for concessions, and in both House and Senate placed his own men in the chair. The legislature approved his proposal for a thirty-million-dollar bond issue to provide farm roads, increased hospital and other institutional support, and free school books, levying a severance tax and higher gasoline taxes to pay for the program. Behind Huey were the people, and the people wanted these things.

And with the people behind him, Huey expanded ominously. Defying rule and convention, he personally directed strategy from the floors of the House and Senate. Once he bragged that he was the state constitution now, and again that he had bought a legislator like a sack of potatoes. He coerced banks which hesitated to make the state a tideover loan. When the legality of his free textbook law was challenged because it included parochial schools among the recipients, he argued his own case before the United States Supreme Court and won brilliantly. Without constitutional authority, he ordered the state militia into the unfriendly, wide-open parishes adjoining New Orleans and closed the casinos until the gamblers co-operated.

All this was shocking enough to those Louisianians who favorably recalled less troublesome days and ways. But when Huey summoned the legislature into special session to enact a five-cent occupational tax on oil to aid "the sick, the halt, the blind, and the children," all hell broke loose. A barrel-house free-for-all took place on the floor of the House when Long's Speaker, smelling impeachment in the air, declared the House adjourned sine die. Bloody-faced legislators groped blindly for assailants who had struck them from behind. Men were felled by inkwells, canes, bare fists. A protesting representative hopped from desk to desk like a mountain goat, vainly trying to reach the Speaker and wreak personal vengeance on him. Men were cursing, screaming, some sobbing in anger.

The next day the Speaker decided that the House had not adjourned, and the House proceeded to impeach Huey Long. The charges ranged from the grave to the ridiculous. Huey had sought to bribe legislators. He had plotted the murder of an opposition senator. He had misused, misapplied, and misappropriated state funds. He had squandered monies allocated to a national governors' conference in New Orleans on a riotous, bosomy party, testimony concerning which left some governors red-faced. He had acted unbecomingly in public places, even to the extent of getting cockeyed drunk. Without authority he had ordered the classical old governor's mansion torn down to make way for a new one. He habitually used unquotable profanity, required signed, undated resignations from his political appointees, made illegal loans. The House impeached.

Huey fought back with promises, intimidation, and circulars, distributed by the hundreds of thousands by state employees to the faithful. Again he barnstormed Louisiana. His primary targets, not altogether without justification, were Standard Oil, the newspapers—particularly the New Orleans newspapers—and the old political guard.

To most of the state it looked as if Huey was finished. Then, dramatically, he produced a round robin, signed by fifteen senators, who declared that no matter what evidence was submitted to the Senate they would not vote to convict the governor because they believed the charges against him were invalid. The number was one more than enough to prevent the two-thirds majority necessary for conviction. The deserving fifteen reaped earthly rewards, and never again was Huey in dire political danger.

From this fiasco emerged the dictator, vindictive and intent upon a domination that could not again be challenged. No holds had been barred by either side in the impeachment fight. From now on there were to be no holds except those in which Huey was master. The impeachment fight technique would be improved upon later, but never radically altered. Frighten the wavering legislator by appealing over his head to the voters. Woo him with certain gratuities to be arranged on the side. What was the legislature, anyway? Just a hodgepodge of ward heelers from New Orleans, a scattering of lawyers, a couple of wagonfuls of simple-minded and simpleton farmers, most of them alike in that they had a price. Own them. Fashion them into a ready blade with which to carve empire.

Louisiana's frightened, vengeful governor surrounded himself with a half-dozen gun-ready, slugging bodyguards. He established a weekly newspaper, the *Louisiana Progress,* staffed it principally with skillful, conscienceless young newspapermen, and sicced it on his enemies. State employees found it good insurance to subscribe to the *Progress,* the number of subscriptions depending upon the size of their salaries, but with a minimum of ten to be sold, eaten, or used as wallpaper. No opponent big enough to be worthy of notice escaped its libeling. The voters of the nation's most illiterate state could understand its cartoon obscenities even when they couldn't spell out the text.

The public-works program went into high gear. The depression was rocking Louisiana. Public works meant needed jobs. And the administration could count on at least five votes for each employee; the votes of the aunts and uncles and cousins and wives and children of job holders who made it clear to their relatives that their fifteen to thirty dollars a week was secure only so long as they could prove their loyalty with political performance.

The first program was followed by a second and more ambitious one: a sixty-eight-million-dollar highway construction project, a five-million-dollar skyscraper capitol, and another twenty million dollars in assorted projects, all to be financed by an additional three-cent hike in the gasoline tax. With a year and a half yet to serve as governor, and with the opposition organizing against the program, Huey decided to run for the United States Senate with the state program as his platform.

The use of the sound truck and the financial strangulation of the enemy city of New Orleans were the principal innovations of the campaign. Conservative, goateed, seventy-year-old Joseph Ransdall, the incumbent whom Huey dubbed "Feather Duster," burbled unavailingly. Huey won hands down; and when his inimical lieutenant governor claimed the governorship because of Long's election to the Senate, Huey called out the state police and the National Guard, read the lieutenant governor out of office, and put in the president pro tempore of the Senate as acting governor. He designated his old benefactor, O. K. Allen of Winnfield, as the apostolic choice for the next full term.

. . .

The wider horizon beckoned. In January 1932, the Kingfish from Louisiana breezed into Washington. For the next three and one-half years he performed simultaneously in two rings of a dazzling political circus, the capital of Louisiana and the capital of the nation. He soon broke with President Roosevelt, each sensing in the other a challenge, and from the Senate floor ridiculed "Prince Franklin, Knight of the *Nourmahal,*" and his New Deal, unconcernedly violating the Senate's rules of personal decorum by lampooning such administration stalwarts as Carter Glass, Henry Wallace (Lord Corn Wallace), Harold Ickes (the Chicago Chinch Bug), Hugh Johnson (Sitting Bull), Joe Robinson, and Pat Harrison. No senator could match him in debate or in monopolizing the front page. Day after day Huey made news.

Sometimes amusing news, as in the controversy over whether corn bread should be dunked or crumbled in turnip-greens potlikker. Sometimes bad news for Huey, as when an unidentified guest at a Sands Point, Long Island, club resented with hammering fists the Kingfish's impatient and misdirected attempt to make use of a urinal before the other had moved aside. On another occasion his national and state prestige sagged momentarily when the Old Regular machine in New Orleans rebelled, returned its mayor, T. Semmes Walmsley, to office, and Walmsley followed up his victory by journeying to Washington and waiting around unavailingly to thrash the well-guarded "yellow coward."

In 1934 Long formalized the program which he hoped would eventually win him the presidency. The hazy concept of a national redistribution of wealth, presented fifteen years before by the obscure state senator from Winn Parish, took definable shape in a national "Share Our Wealth" organization. No dues were necessary. Huey produced the expense money as easily as the nation disgorged the followers, both by the hundreds of thousands. No matter that the Share Our Wealth program was demonstrably impracticable as presented. It *was* believable: a limitation of fortunes to $5,000,000; an annual income minimum of $2,000 to $2,500 and a maximum of $1,800,000; a homestead grant of $6,000 for every family; free education from kindergarten through college; bonuses for veterans; old-age pensions, radios, automobiles, an abundance of cheap food through governmental purchase and storage of surpluses. The Share Our Wealth members had their own catchy song, "Every Man a King," and their own newspaper, the mudslinging *Louisiana Progress,* expanded now to the *American Progress.*

The movement was nothing less than a new political party, heir to the yearnings and frustrations of the Populists, the Whiskey Rebels, the Know-Nothings, the Free Silverites, of all the have-nots of capitalism. Almost single-handed, Long won the election of Hattie Caraway of Arkansas to her deceased husband's Senate seat. The Share Our Wealth clubs began cutting across old lines in Mississippi, Alabama, Georgia. The New Deal became worried and began to use its Louisiana patronage accordingly.

By legislative action Long made sure that no federal relief money could be obtained by any Louisiana municipality or county except with the approval and supervision of an agency of his own. The administration retaliated by withholding Public Works Administration project funds. Revenue agents roved through Louisiana from 1932 until long after Long's death, and with eventually decisive results. A Senate committee timorously held hearings in New Orleans relative to the corruption which accompanied the election to the Senate of a Long ally, John Overton; and, after being defied, browbeaten, and ridiculed by Huey and his jibing lieutenants, exonerated Overton with a weak-kneed finding that he "had not personally participated in or instigated any fraud."

As the Share Our Wealth chorus swelled, Huey, like a wise military tactician, took care to protect his rear. In a spectacular, degenerative series of special sessions in 1934 and 1935, his legislature reduced Louisianians almost literally to the status of Indian wards. Together with this final elimination of the actualities of democratic self-government—to the unconcern of a majority of the unconsulted electorate—came new benefits: homestead tax exemption, theoretically up to two thousand dollars; abolition of the one-dollar poll tax; a debt moratorium act; and new taxes—an income tax, a public utilities receipts tax, and an attempted "two cents a lie" tax on the advertising receipts of the larger newspapers, which the United States Supreme Court pronounced unconstitutional.

Perhaps it seems inconceivable that any legislature, no matter how great the material rewards for its complaisant majority, could have so completely surrendered a people's political powers and economic and personal safety to one man. But Louisiana's legislature did. Administration-designated election supervisors were given the sole right of selecting voting commissioners, sole custody over the ballot boxes themselves, and the privilege of designating as many "special deputies" as might be necessary to guard the polls. Huey's figurehead governor, O. K. Allen, was given the power to call out the militia whenever he—or Huey—wished. The governor could—and did—expand the state police force into a swarm of private agents, some uniformed and some not, their number and the identity of the ununiformed alike a secret. The state attorney general was empowered to supersede any district attorney in any trial. The State Tax Commission was given the right to change any city or county tax assessment, so that a misbehaving corporation or individual might know just who held the economic stranglehold. An ironically designated civil service board was created, with appointive control over all fire and police chiefs, and a school budget committee with the right to review the appointments of every school teacher and school employee. The governor was even enabled to replace the entire city administration of Alexandria, a recalcitrant municipality in which Huey had once been rotten-egged. There were other repressive measures, many others. But these are sufficient to indicate what had happened to self-government in Louisiana.

It is perhaps a corollary that in the last year of his life Long became obsessed with a fear of assassination. He increased his armed bodyguard and took other unusual precautions to insure his personal safety. In July 1935, he charged on the floor of the Senate that enemies had planned his death with "one man, one gun, and one bullet" as the medium, and with the promise of a presidential pardon as the slayer's reward. This plot, he said, was hatched in a New Orleans hotel at a gathering of his enemies. A dictograph, concealed in the meeting room, had recorded the murderous conversation. I was at that meeting. It was a caucus of die-hard oppositionists, dolefully trying to decide what to do for the next state campaign. And the "plotting" was limited to such hopefully expressed comments as "Good God, I wish somebody would kill the son of a bitch."

And somebody did. That July, the white horse of death, foreseen by a state legislator earlier in the year, was but two months distant. On the night of September 8, a slender, bespectacled man in a white suit stepped from behind a marble pillar in the capitol as Long, accompanied by his closest aides and bodyguard, hurried to the governor's office. Dr. Carl Austin Weiss, the man in the white suit, drew a small pistol and fired once. Seconds later, the assassin lay dead, his body and head riddled by sixty-one shots. Huey Long staggered away with one bullet wound, perhaps a second, in his stomach. Thirty hours later he died.

This hideous thing that we remember as the rough-shod reign of the Kingfish was not hideous in its beginnings. Whether or not Huey Long himself was ever sincere in his protestations for the poor and downtrodden is, basically, beside the point. For he led a social-economic revolution in Louisiana; and after his death the entire South was debated ground.

It was not his political genius and ruthlessness alone that made him possible. There were two other factors equally important.

The first factor was that, after two hundred years, the people of Louisiana were ready and waiting for a messiah who would translate their needs into accomplishments. Theirs was the groundswell of the little people, a people undisturbed by his tactics as long as they got the roads, the free bridges, the hospitals, the free school books, the public works; as long as the men whom he pilloried and broke and banished were identified with the leaders of the past, bumbling representatives of an indifferent, negative ruling class. The little people shrugged at graft because of their certainty that there always had been graft of a kind. This time, whatever the politicians skimmed off the top, they were getting theirs too. And they were getting something else. Revenge. A fantastic vengeance upon the Sodom and Gomorrah that was called New Orleans. A squaring of accounts with the big shots, the Standard Oil and the bankers, the big planters, the entrenched interests everywhere. Huey Long was in the image of these little people. He talked their language. He had lived their lives. He had taken them up to the mountaintop and shown them the world which the meek would inherit.

The second factor was the make-up of the forces actively opposed to Long. His disunited enemies had difficulty from beginning to end to maintain an alliance that had its base in military necessity alone. We were strange bedfellows: cynical spoils politicians of the Old Regular ring in New Orleans; ardent, idealistic New Dealers; inept leaders of the country parishes, turned out in short grass; nonpolitical gentility awakened from their slumbers by rude knocking; the hitherto secure representatives of Big Business; honestly disturbed, solid bourgeoisie. Our combined cries for good government made a dissonant chorus. Huey bowled us over like ten-pins, with rare misses, from the time of the failure of the impeachment proceedings to his assassination.

Looking back, I know now that part of our failure arose from an unwillingness to approve any Long-sponsored proposal for change, regardless of its merits. We offered none of our own except a plea for democratic rule, and that sounded hollow in contrast. Yet, at the end, it became the one thing of importance to Louisiana.

And Long triumphed over men far wiser politically than we. President Roosevelt and his pulse-feeler, Jim Farley, became uneasy about Long's threat soon after the Share Our Wealth movement overran the borders of Louisiana. On the Senate floor he made the most adroit, belligerent, and fluent opponent look and sound like a political freshman.

Even had Huey Long relied only upon his mesmeric appeal to Louisiana's masses and his ability to make promised delivery of the material things those masses wanted, it is probable that he could have dominated his state as completely and for at least as long as he did. But he was not content to rely upon these weapons alone. His compelling lust for power as such—a primary, animating force in his political life—and the intense vindictiveness which from the start characterized his public career lured him to a morally indefensible position.

When impeachment seemed a certainty in those early months as governor, he simply bought and paid for enough legislators "like sacks of potatoes" to prevent the majority vote necessary for conviction. From then on, Long bought those whom he needed and could buy, and crushed those who had no purchase price or whose price was too high.

Nor was the control of a governor, a majority of legislators, a court majority enough. It should be repeated that no public officeholder, no teacher, no fire chief or fireman, no police chief or policeman, no day laborer on state projects held his job except in fee simple to the machine. Except among the political job holders, he used this economic power sparingly. Yet even private citizens made their living by his sufferance. Long could have taxed to extinction any business, large or small, and business knew it. Men could be—and were—arrested by unidentified men, the members of his secret police, held incommunicado, tried, and found guilty on trumped-up charges. A majority of the State Supreme Court became unabashedly his. Through his State Printing Board he cracked an economic whip over the rural and small-town press, lashing all but a few into sullen silence. A thug, making a premeditated skull-crushing attack upon a Long opponent, could draw from his pocket in court a pre-signed pardon from the figurehead governor. Entire city administrations could be removed, not by the electorate but by legislative action.

In the end, these things indirectly destroyed Huey Long himself. There are many conflicting tales as to why and how he was killed. This much is a certainty: His assassination was not plotted. It is not probable that Dr. Weiss went to the capitol the night of September 8, 1935, deliberately to kill Long. But he must have intended to protest a grave injury, the double-barreled kind of injury Long delighted in inflicting. Dr. Weiss's father-in-law, an implacable enemy of Long, had been gerrymandered out of his judgeship. Two of the judge's daughters had been dismissed from their teaching positions in further retaliation. And worse, Long had circulated noisome rumors about the family's ancestry.

Political punishment compounded with savage slander—an old, tested formula for reducing enemies to impotence. But this time the formula distilled a deadly reaction. Those who knew young Dr. Weiss best say that he could have sought Long only to protest verbally or with his fists this grave slander. They say that he could have drawn his gun only because the bodyguards threatened him. Few people in Louisiana believe that the full, true story has been told, for Long's henchmen were the only spectators. Perhaps the single bullet, fired from Weiss's small pistol, fatally wounded Long. Perhaps there was a second wound, as many Louisianians believe, caused by a ricocheting bullet from a bodyguard's gun. One bullet, two bullets. It is unimportant now; it was unimportant even then. Out of the terror he created, out of the driving passion to destroy other men, out of the futility that warped the minds of the Louisianians who opposed him, Huey Long himself forged the weapon which felled him.

And it need not have been so. He might have served Louisiana and the South as had no other political leader. Before the numbed thousands of his followers, the worn and credulous who milled across the grounds of the capitol, Gerald L. K. Smith, the grasping opportunist who directed the Share Our Wealth clubs, spoke an epitaph deserving to have been said of a better man by a better man:

> "His body shall never rest as long as hungry bodies cry for food, as long as lean human frames stand naked, as long as homeless wretches haunt this land of plenty."

Close beside the bier crowded the thieves and sycophants of the inner circle. Beyond wept the poor.

Toward what was this man thrusting? The political goal is discernible. It was the presidency of the United States. But what of the goal as president? Was the Share Our Wealth movement only a cynical vote-getting scheme? Or did the attractive packaging decorate a basic belief in a redistribution of the national income and national benefits, implanted in the mind of a poor farmer's son in Winn Parish fifteen years before?

My own conviction is that Huey Long was no true revolutionary. Power for power's sake was his mastering god. No revolutionary but—the word is used not loosely but gingerly—a dictator. A dictator, *sui generis,* the first truly such out of the soil of America. Had all Americans lived some of those years under him, democracy would be more secure today, because democracy would have come to have a more precious meaning.

Excerpted from Isabel Leighton, ed., *The Aspirin Age: 1919–1941* (New York: Simon and Schuster, 1949), pgs. 339–363.

Sam Rayburn

INTEGRITY

Bald head sweating, Sam Rayburn, "Mister Speaker," gaveled the House of Representatives to order on August 12, 1941. An historic vote was at hand. In 1940 Congress had narrowly authorized President Franklin D. Roosevelt to institute the first peacetime draft in U.S. history. Draftees were to serve a year. Now the president was breaking his word, as the soldiers in the House visitor's gallery above the chamber saw it, asking Congress to extend their service a year or more longer. "We, the Mothers of America Mobilized" had also sent a deputation to monitor the debate. They wanted their boys to come home, and a majority of the House appeared to agree with them. The president, having secretly left Washington for a meeting with Churchill, could not lobby undecided congressmen. "The burden," Robert Dallek writes, "fell on Sam Rayburn . . . "

RAYBURN WIELDS AN IRON FIST OVER HOUSE TO JAM THROUGH DRAFT EXTENSION BILL: that *Cleveland Press* headline captures what happened that afternoon. The bill passed by one vote, and only because the Speaker used his mastery of House rules to outmaneuver its opponents, at a crucial point refusing to recognize their spokesman. Continental Europe had fallen to Hitler. His armies were driving toward Moscow. Japan loomed menacingly in the Pacific. And yet the U.S. House, reflecting public sentiment, might have ended the draft but for the will of one man. "Sam Rayburn literally played the role of dictator within the framework of representative government, for the safety and good of the government itself," *Time*'s congressional reporter wrote. History vindicates that verdict.

No calling that permits the rise of a Sam Rayburn (1882–1961) can be all bad. Over his forty-eight year career in the House, nineteen years as Speaker, Rayburn championed that ever-bulging political demographic, the little guy. "We were always . . . at home, and everybody worked like the devil," he said of his childhood on a cotton farm in northeast Texas. "That's what made me determined to give the average man a break." In 1956 Rayburn, who had ten siblings, was touring his one-room schoolhouse with a visitor. Pointing to the initials "W.C.R." carved into one of the desks, the visitor asked, Did a Rayburn do that? "You won't find Rayburn initials on any desks," the old man said, waving the thought away. "No Rayburn ever cut a desk. If any of us ever did that, our little mother would have worn out our asses with a rod."

No Rayburn ever cut a desk, but Sam Rayburn was not the unmitigated saint Robert A. Caro depicts below. Caro favors a light vs. dark dramatic structure in his multi-volume biography of Lyndon B. Johnson, with Johnson as the dark. Rayburn, Johnson's political godfather, furnishes the light of volume one. Yet the politician who counseled new congressmen to "go along" to "get along" dirtied his hands for his party—as Caro details elsewhere in *The Path to Power*. A footnote in the standard biography of Rayburn, by D. B. Hardeman and Donald C. Bacon, contains the revealing reminiscence of Ray Peel, who "performed political chores for Rayburn": "Someone like [a Texas oilman] could come up and visit him and say, 'Now Sam, you are going to need money to get somebody elected in Idaho. Here is $2,000 in cash.' Of course that is not a bribe in any sense of the word. Mr. Rayburn put it in his pocket and when . . . he got to Washington he would give it to somebody to help the guy in Idaho get elected."

Max Weber, the German sociologist, and Sam Rayburn don't often share the same sentence. Still, this anecdote illustrates Weber's distinction between the "ethics of responsibility" practiced by politicians and the "absolute ethics" of Christian teaching. By the latter, Rayburn did wrong in accepting that cash. By the former, he did right. The cash might have elected the Democrat from Idaho—and a Republican might have won his seat without it.

Who would have helped the little guy more? Rayburn, "Mr. Democrat," never doubted the answer. The Christian's business is his personal salvation. The politician has a wider responsibility. Purity of heart won't raise the minimum wage. Did Rayburn help the oil man who gave him the $2,000? Almost certainly—if only by voting to maintain the oil depletion allowance, a tax break for oil producers. Seen this way, the $2,000 looks like a bribe—but a bribe with politically offsetting results, which has a different moral status than a bribe that stayed in Rayburn's pocket. Rayburn lived frugally and left an estate of $15,000. He risked his soul to gain Democrats.

"Nobody dies of lumbago," the Speaker told reporters in September 1961 before checking in to the Baylor University Medical Center, where doctors found he had cancer of the pancreas. Though he'd hoped "to die with my boots on, and a gavel in my hand," he died in a small hospital in Bonham, his hometwon, six weeks later.

Did Rayburn ever do anything for you? a reporter asked the man digging Rayburn's grave. The man tossed off a shovelful of the black soil. "Did he do me any favors? Lots of them. I guess the best thing he did—what I liked the most was just being recognized by the man when he'd see me. And when I used to drive a truck, at the Red River project, and they owed me $600, he saw to it that I got it. A poor man don't forget a thing like that." Nor will you forget Sam Rayburn after reading Robert Caro's stirring portrait.

RAYBURN

Robert A. Caro

Rayburn. Rayburn who hated the railroads, whose freight charges fleeced the farmer, and the banks, whose interest charges fleeced the farmer, and the utility companies, which refused to extend their power lines into the countryside, and thus condemned the farmer to darkness. Rayburn who hated the "trusts" and the "interests"—Rayburn who hated the rich and all their devices. Rayburn who hated the Republican Party, which he regarded as one of those devices—hated it for currency policies that, he said, "make the rich richer and the poor poorer"; hated it for the tariff ("the robber tariff, the most indefensible system that the world has ever known," he called it; because the Republican Party "fooled . . . the farmer into" supporting the tariff, he said, the rich "fatten their already swollen purses with more ill-gotten gains wrung from the horny hands of the toiling masses"); and hated it for Reconstruction, too: the son of a Confederate cavalryman who "never stopped hating the Yankees," Rayburn, a friend once said, "will not in his long lifetime forget Appomattox"; for years after he came to Congress, the walls of his office bore many pictures, but all were of one man—Robert E. Lee; in 1928, when his district was turning to the Republican Hoover over Al Smith, and he was advised to turn with it or risk losing his own congressional seat, he growled: "As long as I honor the memory of the Confederate dead, and revere the gallant devotion of my Confederate father to the Southland, I will never vote for electors of a party which sent the carpetbagger and the scalawag to the prostrate South with saber and sword." Rayburn who hated the railroads, and the banks, and the Republicans because he never forgot who he was, or where he came from.

Forgetting would have been difficult. He was born, on January 6, 1882, on a forty-acre farm in Tennessee whose worn-out soil could not support so many children—he was the eighth of eleven—and in 1887, the Rayburns moved to a forty-acre farm in Texas, in Fannin County, northeast of Dallas. (The thousand-mile train trip to Texas provided him with one of his most enduring memories; from the train windows, he was to recall, he saw "the people . . . on their trek west, all their earthly belongings heaped on covered wagons, men in plainsmen's outfits with wide-brimmed hats and guns on their shoulders, leading the oxen.") The first year in Texas almost finished the Rayburns: floods covered the fields, and boll weevils feasted on the cotton that survived—and out of the forty acres, only two-and-a-half bales. Although Fannin County soil was deep, rich loam, and the rainfall plentiful, forty acres was inadequate for a large family when the interest on the mortgage was 10 percent and cotton was selling for nine cents a pound. The Rayburns managed to hold the farm year after year only because the whole family, even five-year-old Sam, worked in the fields.

Except for four months each year in a one-room, one-teacher schoolhouse, Sam Rayburn spent his boyhood in the cotton rows. In the spring, he plowed—plowed while he was still so small that his weight couldn't keep the plow point in the ground and he had to strain to hold it down as the mules yanked it forward. In the summer, under the searing Texas sun, he worked with a hoe, chopping at the plants to thin them out, going to bed at night with an aching back, knowing that at daybreak he would be out with the hoe again. And in September, he would be in the rows on his knees—crawling down the rows, dragging behind him a long sack, while he picked the cotton—in the rows day after day, knees raw and bleeding from the crawling, hands raw and bleeding from the picking, back aching even worse than from the chopping. "I plowed and hoed from sun till sun," Sam Rayburn was to recall. "If some of our city friends who talk about the beauty and romance of farm life would go out and bend their backs over a cotton row for ten or twelve hours per day and grip the plow handles that long, they would see how fast this romance they have read in the novels would leave, and how surely it would come down to a humdrum life of work and toil." Work and toil—and little to show for it, thanks to the government's tariff and currency policies. The injustice that farmers felt was embodied in these policies—and that made northeast Texas a stronghold of the People's Party—was exemplified by the inclusion of steerhides on the "free" (unprotected by tariff) list, which meant that farmers received little for their steerhides, and the inclusion of the shoes manufactured from steerhides on the protected list, which forced farmers to pay high prices for shoes. Cotton prices were kept low, too. When, after a year's work in the fields by the entire family, its cotton went to the gin, the Rayburns might have left, after paying the furnishing merchant and the mortgage holder and the railroad's cruelly high freighting charges, *in a good year,* as much as twenty-five dollars to show for the year's labor.

And it wasn't the work and toil—or the poverty—from which he suffered most. Except when telling stories about the war (the most prominent object in the living room was a framed picture of General Lee), his father, the bearded Confederate veteran, was a gentle but very silent man, and his mother ("Hard Boss," the family called her because of her rigidity), who loved and was devoted to her children, was careful to conceal her affection; to Sam's parents, a biographer says, "any show of sentiment toward young children was a sign of weakness." All through his boyhood, Sam's life was the cotton fields—the fields and little else. If, Sunday, chores were light, they were supposed to be replaced not by play but by piety. "Many a time when I was a child and lived way out in the country," Sam Rayburn later recalled, "I'd sit on the fence and wish to God that somebody would ride by on a horse or drive by in a buggy—just anybody to relieve my loneliness." Terrible as were the toil and the poverty, the loneliness was worse. Poverty, he was to say, only "tries men's souls"; it is loneliness that "breaks the heart. Loneliness consumes people."

In the bleakness and boredom of Sam Rayburn's childhood, there stood out a single vivid day.

Fannin County's Congressman was Joseph Weldon Bailey, who, as Minority Leader of the House of Representatives, "dominated the Democratic minority like an overseer and conducted himself like a conqueror," and was expected, if the Democrats won control of Congress, to become Speaker. Bailey was one of the greatest of the great Populist orators. When he spoke in the House, it was said, "his tones lingered in the chamber like the echo of chimes in a cathedral." In 1894, when Sam Rayburn was twelve, Bailey spoke in Bonham, the county seat. And Sam Rayburn heard him.

He was to remember, all his life, every detail of that day: how it was raining so heavily that his mule took hours to cover the eleven miles to town; how he felt when he arrived at the covered tent "tabernacle" of the Bonham Evangelical Church, where Bailey was speaking. "I didn't go into that tabernacle. I'd never been to Bonham since we bought the farm, and I was scared of all the rich townfolks in their store-bought clothes. But I found a flap in the canvas, and I stuck there like glue while old Joe Bailey made his speech." And most vividly of all, he remembered Joe Bailey. "He went on for two solid hours, and I scarcely drew a breath the whole time. I can still feel the water dripping down my neck. I slipped around to the entrance again when he was through, saw him come out, and ran after him five or six blocks until he got on a streetcar. Then I went home, wondering whether I'd ever be as big a man as Joe Bailey."

Passing the barn the next morning, his brothers heard a voice inside. Looking through the door, they saw their little brother standing on a feeding trough, practicing a political speech. From the day he heard Joe Bailey, Sam Rayburn knew what he was going to be. Knew precisely. He told his brothers and sisters, and friends; as one recalls his words, "I'm going to get myself elected to the state legislature. I am going to spend about three terms there and then I want to be elected Speaker. After that, I am going to run for Congress and be elected." He would be in the House of Representatives, he said, by the age of thirty. And eventually, he said, he would be its Speaker, too. Sam's ambition became a joke on the Rayburn farm; his brothers and sisters would stand outside the barn and laugh at the speeches being made inside. But the speeches went on. And in 1900, when he was eighteen years old, Sam Rayburn, standing in a field with his father one day, told him he wanted to go to college.

His father said that he had no money to send him. "I'm not asking you to send me, Pa," Sam said. "I'm asking you to let me go." The cavalryman's back was stooped from the fields now; he was old; two of his eight sons had already left the farm; the loss of a third pair of strong hands would be hard to bear. "You have my blessing," he said. On the day Sam left, his clothes rolled up and tied with a rope because he had no suitcase, his father hitched up the buggy and drove him to the railroad station. A silent man, he stood there silently until the train arrived and his son was about to board it. Then he suddenly reached out and pressed some bills into his son's hand. Twenty-five dollars. Sam never forgot that; he talked about that twenty-five dollars for the rest of his life. "God knows how he saved it," he would say. "He never had any extra money. We earned just enough to live. It broke me up, him handing me that twenty-five dollars. I often won-

dered what he did without, what sacrifice he and my mother made."
And he never forgot the four words his father said to him as he
climbed aboard the train; he was to tell friends that he had remembered them at every crisis in his life. Clutching his son's hand, his father said: "Sam, be a man!"

Tuition at East Texas Normal College, a handful of buildings on a
bleak prairie, was twelve dollars a month; to supplement his parents'
gift, he got a job sweeping out a nearby elementary school, and became the college's bellringer, running up to the bell tower every forty-
five minutes to signal the end of a class period. Unable even with
those jobs to stay in school, he dropped out, and taught for a year in a
one-room school to earn money, then returned, to take a heavy load of
courses and graduate with his class. (He was so ashamed of his only
suit and its frayed elbows that he tried to avoid attending the graduation ceremony.) Then he got another teaching job, this one in Fannin
County, held it for two years, and in 1906, at the age of twenty-four,
announced for the legislature.

He campaigned on a little brown cow pony, riding from farm to
farm. Unable to make small talk, he discussed farm problems, a short,
solid young man with a hairline that was already receding, and
earnest brown eyes. At each farm, he asked who lived on the next
farm, so that when he got there, he could call them by name. Two in-
cidents in the campaign showed that he had not forgotten his father's
four words of advice. A man approached him one day and said that a
ten-dollar contribution to an influential farmer would ensure the
votes of the farmer's relatives. "I'm not trying to buy the office," Rayburn replied. "I'm asking the people to give it to me." He and his opponent, Sam Gardner of Honey Grove, became friends and, near the
end of the campaign, rode from town to town together in a one-horse
buggy; arriving in a town, they would take turns standing in the back
of the buggy and speaking. In one town, Gardner became ill and
spent three days in bed. Although Gardner appeared to be leading,
Rayburn didn't use the three days to campaign; he spent them with

Gardner, nursing him. Gardner was to be a friend of Sam Rayburn's all his life.

The votes were cast on a Saturday, but, because the ballot boxes had to be brought in to the county clerk's office in Bonham, and the ballots counted by hand, the results would not be announced until Tuesday. Sam arranged for a friend with a fast horse to bring the news the eleven miles to the Rayburn farm. On Tuesday, he sat with his family in the living room, waiting for the hoofbeats that would announce his destiny. It was victory, by 163 votes.

In Austin, Sam Rayburn didn't forget where he came from. Enlisting in the small band which fought "The Interests" and talked of "The People," he introduced bills to regulate railroads and banks. Unlike some of that band, he never sold out. Years later, when someone mentioned that Rayburn's father had not left him much of an inheritance, Rayburn quickly corrected him—his father, he said, "gave me my untarnished name." He kept it untarnished. He wouldn't drink at the Driskill, and wouldn't live there; rooming at a cheap boardinghouse below the capitol, he shared a small room to save his five-dollar-per-day salary for tuition at the University of Texas Law School. After paying his tuition, he was to recall, he had so little money that once, after offering to buy a soda for a Representative named Pharr, he realized that he had only a nickel to his name; "so when we got to the counter, I told Pharr I wasn't feeling so well and would not take anything. He went on and got his drink and I paid for it. . . . I don't know what I'd have done if he had ordered a dime drink." But when, shortly after he had obtained his law degree and joined a law firm, one of his partners handed him the largest check he had ever seen as his share of a monthly retainer from the Santa Fe Railroad, he handed it back—and added that he would never "accept a dollar of the railroad's money." To his partner's request for an explanation, he replied: "I said to him that I was a member of the legislature, representing the people. . . ." Legislators were routinely presented with free railroad passes; Rayburn returned his, even though, at the time he refused his pass, he was desperately lonely in Austin and unable to return home because he could not afford the fare. (His mother approved. "We often wish for you to be with us," she wrote, "but we would rather wait a little longer than for you to accept free passes.") It was while he was in Austin, where legislators were bought wholesale, that there was first heard a saying that men would be repeating for fifty years: "No one can buy Sam Rayburn."

He didn't forget where he came from—or where he was going. He discussed his ambitions with his fellow members of the Texas House of Representatives as bluntly as he had done, years before, with his brothers and sisters. He wanted to be Speaker of the House, he said, and he told them quite frankly why: "I've always wanted responsibility because I want the power responsibility brings."

Not only did he know what he wanted, he knew—seemed to know instinctively—how to get it. Like Lyndon Johnson's father, Sam Johnson, he had an instinctive gift for the legislative process, but, unlike Sam Johnson, he was not a romantic or a dreamer. When he helped someone, he insisted on help in return, even when the recipient of his aid was his idol.

Arriving in Austin, Rayburn found his idol on trial there: debate was raging over the threatened legislative investigation of Joseph Weldon Bailey, now a United States senator accused of selling out to the railroads and to Standard Oil. Rayburn, who throughout his life was to refuse to believe those charges, offered his support to Bailey's legislative lieutenants, pointing out that, as the representative from Bailey's old district, his opinion might carry more weight than that of the average freshman legislator. But in return for his support, he said, he wanted more than might be given the average freshman legislator. He gave his support—and proved, during his first days in the legislature, a very effective, if quiet, figure in Bailey's defense. And he got what he wanted in return. The backing of Bailey's lieutenants gave him, in his first term in the legislature, the chairmanship of a key legislative committee.

A committee chairman's power was used to build more power. Legislators who received favors from him were expected to give favors in return. And the favors Rayburn asked for were, like the favors he gave, shrewdly chosen. Hardly had he arrived in the Texas House, it seemed, when he was a power in it, thanks to a gift—a rare gift—for legislative horsetrading.

He had other gifts, too—in particular, a very unusual force of personality.

In part, that force was physical. Sam Rayburn was a short man—five-foot-six-inches—but his body was broad and massive, the chest and shoulders so broad and thick that they bulged through the cheap fabric of his suits. His head, set on a bull neck, was massive, too, and seemed even more massive than it was, for already, in his twenties, he was going almost completely bald, so that the loom of the great bare skull was unsoftened by hair. His wide, heavy face could be pleasant in private, but in public it was expressionless, immobile, grim; so hard were the thin line of the lips and the set of the wide, jutting jaw that, except for the eyes that smoldered in it, it might have been the face of a stone statue—and it exuded an immense, elemental strength.

That aura was not dispelled by Sam Rayburn's character.

Already men were whispering about his temper. When he lost it, and he lost it often, a deep flush would rise along the bull neck and completely cover the great head, and the lips, so grim, would twist in a snarl, and the voice, so low, would rasp. "In dark moods," one observer was to write, "his profanity was shattering," and as he cursed, he spat—and, as the observer tactfully put it, "If a . . . cuspidor was handy, that was fine. If there wasn't, it was too bad." In a rage, "Mr. Rayburn's face blackened in a terrible scowl and his bald head turned deep red. . . . That was the way he looked in a rage, and few cared to see such a mien turned upon themselves." When he lost control of that temper, he was deaf to reason; not even considerations of career or ambition could stand before it. The most feared figure in Austin was the recently retired governor, Tom Campbell; the ruthlessness he had exhibited in the statehouse, rumor had it, had not been tempered since he had become lobbyist for the state's banking interests—and the power of those interests still enabled him to punish opponents. Rayburn, fighting bank-sponsored legislation in his committee, and pushing his own, became an opponent. Campbell planted in cooperative newspapers stories that Rayburn was fighting in committee because he was afraid to fight in the open—articles that Rayburn considered an attack on his personal honor. Friends aware of his temper urged him not to lose it; Campbell, they warned him, had de-

stroyed the careers of other men who had opposed him even indirectly. Rayburn thereupon took the floor of the House with a speech
that was not indirect. His own bills, he said, "are in the interest of the
people, and I will stand here day by day and vote for them. . . . It matters not to me what Mr. Campbell's views are." Pausing, he raised his
great head and stared straight at Campbell, who was sitting in the
gallery, not speaking again until everyone in the chamber was staring
at Campbell, too. Then he said: "It matters not to me whether Tom
Campbell stands for a measure or against it. Tom Campbell, in my
opinion, is the least thing to be considered in legislation." The temper,
the aura of immense strength, the legislative cunning, the implacable
standards: in Austin, men learned that they couldn't buy Sam Rayburn—and that they couldn't cross him.

Nor was his temper the only striking aspect of Sam Rayburn's
character. His colleagues talked not only of his rage but of his rigidity.

His standards were very simple—and not subject to compromise.
He talked a lot about "honor" and "loyalty," and he meant what he
said. "There are no degrees in honorableness," he would say. "You are
or you aren't." Harsh though that rule was, he lived up to it—says
one of his fellow legislators: "He had a reputation for honesty and fair
dealing. You could always swear by anything Sam told you"—and he
insisted that others live up to it, too. "Once you lied to Rayburn, why,
you'd worn out your credentials," an aide says. "You didn't get a second chance." His colleagues learned, however, that if they paid Sam
Rayburn what they owed him, they would never be short-changed;
his friendship, they learned, was a gift to be cherished. "If he was
your friend, he was your friend forever," one man was to say. "He
would be with you—*always*. The tougher the going, the more certain
you could be that when you looked around, Sam Rayburn would be
standing there with you. I never met a man so loyal to a friend."

He used the words "just" and "fair" a lot, and his colleagues
learned that he meant those words, too. "Whether or not he liked an
issue was actually immaterial," a friend said. "He kept saying he
wanted to find out what was *right*—and after a while, you realized:
by God, he was trying to do just that."

He would spend "about three terms" in the legislature, he had told his brothers and sisters so many years before, and then he would be elected Speaker. During his third term, he ran for Speaker. His speech in the well of the House was to the point. "If you have anything for me," he told his colleagues, "give it to me now." It was a personal appeal, and the response was personal. Bailey's weight was behind him, but that was not a decisive factor—not for a candidate supported by none of the state's major power interests. "Sam Rayburn was elected," says one of his colleagues, "because of the simple respect everyone had for him." (For a moment, the iron façade cracked and the emotion beneath it showed—but only for a moment. When the vote was announced, recalls a friend, "Sam jumped up and gave a cotton-patch yell and then sat down real quick—like he was ashamed of himself." There was another brief crack—during his acceptance speech. "Up in Fannin County there is an old man already passed his three score, and by his side there sits an old woman at whose feet I would delight to worship," he said. "For them also I thank you.")

A Speaker's power was used to get more. That power (the Speaker's "rights and duties") had been undefined; when, at his direction, they were defined now—by a committee of his friends—the definition gave the Speaker unprecedented power. He had no reluctance to use it. He himself recalled that "I saw that all my friends got the good appointments and that those who voted against me for Speaker got none." Even supporters could not threaten him; when he turned down their nominee for a clerkship, their spokesman told him, "If you don't appoint her, I'll get up a petition signed by a majority." "I don't give a damn if every member signs your petition," Rayburn replied. "I still won't appoint her." And he knew what he wanted to use his power for: during his single year as Speaker, the Texas House of Representatives passed significant legislation regulating utilities, railroads, and banks—including bills whose passage the Populists had been urging, without hope, for years.

A single year: he had, after all, told his brothers and sisters that he would be in Congress by the age of thirty, and now, in 1912, he was thirty. He appointed a committee to redraw the boundaries of congressional districts, and the committee removed from the Fannin County district the home county of the state senator who would have been his most formidable opponent. Running for Congress, he evoked his destiny. "When I was a schoolboy," he said, "I made up my mind that I was going to run for Congress when I was thirty. . . . I have reached that age, and I am running for Congress. I believe I have lived to be worthy of your support. I believe I will be elected." He displayed a quiet but effective wit: "I will not deny that there are men in the district better qualified than I to go to Congress, but, gentlemen, these men are not in the race." And he was elected.

★   ★   ★

Decades later, when Sam Rayburn was a legend, one aspect of the legend, fostered by the brief, almost cryptic terseness of his rare speeches, was taciturnity, at least in public. And the reporters who created the legend, who had not known Sam Rayburn when he was a young congressman, assumed that such taciturnity had always been a Rayburn characteristic.

It hadn't. He had been in Congress less than a month, in fact, when he took the floor. He was aware, he said, of "the long-established custom of this House, which . . . demands that discussions . . . shall be left . . . to the more mature members," but he was going "to break" that custom—to "refuse to be relegated to that lockjawed ostracism." He was refusing, he said, because he represented 200,000 people, and they needed someone to speak for them—and, in his speech, which lasted for almost two hours, he did indeed speak for them, pouring out all the bitterness and resentment that had, a generation before, made the northeast corner of Texas a stronghold of the Texas Alliance and of the People's Party.

The issue was the tariff. The House, newly Democratic, was, under the spur of the newly inaugurated Woodrow Wilson, debating the Underwood Bill, which would begin to reform the tariff laws that Populists hated by, for example, placing shoes as well as steerhides on the free list.

The Republicans "talk about the hard deal the producer is getting in this bill," Rayburn said. The Republican Party, he said, is always "willing and anxious to take that small rich class under its protective wing, but unwilling at all times to heed the great chorus of sad cries ever coming from the large yet poor class, the American consumer." What's wrong, he demanded, with reducing the price of the shoes a man "must buy to protect the feet of his children?" The system that kept that price high was "the most indefensible system the world has ever known." Under it, "the poor man ... is compelled to pay more than the rich man," and "manufacturers fatten their already swollen purses with more ill-gotten gains wrung from the horny hands of the toiling masses," from the people who "have forever been ground under the heel of taxation with a relentless tread."

He was especially bitter about the Republicans' attempt, then in full stride, to persuade the farmer that tariffs were really in his best interest. The Republicans "talk about the farmer," he said. What did they know about the farmer? "What consideration have they shown him?" They would find that they underestimated the farmer, he said; they would learn, to their shock, that "they are dealing with a thinking and intelligent class." The Democratic Party, "the party of the masses," was in power at last. Its representatives were "men who came from every walk of life, and who were fresh from the people, who knew their hopes and their aspirations, and their wants, and their sufferings." Its president was "clean and matchless" with "the great heart and mind that he could interpret the inarticulate longings of suffering humanity." The Democrats would pass the Underwood Bill, reduce the tariffs, break up the "swollen fortunes," destroy the "trusts," lift the load from the bending backs, the "stooped and weary backs," of the farmers and laboring class.

Decades later, when Sam Rayburn was a legend and reporters constantly quoted his advice to young congressmen—"To get along, go along"—one aspect of the legend was the assumption that when *he* was a young congressman, he had "gone along," that he had subordinated his own views to those of his party and its leaders.

He hadn't. As a young congressman, he had "gone along" with no one—not even with the president, the president of his own party, whom he idolized.

During his second year in the House, he wrote—himself, with no staff assistance—a bill embodying the old People's Party dream of intensified government regulation of railroads, by giving the government authority over the issuance of new securities by the railroads. Happening, by chance, to see the bill, Louis D. Brandeis, then one of President Wilson's advisors, thought it so good that, says Wilson biographer Arthur Link, it was made one of the three measures that formed the centerpiece of the president's campaign against the trusts. Despite the opposition of the senior member of the Texas delegation, the popular and powerful John Nance Garner, Rayburn pushed the bill to passage in the House; in a note hand-delivered to Rayburn, the president said he had watched Rayburn's fight "with admiration and genuine appreciation," and for some months thereafter invited him frequently to the White House. But the heady moment passed. Railroad lobbyists killed the bill in the Senate, and by the following year, Wilson had had second thoughts; Rayburn was told that the president did not want the bill re-introduced. Although he knew that without White House support the cause was lost—as, indeed, it proved to be—Rayburn refused to stop fighting for it; he introduced the bill anyway. This was an embarrassment to the White House; Rayburn was told the president did not want the bill actively pushed. Rayburn actively pushed it. The president sent the message again—via a messenger whose orders he was sure would be obeyed: the leader of Rayburn's own state delegation, Cactus Jack Garner himself. Rayburn continued pushing. Then Wilson summoned the obstinate freshman to the White House to give him the order face to face. If Wilson received an answer at all, it was a short one; Rayburn was to recall replying in a single sentence: "I'm sorry I can't go along with you, Mr. President." Turning his back on his "clean and matchless" idol, he walked out of the room without another word.

Angered by his recalcitrance, President Wilson threw the weight of the White House behind Rayburn's opponent in the next Democratic primary. Holding his seat nonetheless, Rayburn, on his return to Congress, introduced half a dozen railroad bills against the president's wishes, secured the passage of several, and was eventually to play a crucial role in winning the eight-hour day for railroad workers. Admiring colleagues gave him a nickname: "The Railroad Legislator." And he was active—defiantly and eloquently active, often against the wishes of party leaders—in other areas, including the creation of the Federal Trade Commission.

One aspect of the legend that *was* true was his personal integrity. Men learned in Washington what they had learned in Austin: no one could cross Sam Rayburn—and no one could buy him. Lobbyists could not buy him so much as a meal. Not even the taxpayer could buy him a meal. Spurning the conventional congressional junket, Rayburn would during his forty-eight years in Congress take exactly one overseas trip—a trip to inspect the Panama Canal that he considered necessary because his committee was considering Canal legislation—and on that trip he insisted on paying his own way. He refused not only fees but travel expenses for out-of-town speeches; hosts who, thinking his refusal *pro forma,* attempted to press checks upon him quickly realized they had made a mistake: the face, already so hard, would become harder; Rayburn would say, "I'm not for sale"—and then he would walk away without a backward glance, as he had walked away from a president. His integrity was certified by his bankbook. At his death, at the age of seventy-nine, after decades as one of the most powerful men in the United States, a man courted by railroad companies and oil companies, his savings totaled $15,000.

Sam Rayburn's blocky figure—pounding along the Capitol corridors with strides that one observer likened to the pumping of a piston—seemed broader now, even more massive, the face beneath the bald skull even more grim and hard. The impression of physical strength was not misleading. Once, two big congressmen—one was a 230-pound six-footer, Thomas Blanton of Texas, the name of the other has been lost in time—got into a fistfight. Stepping between them, Rayburn pushed them apart. Then, bunching each man's lapels in one hand, he held them apart, his arms rigid. Standing between two men almost a head taller who were thrashing furiously in his grip, he held them, each with one hand, until they had quieted down, as effortlessly as if they had been two crying babies. But it was not his physical strength that most impressed his colleagues. About his integrity, one said: "Amidst the multitude, he was the incorruptible." About his accomplishments when he was still new on the Hill, another said, introducing him on the floor for a speech in 1916, during his second term in Congress, "He is a member young in years, but old in accomplishment." In a body in which seniority or powerful friends ordinarily determined a member's standing, Sam Rayburn, who possessed neither, was already, solely because of the strength of his personality, a formidable figure.

★   ★   ★

He was going to need this strength.

As a boy, he had vowed that he would become Speaker of the House of Representatives. Now, as he stood each day amidst the milling and confusion of the House floor, there loomed above him, so aloof and alone on the topmost tier of the triple-tiered white marble dais, the single, highbacked Speaker's chair. From the day he arrived in Congress, he wanted to be in that chair, wanted the Speaker's gavel in his hand. He knew how he would wield it—just as he knew for whom: for the People, against the Interests. For years, no Speaker had dominated the House, and the result was confusion and ineffectiveness; it was during his early years in the House that Sam Rayburn, in a private conversation, suddenly burst out: "Someday a man will be elected who'll bring the Speakership into respectability again. He'll be the real leader of the House. He'll be master around here, and everyone will know it." He knew himself to be capable of such mastery: had he not, after all, demonstrated it already, in another Speaker's chair? He felt, moreover, that the high-backed chair and the gavel were his destiny; had not every other element of his boyhood prediction—election to the Texas House, to its Speakership, to the national Congress—already been fulfilled?

His first years in the House may have given him the illusion that the fulfillment of that destiny was not far off. During those years, he had dealt with a president and with presidential advisors, had seen his name in the Eastern press, had become somewhat of a figure in the House. Now reality set in—the long reality.

In 1918, the Democrats lost control of the House of Representatives. They were not to regain it for twelve years. For twelve years, Sam Rayburn would be in the minority.

A minority congressman of insignificant seniority had power to realize neither his dreams for others nor his dream for himself. There was no way of circumventing, no way of battering down, this fact. John Garner had said, "The only way to get anywhere in Congress is to stay there and let seniority take its course." Rayburn had not wanted to believe that. Now he learned that he had no choice. As the prosperity of the twenties waxed brighter, so did the fortunes of the Grand Old Party, the party identified with the glow: Harding was succeeded by Coolidge, and Coolidge by Hoover, and Republican majorities in Congress grew and grew and grew again—and Democratic congressmen were allowed little voice in its affairs. Sam Rayburn, who had rushed toward his destiny, was going to have to wait.

The waiting was made harder by the lack of assurance that it would ever be rewarded. Rayburn could remember when, at thirty, he had been the youngest congressman; he had still been young—thirty-six in 1918—when the waiting began. Now he was no longer so young: he passed forty and then forty-five. And instead of growing closer, his goal seemed to be receding before him. After the 1928 elections, when Hoover beat Smith, there were only 165 Democrats left in the House, to 269 Republicans; never had the party's prospects of regaining control of the House seemed more remote. Nor, of course, would a Democratic victory in itself end Rayburn's waiting. He was not the first Democrat in line for the Speakership; he was not even first within the Texas delegation—if the Democrats turned to Texas for a Speaker, they would turn to the delegation's most powerful and most senior member, the popular Garner, who had been in Congress since 1902.

If a Democratic victory did come to pass, moreover, would he still be in a position to take advantage of it? Would he still be in Congress? He had already had several close primary races, and it seemed to him, pessimistic as he was by nature, inevitable that he would one day lose. "My ambition has been to rise in the House," he wrote to one of his sisters in 1922. "But nobody can tell when the Democrats will come into power and then a race every two years—they will finally get a fellow in a district." So many men had waited patiently for the tides of history to turn—and had been defeated before the turn came. Had been defeated, or had become ill, or had died. So many men who had once dreamed of rising to the Speaker's chair had died without achieving their ambition. Was he to be only one of these?

Waiting was hard enough. He had to wait in silence. Seniority might one day lift him to the chairmanship of his committee. Seniority alone would never enable him to climb the triple dais. The Speaker was elected by a vote of the majority party, a vote based not only on seniority but on popularity, particularly among the party's influentials. He needed friends. He couldn't make enemies. He needed friends not only for his own dreams but for the dreams he dreamed for what he had referred to as "the large yet poor class." Even if he became committee chairman—even if he became Speaker—the forces which would oppose him, the Interests he hated, would be strong. If he wanted not just to hate them but to beat them, he would need allies among his colleagues; he would need, in fact, every ally—every friend—he could get. The savagery with which he fought made enemies. He would have to stop fighting. Sam Rayburn, who had never bided his time, who had rushed to fight the oppressors of "the People," was going to have to bide his time now. This man who so hated to be licked, who said that being licked "almost kills me," was going to have to take his lickings now—take them in silence.

He waited. He had made so many speeches during his first six years in the House; during these next twelve, he made so few; entire sessions would pass without the representative of Texas' Fourth Congressional District taking the floor. And he was hardly more loquacious in private. He took to standing endlessly in the aisle at the rear of the House Chamber, his elbows resting on the brass rail that separated the aisle from the rows of seats, greeting passing members courteously, listening attentively to their problems, but saying very little himself; if he was pressed to say something, his words would be so few as to be cryptic. Those twelve years were the years in which the legend of Sam Rayburn's taciturnity was born. The heavy lips compressed themselves into a thin, hard line, so grim that even in repose the corners of his mouth turned down. The Republicans passed legislation raising the tariffs again, helping the railroads; the lips of the "Railroad Legislator" remained closed. Men who had not known him before had no idea how much strength it took for him to keep them closed. When Silent Cal Coolidge noted that "You don't have to explain something you haven't said," Rayburn told people that that was "the smartest thing he'd ever heard outside of the Bible." He took to quoting the remark himself; he talked sometimes about men who "had gotten in trouble from talking too much." Was he reminding himself what he was doing—and why he had to do it?

There was no more breaking of House customs, no more defiance of party leaders. He had disregarded Garner's advice once. Now he sought it, became the older Texan's protégé. His hotel, the Cochran, was the Washington residence of many prominent members of the House. In the evenings, they would pull up easy chairs in a circle in the lobby and talk; Rayburn made it his business to become part of that circle: a respectful, advice-asking, attentively listening part. If he felt he knew as much as they, they never knew it. In later years, he would frequently quote a Biblical axiom: "There is a time to fish and a time to mend nets." This was net-mending time for him—and he mended them. The House hierarchy came to look upon him with paternalistic fondness. And these older men learned that on the rare occasions on which Sam Rayburn did speak, there was quite a bit of sense in what he had to say. They saw, moreover, that he had what one observer was to call an "indefinable knack for sensing the mood of the House"; he seemed to know, by some intuitive instinct for the legislative process, "just how far it could be pushed," what the vote on a crucial bill would be if the vote was taken immediately—and what it would be if the vote was delayed a week. Asked decades later about this knack, he would reply: "If you can't feel things that you can't see or hear, you don't belong here." He never discussed this knack then—or admitted he had it—but the older men saw he did. And the older men learned they could depend on him—once he gave his word, it was never broken; Garner tendered him his ultimate accolade: "Sam stands hitched." Garner and other Democratic leaders admitted him to the inner circles of House Democrats, "employed him," as one article put it, "to do big jobs in tough fights, and were repaid by his hard-working loyalty." It was during these years that, when some young member asked him for advice on how to succeed in Congress, he began to use the curt remark: "To get along, go along."

He used his growing influence to make friends among young congressmen, but the alliances thus struck were made very quietly. Recalls one congressman: "He would help you. If you said, 'Sam, I need help,' he might say, 'I'll see what I can do.' He might just grunt. But when the bill came up, if you had needed some votes changed, the votes were changed."

More and more now, other congressmen turned to him. Said one, Marvin Jones:

> The House soon spots the men . . . who attend a committee session where there isn't any publicity, who attend during the long grind of hearing witnesses, who day after day have sat there. . . . Men will come in and out of an executive session, but there are only a few men who sit there and watch every sentence that goes into the bill and know why it went in. . . . The House soon finds out who does that on each committee.

A congressman, required to vote on many bills he knows little about, "learns to rely heavily on those few men," Jones was to say. "I could give you some of the names of those men. . . . There was Sam Rayburn. . . ."

★   ★   ★

"To get along, go along"—wait, wait in silence. It was hard for him to take his own advice—how hard is revealed in the letters he wrote home. "This is a lonesome, dark day here," he wrote.

> You wouldn't think it, but a fellow gets lonesomer here, I think, than any place almost. Everybody is busy and one does not find that congeniality for which a fellow so thirsts. . . . It is a selfish, sourbellied place, every fellow trying for fame, perhaps I should say notoriety . . . and are ready at all times to use the other fellow as a prizepole for it. . . . I really believe I will here, as I did in the Texas Legislature, rise to a place where my voice will be somewhat potent in the affairs of the na-

tion, but sometimes it becomes a cheerless fight, and a fellow is almost ready to exclaim, "what's the use!"

He wrote that letter in 1919. The cheerless fight had just started. He would have to fight it for twelve more years. But he fought. He took his own advice. He waited in silence, waited and went along, for twelve years, acquiring not only seniority but friends, until on December 7, 1931, the day on which, thanks to Dick Kleberg's election, the Democrats regained control of Congress, the day Lyndon Johnson came to Washington, he became not Speaker—it would be another nine years before Sam Rayburn became Speaker—but chairman of the House Interstate Commerce Committee. One more year of waiting was required, because of the general governmental paralysis during Herbert Hoover's last year in office. But on March 4, 1933, the new president was sworn in—and then, after all those years of waiting, Sam Rayburn showed what he had been waiting for.

At Roosevelt's direction, legislation had been drafted giving the federal government authority to regulate the issuance of securities for the protection of those who bought them. Rayburn, who had seen so many financially unsophisticated farmers invest the little spare cash they had been able to scrape together in worthless stocks or bonds, had fought for similar legislation more than twenty years before—not only in Austin but in Washington; it was, of course, over his attempt to give the federal government authority over the issuance of railroad securities that the freshman congressman had defied Woodrow Wilson. That attempt had been unsuccessful, as had decades of Populist outcry for meaningful federal legislation; in the face of Wall Street opposition, the most Populists could get was state "Blue Sky" laws (the Texas law had, of course, been authored by the Gentleman from Blanco County). But when he had made that attempt, Rayburn had been a junior member of the Interstate Commerce Committee. Now he was its chairman. There was uncertainty over which committee had jurisdiction over Roosevelt's proposed "Truth-in-Securities" Act, but Speaker Henry Rainey was a friend of Rayburn's. "I want it," Rayburn told him. Rainey gave it to him.

His first difficulty was with the legislation itself, a poorly drafted bill as confusing as the problems it was trying to solve, and almost completely lacking in any effective enforcement measures. Attempts to patch it up had been hamstrung by Roosevelt's reluctance to offend the man he had asked to draft it, an old Wilsonian Democrat, Huston Thompson, and since no one knew what to do, the measure seemed likely to die. Then Rayburn paid a visit to Raymond S. Moley, one of Roosevelt's advisors.

Rayburn knew what to do, Moley was to recall. The bill "was a hopeless mess," Rayburn said, and the patching-up should stop. A new bill should be written from scratch, he said, and it should be written "under [his] direction" by new draftsmen, experts in the complicated securities field.

Moley agreed with Rayburn's analysis, but felt he could not bring in new draftsmen unless he could find a way around Roosevelt's reluctance to ease out Thompson. Moley was unwilling to spell out the problem—but he found that he didn't have to. Before he "went ahead on the draftsmen business," he said, "it would have to be understood that I was acting directly on his, Rayburn's, authorization, not the president's. For all his seeming slowness, there isn't much Sam misses. He laughed appreciatively. 'All right,' he said, 'you've got it.'" On a Friday in early April, three young men began working on a new bill: a Harvard Law School professor, James M. Landis, and two lawyers expert in the securities field, Thomas G. Corcoran and Benjamin V. Cohen. On Monday, they presented their work to the Interstate Commerce Committee.

Questions from the puzzled committee members about the immensely technical draft lasted all day. All day, the committee's chairman sat silent. Trying to read his face for clues, the young men found none. They were discouraged. Moley had learned what lay behind the seeming slowness, but they hadn't, and to them Rayburn seemed, in Cohen's word, a "countryman"—incapable of understanding so complex a subject. At the end of the day, the chairman asked the young men to wait outside; after a while, he came out, and told them that the committee had approved their work and wanted them to turn it into a finished bill. He said no more; only later did Landis learn that "it was Sam Rayburn who decided that this was a bill worth working on."

Rayburn said he wanted them to work with a House legislative draftsman, Middleton Beaman. Beaman was a Rayburn man. "I had thought I knew something of legislative draftsmanship until I met him," Landis was to say. "For days," in his office, "deep in the bowels of the old House Office Building," Beaman, a "rough, tough guy, would not allow us to draft a line. He insisted instead on exploring the implications of the bill to find exactly what we had or did not have in mind. He probed. . . ." This was, Landis recalls, "exasperating." The young men began to suspect "that this delay bore symptoms of sinister Wall Street plotting." Rayburn's demeanor did not alleviate their suspicions. Dropping by Beaman's office, he would pick up a draft paragraph and stand there studying it. He didn't, Landis could see, "know anything about securities," and they felt he didn't understand what he was reading; if he did, he certainly gave no sign of it. Sometimes he gave them a word or two of advice, but it was advice so simple, so unsophisticated, that they could hardly keep from laughing at it. He said that "He wanted a strong bill, but he wanted to make sure it was right, that it was fair, that it was just," Cohen says. He gave no sign of approval, either. The grim face beneath the gleaming bald skull was as immobile as a mask. They didn't know what to make of him, this man of whom Beaman, and Beaman's assistants— and everyone else they talked to—seemed so unaccountably afraid, but he certainly didn't seem to be on their side.

Their suspicions were seemingly confirmed when Rayburn agreed to Wall Street demands that its representatives be given a hearing to present their views on the draft bill. Suspicion turned to apprehension when they heard that the Street's views would be presented by three of its most prominent attorneys, led by the feared John Foster Dulles himself. They would have to rely for their defense on this slow, stolid farmer.

And then came the hearing. "I confess that when I went in that morning to the hearing, I was scared," Landis was to recall. "After all, I was something of a youngster." The hearing was closed, and no records of it exist, but those who were there agree. Two men, John Foster Dulles of Sullivan & Cromwell and Sam Rayburn of Bonham, were the principal antagonists—and the Dulles who stalked into that hearing room slunk out of it. And after the hearing, there came the moment that, Landis was to say, "I'll never forget," the moment when he found out what was behind the mask.

"I went back to my little cubbyhole down in the sub-basement.... About twenty minutes later, I got a call from Sam Rayburn, to come up to his office. Well, naturally, I was worried. I thought maybe all our work was down the drain." But Rayburn said that the work was just fine, and that they should get right on with it. For the first time, there was an expression on Rayburn's usually expressionless face. It was a snarl. He began talking about Dulles and about Wall Street lawyers, and he cursed them, "in very obscene language."

"Now Sam didn't know anything about securities," Landis was to say, recalling that meeting, "but Sam was an expert on the integrity of people.... He knew when a man ... was telling the truth.... He had no patience for men who were not sincere and honest. And this is what he expressed to me, at that time...." He had not, Landis was to say, known Rayburn "too well up to that time. I got to know him quite well later on. He was an expert in ... procedure—oh, absolutely an expert in matters of procedure! He was an expert in procedure, and sizing up the motives of what made human beings tick."

An expert on human beings. With the full twenty-four-member committee susceptible to Wall Street pressure, he delegated the Truth-in-Securities Bill to a subcommittee—the right subcommittee: as its chairman, he named himself; as its other four members, he named four congressmen he knew he could dominate, four who would bow to his personality rather than to Wall Street. When, in the showdown, they did, and reported the young men's bill favorably to the full committee, he told the young men which committee members to approach, and how to approach them. Says Thomas Corcoran, whose expertise in handling men was to become legendary in Washington: "Sam was a genius in handling men. He would send you to see a guy, and he would tell you exactly what the guy was going to say, and in what order, and he'd tell you how to answer each point. And the guy would say exactly what Sam had told you he was going to say, and if you just answered exactly what Sam told you to answer, you could just see these conservative sons-of-bitches coming around right before your eyes." He told them which committee members not to bother approaching—because they would never come around. And these he handled in a different manner; his weapon was the gavel, and, almost half a century later, the young men can still remember its harsh crash as their champion swung it in their defense. During the Hundred Days, his chairmanship was a "temporary dictatorship," writes Michael E. Parrish in his *Securities Regulation and the New Deal.* "Even under normal circumstances a powerful chairman, [he] dominated the ... committee as never before." Still other committee members didn't understand the incredibly complex bill, with its pages of detailed technical regulations governing securities issuance—but they felt it was not necessary that they understand. Rayburn told them it was a good bill, and they trusted Sam. The hearings the committee held on the bill—before reporting it favorably to the full House—were so brief that Moley years later was to write incorrectly that none had been held.

An expert in procedure—oh, absolutely an expert in matters of procedure. The young men had anticipated problems in the full House because of the legislation's complexities; "If you amended Section 7, it might have an effect on Section 2 and 13, and so on," Landis was to say. But, thanks to Rayburn, the complexities made passage easier, not harder. As Landis recalls: "Because of its complexities, and the danger that an unstudied amendment, apparently fair on its face, might unbalance the articulation of its various sections," the bill was introduced under a special rule that "permitted the consideration of amendments only if they had the approval of the committee chairman." No such approval was forthcoming. Landis, watching with apprehension from the gallery, saw that "Rayburn had complete control of the situation." To his astonishment, the bill passed "with scarcely a murmur of dissent."

The young men had anticipated more problems—all but insoluble problems—in the conference committee, in which five-member delegations from the House and the Senate met to try to reconcile their conflicting versions of the same bill, for the Senate bill was, in effect, Huston Thompson's original, "hopeless" bill, which was thoroughly approved by the distinguished chairman of the Senate delegation,

Duncan U. Fletcher, of Florida. But there were procedures for a conference committee also.

Few men knew them. "If they exist, and documentary evidence to that effect is to be found in *Hine's Precedents,* they are observed as much in breach as in conformance," Landis was to write years later, after he had become a veteran of conference committees. But one of the men who knew them was Sam Rayburn.

Taking advantage of them was made easier because Fletcher, a courtly southern gentleman, suggested that Rayburn be chairman for the first meeting. Rayburn said that the first question to be decided was, as Landis puts it, "what document"—House version or Senate version—"you would work from, which was a very important issue, really a basic issue." Rayburn "quietly asked Senator Fletcher if he did not desire to make a motion on this matter." Apparently unaware of the trap into which he was walking, the seventy-five-year-old Fletcher replied that he certainly did so desire: he moved that the Senate bill be made the working draft.

"Motion moved," Rayburn said quickly. "Motion seconded?" It was seconded. "Vote on the motion." The vote was, of course, a tie; all five Senate members voted in favor of the motion; all five House members voted against it. Since it was a tie, Rayburn said, the motion was lost; consequently, the House bill would become the basic draft. Had a House member made the motion, and a tie vote resulted—as, of course, it would have—the Senate bill would have become the basis for negotiations; by luring a senator into making the motion, Rayburn had won a crucial point before the conferees had more than settled into their seats. "Except for an occasional reference to its provisions," Landis was to reminisce, "that was the last we heard of the . . . Senate bill."

The Senate delegation included not only Fletcher but such big names as Carter Glass of Virginia, James Couzens of Michigan and Hiram Johnson of California. "The House had no such distinguished personalities except for Sam Rayburn," Landis was to say. But that one was enough. While Fletcher had apparently intended that, at succeeding meetings, he and Rayburn would alternate in the chair, he was too much of a gentleman to put himself forward; and, as Landis puts it: "Absent any request from him, Rayburn continued to guide the proceedings."

Aides were guided with an iron hand. Once, desperate because their handiwork was being ignored, two Senate staffers who had worked on the Thompson bill attempted to put their draft in front of the committee members. Rayburn spoke to them, in Landis' phrase, "rudely but firmly"; the attempt was not repeated. Senators were guided with deference: deference in tone, in solicitation of their opinions—in all matters except matters of substance. The atmosphere of most conference committees is tense, Landis was to write: in this committee, "thanks to Rayburn's guidance," and the respect he showed for everyone's opinions, "friendships developed," and the tension dissolved. And so did the opposition. On every crucial point, the final bill was the House bill. On May 27, 1933, Roosevelt signed it into law—and after decades of fruitless discussion, government regulation of the issuance of securities was a reality. In the public mind, Rayburn was associated hardly at all with the dramatic months immediately after Roosevelt's inauguration, during which so much legislation that was to change the shape of American life was rushed through Congress. But to the young men who had seen what he did, he was one of the heroes of the Hundred Days.

The next year brought the introduction of legislation for governmental regulation of the exchanges on which securities were traded. Tough as the fight had been in 1933, the fight in 1934—for the creation of a Securities and Exchange Commission, and an end to the operation of the Stock Exchange as a private club, run by and for the benefit of its members, often at the expense of the public—was tougher. The business community moved against Rayburn in his own committee, and almost beat him there. He had to use every ounce of persuasiveness he possessed—and every lever of power—to break the revolt in the committee. Then, in angry scenes on the House floor, he compromised and compromised and compromised again—and never compromised on the crucial point. He maneuvered like a master in another conference committee. And the Securities Exchange Act of 1934 joined the Securities Act of 1933 on the nation's statute books.

Nineteen thirty-five was the year of the Public Utilities Act—the bill to curb the power of giant utility holding companies over their operating subsidiaries. To Populists, these holding companies symbolized the entrenched economic power of the Northeast—and its effect on "The People" throughout the country. Electric rates were unjustly high for consumers—and particularly for farmers—because of the siphoning off of local power companies' cash by the holding companies up in New York; electricity was unavailable to most farmers because the decision-makers in New York, interested only in profit potential, saw too little in rural electrification. For decades, Populist legislators had attempted to enact state legislation to curb utilities—and had been defeated in almost every significant attempt by the utilities' awesome power in state capitals; as a member of the Texas State Legislature twenty years before, Rayburn himself had fought unsuccessfully against them. Rayburn knew now that only the power of the federal government could curb the power of the holding companies, and now, at last, there was a president who knew it, too (as governor of New York, Roosevelt had fought these giants in their lair, and had lost). The president demanded, and Corcoran and Cohen drafted, and Rayburn and Senator Burton K. Wheeler, the old Populist from Montana, introduced legislation that included a clause—dubbed the "Death Sentence" clause—which gave the Securities and Exchange Commission power to compel the dissolution of holding companies.

The mere mention of lobbyists brought the deep red flush to Rayburn's head; wrote a friend, "He hates [them] with a venomous hatred." Nineteen thirty-five was the year of the utility lobby. "You talk about a labor lobby," Roosevelt said. "Well, it is a child compared to this utility lobby. You talk about a Legion lobby. Well, it is an infant in arms compared to this utility lobby." This was, he said, "the most powerful, dangerous lobby . . . that has ever been created by any organization in this country."

The lobbyists played dirty—it was during the Death Sentence fight that there began the first widespread whispers that the president was insane—and they played rough. The flood of almost a million messages that inundated congressmen was reinforced by the threat direct: congressmen were told bluntly that money, as much as was needed, would be poured into their districts to defeat them in the next election if they voted for the Public Utilities Act. This time, Rayburn's control of his committee was broken. When, after six weeks of bitter hearings, the bill was reported out, it came to the floor with the Death Sentence provision removed, and the bill emasculated.

I hate to be licked. It almost kills me. Three times, against the wishes of congressional leaders of his own party, Rayburn demanded a roll call on the Death Sentence. He had the White House on his side—on Roosevelt's orders, Corcoran was working tirelessly beside him—and Senator Hugo Black's hearings were providing the White House with new ammunition as they revealed that the utilities had spent $1.5 million to generate the "spontaneous" mailings, which had actually been produced by using names picked broadscale from telephone directories. But in Texas, newspapers were calling him a Communist, and accusing him of trying to "murder" a great enterprise. John W. Carpenter, president of Texas Power & Light, asked a banker in Rayburn's district "to estimate how much it would cost to beat Sam Rayburn. . . . He said they had the money to do anything." With a storm of abuse rising about him in the House Chamber (and with Carpenter and other utility executives sitting in the House gallery, their presence a silent warning to the congressmen), he lost all three roll-call votes by overwhelming margins. But there was still the conference committee. No friends were made in this one; so bitter did feelings run during its two months of meetings that other members barred Cohen and Corcoran, the bill's drafters, from the committee room. But the bill that emerged from the conference—and that was passed—while far short of what Roosevelt and Rayburn had originally hoped for, nonetheless contained the mandate they wanted for the SEC to compel holding companies' reorganization. Sam Rayburn issued a rare public statement: "With the Securities Act of 1933, the Stock Exchange Act . . . of 1934, and this Holding Company bill to complete the cycle, I believe that control is restored to the government and the people, and taken out of the hands of a few, and that the American people will have cause to believe that this administration is trying and is establishing a government of the people, by the people and for the people."

Rayburn received little credit at the time for his role in the passage of this legislation. "Few people, if they depend on the public prints for their information, know much about him," the *New York Times* noted. "It is doubtful if there is any member of his ability who is less conspicuous, less self-heralded, and less known outside the influential group with which he is immediately in contact." And he has received little credit from history, in part because he left almost no record of his deeds in writing; not in memoirs, not even in memos—as David Halberstam says, he "did all his serious business in pencil on the back of a used envelope." (When asked how he remembered what he had promised or what he had said, he would growl: "I always tell the truth, so I don't need a good memory to remember what I said")—in part because, shy, he shrank from publicity: "Let the other fellow get the headlines," he said. "I'll take the laws." It is possible to read detailed histories of the New Deal and find hardly a reference to Sam Rayburn.

Occasionally, when he was old, he would refer to what he had done. In 1955, Drew Pearson was interviewing him about the regulatory commissions when Rayburn suddenly blurted out: "I was in on the borning of every one of those commissions. . . . I wrote the law that passed the Federal Communications Commission and the Securities and Exchange Commission. . . . I wrote the law for the Civil Aeronautics Board. . . ." But the people to whom he was speaking would not usually understand what the old man was talking about. During the Eisenhower administration, a young congressional aide was expounding on the brilliance of John Foster Dulles when Rayburn suddenly said: "I cut him to pieces once, you know." What do you mean? the aide asked. When was that? The old man grunted and refused to answer. But his name is on the Securities Act of 1933 (the Fletcher-Rayburn Act), and the Securities Exchange Act of 1934 (the Fletcher-Rayburn Act), and the Public Utilities Act of 1935 (the Wheeler-Rayburn Act), and on other pieces of New Deal legislation that, for a while at least, took control "out of the hands of a few," and restored it to "the people." And those who fought beside him knew what he had done. SEC Chairman William O. Douglas was to recall that "[We] called it affectionately the 'Sam Rayburn Commission,' since he had fathered [it]." The three great pieces of legislation embodied principles for which the People's Party—the party of the great orators, Bryan and Tom Watson and Old Joe Bailey—had been fighting for half a century. But the Populist perhaps most responsible for the achievement represented by their collective passage was the least eloquent of Populists: the man who had achieved the power to bring their dreams to realization not by speeches but by silence. (Rayburn, of course, gave credit to someone else—in his own, quiet way. Although over the course of his many years in Washington, autographed photographs of many notables had joined the pictures of Robert E. Lee on his office walls, in his home back in Bonham, resting on his desk, there was, after all these years, still only one picture, the picture of Sam Rayburn's first hero. But now, when Congress adjourned and he came home and unpacked his suitcase, he lifted out of the suitcase and placed beside the picture of Robert E. Lee a picture of Franklin D. Roosevelt.)

Even before he had attained power, Sam Rayburn, with his grim face beneath the gleaming bald head, had been a formidable figure. Now there was power behind the presence—substantial power: the committee chairmanship as well as patronage on the grand scale, for he had been given not only the naming of some commissioners and top staff members of the new regulatory agencies, but a voice in the White House dispensation of patronage to other congressmen; a columnist noted that while his aversion to publicity made him "a man in the shadows," he was one of the handful of congressmen "who made the wheels go around" in the House. The full force of his personality, held under check so long, was unleashed at last. On the issues he cared deeply about, he was immovable. "If you were arguing with him and raised a point, he'd give you an answer," says a fellow congressman. "If you raised the point again, you'd get the same answer again. The exact same answer. You realized, that was the conclusive remark. That was the end of that conversation." He almost never raised his voice, and he never threatened; the most he might say—in a low, mild, almost gentle, tone—was, "Before you go on here, I want to tell you this—you are about to make a mistake, a very big mistake." And he never asked for anything, a vote or a favor, more than once. If you turned Sam Rayburn down once, men learned, he would never ask you again—for anything.

He would never ask a man to do anything against his own interests. "A congressman's first duty is to get re-elected," he would say, and he would advise young congressmen: "Always vote your district." If a congressman said that a vote Rayburn was asking for would hurt him in his district, Rayburn would always accept that excuse. But Rayburn knew the districts. And if the excuse wasn't true, Rayburn's rage would rise. Once, for example, it erupted against a congressman from a liberal district who took orders from the district's reactionary business interests only because he didn't want to offend them. The congressman had often used the excuse of public opinion in his district, and, because Rayburn had never challenged him on it, and had stopped asking for his support, was under the misapprehension that Rayburn believed that excuse. One evening, however, after the congressman had voted against a bill Rayburn supported, he approached Rayburn, who was standing with a group of friends, and with a winning smile said he sure wished he could have voted with him, but that such a vote would have hurt him in his district. Rayburn did not reply for a long moment, while the deep red flush started to creep up his head. Then, says one of the men who were standing with Rayburn, in a recollection confirmed by another, Rayburn said:

"Now, I never asked for your vote on this bill. I never said a word to you about this bill. I knew you wouldn't vote for this bill, and I never said a word to you about it. But you came across the room just now and told me you wish you could have voted with me.

"So I'm going to tell you something now. You *could* have voted with me. I've known that district since before you were born, and that vote wouldn't have hurt you one bit. Not one bit. You didn't vote with me because you didn't have the guts to."

The flush on the huge head was so dark now that it looked almost black. The men standing with Rayburn backed away. "So don't you come crawling across the room telling me you wish you could have voted for the bill. 'Cause it's a damn lie. It's a damn lie. And you're a

damn liar. You didn't vote for the bill 'cause you didn't have the guts
to. You've got no guts. Let me tell you something. I didn't raise the issue, but you did. You came across the room. So let me tell you something. The time is coming when the people are going to find out that
all you represent is the Chamber of Commerce, and when they find
that out, they're going to beat your ass."

A young state legislator who had considered challenging the congressman for his seat had dropped the idea because he didn't have
enough political clout. Not a week after his confrontation with Rayburn, the congressman walked into the House Dining Room for
lunch and saw the legislator sitting there—at Rayburn's table. When
the legislator returned home, he had all the clout he needed, and the
congressman's political career was over. Rayburn drove him not only
out of Congress, but out of Washington. He tried to stay on in the
capital, looking for a government job or a lobbying job, but no job
was open to him. And none would ever be—not as long as Sam Rayburn was alive.

The temper—backed by the political power—made men afraid of
Rayburn. They tried to gauge his moods. "When he would say 'She-
e-e-e-t,' drawing the word out, I knew he was still good-natured," recalls House Doorkeeper "Fishbait" Miller. "But if he said it fast, like
'I don't want to hear a lot of shit from you,' I knew I was in trouble."
Some congressmen, says House Sergeant-at-Arms Kenneth Harding,
were "literally afraid to start talking to him." Says Harding: "He
could be very friendly. But if he was frowning, boy—stay away. I
mean, if he was coming down a corridor and he was frowning, people
were literally afraid to start talking to him. They feared to get close to
him. They were afraid of saying the wrong thing." And if the great
heavy head wore not only a frown but that dark red flush, "when he
came down a corridor," it was "a stone through a wave. People would
part before him."

But if men who saw Sam Rayburn only in the halls of Congress
feared him, men who also saw him outside those halls pitied him.

As a child, loneliness had been what he dreaded most. "Loneliness breaks the heart," he had said. "Loneliness consumes people." Now he was a man, who had attained the power he had so long sought. But he had learned that even power could not save him from what he dreaded.

During the hours in which Congress was in session, of course, he was surrounded by people wanting to talk to him, clamoring for his attention, hanging on his every word.

But Congress wasn't always in session. It wasn't in session in the evenings, or on weekends. And when Congress wasn't in session, Sam Rayburn was often alone.

He had wanted so desperately not to be alone. He had wanted a family—a wife and children. Driving through the Washington suburbs with a friend not long after he first arrived in the capital, he had said, as they passed the Chevy Chase Country Club, "I want a house that big," and when the friend asked him why, he said, "For all my children." Adults, another friend says, "were scared of Rayburn, but children weren't. They took to him instinctively. They crawled all over him and rubbed their hands over his bald head." He would sit talking to a little girl or boy for hours—with a broad, gentle grin on that great, hard face to which, it sometimes seemed, no man could bring a smile. Friends who saw Sam Rayburn with women realized that his usual grim demeanor concealed—that, in fact, the grimness was a mask deliberately donned to conceal—a terrible shyness and insecurity. He was always afraid of looking foolish; he would never tell a joke in a speech because, he said, "I tried to tell a joke once in a speech, and before I got through, I was the joke." And this fear seemed accentuated when he was with women. He had fallen in love once—with the beautiful, dark-haired, eighteen-year-old sister of another Texas congressman, his friend Marvin Jones; Rayburn was thirty-six at the time. Although he wrote Metze Jones regularly, nine years passed before he asked her to marry him; friends say it took him that long to work up the nerve. And when—in 1927, when Rayburn was forty-five—they finally became engaged, he asked her to make the engagement short; "I was in a great hurry to get married . . . before she changed her mind," he wrote a friend. The marriage lasted three months. Rayburn never spoke of what had happened; so tight-lipped was he on the subject that most men who met him in later years never learned he had been married. (Once, when he was an old man, he was talking to a group of Girl Scouts, one of whom asked why he wasn't married. "Oh, I'm so cranky that nobody would have me," he said. "*I'll* marry you," one of the girls said. Rayburn laughed.) Fishbait Miller, who knew about the marriage—in working with Rayburn for thirty years, he learned things about Rayburn despite Rayburn—says that even after Metze remarried, Rayburn "kept watch over her from a distance"; when her daughter from the second marriage contracted polio, the girl was admitted immediately to the famed polio treatment center at Warm Springs despite the long wait-ing list. ("It is true that someone can be powerful and you can feel very sorry for him," Miller says. "I felt sorry for Rayburn because he lost the woman he loved.") For years thereafter, Rayburn had not a single date. He may, in fact, never have had more than a few scattered dates; no one really knows. After Metze left him, Sam Rayburn was alone. He moved into two rooms in a small, rather dingy apartment house near Dupont Circle, where he lived for the rest of his life.

He could, of course, have gone to parties, but his belief that he could not make small talk, his fear that he would make a fool of him-self if he tried, made parties an ordeal; he talked for years about the first Washington cocktail party he had gone to, back when he was a freshman congressman. "I never felt that [the hostess] knew, or cared, whether I was there or not. So I stopped going [to parties]."

He tried to prolong the hours he spent on Capitol Hill. Jack Gar-ner's old "Board of Education" had been disbanded, but a few con-gressional leaders still gathered for a drink at the end of the day, and Rayburn was always there. But the others would leave rather quickly; they had wives, and families, and social engagements, to go to. (Ray-burn tried never to let them see that he did not; he never asked them to stay, often made a point of leaving early himself, as if he too had somewhere else to go.)

"The tough time was the weekends, when everyone went home to his wife," says D. B. Hardeman, who was to become his aide during the 1950s. During those later years, Rayburn's position as Speaker provided him with a staff, and on weekends he would telephone its members, aides like Hardeman and John Holton, House Doorkeeper Miller or Sergeant-at-Arms Harding; he would sound very jovial on the phone, asking them to go fishing with him in some lakes down near the Maryland shore, or to come over for Sunday breakfast and read the Sunday papers with him. Asking was very hard for Sam Rayburn, however, and although the aides would accept his invitations ("Sometimes I had something planned, but I would come because I knew he had nothing to do," one says), he did not ask often. The pride which made it so hard for him to issue an invitation made it hard for him even to accept one: his aides would, of course, invite him to their homes, but he could not accept too often; he didn't want anyone to get the idea that he didn't have anything to do. (His aides knew the truth, however; Rayburn would sometimes instruct Hardeman or Holton to come to the office on a Sunday, on the pretext that there was work to do, but, often, there wasn't; the young men would watch him opening all the drawers of his desk, and taking out every paper, "looking for something to do.") Says Ken Harding: "He had many worshippers, but very few close friends. You held him in awe. You didn't dare get close to him. People feared to get close to him, because they were afraid of saying the wrong thing. And because people were afraid to get close to him, he was a very lonely guy. His life was a tragedy. I felt very, very sorry for Sam Rayburn."

During the 1930s, he did not yet have a staff that he could telephone. For a while, he made an effort to round up weekend fishing parties from among the Texas congressmen, driving down to the Maryland lakes on Saturday and sleeping over in cabins Saturday night. "Those who went along for the first time were stunned by the change in Rayburn's personality," a friend writes. "Solemn, laconic and brief in the Capitol, on the road he was talkative, humorous and a great tease."

But how many times could he ask people to come—and if he was turned down once by someone, no matter how legitimate the excuse, how graciously it was made, how could Sam Rayburn ask again? So if he went to the Maryland lakes, he usually went alone; in a letter to a friend in Texas, these words burst out of him: "God what I would give for a tow-headed boy to take fishing!" And often, during the thirties, he would spend his weekends in Washington, taking long walks, a lonely figure wandering for hours through the deserted streets, his face set grimly as if he wanted to be alone—as if daring anyone to talk to him.

Excerpted from Robert A. Caro, *The Years of Lyndon Johnson: The Path to Power* (New York: Alfred A. Knopf, 1982), pgs. 307–333.

Franklin Delano Roosevelt

MAN OF THE CENTURY

"[Y]ou'd go into some small mountain cabin," the reporter Peter Lisagor recalled of the West Virginia of 1960, "and about the only picture on the wall would be a picture of Franklin D. Roosevelt." In the Mountain State's decisive Democratic primary that year, John F. Kennedy labored under two handicaps. His opponent, Minnesota Senator Hubert H. Humphrey, not only had a stronger claim than Kennedy to FDR's liberal mantle; like the overwhelming majority of West Virginians, Humphrey was a Protestant. Kennedy was stuck with his Catholicism, so he turned to a Washington car salesman to help him get right with the local deity. Sounding, to Humphrey, "like a precise echo of fireside chats heard on crystal sets and Emerson radios," Franklin Roosevelt, Jr. made ads and broadcast speeches for Kennedy that lifted the pope off his shoulders. It was, a Kennedy aide said, almost like "God's son coming down and saying it was all right to vote for this Catholic." Especially in the coal mining counties, which, breaking Republican ties dating to the Civil War, went Democratic after FDR endorsed the right to organize unions, crowds gathered to see and touch his namesake. "Roosevelt" worked its magic for Kennedy, who carried the state, all but clinching the Democratic presidential nomination. Observers credited FDR, Jr. with persuading enough voters that JFK "represented FDR's second coming."

After November 22, 1963, about the only picture my Boston Irish parents had on their walls was a framed *Parade* magazine cover titled "The Two Johns of the 20th Century," depicting Pope

John 23rd and John F. Kennedy sowing seeds into the furrows of a ploughed field. Religion was all people like my parents had in common with John F. Kennedy, and, excepting religion, West Virginia miners might have lived on a different planet from Franklin Roosevelt. The patrician Bushes play at being ordinary Joes who just happen to be related to the Queen of England; Bush Sr. nibbled pork rinds, Junior drops more *g*'s the farther south he goes. John Kennedy did not pretend to be an average guy; nor did Roosevelt, the Hyde Park squire. Yet these sons of privilege have been the presidents taken to the hearts of ordinary Americans, Kennedy for his stolen promise, FDR for giving a New Deal to people in West Virginia cabins and Boston tenements and for what, unlike Social Security and the TVA, died with him in 1945—his infectious confidence. The first radio president, FDR reached Americans in their homes, his voice warm, his tone commanding, a confiding Moses.

Doris Kearns Goodwin has traced FDR's unfailing confidence to the emotional resources and challenges of his childhood. His mother's epic love both sustained and crowded him, making him adept at preserving his autonomy through "secrecy, manipulation, charm, negotiation, avoidance, and control." Thus endowed, he developed what Freud called "the feeling of a conqueror, that confidence of success that often induces real success." All he lacked to prepare him for his rendezvous with destiny was suffering and will. They came at age thirty-nine, when he was crippled by polio and "came to empathize with . . . people to whom fate had dealt a difficult hand," and refused to be defeated by it. These gifts of nurture and circumstance became national assets during the Great Depression, communicating his certainty of better days to come and his concern for all in struggle. "Roosevelt is my friend," someone chalked on the side of a boxcar in the Denver train yards. He spoke for millions.

In the excerpt below, the closing pages of *Franklin Delano Roosevelt: Champion of Freedom,* Conrad Black delivers something readers want from biography but rarely get from biographers—the set-piece summing up. Even rarer, like the father of biography,

Plutarch, and its modern pioneer, James Boswell, Black rises to his subject's greatness.

WHAT MADE FDR GREAT
Conrad Black

Franklin D. Roosevelt was the most important person of the twentieth century, because of his achievements as one of America's greatest presidents and its most accomplished leader since Lincoln. This greatness rests on seven achievements.

First, he was, with Winston Churchill, the co-savior of Western civilization. He persuaded his countrymen to assist their natural allies in 1940 in order to stay out of war themselves. In order to see out the war emergency, he professed to be drafted to an unprecedented extension of his presidential tenure—a third term. Having pledged to avoid war by helping Britain and the Dominions fight for the common cause, his progressive provocations of the Axis, lawful and benign as they were, were almost artistically executed. Britain could not have remained in the war without his support. He extended U.S. territorial waters 1,800 miles out into the Atlantic and attacked German ships when they were detected, and imposed on Japan an embargo on the sinews of war—oil and scrap metal. This made it almost certain that America would be attacked. He knew this to be the only method of winning the war for the West, and the Japanese, German, and Italian governments, in their aggressive stupidity, played into his hands.

With the help of the eloquence and courage of Churchill and the British and of the revulsion against Hitler's inhumanity, Roosevelt led American opinion from profound isolationism in 1937 to accepting war rather than an Axis victory in 1941, even before Pearl Harbor galvanized the nation. This was arguably the greatest political tour de force in the history of democratic government, as even Stalin recognized in his main toast to Roosevelt at Teheran. His technique of getting ahead of public opinion, pulling it partly behind him while denying his views had evolved, allowing a brief respite and then moving again, was conceived and perfected in this period.

This anchoring of the United States in the world was Franklin D. Roosevelt's second great achievement. His permanent defeat of the isolationists by representing them as Hitler dupes before the war, who would bring the world to war again if heeded in 1945, and by placating them with an international organization designed to make the world seem less dangerous, was the greatest achievement for world stability since the Battle of Waterloo.

The reason the second half of the twentieth century was so greatly more successful than the first half was precisely because of the stabilizing power of the United States, providing deterrence and containment in Europe and the Far East. In the postwar world in which Roosevelt had conditioned America to play its full part, the Soviet Union gradually crumbled, without a major war. And China, whose status as a Great Power Roosevelt was the first important foreign leader to champion, developed a capitalist growth economy, and progressed syncopatedly toward greater political liberalism.

Roosevelt's third great achievement was the reinvention of the American state. Before bringing the United States out of the immaturity of isolation and into the world, where it could defend its interests and assume its responsibilities, Roosevelt had to bring the United States out of the Great Depression. In doing so, he involved the government in many areas where its presence had been limited or non-existent— industrial recovery, reflation, large-scale workfare programs, Social Security, reform of financial institutions, rural electrification, flood and drought control, stabilization of farm production and prices, conservation, refinancing of home mortgages and farm loans, reform of working conditions, public sector development and distribution of hydroelectric power, and generous treatment of veterans.

The New Deal was certainly not an unqualified success. The initial core of the program, the National Industrial Recovery Act and the Agricultural Adjustment Act, were successful to only a limited extent. But most of the programs in the areas enumerated were overwhelmingly successful. By later standards, the New Deal was passing but not brilliant economics. As crisis management and preservation of a civil society, it was a masterly success. Only a leader of immense political dexterity could have presented such a smorgasbord as a coherent program and retained political capital while sorting out conflicting policies. There were many useful innovations, including the application of participatory democracy in crop production restraint programs, and the great scope of workfare projects, from theater companies to the preservation of the whooping crane.

The collective effect of these measures gradually alleviated the Depression in America and prevented a recurrence of a similar catastrophe.

Roosevelt redefined American government as the conservator of last resort not only of public order but of national confidence, and of at least a minimalist concept of social justice. He restored the confidence of Americans in their country, and in their government as a vital and active promoter of an equitable society, and a corrective to economic and natural disasters. No other American president has had anything remotely like as important a reform record.

Roosevelt stole the arguments of the left, enacted very diluted legislative versions of them, and deprived the left of any possibility of political success. It was not just a witticism when Socialist Party leader Norman Thomas said that Roosevelt was carrying out the Socialist Party's program—"in a coffin."

By channeling all the public's resentment at the consequences of the Great Depression into an impersonal cul-de-sac, Roosevelt preserved the moral integrality of the nation so he could focus alarm and moral outrage on America's real enemies: the conquering foreign dictators. He was both the savior of American capitalism and the foremost reformer in the country's history. Thus did he deliver the country from overexposure to the extremes of right and left. American capitalism ceased to be a menace to itself and became an unambiguous engine to greater and better-distributed national prosperity.

It was illustrative of Roosevelt's singular political genius that he completed the recovery from the Depression by accelerating rearmament to prepare the country for world war. It was the tactical triumph of using the fear of one enemy (Hitler and the Japanese) to rout another (domestic unemployment and underproduction), thus preparing the military defeat of the first. His political legerdemain was so refined that no one realized what he was doing, and his mastery of the scene, as Churchill called it in his eulogy, was such that he confided in no one as he engineered this maneuver. He began the complete emancipation of African-Americans in the same way, using the exigencies of depression relief and the nascent welfare system and then the war to start them up the long ladder to equality of opportunity.

In this third achievement, overcoming the Depression and partially reforming the economic and social system, Franklin D. Roosevelt preserved or restored the good name of democratic government. In the thirties, Roosevelt's was the only democratic government of an important country with any panache, and the only one that actually uplifted the people. This was due to the originality of its programs, and even more to his magnetic personality.

He was also the only leader of a very important country between the mid-thirties and 1940 not ultimately to be ashamed of: neither a dictator nor an appeaser of dictators. Churchill and many others helped to give democracy an overwhelming legitimacy. But in the daunting years from 1933 to 1940 this heavy responsibility rested lightly on the massive shoulders of Franklin D. Roosevelt almost alone.

Roosevelt's fourth great achievement was that he was an almost uniformly successful war leader, far more so than Washington, Madison, Lincoln, or Wilson. (The Indian, Mexican, and Spanish Wars don't bear comparison.) After the initial fiasco at Pearl Harbor, where the local commanders had badly let the country down, and except for the momentary setbacks in the Philippines and at the Kasserine Pass and

Savo Island and Java Sea, American forces were almost never defeated, even when, as in early actions like the Coral Sea and Midway, they were heavily outnumbered.

His strategic insights were almost always accurate, even though he made no pretense to being a military strategist, and he harassed his commanders much less than did Churchill, let alone Stalin and Hitler. His command appointments were excellent. George Marshall, Chester Nimitz, Douglas MacArthur, and Ernest King were personal choices of Roosevelt's, and Dwight Eisenhower was agreed to on Marshall's recommendation. All performed well; most performed brilliantly.

He never wavered on the Germany-first strategy, even on the day of Pearl Harbor. He was an early champion of air power, massively augmenting aircraft production and aircraft carrier construction, and he personally ordered the successful conversion of nine heavy cruisers on the slipways to aircraft carriers, over some reluctance from the Navy Department, vitally accelerating American naval victory in the Pacific.

Roosevelt insisted, against professional advice, on the April 1942 James H. Doolittle air raid on Tokyo, a bold stroke that, though this was not foreseen, contributed to the great victory at Midway. He conceived of and required the very successful Torch landings in North Africa, over the objections of his own military advisors, especially Marshall. He was absolutely correct in insisting upon an early cross-Channel invasion as the only means of defeating Nazi Germany in a timely manner, of ensuring that there would be no separate peace between Hitler and Stalin, and of giving the West its best chance of preventing a Soviet takeover of Germany and even France. He insisted on the Anvil invasion of southern France, over fierce resistance from the British, and was vindicated, as Churchill, in contrast to the intractable Bernard Montgomery, graciously acknowledged at the second Quebec Conference and in his memoirs. He was almost certainly correct in ordering the Philippine invasion, about which Marshall and King were divided. And his experience as assistant secretary of the navy in the First World War had taught him the value of planning for the next war boldly and not on the basis of the preceding one.

From 1940 to 1945, the United States amply fulfilled Roosevelt's exhortation to be the "Great Arsenal of Democracy." It produced 300,000 warplanes, two million trucks, over 100,000 tanks, nearly forty million tons of naval and merchant shipping, over twenty million rifles and pistols and machine guns. As Stalin acknowledged at Teheran, American war production made an indispensable and immense contribution to victory. And it was achieved in a fine and relatively unabrasive partnership between the private and public sectors and business and labor that augured well for the administration's postwar relations with business.

At times of supreme crisis—Pearl Harbor, D-Day, the Battle of the Ardennes—Roosevelt was imperturbable, and he was admired by all his subordinates, even MacArthur and conspicuously George Patton.

At the border between political and military strategy, his acute intuition was his sure guide. It enabled him to judge how long Stalin could be left to take 90 percent of the casualties, as among the Big Three, before he might be tempted to compose his differences with Hitler, as he had done in 1939; and how long the British and Americans could operate on the periphery of the main theater before moving to assure that most of geopolitically useful Europe was in their hands and not Russia's. The management of relations with Stalin and Churchill in these matters, apart from the purely military elements, required almost preternatural insight and finesse.

This led to Franklin Roosevelt's fifth great achievement: his creation of the circumstances that enabled his postwar successors to complete the Allied victory in the Second World War, to liberate Eastern Europe, and to make the world safe for democracy at last. He had done what he reasonably could to bring Stalin into the fold of responsible world leaders. He played a decisive role, with Churchill, in limiting Russian and domestic Communist influence in postwar Italy and France, and he focused from early 1943 on occupying as much of Germany as possible until the British and the Russians, could agree upon the zones of occupation in Germany. He, no less than

Churchill, always recognized the danger of letting the Russians into Western Europe.

While representing a swift postwar departure of American forces from Europe as likely, he prepared for an occupation of a large part of Germany for an indefinite period. He moved decisively to develop atomic weapons. And he was the principal creator of the United Nations, a framework for international cooperation and, to a very limited extent, world government, that could operate according to the wishes of the Allies, if they remained united (as during the Gulf War of 1990–1991). He would have been appalled at the degeneration of the United Nations General Assembly into the Western-bashing forum for Third World dictators that it has largely become. The Latin American "Good Neighbors," British Dominions, and emerging colonies were supposed to assure the British and Americans a durable majority and multilateral legitimacy. They did, for a generation. These two developments for which Roosevelt was ultimately responsible—the nuclear age and the United Nations organization—offered the world at the time he died an ultimate conceptual Manichaean alternative between Armageddon and cooperation.

Roosevelt saw that empires would crumble, though Churchill and de Gaulle (despite his subsequent rationalizations) dissented. He foresaw both the possibility of rivalry with Communism and Communism's ultimate failure. And he saw the potential for China and India. His trusteeship proposal for preparing underdeveloped colonies for independence wasn't taken up, but would almost certainly have been more successful than the many colonial wars that occurred, and the indiscriminate granting of independence to scores of primitive colonies, many of which became failed states. If his successors had studied his views on Indochina, the Vietnam debacle would have been avoided.

In ending American isolation, leading the admission or readmission of France, Germany, Italy, and Japan to the West, and staking out the moral high ground opposite Russia through the Yalta declarations on Poland and Liberated Europe, Roosevelt created the principal elements for victory in the Cold War. If he had been ambivalent about imperialism, had not forced Stalin, when the Russian leader subjugated Eastern Europe, to violate agreements with the Western Allies and arouse American political and public opinion, and had not drawn the United States into an international organization even before the war ended, Stalin might have been able to snaffle up Eastern Europe without bringing an unwinnable war of containment and ideological and military competition down upon himself. In such circumstances, the Soviet era, in Russia and its satellites, could have been prolonged.

This fifth great achievement of Roosevelt's has been obscured by the Yalta myth. Starting the Cold War was a catastrophic mistake by Stalin, but the shock of the breakup of the Grand Alliance and the revelation of Stalin as a double-dealing enemy created the opportunity for the systematic defamation of Roosevelt. The deceased president became a catchment for the evasions of the complicit and for the demagogy of the unscrupulous, or merely of the uninformed.

Completing Western Allied victory in World War II by almost bloodlessly defeating the Soviet Union required great skill and perseverance from many of Roosevelt's successors and many Allied statesmen. But the West always held the advantage in this contest.

Most of the key American figures in the Cold War were Roosevelt's protégés, or at least emulators, who learned much from him. This was directly the case with Truman, Eisenhower, Marshall, Dean Acheson, and Lyndon Johnson; and indirectly with John Kennedy and with other younger men who did not know Roosevelt but served in junior military ranks in World War II and studied him, such as Richard Nixon, Henry Kissinger, Gerald Ford, Ronald Reagan, and the senior George Bush.

★   ★   ★

Churchill's setback in the 1945 British election highlighted Roosevelt's sixth claim to greatness—his unmatched mastery of the American political system. Churchill had never led a political party in a general election before, and Britain had not had an election since 1935. Roosevelt faced the voters twice during the war and never lost touch with American opinion.

Roosevelt well knew the public's impatience, but the world was as-tounded by Churchill's electoral defeat, though Roosevelt, as he warned Churchill at Teheran, would not have been. De Gaulle would generously and fairly write "[Winston Churchill's] personality, identi-fied with a magnificent enterprise, his countenance, etched by the fires and frosts of great events, were no longer adequate to the era of mediocrity."

Stalin, who in July 1945 must have been consolable to see the back of Churchill when he abruptly left the Potsdam Conference, said that "Western democracy must be a wretched system if it could exchange a great man like Churchill for Attlee."

Churchill himself initially envied Roosevelt his death while unde-feated but soon said that if the people wanted Attlee, they could have him, and that that was why Britain had fought and won the war.

Roosevelt never had to think in such terms, so sure was he of his ability to keep the public's approval. Remote and unrepresentative of the country though he was in his tastes and manner, he was an intu-itive and tactical political genius and an electrifying political person-ality.

In twelve years as president, Roosevelt's only significant political defeats were on the Supreme Court packing bill and his attempted party purge in 1938. These are minor (and temporary) setbacks against an avalanche of electoral and legislative success with nothing slightly resembling a precedent or a sequel in American history, nor, probably, in any other of the great democracies.

Lyndon Johnson had great legislative success, with more ambigu-ous practical consequences, apart from civil rights, but couldn't carry public opinion very far. Ronald Reagan could stir and shape national opinion and was an important president, but his entire program was essentially tax reduction and simplification and an arms buildup. Roosevelt governed more than four years longer, far more radically and in much more complicated times than Reagan.

Roosevelt was a master of every aspect of American politics. He knew how to maneuver with the congressional leaders, how to mobi-lize public opinion, how to frame and time legislation, how to take care of the machine captains and ward heelers. He had an uncanny intuition of where public opinion was and where and how fast it could be led.

He was cautious and occasionally pusillanimous, vindictive, or simply mistaken. But his shortcomings are vastly outweighed by the countless times he moved opinion, cajoled the Congress, and achieved what had not been thought possible in good or great and often vital causes.

His record of four consecutive presidential election victories, his seven consecutive congressional election victories, the huge crowds that always came out to see and cheer him throughout his long reign, attest incontrovertibly to his genius at operating every lever of the vast and intricate political machinery of the United States. His insight into common men was the more remarkable because he was certainly not one of them, and never pretended for an instant that he was.

Rather, he presented himself as a constructive aristocrat, though, as Acheson pointed out, of the European, not the bourgeois British, variety. He had the nobility of spirit and outlook becoming to the scion of a famous family, but without the effete snobbery, idleness, or venality the public often impute to the hereditary rich.

He was unfailingly courteous, and sincerely considerate of the disadvantaged. He could set almost anyone at his ease, but struck some other gentlemen, such as Acheson, and some people of other backgrounds, like Ernest Hemingway, as presumptuous and condescending by his familiarity, which, because of his office, could not be contradicted or reciprocated.

But to the overwhelming majority of people of every description, his personality, on encountering it, was, as Churchill said, "like opening your first bottle of champagne." Since he was not altogether close to anyone, but generally well disposed to most people, he was completely independent of individual relationships but had a clear idea of how to appeal to masses of people. Thomas Mann, the German novelist, was captivated by him—his combination of power, sensitivity, and physical vulnerability, his liberality in an age of dictators, and the immense popularity he had earned in his own country. Mann wrote: "When I left the White House after my first visit (June 30, 1935), I knew Hitler was lost. . . . I shall be eternally grateful to Roosevelt, the

born and conscious enemy of the Infamous One, for having maneuvered his all-important country into the war with consummate skill."
This general view was shared by people all over the world who saw
him as the shining hope for liberation, peace, and justice. They were
not wrong, and despite some disappointments, he did not fail them.

He also had great style. His powerful, handsome, animated appearance, cigarette holder at a rakish upward angle, flamboyant gestures, hearty and contagious laugh, skill at repartee, and evident love
of his work and his job, made him an irresistible personality. Even
some of his sartorial flourishes, the fold in his hat, his naval cape, a
walking stick, were widely emulated. His idea of how to be president
was to be himself. He loved virtually every aspect of the job, and felt
he held it by a unique combination of personal determination, popular adherence, and natural right, even predestination. He could not
conceive that everyone would not like to be president.

He became and long remained the most publicized and visible person in the world, though rivalled in this at times by Hitler and
Churchill. His confidence, flair, and sure judgment of occasion
caused him never in over twelve years to embarrass himself publicly.
His physical presence, eloquence, and command of his position and
tasks were all, and at all times, impressive. This conferred upon him a
unique status as a public personality.

He was always confident but never vain or apparently domineering, and rarely ill-tempered. His position and the stylish, supremely
confident way he filled it made FDR an unrivalled personality in the
United States throughout his presidential years.

He was a natural leader. As Isaiah Berlin wrote, all through the
terrible years of his presidency, he never once appeared to experience
a moment of fear. This impression is not contradicted in his corre-
spondence or the memoirs and recollections of his closest collabora-
tors and family. He is alleged to have said: "If you have spent six
months on your back trying to move one toe, nothing seems difficult."

He was a phenomenon, and as in other fields, it was difficult to
know when his unfailing intuition left off and cunning analysis began. He was a brilliant phrasemaker and epigrammatist, often find-

ing the expression that would electrify the country: "a New Deal for the American people. . . . Nothing to fear but fear itself. . . . The good neighbor . . . rendezvous with destiny . . . one third of a nation . . . the dagger struck into the back of its neighbor . . . the great arsenal of democracy . . . the day of infamy." When pressed, as on D-Day, he could rise to heights of Lincolnian eloquence.

He kept his own counsel politically after the death of his chief advisor, Louis Howe, and was in little need of anyone else's, as he demonstrated when he dispensed with Jim Farley and then Ed Flynn as party chairman. In this field, as he outwitted first the conservatives and then the isolationists, he didn't need advisors, only executants.

He led a steady progression from the depths of the Depression to postwar optimism and prosperity, each step accomplished with an almost imperceptible shuffling of the domestic political deck. Like that of a great acrobat, Roosevelt's virtuosity and ultimate success became obvious only when his performance was over and he had left the stage. The change in America and the world from when he entered office to when he departed it, largely traceable to his conduct of the U.S. presidency, was from night to day.

It would be astonishing, given his Protean attainments, if Franklin Roosevelt were not the repository of remarkable human qualities. His achievement in triumphing over polio while disguising its effects has been amply recounted. That he could not stand for more than about forty-five minutes at a time after 1921 and "walked" with extreme awkwardness, as if on stilts, yet managed to project the impression of great strength and vigor, is astonishing, even allowing for the cooperativeness of the press. This was an era when a physical handicap was perceived as an electoral liability. No one can know to what solitudes, renunciations, and inhibitions he was subjected, and what feats of will and courage were necessary to surmount them.

Winston Churchill, in his eulogy, said that not one man in a generation in Roosevelt's physical condition could have made himself "indisputable master of the scene." He could have added that in all history no one else, building upon the power of the country he resurrected, and which quadrennially renewed its support of him, so transcended his illness and projected his personality and ideals that they positively touched the life of virtually every person in the world.

This is submitted as Franklin D. Roosevelt's seventh great achievement—not only the courage and determination to prevail over his disability while disguising its extent, but the implications of his triumph for all who strive against heavy odds, whether medically afflicted or not. The importance of his example is immeasurable and almost inexpressible, but it is real to anyone who considers it, even so inhumane a person as Stalin.

Roosevelt would have been particularly gratified when, on the tenth anniversary of his death, his old law partner Basil O'Connor announced at Warm Springs the development of the Salk vaccine, which prevented polio and won the Nobel Prize for its discoverer. This was Roosevelt's ultimate victory over his illness and would not have occurred, at least until decades later, without him, so successful were his fundraising efforts. For years after his death the Warm Springs Foundation met with Roosevelt's chair unoccupied, in silent memory of the founder.

When Roosevelt assumed the presidency, as Eleanor Roosevelt remarked, the United States was in the depths of economic and psychological depression, but he was vital and irrepressible. Gradually, Roosevelt suffused the government and the country with his determination and optimism. And when, in his fourth term, he had transferred all his strength to the nation he served, and was worn down, and he died, the United States had a high and fixed purpose in the world, and enjoyed unexampled prosperity—more than twice as great as when he entered office and more generously distributed. It exercised a military, economic, popular cultural, and moral influence in the world unprecedented in the history of the nation-state, and had triumphed over every foreign and domestic enemy.

American capitalism was no longer a self-destructive force, and the foundations were laid for the final emancipation of the African-Americans. Apart from his indulgence of high taxes to deal with the economic and war emergencies, Roosevelt's successors have retained virtually all his reforms, no matter how strenuously some resisted them when they were introduced.

Franklin Roosevelt's place in American history is with George Washington and Abraham Lincoln. Few now dispute that in saving American democracy and capitalism from the Great Depression, and bringing America to the rescue and then the durable protection of the civilized world, Franklin Delano Roosevelt belongs in the same pantheon as the father of the country and the savior of the Union and emancipator of the slaves.

A. J. P. Taylor was right to credit Roosevelt with strategic genius but exaggerated when he wrote that "of the great men at the top, Roosevelt was the only one who knew what he was doing; he made the United States the greatest power in the world at virtually no cost." All the principal leaders had clear objectives, and nearly three hundred thousand American war dead and three hundred billion dollars were a heavy cost, if modest compared with what had afflicted some other countries, and to what the cost of defeat would have been.

Because Franklin D. Roosevelt rescued America from the Depression, it could then lead the democracies to victory in war. Roosevelt created the circumstances in which America and the other democracies could win the peace and lead the world to a happier time than it had ever known before. America and its allies would promote human rights and the economics of generally distributed wealth everywhere in the world. To remake the world was a vast ambition that is still unfolding. Winston Churchill was prophetic when he said in his eulogy that the consequences of Franklin Roosevelt's astonishing career "will long be discernible among men."

Excerpted from Conrad Black, *Franklin Delano Roosevelt: Champion of Freedom* (New York: PublicAffairs, 2003), pgs. 1122–1131 and 1133–1134.

Eleanor Roosevelt

REFORMER

Jack Paar's obituaries reminded us that Eleanor Roosevelt was once a guest on the *Tonight* show. It was during the 1960 presidential campaign, and Mrs. Roosevelt sat in the same chair lately filled by Buddy Hackett, Cliff Arquette, and the author of *Never Trust a Naked Bus Driver.* Jack was awestruck. MRS. ROOSEVELT! At one point he asked if she'd mind if he broke for a commercial. She put him at his ease, saying she understood these things were done. She was there to talk up John F. Kennedy's candidacy, and if Jack had known of a telegram she had sent Kennedy earlier in the year he might have made something of it. She was cool to the author of *Profiles in Courage* for lacking the courage to stand up to Joe McCarthy, and in her syndicated column had asserted that his father was buying the nomination for him. Kennedy had written her to complain. He received this telegram back: "MY DEAR BOY I ONLY SAY THESE THINGS FOR YOUR OWN GOOD. I HAVE FOUND IN LIFE- TIME OF ADVERSITY THAT WHEN BLOWS ARE RAINED ON ONE, IT IS ADVISABLE TO TURN THE OTHER PROFILE."

As an historic figure Eleanor Roosevelt emerged in the early 1920s, after her husband contracted polio. As FDR withdrew from politics, ER entered it. She did not run for office. She lent her name, energy, organizational skill, and, overcoming her trembling hands and nervous giggle, oratory to feminist causes and Democratic party politics—and she succeeded. Eleanor was already an accomplished political wife: her husband had served eight years in the administration of Woodrow Wilson and he had been Ohio Governor James M. Cox's running mate in the 1920 presidential election. But, Blanche Wiesen Cook writes, now she was about to "become famous not as FDR's wife, but as a major political force to be reckoned with."

ER, POLITICAL BOSS
Blanche Wiesen Cook

> *"Women must get into the political game and stay in it."*
> — ELEANOR ROOSEVELT

Eleanor Roosevelt began her career as the foremost political woman of the twentieth century convinced that women and men enter politics for different reasons: men to pursue their own careers; women to change society, to improve the daily conditions of life. Impressed by the women she worked with, she came to believe that women's public activities would determine America's future. Not a prewar suffragist herself, she fully appreciated the suffragists' century of struggle, and the grass-roots strategy that ultimately triumphed.

During the 1920s, there were four centers of political power for women in New York State: the League of Women Voters; the Women's Trade Union League (WTUL); the Women's Division of the New York State Democratic Committee, which was dominated throughout the 1920s by five intimate friends, Nancy Cook, Marion Dickerman, Caroline O'Day, Elinor Morgenthau, and Eleanor Roosevelt; and the Women's City Club, an umbrella organization dedicated to social reform and municipal affairs.

A small number of women pulled this network together. They served on the governing councils of each organization and decided on policy and strategy. ER rapidly became a leader of this group, which was made up largely of her own circle of Democratic women. She helped to raise funds, edited newsletters, moderated panels, participated in debates, presented information, toured the state on behalf of candidates and causes, and represented New York at national conventions of political women. To pursue the women's agenda, for six years ER, Nancy Cook, Marion Dickerman, Elinor Morgenthau, and

Caroline O'Day, of the N.Y. State Democratic Committee, went "Trooping for Democracy." In every weather and in every season, they toured New York State in their Democratic blue roadster, which they had bought together, or in O'Day's chauffeured Packard. They toured every county to demand an expanded public-housing program, improved sanitation and sewerage control, frequent and comfortable public transit, new parks and public playgrounds, school lunches and nursing facilities, unemployment insurance, workers' compensation, occupational-safety-and-health legislation, the eight-hour day, protective laws for women workers, mandatory-education laws, child-labor legislation, pure-food-and-milk legislation, the right of women to serve on juries, and equal representation of women on all committees of the Democratic Party.

At first, public speaking was an ordeal for ER. But once she became comfortable at the podium, she was grateful for each opportunity to convey the messages she considered so urgent. Louis Howe, FDR's closest advisor, was her tutor. Initially, he accompanied her when she spoke. He sat in the back of the room and monitored her every move. When her hands shook, he told her to hold the podium, not the paper. When she felt nervous, he recommended that she smile and breathe deeply. She laughed and even giggled inappropriately—at the wrong time, with the wrong sound. That was, he assured her, the worst thing she could do: It sent the wrong message. Howe's advice was specific: Be prepared. Know what you want to say. Say it. And sit down. Never appear nervous.

ER's gifts as a speaker were ultimately the result of her love for people. Because she cared about her audience, she knew that it mattered to make eye contact and to connect directly with everybody in the room. Subsequently she hired voice trainers in an effort to control her pitch and her register. She was soon in demand as a speaker.

Throughout the 1920s, articles about ER and her political work appeared almost weekly in the *New York Times*. She was the subject of news accounts, columns, editorials, profiles in the Sunday *Magazine* section, and letters to the editor. Her public appearances were national news. Because she spoke candidly, her major statements were frequently quoted in full.

Ironically, in her memoirs ER called the chapter devoted to the

1920s, the decade of the most robust political activity she undertook on her own, "Private Interlude." Since she could hardly have meant by that an absorption in private or domestic affairs, this period in her life apparently seemed in retrospect private in the sense that it was hers to do with as she pleased. She neither campaigned for FDR nor served as his surrogate. He was preoccupied with recovery from polio, she was preoccupied with politics. She became famous not as FDR's wife, but as a major political force to be reckoned with.

Yet, the more she achieved, the more she was acclaimed and celebrated in her own right, the more she sought to reassure FDR that she was doing it all for him. On 6 February 1924, for example, ER wrote him a long, rambling letter full of detail about her activities. But she concluded by reminding her husband that she was merely his temporary stand-in. She had been asked to sponsor or attend several memorial services for President Wilson, who died on 3 February. She agreed, though she understood they only wanted FDR's name. She aimed neither to compete with her husband nor to upstage him. Only slowly and reluctantly did ER admit being pleased by her public activities. Much more often she professed a selfless lack of interest in her own work, and her own career, and thereby contributed to our distorted image of her public self. While she was First Lady, she wrote that she was pushed into politics reluctantly—and solely in support of her husband. She never acknowledged her own joy in the game, or her own skills at manipulating the cards.

· · ·

ER spent some part of every day planning strategy for the New York State Democratic Party. In her 6 February 1924 letter to FDR where she minimized her activities, she reported that she, Caroline O'Day, and Nancy Cook had been to a "remarkable dinner" of "600 women from Albany and nearby and all workers!" They saw Governor Al Smith, who asked them to lobby for his new reform program, and ER spent several days in Albany, working out the details. But there was still one piece of additional news, she noted almost as an afterthought: Cordell Hull, the Democratic Party's National Committee chairman in 1924, had invited ER—currently finance chair of the Women's Division—to head a platform committee for women to present their demands at the national convention in June, in New York. She was delighted, though she gave no hint of that to FDR: "I'm up to my eyes in work for the convention preparations and trying to raise our budget which is going to be an endless job."

. . .

In March 1924, the Democratic National Committee proudly announced that it was "the first political group to seek women's views on important questions of peculiar interest to them so that these social legislation planks as incorporated in the national Democratic platform may represent their ideas." And, with considerable public relations fanfare, the leadership announced it had asked Eleanor Roosevelt to chair the women's platform committee.

ER agreed, and determined to base the recommendations for needed social-welfare legislation on the "requests of all women's organizations in the country." She appointed a panel of activist experts. The committee endorsed the League of Nations, and called for the creation of a federal department of education, equal pay for women workers, and the ratification of the child-labor amendment. It called for a forty-eight-hour workweek, wages commensurate with the cost of living and health care, the creation of employment bureaus, and the means to ensure "healthy and safe working conditions."

But in June, their three months' effort was rebuffed by the Resolutions Committee at the convention. For hours ER and her coworkers sat outside the locked doors of the all-male Resolutions Committee and waited to be heard. At dawn the men voted twenty-two to eighteen, for the third and last time, to reaffirm their refusal even to hear the women's proposals. ER wrote that at the convention of 1924 she saw "for the first time where the women stood when it came to a national convention. I shortly discovered that they were of very little importance. They stood outside the door of all important meetings and waited." She spent most of her time during the deadlocked, heat-filled convention—every day the temperature topped one hundred degrees Fahrenheit—trying to seem calm. "I sat and knitted, suffered with the heat and wished it would end." One day, Will Rogers noticed ER and asked: "Knitting in the names of the future victims of the guillotine?" ER was tempted to respond that she was "ready to call any punishment down on the heads of those who could not bring the convention to a close."

★   ★   ★

However much ER's political vigor, new friends, and public prominence might disturb the older members of her family, she herself greeted every new controversy with verve. Eleanor Roosevelt had become a feminist. She fought for women's rights steadfastly and with determination; she championed equality in public and private matters; and she herself used the word "feminist." But during the 1920s, the bitterly divisive Equal Rights Amendment ripped the women's movement apart, obscuring for decades the full dimensions of historical feminism—and ER's leadership role within it.

The vision that inspired the ERA was neither new nor frivolous. On 31 March 1777, Abigail Adams wrote to her husband, John Adams: "I desire you would remember the ladies and be more generous and favorable to them than your ancestors. . . . If particular care and attention is not paid to the ladies, we are determined to foment a rebellion, and will not hold ourselves bound by any laws in which we have no voice or representation." Still, Adams and his friends ignored the ladies. Thomas Jefferson opined: "Were our state a pure democracy there would still be excluded from our deliberations women, who, to prevent deprivation of morals and ambiguity of issues, should not mix promiscuously in gatherings of men."

After the Civil War women were specifically excluded from the benefits of the Fourteenth and Fifteenth Amendments. The Fourteenth Amendment inserted the word "male" for the first time into the Constitution, making it clear that the benefits of "due process" and "equal protection" excluded women. Consistently the courts endorsed this situation. In 1873, the Supreme Court upheld an Illinois statute that prohibited women from practicing law. In *Bradwell* v. *Illinois,* the Court decided:

The harmony, not to say identity, of interests and views which belong, or should belong, to the family institution is repugnant to the idea of a woman adopting a distinct and independent career from that of her husband. . . .

The paramount destiny and mission of women are to fulfill the noble and benign offices of wife and mother. This is the law of the Creator.

The Equal Rights Amendment was introduced in 1923 by the organized militants of the National Woman's Party, led by Alice Paul and over a hundred other women who used civil-disobedience methods to campaign throughout the war years "for suffrage—first." From 1917 until the suffrage amendment was passed in Congress and finally ratified by the states in August 1920, they were the women who kept the suffrage-amendment issue in the headlines. They had picketed the White House, and demonstrated against Wilson everywhere he spoke with banners criticizing him and cauldrons in which to burn the hypocritical words he had used to celebrate democracy while they were being arrested, jailed, brutalized, and force-fed. Largely isolated during the war, assailed as "madwomen," "petticoat Bolsheviks," and traitors, they remained undaunted.

Immediately after suffrage was won, Alice Paul and the militant warriors of the National Woman's Party sought a new amendment, which they believed would erase all the laws that discriminated against women. Paul's original Equal Rights Amendment, as introduced in Congress in December 1923, was as simply worded as its successor during the 1970s: "Men and women shall have Equal Rights throughout the United States and every place subject to its jurisdiction."

One of Paul's most vigorous supporters, Crystal Eastman, believed that "this was a fight worth fighting even if it took ten years," and recognized that its importance could be measured by the intensity of all the opposition to it. And the opposition was immediate: Within twenty-four hours after it was introduced, every member of Congress received a passionate protest against it—signed by the leaders of the seven other major women's-rights and suffrage groups, most notably the social feminists, identified with the League of Women Voters;

and settlement-house reformers, associated with Florence Kelley, Dr. Alice Hamilton, and Jane Addams, who supported protective legislation for women and children. Their goal was to isolate Paul and her movement; Paul's goal was to dismiss them as antifeminists: humanitarians solely concerned with "family welfare."

Entirely allied with the social feminists of the League of Women Voters, and with the effort to achieve protective legislation for women workers, ER and many of the most radical suffragists, women who had devoted their lives to fighting social evils, poverty, racism, cruelty of every kind, now opposed the ERA. They feared it was politically premature and would serve only to destroy the few laws that served to protect women and children in the industrial workplace that they had been able to achieve.

Initially, the political and geographic range on both sides of the battle included Republicans, Democrats, and socialists; southern and northern sensibilities. The equal-rights feminists, led by Alice Paul, southern and conservative by any standard, were joined by Crystal Eastman, Doris Stevens, and Lavinia Dock, radical and socialist by any standard. On the protectionist side, Jane Addams was a liberal social reformer, Florence Kelley was a radical socialist who called herself a Marxist, Narcissa Vanderlip was a rather conventional Republican, and Eleanor Roosevelt represented the progressive wing of the Democratic Party.

The tragedy of the split was that it represented a genuine and irreconcilable difference in strategy in behalf of a shared goal: the improved economic and political condition of women, the achievement of power by women. Feminist activists dominated the battle on both sides.

The ERA-protectionist division resulted from a conflicting understanding of what was possible in an unrestrained capitalist economy. In 1923, despite years of progressive action, there was still no limitation on the number of hours or the conditions of work for women *or* men; and ER and the protectionist feminists—all of whom wanted protective legislation for all—sincerely believed that it was possible to achieve a fair and just administration of a forty-eight-hour workweek by demanding it for women *first*. Equal-rights feminists sincerely believed that shorter hours for women first would result in the loss of jobs for women, who were not as valued as men workers and were not paid on a par with them, and who were therefore required by economic need to work longer hours merely to survive. Although the two sides agreed that women worked in a brutal economy that achieved profits by demanding the longest possible hours for the least possible pay, the battle between them raged in bitter tones of acrimony. The protectionists believed the ERA women were elitists and careerists who cared only for privileged and professional women and were ignorant of and unconcerned about the poor. The ERA activists believed the protectionists were old-fashioned reformers who refused to see that until women were acknowledged equal in law, all reforms to protect women were frauds that could only work against them.

On 16 January 1922, Dr. Alice Hamilton, the United States' leading authority on industrial medicine, wrote a letter to explain her position to the editor of the National Woman's Party journal, *Equal Rights,* Edith Houghton Hooker:

> I could not help comparing you as you sat there [over a "friendly cup of tea"], sheltered, safe, beautifully guarded against even the uglinesses of life, with the women for whom you demand "freedom of contract." The Lithuanian women in the laundries whom the Illinois law . . . permits to work seventy hours a week on the night shift; the Portuguese women in the Rhode Island textile mills, on long night shifts . . . the great army of waitresses and hotel chambermaids, unorganized, utterly ignorant of ways of making their grievances known, working long hours and living wretchedly. To tell them to get what they should have by using their right of contract is to go back to the days of the Manchester School in England, when men maintained that there must be no interference with the right of women and children to make their own bargains with their employers in the cotton mills or at the pitheads. It is only a great ignorance of the poor as they actually are, only a great ignorance as to what is possible and what is impossible under our supposed democracy and actual plutocracy, that could make you argue as you do. . . . [If] you succeed in rescinding all the laws in the country discriminating against women and do it at the ex-

pense of present and future protective laws you will have harmed a far
larger number of women than you will have benefited and the harm
done to them will be more disastrous. . . .

For the next twenty years, Eleanor Roosevelt shared Alice Hamilton's analysis. She too tended to consider the ERA proponents self-
serving aristocrats who cared little and understood less about the
needs of the poor. She was drawn toward the vision of reform created
by that earlier generation of community activists, unionists, and radicals led by Florence Kelley, Jane Addams, Lillian Wald, Rose Schneiderman, and Dr. Alice Hamilton. Although she was the same age as
many of the ERA activists, and was indeed two years younger than
Crystal Eastman, ER understood society the way her earlier mentors
in the settlement-house movement did. Above all, ER believed that
one utopian constitutional amendment, however virtuous, was virtually meaningless in the real political world, and she opposed the idea
of a separate woman's party. Even after 1937, when unionism and collective bargaining caused her to doubt the need for continued opposition to the ERA, she continued to take direction from the Women's
Trade Union League.

ER's position began to change after the passage of the 1938 Fair Labor Standards Act, which provided protective laws that covered
women and men alike. Although she was ready to endorse the ERA
in 1941, she still hesitated because of WTUL leader Rose Schneiderman's continued opposition. But she became impatient with the fight.
In 1944, she consented to the Democratic Party's endorsement of the
ERA, and finally, in 1946, at the United Nations, she publicly withdrew her opposition.

ER's allies were the social activists who long before suffrage had
created such abiding institutions of successful reform as the settlement houses, the National Consumers' League, and the Women's
Trade Union League. They had pioneered such improvements as
public playgrounds, school lunches, medical care in public schools,
the visiting-home-nurse service, sanitation removal, and minimum-
wage and maximum-hour laws for women. They regarded the ERA
as a fantasy that endangered their life's work.

They were practical women who worked vigorously on the margin of politics, where they were allowed to perform. They did domestic housekeeping for the neighborhood, the community, the city, state, and nation. It was that arena to which they were restricted. The health of women and children, the health of the state was considered women's work. And they accepted it. They had not waited for the vote. They did not wait for the ERA. They did what they could to counter the ills of a wretched, mean-spirited society where children were allowed to starve to death; where mothers and infants routinely died unnecessarily; and where acres and acres of tenements, unfit for dwelling, stunted growth and happiness. To do other than what they did every day would have been to accept powerlessness. They had none of the power and prestige of men, but they were not powerless. They were earnest and bold and committed to fundamental change.

★   ★   ★

In 1925, ER's energies were focused on the forty-eight-hour work-week for women: "Aside from all the so-called sob stuff which we have heard here this afternoon," she said at a legislative meeting, "I am convinced that a great majority of the workingwomen of this State are really in favor of this bill. . . . I can't understand how any woman would want to work fifty-four hours a week if she only had to work forty-eight and could receive the same rate of wages."

At the same hearing, the equal-rights feminists Doris Stevens and Rheta Child Dorr opposed ER's interpretation, and argued that the male-dominated labor unions supported the bill so that women would not be able to compete with men. They urged instead that the forty-eight-hour law cover both women and men, so that women would not be unfairly hobbled. In every competitive job, where women had worked with equality during the war years, women were now fired—like, for example, the women workers of the Brooklyn and Manhattan Transit Company, who testified that all laws intended to put women on "easy street" merely put them resoundingly on the street.

The fight in the New York State legislature for the forty-eight-hour bill for women workers became bipartisan when, in 1926, the bill was denied even the courtesy of a vote and Republican Club women protested. ER considered "the courage and independence" the Republican women demonstrated by "refusing to abide by the mandates of their legislative leaders . . . a vindication of the value of women in politics." She also congratulated the Republican women on the "fairness and scientific accuracy" of their six-month-long investigation of labor conditions, which revealed that 95 percent of all women workers favored the forty-eight-hour legislation.

ER believed that a great political bonus resulted from bipartisan unity on the forty-eight-hour bill: It revealed the power of voting women to remind men that they would no longer be allowed to sidestep promises made simply to catch votes, or to "neglect party platforms" so solemnly crafted. ER deplored this "final act of the farce-drama" male politicians "have conducted . . . for many years. I know of no more open, cynical and reckless defiance of definite platform and campaign promise than the refusal even to allow a vote on the 48-hour legislation."

The forty-eight-hour week, and subsequently the battle for a five-day week, seem ordinary and tame demands today. But until the end of the 1930s and the general acceptance of unionism, U.S. workers, women and men, were without real protection of any kind, and routinely worked twelve to fourteen hours a day, six—frequently six and a half—days a week. According to the WTUL's Rose Schneiderman, employers believed that endless toil kept women "out of mischief and that shorter hours would endanger their morals." They believed also "that if working people had rooms with baths they would use the bathtubs in which to keep the coal. . . ." Workers were not supposed to have "leisure" time, and reformers who insisted on maximum-hour and minimum-wage laws were regarded as radical or "parlor pink" if not clearly "Bolshevik."

★   ★   ★

As Eleanor Roosevelt's influence grew, and as her confidence increased, she threw herself into a range of social initiatives aimed at strengthening government protection for women and children. She fought for the Child Labor Amendment, increased support for the

Children's Bureau and the Women's Bureau, and worked to raise state matching funds for the $1.25-million Sheppard-Towner Act to establish maternity and pediatric clinics, and a health-care program for mothers and infants. A great victory for social feminists, who had campaigned for years to decrease the grim rate of infant mortality in the United States, the Sheppard-Towner Act was attacked as "Sovietism," and a dangerous precedent leading to birth control and governmental programs of "social hygiene."

. . .

Every issue involving women was of concern to ER. In April 1925, she went on the radio to describe the significance of the Women's City Club, which she termed a "clearing house for civic ideals." The club conducted its own research on all issues, and held debates and informative lectures. To investigate the issue of outlawing dance halls, for example, the club's members went to numerous dance halls, not as "investigators, but as participants." They discovered, ER noted, "the fascination, the dangers and the surprisingly low percentage of disaster to the girls" despite the "unwholesome surroundings." ER never supported the effort to outlaw dance halls.

She called for equal political education for girls and boys, and noted with pride that "Girls nowadays may be rivals of their brothers in school, sports, and business." But ER lamented they "lag behind in a knowledge and interest in government." She gave as examples her own daughter, Anna, and Governor Smith's daughter Emily, whom she had overheard complaining that politics dominated their fathers' conversations. ER contrasted this attitude with the one that prevailed among "flappers of politically prominent families in England. British daughters not only take a keen interest in their fathers' careers but go out to help in the political battle." She cited the good works of Ishbel MacDonald and Megan Lloyd George in particular, and concluded that if "our American girls are not to be left behind, something must be done to stimulate their interest in civic responsibilities." She thought that daughters of politicians should at least want to be able "to outtalk their fathers."

Eleanor Roosevelt's own sense of responsibility took her beyond strong words to vigorous deeds. In 1926, she made headline news when she participated in a mass picket demonstration of three hundred women in support of striking paper-box makers. Eight notable women "of prominence" were arrested for ignoring a police order "to move on," and charged with "disorderly conduct," including ER, Margaret Norrie, Mrs. Samuel Bens, Marion Dickerman, Evelyn Preston, and Dorothy Kenyon.

ER was proud of the achievements of women. She honored their daring, and their vision. She considered women flyers marvelously courageous, and she promoted women in flight. She herself wanted to fly, and she did. ER was one of the first women to fly at night, and she logged more hours in the air during the 1920s and 1930s than any other woman passenger. But she remained a passenger, much to her regret. FDR's only known vigorous opposition to any of ER's efforts was when she decided to become a pilot. Her friend Amelia Earhart gave her preliminary lessons, and ER actually took and passed the physical examination. But FDR persuaded her that he had sufficient worries without her flying above the clouds at top speed. FDR's opposition to flying was genuine. In 1920, he was horrified when his mother flew from London to Paris, and asked her never to go aloft again. Evidently both women acquiesced to his fear; but ER always regretted not becoming a pilot, because, she said, she liked to be in control of her own mobility.

Increasingly, ER's interests became international. In October 1927, she hosted a meeting of four hundred women at Hyde Park to launch a women's peace movement and support the Kellogg-Briand Treaty to outlaw war. Carrie Chapman Catt was the keynote speaker, and she stirred ER with her call for a crusade against war as mighty as the antislave crusade, as mighty as the suffrage crusade: We must find a way to "end this awful menace to civilization, the disgrace to this century, called war."

For the next ten years, ER was to be one of the most prominent antiwar women in the United States, associated with both Jane Addams's Women's International League for Peace and Freedom, and Carrie Chapman Catt's National Conference on the Cause and Cure of War.

Wherever she went, or whatever her announced topic, whenever ER spoke as the decade of the 1920s drew to a close, she spoke at least in part about world peace. Long before the war clouds gathered, her message was urgent: "The time to prepare for world peace is during the time of peace and not during the time of war."

★   ★   ★

By 1928, the year FDR ran for governor of New York, Eleanor Roosevelt had become a major political force. For six years, she had served as finance chair of women's activities of the New York Democratic State Committee. She was vice-chair of the Woman's City Club of New York, chair of the Non-Partisan Legislative Committee, editor and treasurer of the *Women's Democratic News,* a member of the board of directors of the Foreign Policy Association and the City Housing Corporation.

In fact, in 1928, ER was one of the best-known and highest-ranking Democrats in the United States. She was named director of the Bureau of Women's Activities of the Democratic National Committee, and in July asked to head a Woman's Advisory Committee, to develop Al Smith's presidential campaign organization.

In 1928, ER held, therefore, the most powerful positions ever held by a woman in party politics. In matters of "turfing," which we now recognize as more than symbolic, she demanded and received equality for the women political organizers: Their offices had the same floor space as their male counterparts, and equal comfort. There were windows, carpets, plants; the accommodations were light and airy. The *New York Times* reported that the space allotted to women in the national headquarters of the Democratic party was "said to be the largest headquarters ever occupied by a women's political organization." ER's rooms and those of John J. Raskob, then Democratic national chairman, were "identical in size and location."

Throughout the 1920s ER worked to insure that this equality involve more than floor space. In September 1926, after a bitter struggle for equal representation for women within the New York State Democratic Party, the party convention elected Caroline O'Day vice-chair of the State Committee, and women were voted equal representation with men in 135 of 150 Assembly districts. On a "day of triumph and celebration," ER delivered the convention's banquet speech and hailed the victory as "the breaking down of the last barrier" to equality within the Democratic Party.

But she quickly realized that equal representation had as yet very little to do with equal power. Increasingly distressed by the manipulations of her male colleagues, ER argued that women needed to take tougher, more direct measures.

In April 1928, she published a boldly feminist article in *Redbook*. "Women Must Learn to Play the Game as Men Do" was a battle cry that urged women to create their own "women bosses" in order to achieve real power.

. . .

ER's tone was outraged and unrelenting: Women went into politics with high hopes and specific intentions. They were courted and wooed. But when they demanded and expected real power, they were rebuffed. ER noted: "Their requests are seldom refused outright, but they are put off with a technique that is an art in itself. The fact is that generally women are not taken seriously. With certain exceptions, men still as a class dismiss their consequence and value in politics, cherishing the old-fashioned concept that their place is in the home."

. . .

As for political office, party leaders "will ask women to run for office now and then, sometimes because they think it politic and wise to show women how generous they are, but more often because they realize in advance their ticket cannot win in the district selected. Therefore they will put up a woman, knowing it will injure the party less to have a woman defeated, and then they can always say it was her sex that defeated her. Where victory is certain, very rarely can you get a woman nominated. . . ."

She urged women to "elect, accept and back" women bosses on

every level of party management, in "districts, counties and states. Women must organize just as men organize." ER was aware that the word "boss" might "shock sensitive ears." She did not mean by "boss" some sleazy and easy-to-buy politician, but, rather, a "high-minded leader." And she chose the word deliberately, "as it is the word men understand." She explained in detail her conviction that "if women believe they have a right and duty in political life today, they must learn to talk the language of men. They must not only master the phraseology, but also understand the machinery which men have built up through years of practical experience. Against the men bosses there must be women bosses who can talk as equals, with the backing of a coherent organization of women voters behind them."

. . .

ER argued that women could achieve real power only by organization and endless work. Male hostility to women was only partly responsible for women's failure to achieve power. Women seemed to ER reluctant to claim power. She dismissed the attitude of those women who professed "to be horrified at the thought of women bosses bartering and dickering in the hard game of politics with the men." She was cheered by the fact that "many more women realize that we are living in a material world, and that politics cannot be played from the clouds." She understood that the task was hard and that the role of women in public life was difficult. Women's lives, to begin with, ER noted, were always "full of interruptions." Home, children, meals to prepare, dinner parties to arrange. She was aware of the double standards, and the double-job burdens. And so, she argued, women have to be more organized, more methodical, and, yes, more hardworking than men. She was adamant: "Women must learn to play the game as men do."

. . .

But publicly ER understood and always worked within the limitations of her time, and her marriage. Publicly she denied to the end of her life that she ever had, or ever wanted, real political power. She acknowledged that she worked for those issues that she believed in, but not once did she profess to enjoy the game. She never acknowledged that it satisfied her own interests, served her own needs, or that she delighted even in the rough-and-tumble of the deals and battles. Nevertheless, she expressed dismay whenever she or other women were bypassed or ignored and men took credit for their efforts and ideas.

★   ★   ★

If ER's controversies affected her husband's own campaign for New York's governorship against Albert Ottinger, the popular Republican state attorney general, neither referred to them. Although ER distanced herself from FDR's race and campaigned exclusively for Smith, she had played a critical part in FDR's nomination. If ER had not encouraged him to run, he would not have done it. FDR had refused all entreaties for months, believing that he needed two more years of serious exercise to walk again. (Also, he had invested over $200,000 of his capital in the polio-treatment center he had established in Warm Springs, Georgia, and wanted to make it work.) He resisted even after the Democratic national chair, John J. Raskob, offered to pay all his debts and contribute significantly to the center at Warm Springs; and he resisted after Herbert Lehman offered to run as lieutenant governor and promised to take over whenever FDR wanted to return to Warm Springs. His family and advisers opposed his candidacy. Only FDR's daughter, Anna, was positive: "Go ahead and take it," she wired. FDR wired back: "You ought to be spanked."

ER was never certain what FDR's return to public office would mean to her own life, but when she appeared for the opening ceremonies of the New York state convention in Rochester on 1 October, Smith and Raskob "begged" her to call her husband. He had avoided them all day, refused all their calls. They were told he was out, and he never returned their messages. There was no doubt what her call would mean. She did not hesitate.

That evening, ER was put through to her husband within minutes. FDR told her, "with evident glee," that he had kept "out of reach all day and would not have answered the telephone if I had not been calling." She replied that she was with Smith and Raskob, and without apology handed the phone to Smith and fled to catch her train for New York City. In 1949, ER wrote, "I can still hear Governor Smith's voice saying: 'Hello Frank,' as I hurried from the room. . . . I did not know until the following morning when I bought a newspaper that my husband had been persuaded finally to accept the nomination."

. . .

ER's loyalty to FDR, and to what she truly believed was best for him, involved her perception of his physical progress, which had reached its limit, and her conviction that his return to political life would enhance his health and well-being. After seven years of struggle, he could walk short distances supported by canes and braces, and the strong arms of his sons and associates. But his legs had no real mobility, no actual strength. Moreover, she believed that one must do "what comes to hand," which did not reflect a careless regard for fate but, rather, her sense of obligation and responsibility to the mysteries and vagaries of opportunity. It would be wrong, ER believed, to disregard destiny, when it so specifically called.

At Warm Springs on 2 October, when FDR was nominated by acclamation and decided not to decline, nobody was pleased. Missy Le-Hand, FDR's secretary, wanted FDR free to concentrate on his health; Louis Howe believed the Republicans would win and wanted to avoid another personal defeat for the man he wished to help make president. Howe wired: "BY WAY OF CONGRATULATIONS DIG UP TELEGRAM I SENT YOU WHEN YOU RAN IN SENATORIAL PRIMARIES"—a reference to FDR's failed race in the 1914 Democratic primary for U.S. senator from New York.

According to his mother, Warm Springs went into instant mourning until "Franklin's cheery voice was heard to remark, 'Well, if I've got to run for Governor, there's no use in all of us getting sick about it!'"

Once FDR decided to run, he ran with vigor, and all his allies rallied to support his decision. His mother wrote that, no matter what,

"I do not want you to be defeated!" She assured him that "all will be well whatever happens." And, with a mother's commitment that tells us much about the origins of FDR's unrivaled sense of security, she wrote: "Now what follows is *really private*. In case of your election, I know your salary is smaller than the one you get now. I am prepared to make the difference up to you."

ER publicly distanced herself as far as possible from her husband's decision, and told the press that she was "very happy and very proud, although I did not want him to do it. He felt that he had to. In the end you have to do what your friends want you to. There comes to every man, if he is wanted, the feeling there is almost an obligation to return the confidence shown him. . . ." When asked if it was because of her last-minute phone call that he changed his mind, she denied it all: "I never did a thing to ask him to run. Franklin always makes his own decisions."

ER answered questions about her own role in FDR's campaign: "I have plenty to do with the job I am handling now for the national campaign. . . . I do not think I will change my plans, but I may make a few speeches later for my husband. If I can be of any help I shall be glad to give it."

As ER had anticipated, the excitement of his nonstop campaign energized FDR. He told his mother: "If I could campaign another six months, I believe I could throw away my cane."

But the election of 1928 was such a total disaster for the Democrats on every level that ER and FDR left party headquarters at midnight on election day convinced that he too had been defeated. They had been watching the returns in New York City's great armory with Al Smith, who had lost not only the nation but also New York: Bigotry and Prohibition, no less than the celebrated Republican era of prosperity, had ensured his overwhelming defeat. Herbert Hoover went on to win 444 electoral votes to Smith's eighty-seven, and Florida, North Carolina, Texas, and Virginia voted Republican for the first time in history. "Well," Smith said that evening, "the time hasn't come yet when a man can say his beads in the White House."

Only Franklin's mother refused to believe that her son could lose. She waited through the night for the final upstate returns to come in, even though they represented districts that had been devoted to Ot-tinger. FDR and Edward J. Flynn, the colorful "boss of the Bronx," had telephoned upstate sheriffs threatening to investigate their suspi-ciously tardy returns. But Flynn also left before they came in. Only Sara Delano Roosevelt stayed through the early-morning hours as the votes trickled in. She sat in a darkened corridor, alone with a few party stalwarts and the counting staff, until 4 A.M., and was the only member of the family who heard the tally that announced her son's election. Governor Franklin Delano Roosevelt carried New York State by 25,564 votes, even though Smith lost it by 103,481.

★   ★   ★

ER's initial response to Smith's defeat and FDR's victory was com-plex. For over nine months, she had worked daily and imaginatively for the Smith campaign. ER hated to lose. It was not merely Smith's personal loss, or her own, but the continued defeat on the national level of all the social programs she championed. ER understood that progressive Democrats needed to regroup and reorganize. They would all have to try again in four years, and she urged her co-work-ers to begin immediately.

ER was eager to continue the battle, but in terms of her own work, she considered FDR's victory a mixed blessing. She feared that FDR's election to office meant that she would have to withdraw from public life. To reporters, her remarks were restrained, even ungracious: "If the rest of the ticket didn't get in, what does it matter?" "No, I am not excited about my husband's election. I don't care. What difference can it make to me?" In retrospect, she wondered if she had "really wanted Franklin to run. I imagine I accepted his nomination and later his election as I had accepted most of the things that had happened in life thus far; one did whatever seemed necessary and adjusted one's per-sonal life to the developments in other people's lives."

In 1928 a political wife had no accepted place except in the back-ground. ER had grown accustomed to a different role. She was a pub-lisher, an editor, a columnist; she debated on the radio and before large audiences; her opinions were forthright and specific. She had a following, and people relied on her views and depended on her leadership. Was ER seriously meant to become again the dutiful wife at home with the children, silent by the radio, while her husband and all their friends were engaged in the work she most enjoyed? It was impossible. She could not abide the thought. She resented even contemplating it. And so the Roosevelt partnership departed yet again from tradition. ER never withdrew from the public sphere.

Excerpted from Blanche Wiesen Cook, *Eleanor Roosevelt Volume One: 1884–1933* (New York: Viking Penguin, 1992), pgs. 338–380.

Harry S. Truman

GRIT

In this excerpt from his Pulitzer Prize-winning biography, *Truman,* David McCullough puts us on Harry Truman's train for the whistle-stop campaign of 1948. Franklin Roosevelt's death made Truman president in April 1945; he had not sought the office and in his first two years fumbled badly. "To err is Truman," went the gibe. He tried to talk General Dwight D. Eisenhower into running in his place. McCullough cites a report that he even offered to run as Ike's vice president. But the GOP takeover of Congress in 1947 brought out the fighter in him, and this is what he said on being nominated at the Democrats' convention in Philadelphia: "Senator Barkley and I will win this election and make these Republicans like it." Alben Barkley, the Kentucky senator, was his second choice for vice president. His first, Supreme Court Justice William O. Douglas, turned him down. "Reportedly Douglas had told others he did not want to be number two to a number two man," McCullough writes.

Truman's party split in three in 1948: Truman in the center; Henry Wallace, whom Truman displaced as FDR's vice president in 1944, running as the nominee of the Progressive Party on the left; and South Carolina governor J. Strom Thurmond running as a Dixiecrat on the right. The three candidates would divide the normal Democratic vote, ensuring a Republican landslide. Even members of his own family thought Truman would lose to the Republican nominee, New York governor Thomas E. Dewey, and the pollsters and pundits agreed. "It will be the greatest campaign any President ever made," Truman wrote his sister. "Win, lose, or draw people will know where I stand. . . ."

FIGHTING CHANCE
David McCullough

The *Ferdinand Magellan* was the only private railroad car ever fitted out for the exclusive use of the president of the United States. Eighty-three feet in length and painted the standard dark green of the Pullman Company, it had been built originally in 1928 as one of several luxury cars named for famous explorers—*Marco Polo, David Livingstone, Robert Peary*—then taken over by the government for Franklin Roosevelt's use during wartime, in 1942, when it was completely overhauled to become a rolling fortress.

To Truman, who loved trains and loved seeing the country, it was the perfect way to travel, and one he had enjoyed frequently since becoming president. There had been a memorable night of poker with Churchill on the way to Missouri for the "iron curtain" speech, the long "nonpolitical" swing west in June. More recently, he had made a quick one-day tour of Michigan for a Labor Day speech at Detroit's Cadillac Square, to open his campaign for reelection. Yet for all the miles covered, the days and nights spent on board the *Magellan,* these prior expeditions had been only prologue to the odyssey that began the morning of Friday, September 17, 1948, when the *Magellan,* at the end of a seventeen-car special train, stood waiting on Track 15 beneath the cavernous shed of Washington's Union Station. In June, he had gone 9,000 miles. Now, on what was to become famous as the Whistle-stop Campaign, he would travel all told 21,928 miles, as far nearly as around the world—as far nearly as the voyage of Magellan.

The odds against him looked insurmountable. The handicaps of the Truman campaign, wrote columnist Marquis Childs, one of the writers on board, "loomed large as the Rocky Mountains." Henry Wallace and the Dixiecrats had split the Democratic Party three ways. Conceivably, New York and the South were already lost to Truman. The victory of the Republicans in the elections of 1946 had been resounding, and ever since the Civil War, the party winning the off-year election had always gone on to win the presidency in the next election. At Washington dinner parties, as Truman's wife, Bess, had heard, the talk was of who would be in the Dewey cabinet. Some prominent Democrats in Washington were already offering their homes for sale. Even the president's mother-in-law thought Dewey would win.

In the West, where Truman had made an all-out effort in June, predictions were that at best he might win 19 of the 71 electoral votes at stake. Only Arizona, with 4 votes, looked safe for Truman. And the West was essential.

A Gallup Poll of farm voters gave Dewey 48 percent, Truman 38. And the farm vote, too, was essential.

On September 9, a full week before Truman's train departed Washington, Elmo Roper, a widely respected sampler of public opinion, had announced his organization would discontinue polling since the outcome was already so obvious. "My whole inclination," Roper said, "is to predict the election of Thomas E. Dewey by a heavy margin and devote my time and efforts to other things." The latest Roper Poll showed Dewey leading by an "unbeatable" 44 to 31 percent. More important, said Roper, such elections were decided early.

> Political campaigns are largely ritualistic. . . . All the evidence we have accumulated since 1936 tends to indicate that the man in the lead at the beginning of the campaign is the man who is the winner at the end of it. . . . The winner, it appears, clinches his victory early in the race and before he has uttered a word of campaign oratory.

The idea that the campaign was "largely ritualistic," a formality only, became commonplace. *Life,* in its latest issue, carried a picture of Governor Dewey and his staff under the headline: "Albany Provides Preview of Dewey Administration."

Yet, inexplicably, Truman had drawn tremendous crowds in Michigan on Labor Day. A hundred thousand people had filled Cadillac Square. By train and motorcade he rolled through Grand Rapids, Lansing, Hamtramck, Pontiac, and Flint, where to Truman and his staff the crowds were even more impressive. "Cadillac Square . . . that was *organized*," remembered Matt Connelly. "But we rode from there up to Pontiac . . . [and] from Detroit to Pontiac I'd see people along the highway. This was not organized and there were a lot of them out there!" According to police estimates the turnout at Truman's six stops in Michigan totaled more than half a million people.

Often, in later years, the big Truman crowds would be remembered as a phenomenon of the final weeks of the campaign. But this was a misconception. They were there from the start, in Michigan and in traditionally Republican Iowa—in Davenport, Iowa City, Grinnell, Des Moines—beginning September 18, his first full day heading west.

"Newsmen were nonplused," reported *Time*. "All across Republican Iowa large crowds turned out . . . a good deal of the cheering was enthusiastic."

The main event of the day was the National Plowing Contest at Dexter, forty miles west of Des Moines, where Truman spoke at noon, in blazing sunshine, standing front and center on a high, broad platform, a sea of faces before him, a giant plowing scoreboard behind. The crowd numbered ninety thousand.

The long horizons were rimmed with ripening corn. The atmosphere was of a vast county fair in good times, with throngs of healthy, well-fed, sun-baked, and obviously prospering people enjoying the day, as dust swirled in a steady wind and more families arrived in new trucks and automobiles. Lined up in an adjoining field, their bright colors gleaming in the sun, were perhaps fifty private airplanes.

It was a Republican crowd. Iowa had a Republican governor. All eight Iowa representatives in Congress, and both senators, were Republicans. In the last presidential election Iowa's ten electoral votes had gone to Dewey. But more important to Truman, nearly all his audience were farmers and in the Great Depression, he knew, Iowa farmers had voted for Roosevelt.

Years before, in 1934, when he had been running for the Senate the first time, a St. Louis reporter had written, "In a fight this quiet man can and does hurl devastating fire." Now at Dexter he ripped into the Republican "gluttons of privilege . . . cold men . . . cunning men," in a way no one had heard a presidential candidate speak since the days of William Jennings Bryan. The difference between Republicans and Democrats was a difference in "attitude":

> You remember the big boom and the great crash of 1929. You remember that in 1932 the position of the farmer had become so desperate that there was actual violence in many farming communities. You remember that insurance companies and banks took over much of the land of small independent farmers—223,000 farmers lost their farms. . . .
>
> I wonder how many times you have to be hit on the head before you find out who's hitting you? . . .
>
> The Democratic Party represents the people. It is pledged to work for agriculture. . . . The Democratic Party puts human rights and human welfare first. . . . These Republican gluttons of privilege are cold men. They are cunning men. . . . They want a return of the Wall Street economic dictatorship. . . .

It was language that, to many, seemed oddly archaic and out of place in the midst of such obvious prosperity. The *Des Moines Register* would point to the "incongruity of being a prophet of doom to an audience in time of harvest of bumper crops." Truman, it was said, was sadly miscast as the new Bryan, his speech "harsh and demagogic."

. . .

Afterward, in a tent behind the platform, a perspiring president in his shirtsleeves pulled up a wooden folding chair to a long table with a red-check cloth and ate country fried chicken and prize-winning cake and pie with thirty farmers and their wives. Asked if he would please speak again, only on a more personal level this time, Truman agreed and returned to the platform.

Was it true he had once been able to plow the straightest furrows in his part of Missouri, he was asked. Yes, said Truman, but only according to an exceedingly partial witness, his mother. But he did have a reputation, he said, for never leaving a "skip place" when he sowed wheat. "My father always used to raise so much fuss about a skip place."

He talked of the 12-inch, horse-drawn gang plow he rode at Grandview and how it had taken him sometimes four days to plow a field. He didn't want to go back to those days. "I don't want to turn back the clock. I don't want to go back to the horse and buggy age, although some of our Republican friends do," he said, and this brought a warm cheer.

"He was delightful and the people were delighted," wrote Richard Rovere of *The New Yorker,* who had thought the earlier speech "deplorable."

Truman had begun the day at 5:45. There had been six stops and six speeches before Dexter. After Dexter, he spoke at Des Moines, Melcher, and Chariton, Iowa. "At each stop," reported the Des Moines *Register,* "the listeners massed for his rear platform talk were larger than the town's population."

"You stayed at home in 1946 and you got the 80th Congress, and you got just exactly what you deserved," he said at Chariton. "You didn't exercise your God-given right to control this country. Now you're going to have another chance."

He was on a crusade for the welfare of the everyday man, he said next, across the state line, at Trenton, Missouri. At Polo, Missouri, just after 8 P.M., he told the delighted crowd he had not been sure whether he would be able to stop there, but that the railroad had finally consented. It was his thirteenth speech of the day and he was sounding a little hoarse.

. . .

He had just one strategy—attack, attack, attack, carry the fight to the enemy's camp. He hammered the Republicans relentlessly, in speeches at Grand Junction, Colorado; Helper, Springville, and Provo, Utah. "Selfish men have always tried to skim the cream from our natural resources to satisfy their own greed. And ... [their] instrument in this effort has always been the Republican Party," he charged at Salt Lake City, to a standing-room-only crowd in the cavernous Mormon Tabernacle. At Ogden, he warned of "bloodsuckers who have offices in Wall Street." The 80th Congress, he said at Reno, Nevada, was run by a "bunch of old mossbacks still living back in 1890."

At both Grand Junction, Colorado, and the Mormon Tabernacle in Salt Lake City, he reminisced about Grandfather Solomon Young and his journeys over the plains, his friendship with Brigham Young. "Oh, I wish my grandfather could see me now," he said spontaneously at Salt Lake, and the audience first laughed, then broke into prolonged applause. "Those pioneers had faith and they had energy," he said, seeming himself to embody an excess of both qualities.

He expressed love of home, love of the land, the virtues and old verities of small-town America, his America. "Naturally, if we don't think our hometown is the greatest in the world, we are not very loyal citizens. We all should feel that way," he told the loyal citizens of American Fork, Utah.

"You don't get any double talk from me," he declared from a brightly decorated bandstand first thing in the morning sunshine at Sparks, Nevada. "I'm either for something or against it, and you know it. You know what I stand for." What he stood for, he said again and again, was a government of and for the people, not the "special interests."

He was friendly, cheerful. And full of fight.

"You are the government," he said time after time. "Practical politics is government. Government starts from the grass roots." "I think the government belongs to you and me as private citizens." "I'm calling this trip a crusade. It's a crusade of the people against the special interests, and if you back me up we're going to win. . . ."

. . .

The crowds would be gathered at station stops often from early morning, waiting for him to arrive. Men and boys perched on rooftops and nearby signal towers for a better view. There would be a high school band standing by, ready to play the national anthem or

"Hail to the Chief," or to struggle through the "Missouri Waltz," a song Truman particularly disliked but that it was his fate to hear repeated hundreds of times over. His train would ease into the station as the band blared, the crowd cheered. Then, accompanied by three or four local politicians—usually a candidate for Congress or state party chairman who had boarded the train at a prior stop—Truman would step from behind the blue velvet curtain onto the platform, and the crowd, large or small, would cheer even more. One of the local politicians would then introduce the president of the United States and the crowd would cheer again.

. . .

"Give 'em hell, Harry!" someone would shout from the crowd—news accounts of his promise to Senator Barkley to "give 'em hell" having swept the country by now. The cry went up at one stop after another, often more than once—"Give 'em hell, Harry!"—which always brought more whoops, laughter, and yells of approval, but especially when he tore into the 80th Congress.

("I never gave anybody hell," he would later say. "I just told the truth and they thought it was hell.")

. . .

Pounding his way across Texas, Truman had seemed to gather strength by the hour and give more of himself to the campaign with every stop. He was fighting for his political life and having a grand time at it.

At San Antonio an estimated 200,000 people filled the streets, and at a dinner that night at the Gunter Hotel, speaking spontaneously and simply of his feeling for people and his wish for peace, Truman achieved what Jonathan Daniels called "an eloquence close to presidential poetry."

> Our government is made up of the people. You are the government, I am only your hired servant. I am the Chief Executive of the greatest nation in the world, the highest honor that can ever come to a man on

earth. But I am the servant of the people of the United States. They are not my servants. I can't order you around, or send you to labor camps or have your heads cut off if you don't agree with me politically. We don't believe in that. . . .

I believe that if we ourselves try to live as we should, and if we continue to work for peace in this world, and as the old Puritan said, "Keep your bullets bright and your powder dry," eventually we will get peace in this world, because that is the only way we can survive with the modern inventions under which we live.

We have got to harness these inventions for the welfare of man, instead of his destruction.

That is what I am interested in. That is what I am working for.

That is much more important than whether I am President of the United States.

・ ・ ・

It had been known for some while that *Newsweek* magazine was taking a poll of fifty highly regarded political writers, to ask which candidate they thought would win the election. And since several of the fifty had been on the train with Truman during the course of the campaign—Marquis Childs, Robert Albright of the *Washington Post,* Bert Andrews of the *New York Herald Tribune*—there had been a good deal of speculation about the poll.

Of the writers polled, not one thought Truman would win. The vote was unanimous, 50 for Dewey, 0 for Truman. "The landslide for Dewey will sweep the country," the magazine announced. Further, the Republicans would keep control in the Senate and increase their majority in the House. The election was as good as over.

For months efforts had been made to persuade Eleanor Roosevelt to say something, anything, to help Truman—efforts that Truman himself refused to have any part in—but all to no avail. From Paris, where she was attending the United Nations session, she wrote to Frances Perkins that she had not endorsed Truman because he was "such a weak and vacillating person" and made such poor appointments. Now, at the last minute, she changed her mind, hoping to help the Democrats to carry New York.

"There has never been a campaign where a man has shown more personal courage and confidence in the people of the United States," she said in a broadcast from Paris.

The scene of the final rally of the campaign, and the last platform appearance Harry Truman would ever make as a candidate for public office, was the immense Kiel Auditorium in St. Louis, where there was not an empty seat.

Discarding the speech efforts of his staff, he went on the attack, lashing out one last time at the Republican Congress, the Republican press, the Republican "old dealers," and the Republican candidate. The stomping, cheering crowd urged him on.

He felt afterward that he had done well. In any case, he had done the best he knew how.

★   ★   ★

The odyssey was over. Sunday, October 31, Halloween, was spent at home at 219 North Delaware Street. "Home!" remembered Truman's daughter, Margaret. "I couldn't believe it."

Truman worked on an election-eve radio address to be delivered from the living room the following night.

> From the bottom of my heart I thank the people of the United States for their cordiality to me and their interest in the affairs of this great nation and of the world. I trust the people, because when they know the facts, they do the right thing. . . .

Election day, up at five, he took his usual morning walk, read the papers, and had breakfast. Then, trailed by a swarm of reporters and photographers, he, Bess, and Margaret went to Memorial Hall three blocks away on Maple Avenue and voted.

A final Gallup Poll showed that while he had cut Dewey's lead, Dewey nonetheless remained a substantial five points ahead, 49.5 to

44.5. The betting odds still ranged widely, though generally speaking Dewey was favored 4 to 1.

The *New York Times* predicted a Dewey victory with 345 electoral votes. "Government will remain big, active, and expensive under President Thomas E. Dewey," said the *Wall Street Journal*. *Time* and *Newsweek* saw a Dewey sweep. The new issue of *Life* carried a full-page photograph of Dewey, "the next President," crossing San Francisco Bay by ferry boat. Alistair Cooke, correspondent for the *Manchester Guardian,* titled his dispatch for November 1, "Harry S. Truman, A Study in Failure."

★   ★   ★

The country was flabbergasted. It was called a "startling victory," "astonishing," "a major miracle." Truman, said *Newsweek* on its cover, was the Miracle Man.

Truman carried 28 states with a total of 303 electoral votes, and defeated Dewey in the popular election by just over 2,100,000 votes. In the final tally, Truman polled 24,105,812, Dewey 21,970,065.

He had won against the greatest odds in the annals of presidential politics. Not one polling organization had been correct in its forecast. Not a single radio commentator or newspaper columnist, or any of the hundreds of reporters who covered the campaign, had called it right. Every expert had been proven wrong, and as was said, "a great roar of laughter arose from the land." The people had made fools of those supposedly in the know. Of all amazing things, Harry Truman had turned out to be the only one who knew what he was talking about.

Actress Tallulah Bankhead sent Truman a telegram: "The people have put you in your place." Harry Truman, said the radio comedian Fred Allen, was the first president to lose in a Gallup and win in a walk.

Excerpted from David McCullough, *Truman* (New York: Simon & Schuster, 1972), pgs. 653–654, 656–663, 675–676, 694, 702–703, 710.

Dwight Eisenhower

HIDDEN HAND

"Don't worry, Jim, if that question comes up, I'll just confuse them."
—PRESIDENT EISENHOWER, speaking to his press secretary,
James Hagerty, before a March 1955 press conference

"Ike, we hardly knew ye!" That was the effect Fred Greenstein's book, *The Hidden Hand Presidency* (1981), had on many of us who saw Dwight Eisenhower through the eyes of our Stevenson-smitten parents as, in John F. Kennedy's private estimation, a "non-president" who left governing to his cabinet while he played golf.

This was the visible Ike, who, in Dwight McDonald's parody, would have begun the Gettysburg Address this way: "I haven't checked the figures, but eighty-seven years ago, I think it was, a number of individuals organized a governmental set-up here in this country, I believe it covered eastern areas, with this idea that they were following up based on a sort of national independence arrangement and the program that every individual is just as good as every other individual."

Using sources ranging from public archives to private inter-views to Ike's diary, Greenstein unveiled a hidden Ike—lucid in speech and thought, prudent in policy, a subtle politician who, through seeming not to exercise power, got things done without bearing the onus of doing them. Building on the work of Green-stein and other revisionists, Stephen Ambrose, in his 1990 one-volume biography, pronounced Ike "one of the outstanding leaders of the western world in this century." That was by then a consensus view. Shortly after he left office a poll of presidential historians ranked Eisenhower with Chester Arthur; twenty years later the historians ranked him ninth among the ten greatest presidents.

Eight years of peace in a time when Cold War tensions rarely fell below harrowing, eight years of prosperity mitigated by recession, eight years of what one historian calls "the American High," the pursuit of happiness in big-finned cars and split-level homes by couples raised in depression and war to expect self-denying lives—what's not to like about Ike? Nostalgia for the lost Eden of the fifties has rubbed off on his reputation.

African-Americans, living under Jim Crow segregation in the South and de-facto segregation in the North, did not share in the milk and honey. White politics took no account of their ordeal. They found much *not* to like—and not only about Ike but about the liberal paladin, Adlai Stevenson, who ran against Eisenhower in 1952 on a ticket with a segregationist running mate. Though he selected Earl Warren to be chief justice of the Supreme Court, where Warren orchestrated the historic *Brown v. Board of Education* school desegregation decision of 1954, Eisenhower called the appointment "the biggest damn fool mistake." He could not, as the Court did in *Brown*, transcend white complacency toward the legal apartheid of black Americans. Seeking harmony as an end in itself, he seemed more concerned with placating the prejudice of southern whites than he was sympathetic to its southern black victims. While the Court was considering *Brown*, Eisenhower even went so far as to invite Warren to a White House dinner with the lead attorney defending the segregationist practices at issue in the case, and asked Warren privately to consider the feelings of white southerners in reaching his decision. "These are not bad people," he said. "All they are concerned about is to see their sweet little girls are not required to sit in school alongside some big overgrown Negro." Shocking now, such views were all-too-conventional then.

While Ike said he would do "my very best" to enforce the *Brown* decision, James Patterson writes, "this did not move him to action. He told his speechwriter that the Court had set progress back by 'at least fifteen years. . . . We can't demand perfection in these moral things.'" Perfection, no; but equal protection of the laws and equal rights, including the elementary right to vote—the demands of the fledgling Civil Rights movement—surely yes. In *Grand Expectations, The United States, 1945–1974* Patterson faults Eisenhower for not strongly backing the decision, calling his stand "morally obtuse and encouraging to anti-Brown activists."

Still, when he had to act against those "activists" Eisenhower acted, dispatching 1,100 army paratroopers to protect black students from white mobs in the Little Rock integration crisis of 1957. Dixiecrat politicians fulminated; liberals complained that he moved too late and too reluctantly. Nevertheless, his decision ended a cycle of history in which the North had turned its back on segregation in the South. "It was the first time since Reconstruction," Patterson notes, "that federal troops had been dispatched to the South to protect the civil rights of blacks."

The greatest presidents not only lead within their own time but beyond its limits. Lincoln did that during the Civil War in moving from a policy of subordinating anti-slavery to keep the border states in the Union to embracing emancipation. FDR did it in 1940–41 by trespassing the lawful border of his authority to aid Great Britain against Hitler and by slowly bringing an isolationist public to recognize the necessity of war. Ronald Reagan did it in the 1980s by giving lonely voice to a cause more urgent than ever in an age of terrorism, the abolition of nuclear weapons. Eisenhower himself approached this standard by controlling defense spending out of a conviction that "every dollar spent on weapons" is a dollar not spent on domestic necessities and in warning against the dangers to peace posed by a "military-industrial complex" with a vested interest in war.

In the following excerpt from *The Hidden Hand Presidency,* Greenstein analyzes Eisenhower's fingerprint-free political touch, which most voters, with their Ike-cultivated image of a president above politics, never suspected him of at the time.

IKE'S POLITICAL STRATEGIES

Fred I. Greenstein

Dwight Eisenhower, like Harry Truman, had a desk ornament bearing a motto epitomizing his view of leadership. Rather than "The buck stops here," Eisenhower's declared *"Suaviter in modo, fortiter in re"* (Gently in manner, strong in deed). The motto nicely captures the essence of Eisenhower's approach to leadership, a repertoire of six strategies that enabled him to exercise power without seeming to flex his muscles. The strategies, which were characteristic of Eisenhower the man, enabled him to balance the contradictory expectations that a president be a national unifier yet nevertheless engage in the divisive exercise of political leadership.

For covertly exercising the prime-ministerial side of the chief executive's job Eisenhower employed five strategies: hidden-hand leadership; instrumental use of language; the complementary strategies of refusing in public to "engage in personalities" but nevertheless privately basing actions on personality analyses; and the selective practice of delegation. Together these enabled him to use a sixth strategy that helped make him a credible chief of state—building a public support that transcended many of the nation's social and political divisions.

The individual strategies were not uniquely Eisenhower's. Any single act or utterance of Eisenhower was likely to include more than one strategy, and the six strategies did not exhaust his repertoire. But he fit them together in a way that made his presidential leadership distinctive.

★   ★   ★

Presidents often find it necessary to maneuver in secrecy. Presidents who seek to establish a professional reputation with other leaders as skilled, tough operators, and who want to be recognized by historians as "presidential activists," however, sometimes deliberately stimulate accounts of their tour de force exercises of personal influence. John F. Kennedy used this tactic in his bravura 1962 assault on the steel industry that forced a price increase recision. In 1964 Lyndon Johnson encouraged publicity about his personal mediation of an impending railroad strike, an around-the-clock exercise in which he virtually locked union and management negotiators in the White House cabinet room. Jimmy Carter's intense personal participation in negotiation in the Camp David accords between Egypt and Israel is another example of publicized presidential activism.

Although Eisenhower cultivated the reputation of being above political machination, he was an activist. However, in part because he chose not to publicize his activities and in part because his activities did not always fit the popular conception of an activist, he was not considered one. Commentators usually associate activism with efforts to effect major innovations (usually liberal) in public policy. Eisenhower sought, at least in domestic policy, to restrain policy change, but he was active in doing so. He worked hard, considered it his responsibility to shape public policy, and followed through on his initiatives.

A president who seeks influence and cultivates a reputation for not intervening in day-to-day policymaking will necessarily hide his hand more often than one who seeks recognition as an effective political operator. Eisenhower often camouflaged his participation not only in political activity generally falling outside popularly conceived bounds of presidential leadership, but also in more commonplace political leadership. In either case sometimes he used hidden-hand strategy to conceal his activities from all nonassociates; sometimes it suited his purposes to target his hidden-hand leadership so that selective nonassociates would be made aware of his actions.

An example of simple hidden-hand leadership—one that is a paradigm of Eisenhower influence attempts and has been kept completely secret—was his 1954 effort to influence Senate Democratic Leader Lyndon Johnson, an act which, if exposed, would have been controversial in any administration. Believing that Johnson was straying from the course of "fine conservative government," the president used a wealthy Johnson supporter to coerce him. Employing an intermediary, who concealed from the Johnson backer that Eisenhower had initiated the scheme to influence Johnson, Eisenhower "laundered" his own participation in the exercise. Eisenhower's secretary,

Ann Whitman, took notes on Eisenhower's telephone conversation to Treasury Secretary George Humphrey, during which he told Humphrey to call Texas oil multi-millionaire Sid Richardson, who, Eisenhower noted, "was really the angel for Johnson when he came in." The telephone log summarizing their conversation records these instructions:

> Ask [Richardson] . . . what it is that Tex wants. We help out in drought, take tidelands matter on their side, and tax bill. But question is, how much influence has Sid got with Johnson? He tells Sid he's supporting us, then comes up here and disproves it (yesterday for instance). Perhaps Sid could get him on the right channel, or threaten to get [Texas Governor Allen] Shrivers in a primary and beat him for Senate.

Because Richardson was an old friend of Eisenhower's—they met in 1941—Eisenhower and Humphrey agreed that the latter should talk to Richardson so "it can't be said that DDE is taking advantage of a longtime friendship."

Clearly Eisenhower's efforts to influence Johnson required such discretion. Eisenhower, however, also concealed his involvement in conventional politicking that would not have been controversial if he had been prepared to be viewed as a political professional. In 1957, for example, he sent a letter to Secretary of the Treasury Robert Anderson. Anderson, a Texas lawyer, whom Eisenhower frequently mentioned to associates as the man he felt best equipped to succeed him, had served as secretary of the Navy, and deputy assistant secretary of defense, and had just assumed the Treasury secretaryship. Throughout this period, although ostensibly not a political operative, at Eisenhower's behest, Anderson drew on his long personal friendship with Lyndon Johnson to serve as private administration conduit to and pulse taker of the mercurial Senate Democratic leader by maintaining virtually daily contact with Johnson. This role extended into that of a general behind-the-scenes political aide.

Eisenhower's letter to Anderson contained a detailed set of procedural suggestions for managing congressional relations. The suggestions were originally drafted by Henry Cabot Lodge, who had been a two-term senator and an active figure in securing Eisenhower's nomination. From his post as United Nations ambassador, Lodge regularly and also without publicity advised Eisenhower on strategy and tactics for domestic politics.

In his letter to Anderson, the "apolitical" Eisenhower passed on Lodge's suggestions. They included such standard fare as insisting that department secretaries establish personal friendships with the congressional chairmen whose committees supervised agency operations and also ingratiate themselves with the chairmen's wives; that they grant all favors requested by friendly congressmen immediately if possible, and if not possible, explain why, stressing their desire to be helpful wherever feasible; and that they pay verbal deference to congressional authority when testifying on Capitol Hill but frame their approach to Congress on the premise that congressmen would prefer to be led than to lead.

This not very novel codification of ways to influence Congress would have elicited only modest interest had it leaked from the Kennedy or Johnson White House. In the Jimmy Carter years its release might even have been a reassuring sign that the president was learning the rules of the Washington game. But such directives were inappropriate for a president who avoided being linked with political operations. Consequently, in sending the Lodge memorandum, along with a comment on it by General Persons, Eisenhower instructed Anderson to study the documents carefully, and after doing so, "I request that you personally destroy them both. I am particularly anxious that no word of any concerted effort along this line ever reach the outside because a leak would tend to destroy the value of the effort." Eisenhower noted, however, that Anderson was free to communicate the contents to his staff, but with a key qualification, "[A]s your own ideas."

Eisenhower used the targeted variant of hidden-hand leadership in which he and his team concealed his maneuvers from only some outsiders (in this case the general public, but not from the person he wished to influence) in a 1953 exchange with South Carolina Governor James Byrnes, a 1952 Eisenhower supporter who had protested an administration executive order instituting racial integration in Southern federal facilities. In a letter to Byrnes Eisenhower stressed that he was acting out of a conviction about what was constitutionally required of him and not because he was insensitive to Southern mores or because his high personal regard for Byrnes had weakened.

Eisenhower discussed with a White House aide the possible impact his message would have if made public. He decided to have the letter marked "personal and confidential." "After all," he pointed out, "we are not after publicity for this particular letter; what we want is the governor to go along with us completely in the enforcement of federal regulations." The concluding sentence of his interoffice memorandum to the aide perfectly captures Eisenhower's predilection to defuse conflicts rather than bring them to a head: "Our job is to convince; not to publicize."

Eisenhower himself believed that this kind of hidden-hand strategy had been responsible for the termination of the Korean conflict. When Eisenhower entered the White House, he was convinced that the Chinese forces were so well entrenched on the current truce line that a negotiated settlement was the best course of action. The alternative possibilities of bloody fighting for limited gains or a major assault on the mainland that at worst could escalate into a global war and at best might unify Korea, thus leaving the United States with unwanted control of North Korea, seemed to him to be wholly inappropriate. But the truce talks were stalled, and no obvious Chinese advantage was to be gained in reopening them. After considering the possibility of using tactical nuclear weapons on North Korean troop concentrations and being persuaded that such a course of action would be repugnant to the NATO allies, Eisenhower records that he conveyed an unpublicized message to the Chinese through indirect channels. Proceeding on the premise that China would not relish nuclear devastation of its industrial and military concentrations and would expect a new American regime led by a general to be more bellicose than Truman's, he acted in a way calculated not to arouse NATO fears of an expanded war, but even so to create among the Chinese the expectation that if they did not negotiate a settlement they would bear unacceptable costs. As he put it:

In India and in the Formosa Straits area, and at the truce negotiations at Panmunjom, we dropped the word, discreetly, of our intention . . . to move decisively without inhibition in our use of weapons, and . . . no longer be responsible for confining hostilities to the Korean Peninsula. . . . We felt sure that it would reach Soviet and Communist ears.

There is no way short of examining Communist sources to prove that this strategy was effective. Eisenhower felt it had been, since, almost immediately after the signals were issued in February 1953, the Chinese became more open to negotiations. A truce settlement was agreed upon by the summer of 1953.

Hidden-hand tactics also helped Eisenhower to conceal his part (indeed the part of the United States) in the overthrow of the Mossadegh government in Iran in 1953 and of the Arbenz government in Guatemala in 1954. In neither instance did the mainstream American media even suggest that these operations were initiated by America, much less by Eisenhower.

Hidden-hand leadership, whether simple or targeted, by an ostensibly nonpolitical president can, however, cut two ways. While it may permit the president to achieve what would be a controversial outcome without backlash, it also has intrinsic limitations in situations where the object of influence can best be persuaded if he thinks the action urged on him is one the president wants him to take.

The strategy failed when Eisenhower tried indirectly to dissuade Richard Nixon from running for vice president in 1956.

In February 1956, before Eisenhower had announced his own candidacy for reelection, he suggested to Nixon that his chance of becoming a winning Republican presidential candidate in 1960 would be greater if, rather than running for a second vice presidential term, he establish independent status as secretary of a major cabinet department, adding with matter-of-fact detachment, "if we can count on my living five years." Recapping this conversation to party chairman Leonard Hall, Eisenhower talked about another reason for removing Nixon from the ticket: to get a stronger running mate and groom an alternate 1960 candidate for the presidency. Robert Anderson, as usual, was his first choice. He also was fascinated with the notion that it might be possible to crack the New Deal coalition by enlisting a conservative Democrat and Roman Catholic, Ohio Senator Frank Lausche.

Although Eisenhower preferred an alternative to Nixon as a running mate, he made clear to an aide that he felt "there is nothing to be gained politically by ditching him." Hall, in a massive underestimation of Nixon's tenacity, assured Eisenhower that it would be "the easiest thing to get Nixon out of the picture willingly." Eisenhower replied, "Well, all right, you see him and talk to him, but be very, very gentle." Hall's mission, of course, failed.

Unwilling to depart from his strategic rule of avoiding visible wirepulling within the party and, unwilling to instruct Nixon not to run, Eisenhower succumbed to the pressures of Nixon's many party supporters and to the impact of the write-in votes Nixon garnered in the early primaries. He announced in March that the team would again be "Ike and Dick." Eisenhower deliberately traded one desired result, dropping Nixon, for others, such as preserving his politics-free image and avoiding a factional squabble. And in doing so, he failed to accomplish his goal of obtaining a preferable second-term running mate.

Eisenhower found it natural to express himself straightforwardly and incisively, arraying facts and rigorously justifying his policies and actions. He could do this by using precisely etched prose and he took pride in his capacity to do so. He was, however, also willing to replace clear, reasoned discourse with alternative ways of expressing himself when they better served his purposes. Neither pride in ability nor his natural predilection for clarity kept him from deliberately turning to language that was emotive and inspirational or purposely ambiguous. Verbal expression was his instrument; he refused to indulge his obvious pleasure in analytic thought and clear expression as an end in itself.

I say that clear expression was natural to him because it is the manner he adopted in private circumstances. The personal diary passages he used for self-clarification and that he never released for publication are lucidly written, as are his innumerable prepresidential and presidential memoranda to aides and associates, as well as his letters to his most confidential correspondents. His penchant for clarity also is evident in the many drafts that have been preserved of reports, letters, and speeches that he personally edited to hone the prose.

His dictated list of editorial changes on the first draft of his 1954 State of the Union message shows Eisenhower's work as a word clarifier and also as a stylist striving for public effect. As one of the rare editing efforts in which he explained the reasons for his changes, the list illustrates how in his writing, as in other endeavors, he formulated abstract rules for many of his operating procedures. In the course of transmitting four general and thirty-eight specific instructions for change, he tightened the prose by telling the speechwriter that "sections need to be more distinctly marked" and admonished: "Do not be afraid to say 'I come to so-and-so.' . . . You cannot take the human mind from subject to subject . . . quickly!" And, almost nigglingly, he had the assertion "confidence had developed" changed to "constantly developing confidence" to indicate "continuing action."

Eisenhower also conveyed instructions designed, in a latter-day phrase, to make the speech play better in Peoria. He instructed the speechwriter to eliminate such technical language as "substantial reductions in the size and cost of Federal Government" and "deficit spending" on the grounds that the "man we are trying to reach" better understands the phrases "purchasing power of the dollar" and stability "in the size of his market basket." The changes advanced his aim of expanding his party's base to encompass the upper blue-collar and lower white-collar nucleus of the Democratic Party's coalition.

In addition to using words as instruments for communicating substance and emotions, Eisenhower also sometimes employed them in a fashion similar to his hidden-hand strategy—to create smoke screens for his actions in his role as covert prime minister. Some of his utterances served to obscure sensitive subjects from public view; others conveyed deliberately ambiguous messages that left him freedom of action. Deliberate use of ambiguity and evasiveness were, of course, not unique to Eisenhower. What distinguished him from other politicians was the ability to leave the impression that such utterances were guileless.

His press conferences furnish a good perspective on his use of language to convey ambiguity. The most instructive are those for which transcripts have been kept of the preliminary briefings so that a record is available of what he chose to say and why. But the entire body of his official exchanges with the press reveals his use of ambiguity and other verbal strategies. Some of his press conference practices contributed to the impression that he simply was uninformed, when in fact he was choosing to be ambiguous. He was more disposed than other presidents simply to say that he was not aware of certain issues, including some that had received wide press attention. He also often directed questioners to one of his associates for an answer, suggesting that the issue on which he was being queried was not of sufficient magnitude or "ripeness" to warrant presidential attention: "Well, this is the first I've heard of that," and "You'd better take that up with Secretary X" are common assertions in his press conferences.

The texts of the preliminary briefings make it clear, however, that in claiming ignorance he often was following a practice he used as early as his first press conference on becoming European theater commander in June 1942, which the New York Times described as an "excellent demonstration of the art of being jovially outspoken without saying much of anything." Even then he was sufficiently self-conscious about ways that a leader can use his mode of expression as a tactic to advise others—such as his embarrassingly outspoken subordinate commander, George S. Patton—on verbal comportment. Quoting "an old proverb . . . : 'Keep silent and appear stupid; open your mouth and remove all doubt,'" he advised Patton that "a certain sphynx-like quality will do a lot toward enhancing one's reputation."

Eisenhower's strategy of remaining silent is illustrated in the summary of the briefing before his July 31, 1957, press conference. Aides reminded Eisenhower that Egyptian president Gamal Abdel Nasser had been making speeches criticizing the United States and that the "Egyptians are trying to say [they] have disturbed us." Eisenhower told his briefers that if the question came up, he would say he had not read Nasser's speeches.

Earlier that month, however, his briefers did correctly anticipate a question. On July 17 Eisenhower and his aides discussed an issue that was likely to be on the reporters' agenda, because Secretary of State John Foster Dulles had raised it in his news conference the previous day: the disposition of American missiles in Europe. Eisenhower expressed annoyance that Dulles had "wandered" into a topic he felt should have been a matter for "no comment" on national security grounds. Phoning Dulles to be reminded in detail of what he had said, Eisenhower hung up and told his associates that if the question came up at the press conference, he would "be evasive."

It did and he was. Quoting Dulles, Peter Lisagor of the *Chicago Daily News* noted that the secretary of state "yesterday disclosed that consideration is being given to a plan for establishing nuclear stockpiles of weapons and fissionable materials for NATO powers." How did the president stand on this matter? Lisagor asked. In his reply Eisenhower denied knowledge of the very information he had just confirmed in his conversation with Dulles. "Now I don't know what he told you about a plan," he said. "What we have just been doing is studying means and methods of making NATO effective as a defensive organization. . . . Now that is all there is to that."

Such intentional evasiveness was a standard Eisenhower press conference tactic. Sometimes, as in a March 16, 1955, press conference, he mixed vagueness with ambiguity studiously designed to have different effects on different audiences. The issue was whether, under what circumstances, and with what kinds of weapons the United States would defend Quemoy and Matsu. In his previous news conference, Eisenhower had warned that in the event of a "general war" in Asia the United States was prepared to use tactical nuclear weapons. Just before the following week's conference, the State Department conveyed through James Hagerty, Eisenhower's press secretary, the urgent request that the president not discuss this delicate matter further. Eisenhower reports that he replied, "Don't worry, Jim, if that question comes up, I'll just confuse them."

Joseph C. Harsch of the *Christian Science Monitor* raised the question, asking, "If we got into an issue with the Chinese, say, over Matsu and Quemoy, that we wanted to keep limited, do you conceive us using [atomic weapons] in that situation or not?" Eisenhower responded:

Well, Mr. Harsch, I must confess I cannot answer that question in advance. The only thing I know about war are two things: the most unpredictable factor in war is human nature in its day-by-day manifestation; but the only unchanging factor in war is human nature. And the next thing is that every war is going to astonish you in the way it occurred, and in the way it is carried out. So that for a man to predict, particularly if he has the responsibility for making the decision, to predict what he is going to use, how he is going to do it, would I think exhibit his ignorance of war; that is what I believe. So I think you just have to wait; and that is the kind of prayerful decision that may some day face a president.

The vagueness and ambiguity in this response was contrived to serve several ends. It allowed Eisenhower to sidestep a potentially divisive encounter with right wing "China Firster" Republicans, which would have destroyed his ability to pass such high priority programs as the annual foreign aid appropriation. It also conveyed an ambiguous warning message to the PRC, which would have been delighted to occupy Quemoy and Matsu. Finally, for the American public, the message was a reassuring reminder that any decision taken would reflect the professional judgment of a president who understood the nature of war. Eisenhower and Hagerty recognized that Eisenhower's style in press conferences was well received by the general public, even if it left the impression among Washington cognoscenti that he was obtuse. They, after all, introduced the practice of releasing tapes and kinescopes of presidential news conferences to the public.

"I Do Not Engage in Personalities." This was Eisenhower's curiously phrased way of asserting his strategy of not criticizing others personally, no matter how strong the provocation. He enunciated his rationale to Bryce Harlow after editing a public statement Harlow drafted for him on a currently hot issue. Harlow recalls that Eisenhower

> picked up his pen, leaned forward, and struck out a word. He sat back and said, "Now, Bryce, that's a fine statement. . . . Go ahead and issue it. I made one little change." And I said, "Well, sir, what's that?" He said, "I struck out the word 'deliberate.'" He said, "This is an attack on a person. When you said it was deliberate, what he had done, you were attacking his motives. Never, ever, attack a person's motives, Bryce."

Eisenhower's sensitivity to the costs of handling personalities indelicately is illustrated repeatedly in his statements and actions throughout his public career. The tasks he faced as Supreme Commander Allied Forces Europe were so thoroughly steeped in personality management that, only two months after returning to the United States and becoming Army chief of staff, he advised West Point Superintendent Maxwell Taylor to introduce a course in "practical or applied psychology" to the military academy curriculum. The course was needed, he said, because

> [t]oo frequently we find young officers trying to use empirical and ritualistic methods in the handling of individuals—I think that both theoretical and practical instruction along this line could, at the very least, awaken the majority of Cadets to the necessity of handling human problems on a human basis and do much to improve leadership and personnel handling in the Army at large.

Although wartime leadership was plagued by personality conflicts, Eisenhower made clear many years later that he had deliberately omitted reference to them in his VE-Day Victory Order, which declared, "Let us have no part in the profitless quarrels on which other men will engage as to what country, what service, won the European War." Drawing attention to the reference to "quarrels," he noted in a 1959 letter that the passage "might just as well have contained the word 'individual' as well as 'country' and 'service.'" He stressed that,

"So far as I know I have not, myself, consciously violated the exhortation I then delivered the command." Thus, for example, in spite of the many personal recriminations and invidious comments others introduced into their World War II memoirs, in Eisenhower's own *Crusade in Europe,* "wherever there is given . . . any impression of mine concerning an individual, it invariably winds up with an expression of respect and even admiration."

Eisenhower's fullest statement of the reasons for his rule not to engage in personalities and its basic rationale is in a March 9, 1954, letter to his businessman friend Paul Helms.

> For the past thirteen years I have occupied posts around which there focused sufficient public interest that they were considered news sources of greater or lesser importance. . . . Out of all those experiences, I developed a practice which, so far as I know, I have never violated. That practice is to avoid public mention of any name *unless it can be done with favorable intent and connotation;* reserve all criticism for the private conference; speak only good in public. [Eisenhower's emphasis.]

Then, stating the psychological basis for the practice, he observed:

> This is not namby-pamby. It certainly is not Pollyanna-ish. It is just sheer common sense. A leader's job is to get others to go along with him in the promotion of something. To do this he needs their goodwill. To destroy goodwill, it is only necessary to criticize publicly. This creates in the criticized one a subconscious desire to "get even." Such effects can last for a very long period.

When Eisenhower told Helms he reserved personality "criticism for the private conference," he did not go on to suggest the almost clinical objectivity with which he could analyze and think about the problems of dealing with people who hampered him but whom he refused publicly to criticize. There is no better illustration of how his private and public assertions diverged than the contrast between a 1953 exchange with persistent journalists who sought to foster a confrontation between Eisenhower and Senator Taft and a diary entry he made a month later. Taft, in a speech of May 26, 1953, concerning the stalemated Korean truce negotiations, asserted that if the negotiating team meeting in Korea could not agree on a militarily secure truce line, the United States should "let England and our allies know that we are withdrawing from all further peace negotiations in Korea" because we "might as well . . . reserve to ourselves a completely free hand."

This was typical of the kind of emotional statement by Taft that Eisenhower deplored. He noted in the diary entry that

> [i]n the foreign field, Senator Taft never disagrees with me when we discuss such matters academically or theoretically. . . . However, when we take up each individual problem or case, he easily loses his temper and makes extravagant statements. He always does this when he starts making a public speech—he seems to work himself into a storm of resentment and irritation. The result of all this is that our allies fear him and all he influences. They think he gives McCarthy ideas and McCarthy, with his readiness to go to the extremes in calling names and making false accusations, simply terrifies the ordinary European statesman.

The White House withheld comment on Taft's speech, but Senator John Sparkman, the 1952 Democratic vice presidential candidate, called the speech a "diametric contradiction" of Eisenhower's policy, and the senior Democratic foreign policy spokesman, Senator Walter George, said that Taft was advocating "the road that leads directly to complete isolation and a third world war." In Eisenhower's May 28 press conference, Richard Wilson of Cowles Publications attempted in an extended colloquy to smoke Eisenhower out. Did he, or did he not, agree with the senator? Eisenhower avoided "engaging in personalities" with Taft by being persistently elusive, insisting that Taft's remarks had been misinterpreted by the reporters.

> WILSON: As I read Senator Taft's speech . . . if the present truce negotiations fail, that then we should go it alone.

EISENHOWER: Well now, I am not going to put words in Senator Taft's mouth because I did not read the speech in detail. But I do believe this: when he says go it alone, he *must* mean that we insist on following our own beliefs and convictions in the situation. He certainly doesn't mean we just would throw everybody out. [Emphasis added.]

Wilson persisted, "If I read his speech correctly—in fact, that is what he said exactly." No doubt Taft was referring to the possibility that lack of cooperation by the *Chinese* could force the United States to withdraw from negotiations, Eisenhower speculated. Yes, Wilson replied, but he took Taft's position to be that disagreement between the United States and Great Britain might also be cause for withdrawing.

EISENHOWER: There is something confusing here. I don't believe I had better answer it. I don't understand what could be meant by such a thing. Look—suppose all of us here are friends, and we are trying to get somebody out on the street to agree to something and he disagrees, does that mean we all suddenly here become enemies and break up? I don't understand that!

Straining for precision, Wilson received permission to read directly from Taft's speech, which contained the blanket assertion, "I think we should do our best now to negotiate this truce, and if we fail, then let England and our other allies know that we are withdrawing from all further peace negotiations in Korea." Eisenhower again offered an interpretation of Taft's meaning: it might be that the United States *and* its allies would at some point agree that the negotiations had become fruitless and withdraw from them. "As I say," Eisenhower concluded, "there is some idea there that I am not grasping, and I don't think it is fair to ask me to try to comment on it when I don't."

Eisenhower relentlessly refused to grasp an idea that would force him to disagree publicly with Taft. Later in the news conference when Texas newspaperwoman Sarah McClendon asked if he would read Taft's speech in detail and comment, he replied, "If I had to read all the speeches that are in the papers in detail, I would be pretty badly off," thus terminating the discussion and, as usual, fostering his "above the fray" appearance.

★   ★   ★

World War II presented Eisenhower with a classic leadership dilemma: how to maximize the effectiveness of subordinates who have some personal qualities that make them well suited for the tasks that need to be performed, but who also have flaws that can undermine their performance. The man who was in the best position to evaluate Eisenhower's wartime leadership, European command Chief of Staff General W. Bedell Smith, once described how Eisenhower dealt with this complication by assessing each subordinate's qualities in terms of assets and liabilities and shaping his job so that it exploited the former and minimized the impact of the latter. Smith explained that Eisenhower

> considers his commanders and senior staff officers the tools with which he works and he uses them in accordance with their particular capacity. For example, General Patton, the typical cavalryman with all the ideals and traditions of mobile action and with the dash and flamboyancy of a Custer, was invariably selected as the commander of forces engaged in wide maneuver aggressive action and deep penetration which required great initiative, boldness and a certain disregard of consequences. Other commanders with slightly different qualifications were used on equally important, though less conspicuous assignments which were in keeping with their temperaments.

Personality assessment was virtually a reflexive act for Eisenhower. This propensity is most extensively documented during the war years, when he kept up a regular flow of letters to his immediate superior, General George Marshall, explaining his thinking and actions. The comments on Patton alone are voluminous: For example,

> I doubt that I would ever consider Patton for an army group commander or for any higher position, but as an army commander under

a man who is sound and solid, and who has enough sense to use Patton's good qualities without becoming blinded by his love of showmanship and histrionics, he should do as fine a job as he did in Sicily.

Of the problems of Patton's predecessor as II Corps Commander, General Lloyd R. Fredendall, Eisenhower reflected (shortly before returning him to the United States to command a training unit):

Fredendall . . . is tops—except for one thing. He has difficulty in picking good men and, even worse, in getting the best out of subordinates. . . . I must either find a good substitute for Fredendall or must place in his command a number of assistants who are so stable and sound they will not be disturbed by his idiosyncracies.

Without a Marshall to report to while president, examples of Eisenhower's use of personality analysis in determining how to respond to people and how to employ them tend to be preserved only in fragmentary form. These include his diary notes on Taft; a comment warning his press aide Hagerty that it would be difficult to persuade Agriculture Secretary Ezra Taft Benson to retract an error because he is a "stubborn man and I don't suppose we can get him to do that"; and his warning to the Republican party chairman to be "very, very gentle" with Nixon in discussing his political ambitions.

Nevertheless, from time to time during his presidency Eisenhower devoted a full communication to a personality analysis and how he wanted his associates to act on it. An illustration is his instruction to Dulles that John Sherman Cooper, the new ambassador to India, should "do everything possible to win the personal confidence and friendship" of Prime Minister Nehru because of "the amount of evidence we have that Nehru seems to be often more swayed by personality than by logical argument." Cooper, he stressed, should be protected from any "chores . . . that would almost compel him to show an unsympathetic attitude toward the Premier," on the grounds that if Cooper pursued the "one single *general* objective" of winning over Nehru personally, "that could possibly pay off in big terms" (Eisenhower's emphasis).

In congressional relations, because the committee and leadership way stations are controlled by semiautonomous individuals, each with his own idiosyncracies, personality analysis played a particularly key role. Personal relations based as much on art as spontaneity, for example, were crucial in Eisenhower's establishment of unexpectedly amiable relations with Taft. During the period from which the earlier statement on Taft was made, Eisenhower regularly consulted with him, even insisting that the majority leader feel free to enter the Oval Office unannounced.

Eisenhower's sensitivity to personalities enabled him to identify and therefore bypass blocks in his channels for influencing Congress. One frequent block was Taft's successor as Senate Republican leader, William F. Knowland. Eisenhower recorded in a diary reflection on how great a loss Taft's death in the summer of 1953 had been: "Knowland means to be helpful and loyal, but he is cumbersome. He does not have the sharp mind and the great experience that Taft did. Consequently, he does not command the respect in the Senate that Taft enjoyed." He was regularly irritated by Knowland's simplistic views as well as clumsy leadership. (He told a friend that "Knowland has no foreign policy except to develop high blood pressure whenever he mentions the words 'Red China.'") But he successfully concealed his distaste from Knowland, who in his Columbia Oral History interview made only the conventional observations that Eisenhower was a nonpolitical leader, "sincere" and "without guile."

A week before Taft's death, Eisenhower had made an arrangement intended to circumvent a cumbersome Senate party leader. After a breakfast meeting with Senator Everett Dirksen, Eisenhower recorded that

> I asked him to be "verbal leader" of the middle-of-the-road philosophy (my philosophy) in the Senate. Regardless of the formal leadership, he would be the man to take on all attackers, the champion who would put on armor and get on the white horse and take on the fight.

Dirksen could be especially useful as an ally because his widely publicized tirade against Eisenhower's nomination at the 1952 convention had established his *bona fides* with conservative Republicans. When a strong Taft backer spoke out for Eisenhower's policies, it was persuasive testimony to his congressional colleagues that the administration was acting in a way that was consistent with the principles of the man who had personified traditional Republican principles. On the House side, Eisenhower also established an informal working relationship with a leader he had sized up as being more effective than the aging official party head, Joseph Martin. His choice was the second-ranking Republican, Indiana Congressman Charles Halleck, who in Eisenhower's diary is warmly described as a selfless, "highly intelligent and mentally alert . . . team player."

Eisenhower's analyses of the personalities of members of his official family also were of the greatest importance, particularly in determining the extent and nature of the authority he delegated to subordinates. The thumbnail sketches he made in his private diary four months after taking office of two occupants of major cabinet posts, the secretary of state and the secretary of defense, not only illustrate his characterizations of subordinates but also provide insight into his practice of selective delegation.

Of John Foster Dulles, Eisenhower wrote,

> I still think of him, as I always have, as an intensive student of foreign affairs. He is well informed and, in this subject at least, is deserving, I think of his reputation as a "wise" man. . . . [But] he is not particularly persuasive in presentation and, at times, seems to have a curious lack of understanding as to how his words and manner may affect another personality.

Of Charles Wilson, whose confirmation hearings had been flawed by the first of many verbal faux pas, he observed, "Mr. Wilson is prone to lecture, rather than to answer, when asked a question. This not only annoys many members of Congress, but it gives them unlooked for opportunities to discover flaws in reasoning and argument." But neither man's defects incapacitated him from Eisenhower's standpoint, because he was able to devise ways to use their strengths and neutralize their weaknesses.

★   ★   ★

Eisenhower's wartime experience of commanding a vast intricate organization and his extensive staff experience in the army, an institution with an explicitly elaborate organizational structure, undoubtedly account for the self-consciousness and subtlety with which he approached delegation of authority. First, he was highly attentive to the general need for delegation, if the head of a complex organization is not to be inundated with details. Secondly, he took care not to delegate in a fashion that would dilute his own ability to keep the actions of his associates in line with his own policies, adjusting the degree of his supervision both to the abilities of his associates and to the extent he believed his own participation in a policy area was necessary. Finally, he was highly sensitive to a side effect of delegation, that of sharing credit with subordinates for popular policies, but also (especially important for a president who emphasized his role as chief of state) diffusing blame for unpopular policies throughout the administration rather than allowing himself as chief executive to be the main recipient of blame.

Taking stock of the leadership principles he had practiced and commenting on a *Life* editorial praising his presidency but asking whether he had sometimes been "too easy a boss," Eisenhower stated his view on the general need to delegate in a 1960 letter to Henry Luce. Eisenhower's comments were straightforward extensions of his prepresidential administrative rhetoric and action, exemplified both by his tribute in *Crusade in Europe* to General Marshall's advancement of subordinates who had the capacity to make decisions without constantly referring back to higher authority, and the instruction he gave to his principal aides in June 1942 on assuming American command in Europe that they were "free to solve their own problems wherever possible and not to get in the habit of passing the buck up." Eisenhower pointed out to Luce that "the government of the United States has become too big, too complex, and too pervasive in its influence on all our lives for one individual to pretend to direct the details of its important and critical programming. Competent assistants are mandatory: without them the executive branch would bog down."

Moreover, wholehearted support of subordinates could not be won by "desk pounding":

> To command the loyalties and dedication and best efforts of capable and outstanding individuals requires patience, understanding, a readiness to delegate, and an acceptance of responsibility for any honest errors—real or apparent—those associates and subordinates might make. . . . Principal subordinates must have confidence that they and their positions are widely respected, and the chief must do his part in assuring that this is so.

Eisenhower handled delegation selectively to be sure his policies were satisfactorily carried out. One kind of selective delegation he practiced before and during his presidency consisted of assigning a clearly defined mission to an able subordinate who, in effect, would become more of a deputy than a delegate. The deputy approach is one that Eisenhower used with his first Budget Bureau director, Joseph Dodge. Eisenhower admired Dodge greatly but also had well-developed personal views about how to reshape the budgetary legacy of the Truman administration. Therefore, he sought to establish precise guidelines for Dodge so that when the budget director made decisions, Dodge in effect would be a simple extension of Eisenhower in dealing with the inevitable departmental appeals that follow reductions in budget requests. As Eisenhower wrote to Dodge in 1954,

> It is essential that we understand each other very clearly, because necessarily you must act as my authoritative agent in working on these problems. While, of course, each Department head always has direct access to me, I think it vastly important that if any appeal from your decisions is made, that you must be present at the time—and even more important that you and I approach these problems so definitely from the same viewpoint that the occasions for such appeals will be minimized.

Robert Anderson, as we may infer from Eisenhower's willingness to support him as a successor, also fell in the category of a deeply respected subordinate. During the time he was Treasury secretary, beginning in 1957, Anderson was used as a delegate rather than a deputy and presided over issues of great complexity about which Eisenhower was not minutely informed; he felt as though Eisenhower had given him virtual carte blanche. Anderson, who was also closely associated with Lyndon Johnson during his presidency, compares the two presidents:

> President Eisenhower's background in history was a military one. He came up through all of his life in the atmosphere of having staffs, delegating large amounts of responsibility, assuming large responsibility delegated to him, but having a very tight staff operation. For example, when I was in the Treasury, I have no recollection of the President ever calling me to suggest a policy or anything of the sort. It was always the other way around. . . . On the other hand . . . President Johnson . . . grew up as a congressman. . . . He was not surrounded by either large staffs or where he could say, "I'm going to delegate these responsibilities," because *he* was the congressman, *he* was the senator, *he* was the majority leader. . . . So I think, in President Johnson's administration, there was more of a personalized presidency, a president who by his very nature became more involved in more details, in more operations, and in more procedural matters, than in the days of President Eisenhower.

Not all of Eisenhower's subordinates, however, were extended the same freedom of action that Anderson enjoyed. Although some were left largely to their own devices, others would periodically experience Eisenhower's direct intervention in their activities. As one might expect both from Eisenhower's expert knowledge of national security issues and from his private characterization of Charles Wilson, the first Eisenhower defense secretary had little policy-making leeway. Much of the time Eisenhower treated Wilson neither as a deputy nor as a delegate, but rather as little more than an expediter of detailed presidential instructions.

In his diary entry on the former General Motors chief, Eisenhower observed: "In his field, he is a really competent man. He is careful and positive, and I have no slightest doubt that, assisted by the team of civilian and military men he has selected, he will produce the maximum security for this country at minimum or near minimum cost." The last six words indicate the principal reason the top executive of the nation's largest corporation had been chosen for the Defense Department. Eisenhower did not need a military expert to head a department he knew inside out and to determine overall policy: in this sphere, the president's own background and skills scarcely could be equaled. Thus, following the approach described by Bedell Smith, the "tool" Eisenhower chose to head the largest government department was a man with a record for efficiently managing the nation's largest corporation. Wilson's duties, however, were limited mainly to internal management—making the department function in a businesslike manner—while Eisenhower and those closest to him in the national security policymaking community were responsible for establishing defense policy.

Eisenhower is often quoted as having expressed impatience at Wilson's proclivity to bring problems to the White House that might have been settled by Wilson himself: "Charlie, you run defense. We both can't do it, and I won't do it. I was elected to worry about a lot of other things than the day-to-day operations of a department." It may be true that Eisenhower had to press Wilson to be more independent in the managerial aspects of Defense Department leadership, but it is clear that on major policy issues—ranging from levels of funding to overall strategic stance—Eisenhower personally made defense policy and in doing so entered deeply into organizational and managerial issues. The Eisenhower Library files contain countless communications to Wilson. They commonly are in the form of directives, often defining in minute detail a Defense Department policy, as when, on November 30, 1953, he expressed "shock" at recently having received information "that we now have a proportion of general and flag officers in the Services approximately three times as great as it was in the wartime year of 1944."

The ratio of colonels and captains to overall service strength likewise appears high. This level of rank must also be considered in the executive or overhead category since there are far more captains in the Navy than there are ships and far more colonels in the Army than there are regiments. I am told that the present proportion of colonels and captains in the Armed Services is approximately four times what it was during 1944.

Noting that if the statistics he cited were incorrect he should be informed, Eisenhower pointed out that although personnel costs were small "compared with the gigantic sums involved in the procurement of equipment . . . nevertheless these examples are extremely important as symbols."

Please take a good look at the manning situation in these higher ranks. I'd like to talk to you further about the matter because I'm seriously considering the adoption of an executive policy of limiting nominations in the higher grades to a percentage of those legally authorized.

Considerably more important than Eisenhower's close attention to the ratios of officers in varying ranks, however, were his communications explicitly enunciating major strategic policies in his capacity as commander in chief. On December 21, 1955, for example, after policies concerning ballistic missiles had been promulgated in the National Security Council (NSC) and listed in the actions of the December 1 NSC meeting, Eisenhower sent Wilson a memorandum simply announcing that he had, on further consideration, amended the Record of Action to include an additional item in which the NSC

noted the President's statement that the political and psychological impact upon the world of the early development of an effective ballistic missile with a range in the 1,000–1,700 mile range would be so great that the early development of such a missile would be of critical importance to the national security interests of the United States

and another item stating that

the President directed that the IRBM [Intermediate Range Missiles] and ICBM [Intercontinental Range Missiles] programs should both be research and development programs of the highest priority above others. Mutual interference between these programs should be avoided so

far as practicable, but if a conflict should occur . . . [which] would in
the opinion of the Secretary of Defense, cause major damage to the security interests of the United States, then the matter will be promptly
referred to the President.

The mere ministerial function sometimes played by Wilson as
head of a major cabinet department is perhaps best conveyed in the
language Eisenhower used in informing NSC staff chief Robert Cutler in 1953 of the steps that would be taken to carry out the strategic
and budgetary planning for implementing the New Look—if possible in time for the 1955 budget. Enumerating with his customary
planner's logic a six-step sequence of what should be done, Eisenhower simply began the memorandum by saying, "I *instructed* Mr.
Wilson as follows on the budget matters" (emphasis added).

. . .

Eisenhower delegated substantial power to Secretary of State Dulles,
but with Dulles, as with no other cabinet member, he entered into a
collegial working relationship. Although most accounts of United
States foreign policy between 1953 and 1958 take it for granted that
Dulles was the senior colleague, the reverse was true. The two men
were in daily touch even when Dulles was out of the country on his
many missions as presidential emissary. If they could not talk by telephone because Dulles was overseas, they exchanged coded cables.
Eisenhower often accepted Dulles's advice. They jointly perfected
policies, but Eisenhower made the final decisions and Dulles executed them.

This is firmly documented, as Richard Immerman has shown, by
the record of personal communication between the two—including
telephone conversation transcripts and memoranda—and by the reports of those aides who personally observed them at work. Their response to the downing of a British plane and two American search
planes off Hainan in June 1954 illustrates the dynamics of the collaboration. Dulles, on learning of these events, called the White House.
Eisenhower asked Dulles how he suggested handling the matter.
Dulles's reply was that if the president approved, he would issue "a

protest against further barbarities in attempting to shoot down rescue-type planes." Eisenhower not only already knew of the incident but also had already discussed making a protest with the congressional leaders, who agreed that this should be done. He told Dulles he had asked the leaders to keep the information secret until there had been consultation within the administration and instructed him to send a message to British Foreign Secretary Anthony Eden urging that the British simultaneously release a strong statement. This would increase the impact of the American statement and avoid possible Anglo-American friction. Dulles agreed with this tactic. The two concluded that Dulles, after clearing the policy with Eden, would make the public statement and Eisenhower would delay any comments of his own.

This episode reveals genuine consultation. It also shows that before hearing from Dulles, Eisenhower had already established a course of diplomatic action. Moreover, Eisenhower determined the tactic that was pursued, but Dulles, in implementing Eisenhower's instructions, was the publicly visible actor.

A number of Eisenhower's practices inadvertently or deliberately fostered the impression that Dulles had nearly complete autonomy in making foreign policy and that he was the more skilled and informed of the two with respect to foreign affairs. Much of the detailed content of foreign policy was announced in Dulles's Tuesday press conferences. Eisenhower, who met the press on Wednesdays, explained foreign policy in broad, colloquially stated common-sense terms. He referred questioners to Dulles's remarks of the previous day for elaboration. In fact, however, Dulles's utterances had been cleared in detail with Eisenhower in the course of intense consultation. And if they strayed from Eisenhower's views, Eisenhower "reinterpreted" them in his own Wednesday meetings with the press.

Eisenhower felt so strongly that Dulles should be recognized as an authoritative spokesman of the administration that on one occasion he arranged to take the blame for a Dulles slipup in diplomatic practice. He recounts the event in his diary. He discovered the error in a February 1953 meeting with the retiring ambassador to the Court of St. James, "my good friend, Walter Gifford."

While Eisenhower was still at Supreme Headquarters Allied Powers Europe (SHAPE), he had learned of Gifford's plan to retire as soon as the next administration was in office.

> With this knowledge, I of course was interested in the task of selecting a completely acceptable and useful successor. We started this job shortly after election in early November and it was not long before we determined that all things considered Winthrop Aldrich would be our best bet. This selection was made on the most confidential basis, but to our consternation it was soon public knowledge.

Because Dulles felt the situation embarrassing, he believed a public explanation was in order. Eisenhower authorized him to do this but "put in my word of caution that Walter Gifford would have to be protected and in every possible way."

In the haste to act quickly, Gifford's planned resignation and Aldrich's intended appointment were announced promptly, without clearing the matter with the British. Eisenhower continues:

> This upset the British government very badly—and I must say most understandably. As Anthony Eden pointed out in his informal protest to Walter Gifford, this meant that Britain was being subjected to pretty rough treatment when there was no effort made to get the usual "agreement." He said that with this precedent, any small nation could pursue the same tactics and if Britain should protest, they could argue that since the United States had done this and Britain had accepted it, no real objection could be made. . . . To guard against any such development as this, I am going to advise Anthony, when I see him next month, to lay the blame for this whole unfortunate occurrence squarely on me. He will have the logical explanation that my lack of formal experience in the political world was the reason for the blunder. Actually, I was the one who cautioned against anything like this happening, but manifestly I can take the blame without hurting anything or anybody, whereas if the Secretary of State would have to shoulder it, his position would be badly damaged.

Eisenhower's private communications to Dulles about policy—in contrast to his public rhetoric, which was more broadly humanitarian than Dulles's—also contradict the standard view that Eisenhower was the more conciliatory of the two men. In a March 1958 memorandum, for example, Eisenhower warned Dulles of a "potentially dangerous" situation.

> This is the credence, even respect, that the world is beginning to give ... spurious Soviet protestations and pronouncements. As their propaganda promotes this world confusion the tone of Soviet notes and statements grows more strident. The more the men in the Kremlin come to believe that their domestic propaganda is swallowed by their own people and the populations of other countries, including some we have counted upon as allies, the greater the risk of American isolation.... I personally believe that one of the main objectives of our own efforts should be to encourage our entire people to see, with clear eyes, the changing character of our difficulties and to convince them that we must be vigilant, energetic, imaginative and incapable of surrender through fatigue or lack of courage.

Eisenhower, then, was not more accommodating to the Soviet Union than was Dulles. Nevertheless, Eisenhower recognized that Dulles's demeanor and mode of expression conveyed an impression of harshness and intractability. His 1953 comment that Dulles "is not particularly persuasive in presentation and, at times, seems to have a curious lack of understanding as to how his words and manner may affect another personality" was paralleled by a remark he made to Goodpaster in January 1958: "I sense a difference with Foster Dulles.... His is a lawyer's mind," and he tends to proceed like "a sort of international prosecuting attorney," indicting the Soviet Union for its policies and actions. Eisenhower preferred to present the American position more positively: "Of course, we have got to have a concern and respect for fact and reiteration of official position, but [we] are likewise trying to 'seek friends and influence people.'" In these remarks Eisenhower seems explicitly to have accepted the implicit division of labor in his and Dulles's public utterances. Dulles appeared to be the austere cold warrior, Eisenhower, the warm champion of peace. It was Dulles who issued the bulk of the "get tough" foreign policy statements (placating domestic anti-Communists as well as presenting a firm international position), while amiable Ike could be more effective in his gestures towards international humanitarianism and détente—for example, Atoms for Peace, Open Skies, goodwill trips, and summitry.

The difference in the public images conveyed by Eisenhower and Dulles raises the general issue of how credit and blame were shared in Eisenhower's practice of selective delegation. Stephen Hess views Eisenhower's delegations of authority as an "artfully constructed . . . elaborate maze of buffer zones," adding that "Eisenhower gave himself considerable freedom of action by giving his subordinates considerable leeway to act." The image of a "lightning rod" captures Hess's point even better than "buffer zone."

Dulles was only one object of animosity that in another presidency would have been directed toward the chief executive. Other Eisenhower associates performed the same function—consciously or unconsciously—in their own spheres. Farmers who were rankled by the moves toward decreasing subsidization of agriculture blamed the zealous Mormon elder, Ezra Taft Benson, who served as agriculture secretary for eight years—not Eisenhower. Many of the inevitable irritations produced by White House nay-saying found their target in the staff chief, Sherman Adams. There is no evidence that Eisenhower chose these people because they would be ready targets for critics. Adams and Dulles in fact were succeeded by men of gentle personality. Nevertheless, Eisenhower's underlining in the following passage describing Lyndon Johnson's presidential style in Arthur Krock's memoirs, shows his awareness of how a subordinate's tendency to garner criticism could protect his leader's public support:

Partly because of his incessant ubiquity, Johnson, as much as any president in our history, has closely identified himself and his office with the disasters, foreign and domestic, economic and social, into which the United States has become more and more deeply involved in his time. This . . . is to a considerable degree the consequence of his innate trait of craftiness. But it also is the product of an evasive or soaring loquacity which induces him to utter and write paragraphs when sentences would cover the point or event, and to allow his promises to run far beyond the clear limits of attainment. *Another source of this close identification with all acts, policies and thorny situations is a passion to control every function of government, though subordinates are always available in profusion to take the gaff,* or, without diminishing him, the credit. (Eisenhower's underlining)

The strong personal loyalty engendered in Eisenhower's team players accounted for their willingness to accept criticism for policies that were in fact the president's and that did not arise from their own delegated authority. As James Hagerty recollected,

> President Eisenhower would say, "Do it this way." I would say, "If I go to that press conference and say what you want me to say, I would get hell." With that he would smile, get up and walk around the desk, pat me on the back and say, "My boy, better you than me."

★   ★   ★

In examining Eisenhower's strategies it is no surprise to find him underscoring Arthur Krock's diagnosis that Lyndon Johnson's presidency had ended so painfully because Johnson dissipated public support, among other ways, by identifying "himself and his office with . . . disasters" and "with all acts, policies and thorny situations" despite the availability of subordinates "to take the gaff." In his own presidency, Eisenhower had been helped by gaff-taking subordinates and had even occasionally simulated acts of delegation to deflect controversy. More generally, by keeping the controversial political side of the presidential role largely covert (without, however, abdicating it) and casting himself as an uncontroversial head of state, he maintained an extraordinary level of public support.

This high level is well known: his 64 percent average approval rate in the Gallup polls throughout his eight years; always more approval than disapproval in the monthly Gallup polls asking, "How good a job do you think President X is doing?"; and his two landslide elections. The nature of this support—why people liked him—is less precisely documented. One valuable source of evidence, however, is available in the reports that citizens gave of why they liked or disliked each candidate in the pioneering 1952 and 1956 electoral surveys conducted by Angus Campbell and his University of Michigan associates.

In 1952 Eisenhower, who had been wooed by both parties since World War II because of a powerful public appeal that regularly put him at or near the top of Gallup's annual "most admired American" poll, was mentioned far more often for his human qualities (for example, warmth and sincerity) than for his experience, beliefs, or leadership skills. In 1956, after four years of acquiring governing experience and giving the public an opportunity to reach conclusions about the merits (or lack thereof) of his policies and skills, he was again mentioned more often for what he was as a person than for what he had done or could do as a president. But there was a difference between public responses to him in the 1952 and 1956 polls that puzzled the Michigan voting analysts: references to why Eisenhower was liked were even *more* lopsidedly personal and less political and governmental in 1956 than in 1952. While this difference might have seemed to belie common sense, we can readily see that it follows from his leadership style of refusing to be identified with "disasters" and "thorny situations."

Partisan Democrats would have had less difficulty explaining the findings than did the studiously nonpartisan University of Michigan scholars. They would readily have granted that Eisenhower had maintained his popularity by accentuating the chief of state role. Liberal columnist Marquis Childs, for example, described him as a "captive hero," a term borrowed from an ancient practice in which the powers that be in a country legitimized their political control by capturing a king who served as a reassuring but impotent figurehead.

As we have seen, Eisenhower *did* exercise political leadership. If his economics tended to be laissez-faire, his politics were decidedly though covertly interventionist. Much of his intervention, however, was geared to preventing conflicts before they occurred, or resolving them without associating the mechanics of their resolution with the president and presidency. One example of Eisenhower's hidden-hand interventions bears directly on why it was possible for him to remain popular and to accentuate his apolitical image while in office: the 1953 leak directed to the Chinese Communists to stimulate them to reach a truce agreement. An Eisenhower who was still presiding over a stalemated war of attrition in Korea would neither have been popular nor viewed so often as "good" on purely personal grounds.

. . .

Apart from maintaining support by quietly eliminating irritants that eventually would have tarnished his popularity, Eisenhower was intensely preoccupied with and worked intensely at "public relations," a phrase he used freely to describe actions not only during his nominating campaign and presidency but also during his prepresidential years.

Eisenhower's personal qualities became a staple for journalists virtually as soon as he assumed the European command in 1942. He promptly began to receive mention as a potential candidate for public office, a prospect he was quick to deprecate whenever friends mentioned it. Yet he could not escape awareness of his growing visibility, popularity, and reputation for refreshing informality and openness. Shortly after the invasion of North Africa in the fall of 1942, his portrait appeared on the cover of *Time*. Increasingly, journalists portrayed "Ike Eisenhower" as tough as nails, but delightfully warm; determined to win, but impatient with martial postures; and a modest, all-American leader. In spite of his assertions that he did not want to call personal attention to himself and his policy of encouraging press coverage of his subordinates, laudatory reports of him seemed perversely to increase rather than diminish. Moreover, though he made light of his personal popularity, he also acknowledged that he needed it to carry out his military leadership.

The Eisenhower who disclaims an interest in being publicized, but nevertheless makes it clear that his modus operandi brings him press attention, which he uses in his leadership, is evident in the wartime years. Eisenhower expresses these contradictions in a 1944 letter to his brother Edgar:

To the extent possible in a position such as mine, I have constantly shunned the headlines. This has not been entirely due merely to a sense of modesty, but because of the nature of an Allied Command. Any "glory grabbing" on the part of the top man would quickly wreck an institution such as this. Happily the official requirement has coincided exactly with my personal desire.

At this point, however, his observations undergo a seemingly uncharacteristic derailment. His efforts had *not* kept him out of the headlines. Rather,

one result is that, almost without exception, the 500 newspaper and radio men accredited to this organization are my friends. Quite frequently they seem to be moved by a desire to see that I get "full credit" and so they write special articles and even books.

Journalists, he explains to Edgar, will

eventually turn upon a man who shows any indication of courting them in his own self interest, no matter how "colorful" they may deem him at first. What I am trying to say is that some publicity is mandatory—otherwise, American soldiers would not know they had an American commander, interested in their welfare. The problem is to take it and use it in the amount required by the job; but to avoid distortion and self-glorification.

The importance of publicity used appropriately did not dawn on Eisenhower as late in the war as 1944. On taking his assignment in Europe, Eisenhower arranged that Columbia Broadcasting System executive Harry Butcher be assigned to his headquarters as naval aide. There was no pretense that Butcher, who was in constant touch with the press corps, would have nautical obligations. Butcher even helped prepare the draft of a letter rejecting a suggestion that Eisenhower should appoint a press relations officer to "humanize" himself. "My habit," the letter read, "is to keep my name out of the papers," but there was his usual qualification: personal publicity was acceptable "when military or public relations dictate that I should speak."

Professional public relations men were among the first civilians to gather in the loyal network of businessmen that formed around Eisenhower and participated actively in drafting him to run for the presidency. Notable among them were William E. Robinson, who, after years as an advertising and sales executive at the *New York Herald Tribune,* went on to head his own public relations firm, and Sigurd S. Larmon of Young & Rubicam. When Eisenhower acceded to a presidential candidacy, his campaign for nomination and election made innovative use of spot radio and television commercials. He and his associates also made a consistent effort to improve his ability to "come across" to the American people. His whistle-stop campaign covered more miles than Adlai Stevenson's. And he flexibly experimented with prepared and outlined speeches delivered informally from notes, submitting himself to the guidance of professionals. He used actor and television producer Robert Montgomery to advise him on the mechanics of delivering speeches and experimenting with other ways of reaching the public.

Eisenhower prepared his speeches with an understanding of his public image and endeavored to enhance and maintain it. As president of Columbia University, he had been carefully briefed on the specific content of his admirers' images of him. In 1948 he received 20,000 letters, virtually all urging him to run for president that year. In the summer of 1949 Eisenhower turned these over to the prominent Columbia sociologist, Robert Merton, for analysis by the university's Bureau of Applied Social Research. The bureau report revealed that the letter writers admired Eisenhower for his sincerity and humanity and viewed him as a general who had demonstrated great military competence but who was nonmilitaristic and therefore well suited for civil leadership. Many writers stressed simply that they would be comforted to know he was president, and others talked about him as a "born leader" in terms that led Merton to advise Eisenhower that he fit the classic definition of a charismatic leader. Merton went over the report "with the General almost line by line in two or three sessions," during which Eisenhower evinced keen interest in the findings.

Many of Eisenhower's presidential utterances directly play on the public image of the military hero who is a soldier of peace. On one oc-

casion he compared the primitive rifle in use when he was a lieutenant before America's entry in World War I with the devastating
weapons that had emerged from World War II in order to dramatize
the overriding urgency of avoiding nuclear war. He went on, using
the homely language of a sincere, humane soldier of peace, to reassure
his audience. Granting that the problems of nuclear stalemate have
no "easy answer" and that many contemporary problems "have no
answer at all, at least in the complete sense," he compared the government's responsibility of "doing our best" with "what the ordinary
American family does."

> It has the problems of meeting the payments on the mortgage, paying
> for the family car, educating the children, laying aside some money for
> use in case of unexpected illness. It meets these problems courageously.
> It doesn't get panicky. It solves these problems with what I would call
> courage and faith, but above all by cooperation, by discussing the
> problem among the different members of the family and then saying:
> this is what we can do, this is what we will do, and reaching a satisfac-
> tory answer.

These homilies served to introduce a plain speaking but thoughtful
exposition of the basic lines of foreign and domestic policy, including
warnings against excessive fears of internal Communist subversion
and a penultimate pitch for his legislative program. His concluding
remarks voiced the sturdy patriotism and piety of a turn-of-the-
century Midwestern family, using a figure of speech that echoed the
daily Bible readings of his own childhood:

> I don't mean to say, and no one can say to you, that there are no dan-
> gers. Of course there are risks, if we are not vigilant. But we do not
> have to be hysterical. We can be vigilant. We can be Americans. We
> can stand up and hold up our heads and say: America is the greatest
> force that God has ever allowed to exist on his footstool.

None of this was calculated to appeal to an Adlai Stevenson
egghead supporter, but this was not "the man we are trying to reach."

The 1956 University of Michigan Survey Research Center election study tabulates reports of the number of people interviewed who mentioned the speaking style of the two candidates. While more people mentioned the rhetoric-loving Stevenson, a substantial majority of references to his style were unfavorable ("too high fallutin"), and the fewer references to Eisenhower's style were predominantly positive.

Eisenhower's press conferences consistently reinforced the 1948 letters' characterization of him—sincere, warm, and the distinguished general who always worked for peace. The unpretentiousness of his give-and-take with reporters and his seemingly offhanded reassuring references to his prepresidential experiences are illustrated in this exchange.

Q: Mr. President, there has been some recent interest in the subject of dependents of our military men joining them overseas, sometimes in potential trouble spots around the world; and I wondered if you, as an old soldier, shall we say, believe—[laughter].

THE PRESIDENT: Make no mistake. I am proud of the title [laughter].

Q: It is the "old" I was questioning—[laughter]—believe that there is a military asset in having the wives and children of the servicemen with them overseas: and in the event of a sudden enemy attack, what would their presence mean?

THE PRESIDENT: Of course, to take your last part first, if there is a sudden enemy attack, their presence would cause very acute problems. But let us not forget this: we are in a cold war; we want to present our best foot, let us say; we want people of high morale; we want to look confident.

If every place we sent our soldiers in the world we broke our old custom of letting dependents go along, it would look like we were frightened to death and expecting an attack momentarily.

Some of you here probably may have been in Europe in January 1951, when I went over there; and you will recall, possibly, also that my wife went with me. The tension was so great at that moment— and you may have forgotten—the tension was so great that a few, 2 or 3 months later the head of one of the principal travel agencies of the United States came to me and said that the mere fact that my wife went over there, took a season where there was going to be no travel at all and made it one of the finest travel seasons of their whole career. In other words, the showing of confidence on the part of the leaders and people of a nation—as long as it is not truculent, if you are not being, you might say, bombastic and truculent and ill-mannered—I think that such things as that really encourage confidence.

Whatever intellectuals may have thought of such remarks, they were unquestionably reassuring to the bulk of citizens. After, as before, taking office, Eisenhower's seemingly effortless facility in winning public confidence never stopped him from also working to find additional ways to enhance his support. This accounts for the great care he took in preparing speeches, planning campaigns, and working at the task of exhibiting the buoyant, optimistic side of his personality. Nor did he let his team approach to leadership vitiate his attention to maintaining personal support. He was fully aware that his popularity was essential to his ability to exercise influence over other leaders. As he once noted, "one man can do a lot . . . he can especially do a lot at any particular given moment, if at that moment he happens to be ranking high in public estimation. By this I mean he is dwelling in the ivory tower and not in the dog house."

Excerpted from Fred Greenstein, *The Hidden-Hand Presidency: Eisenhower as Leader* (New York: Basic Books, 1982), pgs. 57–63, 66–70, 73–85, 87–99.

IKE REVISIONISM REVISED

Arthur M. Schlesinger, Jr.

Martin Van Buren, John Randolph of Roanoke once said, "rowed to his object with muffled oars." Phrased less elegantly, this is Fred I. Greenstein's thesis in his influential study of Eisenhower's administrative techniques. Greenstein ascribes six "political strategies" to Eisenhower—"hidden-hand" leadership; "instrumental"—i.e., manipulative—use of language; refusal to engage in personalities; taking action nevertheless on the basis of private personality analysis; selective delegation; and building public support. While the author concedes that these strategies were hardly exclusive to Eisenhower, the loving care with which they are described gives the impression of attributing uniquely to Eisenhower practices that are the stock in trade of political leaders. Thus: "Eisenhower ran organizations by deliberately making simultaneous use of both formal and informal organizations." What president does not?

I do not think that Greenstein fully considers the implications of a "hidden-hand presidency." For in a democracy, politics must be in the end an educational process, resting above all on persuasion and consent. The presidency, in Franklin D. Roosevelt's words, is "preeminently a place of moral leadership." The hidden-hand presidency represents an abdication of the preeminent presidential role. The concept is even a little unjust to Eisenhower, who was not entirely averse to using the presidency as a pulpit.

On the whole, however, as his political confidant Arthur Larson later wrote, "He simply did not believe that the President should exploit his influence as a dominant national figure to promote good causes that were not within his constitutional function as Chief Executive." In consequence, Larson regretfully continued, Eisenhower denied the country the "desperately needed . . . educational guidance and moral inspiration that a President with a deep personal commitment to the promotion of human rights could supply." Larson was talking about civil rights. His point applies equally to civil liberties.

Racial justice and McCarthyism were the great moral issues of the Eisenhower years. Eisenhower evaded them both. This may be in part because of his severely constricted theory of the presidency. But it was partly too because Eisenhower did not see them as compelling issues. He did not like to use law to enforce racial integration, and, while he disliked Joseph McCarthy's manners and methods, he basically agreed with his objectives. His failure, as his biographer Stephen E. Ambrose has said, "to speak out directly on McCarthy encouraged the witch-hunters, just as his failure to speak out directly on the *Brown v. Topeka* [school integration] decision encouraged the segregationists." It can be added that Eisenhower's failure to speak out directly on the Pentagon, at least before his Farewell Address, encouraged the advocates of the arms race.

Yet, whatever his defects as a public leader, we may stipulate that the opening of the papers in the Eisenhower Library and the publication of his diaries reveal an Eisenhower who showed more energy, interest, purpose, cunning, and command than many of us understood in the 1950s; that he was the dominant figure in his administration whenever he wanted to be (and he wanted to be more often than it seemed at the time); and that the very talent for self-protection that led him to hide behind his reputation for muddle and to shove associates into the line of fire obscured his considerable capacity for decision and control.

★   ★   ★

To what end was this political cunning devoted beyond survival? Though his brother Milton had worked in the Roosevelt administration, Eisenhower did not like FDR or the New Deal. Harry Truman had offered to help him get the Democratic presidential nomination, but he chose to run as a Republican. The reason, he used to explain, was his desire to redress the balance in the political system—the balance between the executive and legislative branches and the balance between the federal government and the states, both presumably upset during the age of Roosevelt.

This desire was largely frustrated. Indeed, while Eisenhower generally respected the congressional prerogative, in one area he greatly increased the imbalance between the executive and legislative branches. The doctrine of "executive privilege," by which presidents claim the right to withhold information from Congress, received both its name and its most sweeping execution during the Eisenhower years. From June 1955 to June 1960 Eisenhower officials refused information to Congress forty-four times—more times in five years than in the first hundred years of the republic. And in the most critical area where presidents encroach on the constitutional authority of Congress—the war-making power—Eisenhower faithfully preserved the claims of the Imperial Presidency. He never renounced the idea, advanced by Truman when North Korea invaded South Korea, that the president had inherent authority to send troops into major combat without congressional authorization.

Nor was he more successful in redressing the imbalance between Washington and the states. His Commission on Intergovernmental Relations could find only two minor federal programs, costing $80 million, to recommend for transfer to the states. When Eisenhower departed in 1961, the size of the federal government was about what it had been when he was inaugurated in 1953—and the White House staff was a good deal larger.

So was the deficit. In 1959, despite his passion for balanced budgets, Eisenhower produced the largest peacetime deficit up to that time in American history. The favorite, and most prodigal, of his domestic programs was the Interstate Highway Act of 1956. In 1966, when he compiled an inventory of the twenty-three major accomplishments of his administration, he listed the "most ambitious road program by any nation in all history." No administration was more responsive to the business community, but "business confidence" turned out, as so often, to be irrelevant to economic health. The average annual rate of economic growth slowed from 4.3 percent in the last six Truman years to 2.5 percent in the Eisenhower years.

In domestic policy, historians may well regard Eisenhower's Supreme Court appointments as his most distinguished achievement. Four of his five choices—Earl Warren, John M. Harlan, William J. Brennan, and Potter Stewart—were men of preeminent judicial quality. Eisenhower himself, however, thought little of the Warren Court. He later told Ambrose that his biggest mistake was "the appointment of that dumb son of a bitch Earl Warren." Heaven alone knows what he thought about Brennan. The Court appointments did not make the list of major accomplishments. He did put down "First Civil Rights Law in 80 years." But the Civil Rights Act of 1957 was in fact pushed through his administration by the attorney general, Herbert Brownell, without much presidential understanding or encouragement. He would never have sought broad civil rights legislation like the Kennedy-Johnson act of 1964, Larson has written, because he was "skeptical both of the objective itself and of the method of achiev-ing it—that is, by legislative compulsion."

Eisenhower's other domestic achievement was simply to acquiesce in, and thereby to legitimate, the changes Franklin Roosevelt had wrought in American society. He did little to tackle emerging prob-lems of racial justice, of urban decay, of the environment, of resources and energy at a time when these problems were still relatively man-ageable. Like Washington and Jackson, he left behind a testament to the people in the form of a Farewell Address. Here he famously warned against "the acquisition of unwarranted influence ... by the military-industrial complex." The admonition was prescient, but it was a thought inserted by his ghostwriter, the political scientist Mal-colm Moos. It was not a theme of his presidency nor an item on his list of accomplishments.

Eisenhower in fact had little spontaneous interest in domestic af-fairs. He did what duty required. He was, said Larson, "a man for whom the primacy of the problems of peace and war was instinctive, and for whom domestic political questions were an acquired taste."

It is on his handling of the problems of peace and war that Eisen-hower's enhanced reputation rests. Robert A. Divine conveniently sums up the case for "a badly underrated President" in his *Eisenhower and the Cold War* (1981):

> For eight years he kept the United States at peace, adroitly avoiding military involvement in the crises of the 1950s. Six months after taking office, he brought the fighting in Korea to an end; in Indochina, he re-sisted intense pressure to avoid direct American military intervention; in Suez, he courageously aligned the United States against European imperialism while maintaining a staunch posture toward the Soviet Union. He earnestly sought a reduction in Cold War tensions.

Professor Divine draws a particular contrast with his predecessor, claiming that the demands of foreign policy outran Truman's ability and that the result was "overreaction and tragedy for the nation and the world."

. . .

Revisionists exalt Eisenhower not only over his predecessor but over his successor as well, contrasting Eisenhower's conciliatoriness with Kennedy's alleged bellicosity. N. S. Khrushchev, who was perhaps in a better position to judge, offers a different assessment. "If I had to compare the two American presidents with whom I dealt—Eisenhower and Kennedy—" Khrushchev tells us in his memoirs, "the comparison would not be in favor of Eisenhower. . . . I had no cause for regret once Kennedy became president. It quickly became clear he understood better than Eisenhower that an improvement in relations was the only rational course. . . . He impressed me as a better statesman than Eisenhower."

Winston Churchill stands high on the revisionist hit list of Cold War villains. But Churchill knew Eisenhower well and when he heard that Eisenhower had defeated Adlai Stevenson in 1952 told his wartime private secretary John Colville: "For your private ear, I am greatly disturbed. I think this makes war much more probable." After Stalin's death in March 1953, the new Soviet regime signaled in various ways, as in the Austrian treaty negotiations, interest in the relaxation of tensions. Churchill, now prime minister again, rightly or wrongly perceived a major change in Soviet policy. "A new hope," he wrote Eisenhower, "has been created in the unhappy, bewildered world." "If we fail to strive to seize this moment's precious chances," he wrote in a Top Secret minute, "the judgement of future ages would be harsh and just." Churchill was now an old man (seventy-nine), but he had been around, and his thoughts deserved at least as much respect as those of John Foster Dulles. Eisenhower, who had decided that Churchill was gaga, took the Dulles line. Churchill, Colville noted in his diary, was "very disappointed in Eisenhower whom he thinks both weak and stupid."

When Eisenhower and Churchill met in Bermuda in December 1953, Churchill argued that the policy of strength toward the Soviet

Union should be combined with the hand of friendship. "Ike followed," Colville recorded, "with a short, very violent statement in the coarsest terms." As regards the prime minister's belief that there was a new look in Soviet policy, Eisenhower said, "Russia was a woman of the streets and whether her dress was new, or just the old one patched, it was certainly the same whore underneath. America intended to drive her off her present 'beat' into the back streets." Colville wrote: "I doubt if such language has ever before been heard at an international conference. Pained looks all round."

Eisenhower fully accepted the premises of the Cold War. He appointed the high priest of the Cold War as his secretary of state. He allowed Dulles to appease Joe McCarthy, to purge the Foreign Service, to construct a network of military pacts around the globe, and to preach interminably about godless communism and going to the brink and massive retaliation. Lord Salisbury, the quintessential British Tory and a leading figure in the Churchill cabinet, found Eisenhower in 1953 "violently Russophobe, greatly more so than Dulles," and believed him "personally responsible for the policy of useless pinpricks and harassing tactics the U.S. is following against Russia in Europe and the Far East."

Eisenhower's superiority to the other Cold War presidents, revisionists argue, lay not in the premises of policy but in the "prudence" with which he conducted the struggle. It is true that, as a former general, Eisenhower was uniquely equipped among recent presidents to override the national security establishment. Convinced that excessive government spending and deficits would wreck the economy, he kept the defense budget under control. He knew too much about war to send regular troops into combat lightly, especially on unpromising Third World terrain. Perhaps for this as well as for budgetary reasons—nuclear weapons cost less than large conventional forces—he contrived a military posture that made it almost impossible for the United States to fight anything short of nuclear war.

The doctrine of massive retaliation left the United States the choice, when confronted by local aggression in a distant land, of dropping the bomb or doing nothing. Eisenhower's critics feared he would drop the bomb. Most of the time his preference was for doing nothing—not always a bad attitude in foreign affairs. When the Democrats took over in 1961, they briskly increased conventional forces. Their theory was that enlarging the capability to fight limited wars would reduce the risk of nuclear war. The result was the creation of forces that enabled and emboldened us to Americanize the war in Vietnam. Had the Eisenhower all-or-nothing strategy survived, we might have escaped that unmitigated disaster. Or we might have had something far worse.

Eisenhower's budgetary concerns—"a bigger bang for a buck"—and his skepticism about the regular Army and Navy also had their disadvantages. They led him to rely exceptionally, and dangerously, on unconventional forms of coercive power: upon the covert operations of the Central Intelligence Agency, and upon nuclear weapons.

Instead of sending regular forces into combat abroad, Eisenhower silently turned the CIA into the secret army of the executive branch. The CIA, as originally conceived in 1947, was supposed to concentrate on the collection and analysis of intelligence. Covert action began in 1948 under the Truman administration, and there was more of it than Truman later remembered (or knew about?). But it was mostly devoted to supporting friends—socialist and Christian trade unions, Italian Christian Democrats, anti-Stalinist intellectuals—rather than to subverting foes. As Kermit Roosevelt, the CIA operative in Iran, has written about his project of overthrowing the Mossadegh government, "We had, I felt sure, no chance to win approval from the outgoing administration of Truman and Acheson. The new Republicans, however, might be quite different."

Indeed they were. Where Truman had seen Mossadegh as an honest if trying nationalist, Eisenhower saw him as a tool of Moscow. Eisenhower, as Anthony Eden, the British foreign minister, reported to Churchill, "seemed obsessed by the fear of a Communist Iran." The new president promptly gave Kim Roosevelt the green light. In August 1953 the CIA overthrew Mossadegh and restored the shah. (One result of this disruption of indigenous political evolution in Iran was to stir resentments that after festering a quarter century overthrew the Shah in 1979. By that time Washington would have been delighted if it could have had a Mossadegh rather than a Khomeini.)

His thorough and generally approving biographer Stephen E. Ambrose has noted Eisenhower's "penchant for seeing Communists wherever a social reform movement or a struggle for national liberation was under way." He saw Communists next in the reformist Arbenz government in Guatemala. The domino theory was already forming itself in Eisenhower's mind. "My God," he told his cabinet, "just think what it would mean to us if Mexico went Communist!" Exhilarated by success in Iran, the CIA overthrew the Arbenz regime in 1954.

Exhilarated once more, the CIA helped install supposedly proWestern governments in Egypt (1954) and Laos (1959), tried to overthrow the Indonesian government (1958), and organized the expedition of Cuban exiles against Castro (1960). In December 1955 Eisenhower specifically ordered the CIA to "develop underground resistance and facilitate covert and guerrilla preparations . . . to the extent practicable" in the Soviet Union, China, and their satellites; and to "counter any threat of a party or individuals directly or indirectly responsive to Communist control to achieve dominant power in a free-world country."

The CIA evidently construed the verb "counter" in drastic fashion. There are indications that CIA operatives in 1955 blew up the plane on which Chou En-lai was scheduled to fly to the Afro-Asian conference in Bandung, Indonesia. There is no question about later CIA assassination attempts in the Eisenhower years against Castro and against the Congolese leader Patrice Lumumba. There is no evidence, however, that these operations were undertaken with Eisenhower's knowledge or approval. Given the strong evidence that the CIA so often acted on its own, one may well conclude that assassination was another of its private initiatives.

By 1956 the CIA was spending $800 million a year for covert action as against $82 million in 1952. That same year Eisenhower created a President's Board of Consultants on Foreign Intelligence Activities. Its members were private citizens of unimpeachable respectability.

(One was Joseph P. Kennedy, who remarked about the CIA after the Bay of Pigs, "I know that outfit, and I wouldn't pay them a hundred bucks a week.") The Board promptly commissioned Robert A. Lovett and David Bruce to take a look at the CIA's covert action boom.

Lovett had been secretary of defense and undersecretary of state. Bruce had run the Office of Strategic Services in the European Theater of Operations and was a distinguished diplomat. Their report was stern and devastating. Those who made the 1948 decision to start a program of covert action, Lovett and Bruce said, "could not possibly have foreseen the ramifications of the operations which have resulted from it." CIA agents were making mischief around the planet, and "no one, other than those in the CIA immediately concerned with their day to day operation, has any detailed knowledge what is going on." Should not someone in authority, Lovett and Bruce asked, be continuously calculating "the long-range wisdom of activities which have entailed our virtual abandonment of the international 'golden rule,' and which, if successful to the degree claimed for them, are responsible in a great measure for stirring up the turmoil and raising the doubts about us that exist in many countries of the world today?" If we continue on this course, they concluded, "Where will we be tomorrow?"

Where indeed? Eisenhower's faith in covert action produced mindless international meddling that exacerbated the Cold War, angered American allies, and in later years rebounded fiercely against American interests. Moreover, by nourishing and cherishing the CIA more than any president before Reagan had done, Eisenhower released a dangerous virus in American society and life.

We are sensitive these days about the limitless horror of nuclear war. Revisionist historians condemn Truman for his allegedly unrepentant decision to drop the bomb in 1945. In fact, Truman behaved like a man much shaken by the decision. He had directed that the bomb be used "so that military objectives . . . are the target and not women and children," and he was considerably disturbed when he learned that most of those killed at Hiroshima were civilians.

The day after Nagasaki he ordered that further atomic bombing be stopped. He told his cabinet, as Henry Wallace recorded in his diary, that "the thought of wiping out another 100,000 people was too horrible. He didn't like the idea of killing, as he said, 'all those kids.'" After the cabinet meeting he remarked to Wallace that he had had bad headaches every day. Four months later, when the question came up at cabinet as to how many atomic bombs there were, Truman said that he didn't really want to know.

Nor did he press the production of bombs in the next years. The best estimates of the number of bombs stockpiled in early 1948 range from less than six to two dozen. When the secretary of the Army proposed using the bomb to break the Soviet blockade of Berlin, Truman told him, "You have got to understand that this isn't a military weapon. It is used to wipe out women and children and unarmed people, and not for military use. So we have to treat this differently from rifles and cannon and ordinary things like that." At the worst moment of the Korean War, when the Red Chinese were storming down the Korean peninsula, Truman remarked in casual answer to a press conference question that the United States would employ "every weapon" to end the war. But in fact the Joint Chiefs of Staff (though, as always, it had contingency plans) never recommended the use of the bomb, and Truman, as Gregg Herken writes, "consistently refused to be stampeded by the bad news from Korea into a precipitous decision on its use in the Far East." Reflecting about Korea in 1954, Truman wrote in a private memorandum that, to be effective, the bomb would have had to be used against China. Distinguishing the Korean case from ending the war against Japan, he wrote, "I could not bring myself to order the slaughter of 25,000,000 noncombatants. . . . I know I was *right*."

Revisionist historians are similarly severe in condemning John Kennedy for running the risk of nuclear war to get the Soviet missiles out of Cuba in 1962. They seem strangely unconcerned, however, that Eisenhower used the threat of nuclear war far more often than any other American president has done, before or since. Nuclear blackmail was indeed the almost inevitable consequence of the military posture dictated by "massive retaliation." It is said in his defense that Eisenhower used the threat in a context of American nuclear superiority that minimized the risk. But the same condition of nuclear supe-riority prevailed for, and must equally absolve, Truman and Kennedy.

Eisenhower began by invoking the nuclear threat to end the fight-ing in Korea. He let the Chinese know, he later told Lyndon Johnson, that "he would not feel constrained about crossing the Yalu, or using nuclear weapons." Probably the effectiveness of this threat has been exaggerated. The Chinese had compelling reasons of their own to get out of the war. The decisive shift in their position away from the forced repatriation of prisoners of war took place, as McGeorge Bundy has pointed out, after the death of Stalin in March 1953—and before Eisenhower sent his signals to Peking. In May 1953 General J. Lawton Collins, the Army chief of staff, declared himself "very skep-tical about the value of using atomic weapons tactically in Korea." Eisenhower replied that "it might be cheaper, dollar-wise, to use atomic weapons in Korea than to continue to use conventional weapons." If the Chinese persisted, "it would be necessary to expand the war outside of Korea and . . . to use the atomic bomb." In Decem-ber, Eisenhower said that, if the Chinese attacked again, "we should certainly respond by hitting them hard and wherever it would hurt most, including Peiping itself. This . . . would mean all-out war." A joint memorandum from the State Department and the Joint Chiefs of Staff called for the use of atomic weapons against military targets in Korea, Manchuria, and China.

The next crisis came in 1954 in Vietnam. In March, according to Divine, Eisenhower was "briefly tempted" by the idea of American intervention, refusing, as he put it, to "exclude the possibility of a sin-gle [air] strike, if it were almost certain this would produce decisive results. . . . Of course, if we did, we'd have to deny it forever." As en-visaged by General Nathan Twining of the Air Force and Admiral Arthur W. Radford, the strike would involve three atomic bombs. Opposition by Congress and by the British killed the idea. Whether this was Eisenhower's hope when he permitted Dulles to carry the air strike proposal to London remains obscure. It was at this time that he propounded what he called "the 'falling domino' principle . . . a be-ginning of a disintegration that would have the most profound influences," a disintegration that, he said, could lead to the loss of Indochina, then Burma, then Thailand, Malaya, Indonesia, then Japan, Formosa, and the Philippines. This theory of the future entrapped Eisenhower's successors in the quicksands of Vietnam. The dominos did indeed fall in Indochina, as we all know now. But, with communist China invading communist Vietnam because communist Vietnam had invaded communist Cambodia, the dominos fell against each other, not against the United States.

Whatever Eisenhower's intentions regarding Vietnam, he definitely endorsed in May 1954 the recommendation by the Joint Chiefs to use atomic bombs in case of Chinese intervention if Congress and allies agreed. "The concept" in the event of a large-scale Vietminh attack, Dulles said in October, "envisions a fight with nuclear weapons rather than the commitment of ground forces."

Eisenhower tried nuclear blackmail again during the Quemoy-Matsu crisis of 1955. In March of that year Dulles publicly threatened the use of atomic weapons. Eisenhower added the next day in his press conference, "I see no reason why they shouldn't be used just exactly as you would use a bullet or anything else." In the 1958 replay of the Quemoy-Matsu drama, Dulles said that American intervention would probably not be effective if limited to conventional weapons; "the risk of a more extensive use of nuclear weapons, and even of general war, would have to be accepted."

"The beauty of Eisenhower's policy," Divine writes with regard to Quemoy and Matsu, "is that to this day no one can be sure whether or not ... he would have used nuclear weapons." Nuclear blackmail may strike some as the beauty part, though we did not used to think so when Khrushchev tried it. In Eisenhower's case it was associated with an extraordinary effort to establish the legitimacy of nuclear war. One restraint on the use of the bomb was the opposition of American allies and of world opinion. This resistance Eisenhower was determined to overcome. As Dulles told the National Security Council on 31 March 1953, while "in the present state of world opinion we could not use an A-bomb, we should make every effort now to dissipate this feeling." The minutes of the meeting add: "The President and Secretary Dulles were in complete agreement that somehow or other the tabu which surrounds the use of atomic weapons would have to be destroyed."

Eisenhower's campaign to legitimate the bomb appalled America's British ally. In their Bermuda meeting Eisenhower sought Winston Churchill's support for nuclear war if the Korean truce broke down. Churchill sent Jock Colville to Eisenhower with a message of concern. According to Colville's notes on the meeting, Eisenhower said "that whereas Winston looked on the atomic bomb as something entirely new and terrible, he looked upon it as just the latest improvement in military weapons. He implied that there was no distinction between 'conventional weapons' and atomic weapons: all weapons in due course become conventional." Colville wrote later, "I could hardly believe my ears."

The British were no happier the next year when Eisenhower asked their support for intervention in Vietnam. Churchill, who had received a long letter from Eisenhower lecturing him about Munich and the dangers of appeasement, was unmoved. "What we were being asked to do," he said to his foreign secretary, "was to assist in misleading Congress into approving a military operation, which would in itself be ineffective, and might well bring the world to the verge of a major war." He told Admiral Radford that the British, having let India go, were not about to give their lives to keep Indochina for France. "I have known many reverses myself," he said. "I have not given in. I have suffered Singapore, Hong-Kong, Tobruk; the French will have Dien Bien Phu." The Indochina War, he said, could only be won by using "that horrible thing," the atomic bomb. Eisenhower was enraged.

In December 1954 Eisenhower ordered the Atomic Energy Commission to relinquish control of nuclear weapons to the Department of Defense. At the same time, he ordered Defense to deploy overseas a large share of the nuclear arsenal—36 percent of the hydrogen bombs, 42 percent of the atomic bombs—many on the periphery of the Soviet Union. The movement of American policy continued to disturb our British allies.

According to the official minutes, Lord Salisbury told the cabinet in this period, "Some believed that the greatest threat to world peace came from Russians. He [Salisbury] himself believed that the greater risk was that the United States might decide to bring the East-West issue to a head while they still had overwhelming superiority in atomic weapons."

Eisenhower's persevering effort was to abolish the "firebreak" between conventional and nuclear weapons. Fortunately for the world, this effort failed. By 1964 nearly everyone agreed with Lyndon Johnson when he said, "Make no mistake. There is no such thing as a conventional nuclear weapon."

★   ★   ★

In his first years in the White House, Eisenhower regarded nuclear attack as a usable military option. He had no compunction about threatening such attack. He hoped to destroy the taboo preventing the use of nuclear weapons. But in fact he never used them. As Ambrose points out, "Five times in one year [1954] the experts advised the President to launch an atomic strike against China. Five times he said no." His campaign to legitimate the bomb was happily only a passing phase.

As the Soviet Union increased its nuclear arsenal, Eisenhower came to believe more and more strongly in the horror of nuclear war. The outlook was ever closer, he said in 1956, "to destruction of the enemy and suicide for ourselves." When both sides recognized that "destruction will be reciprocal and complete, possibly we will have sense enough to meet at the conference table with the understanding that the era of armaments has ended and the human race must conform its actions to this truth or die."

For all his early talk about the "same old whore," Eisenhower now sought better relations with the Soviet Union. As Sherman Adams, Eisenhower's chief of staff on domestic matters, later observed, "The hard and uncompromising line that the United States government took toward Soviet Russia and Red China between 1953 and the early months of 1959 was more a Dulles line than an Eisenhower line." But Dulles retained his uses for Eisenhower, both in frightening the Russians and in enabling the president to reserve for himself the role of man of peace.

In his later mood, Eisenhower strove, less anxiously than Churchill and later Macmillan but a good deal more anxiously than Dulles, to meet the Russians at the conference table. In 1953 at the United Nations he set forth his Atoms for Peace plan, by which the nuclear powers would contribute fissionable materials to an International Atomic Energy Agency to promote peaceful uses of atomic energy. This well-intentioned but feckless proposal assumed that atoms for peace could be segregated from atoms for war—an assumption abundantly refuted in later years and the cause of dangerous nuclear proliferation in our own time. In 1955 at the Geneva summit he came up with a better idea, the creative Open Skies plan. A system of continuous reciprocal monitoring, Eisenhower argued, would reduce fears of surprise attack. The Russians turned Open Skies down as an American espionage scheme. In his second term, against the opposition of many in his own administration, Eisenhower fitfully pursued the project of a nuclear test ban.

He resented the mounting pressure from the Democrats and from the Pentagon to accelerate the American nuclear build-up. The Pentagon did not impress him. He knew all the tricks, having employed them himself. He used to say that he "knew too much about the military to be fooled." He refused to be panicked by perennial Pentagon alarms about how we were falling behind the Russians and dismissed the "missile gap" of the late 1950s with richly justified skepticism.

Yet he weakly allowed the build-up to proceed. In 1959 he complained that the Pentagon, after agreeing a few years earlier that hitting seventy key targets would knock out the Soviet system, now insisted on hitting thousands of targets. The military, he said, were getting "themselves into an incredible position—of having enough to destroy every conceivable target all over the world, plus a threefold reserve." The radioactivity from atomic blasts at this level, he said, would destroy the United States too. The United States already had a stockpile of "five thousand or seven thousand weapons or whatnot." Why did the Atomic Energy Commission and the Department of Defense want more? "But then," writes Ambrose, "he reluctantly gave way to the AEC and DOD demands."

In 1960, when informed at a National Security Council meeting that the United States could produce almost 400 Minuteman missiles a year, Eisenhower with "obvious disgust" (according to his science adviser George Kistiakowsky) burst out, "Why don't we go completely crazy and plan on a force of 10,000?" The nuclear arsenal had now grown to a level that the Eisenhower of 1954 had considered "fantastic," "crazy," and "unconscionable." There were approximately 1,000 nuclear warheads when Eisenhower entered the White House, 18,000 when he left.

For all his concern about nuclear war, for all his skepticism about the Pentagon, for all the unique advantage he enjoyed as General of the Armies in commanding confidence on defense issues, he never seized control of the military-industrial complex. "Being only one person," he lamely explained, he had not felt he could oppose the "combined opinion of all his associates." In the measured judgment of the Regius Professor of History at Oxford, the military historian Michael Howard, "The combination of his constant professions of devotion to disarmament and peace with his reluctance to take any of the harsh decisions required to achieve those professed objectives leaves an impression, if not of hypocrisy, then certainly of an ultimate lack of will which, again, denies him a place in the first rank of world statesmen."

Though Eisenhower carefully avoided war himself, he was surprisingly bellicose in his advice to his successors. He told Kennedy before the inauguration not only to go full speed ahead on the exile invasion of Cuba but, if necessary, "to intervene unilaterally" in Laos. So bent was Eisenhower on American intervention in Laos that Kennedy persuaded British prime minister Harold Macmillan to explain to him in detail the folly of such an adventure. When Vietnam became the issue in the mid-1960s, Eisenhower advised Lyndon Johnson to avoid gradualism, "go all out," declare war, seek victory, not negotiations, warn China and the Soviet Union, as Eisenhower himself had done over Korea, that the United States might feel compelled to use nuclear weapons to break the deadlock, and, if the Chinese actually came in, "to use at least tactical atomic weapons." The antiwar protest, Eisenhower declared, "verges on treason." When Johnson announced in 1968 that he was stopping most of the bombing of North

Vietnam, Eisenhower, Ambrose writes, "was livid with anger, his remarks [to Ambrose] about Johnson's cutting and running unprintable." Eisenhower was more a hawk than a prince of peace.

"It would perhaps have been better for him, as in the last century for Wellington and Grant," Sir John Colville concludes, "if he had rested on his military laurels." Walter Lippmann remarked in 1964 that Eisenhower's was "one of the most falsely inflated reputations of my experience," and he was speaking before the inflation was under way. In later years the Eisenhower boom has gathered momentum in cyclical response to a need and a time.

In due course the pendulum will doubtless swing back toward the view of Eisenhower presented in the illuminating early memoirs by men close to him—Sherman Adams's *Firsthand Report* (1961), Emmet Hughes's *The Ordeal of Power* (1963), Arthur Larson's *Eisenhower: The President Nobody Knew* (1968). In these works of direct observation, Eisenhower emerges as a man of intelligence, force, and restraint who did not always understand and control what was going on, was buffeted by events, and was capable of misjudgment and error.

Yet we were wrong to have underestimated Eisenhower's genius for self-presentation and self-preservation—the best evidence of which lies in his capacity to take in a generation of scholars.

Excerpted from Arthur M. Schlesinger, Jr., *The Cycles of American History* (Boston: Houghton Mifflin, 1986), pgs. 387–405.

John F. Kennedy

CHARISMA

In this 1960 piece on John F. Kennedy at the Democratic National Convention in Los Angeles, Norman Mailer wrote about the living Kennedy the way millions came to regard the dead Kennedy, as a talisman of possibility, of what could have been. If Kennedy had lived, the sixties still might have spawned Vietnam, race riots, white backlash, and Richard Nixon. But we will never know, and the Kennedy hero-myth preserves the illusion that one man might have saved us from history. But would that man have been Kennedy? In words that uncannily map Lee Harvey Oswald's psyche, Mailer pictured the dark forces of the American imagination—"the subterranean river of untapped, ferocious, lonely and romantic desires, that concentration of ecstasy and violence which is the dream life of the nation"—as awaiting Kennedy's summons, and when they surfaced in the sixties, they swept away so much of what Americans held to as America that the country might have been better off if Nixon had defeated Kennedy and the haunted normality of the fifties been prolonged magically. However, this is to indulge Mailer's heroic conception of history more than a sensible person should. Marx has the antidote: "Men make history, but not under conditions of their own choosing."

Mailer's essay originally appeared in the October 1960 issue of *Esquire,* and Mailer says it played a small part in electing Kennedy a month later. The following excerpt is taken from *The Presidential Papers,* published in 1963, and now out of print. It should be reissued every presidential season to stir political journalists to emulative acts of imagination.

THE EXISTENTIAL HERO
Norman Mailer

Perspective from the Biltmore Balcony: The Colorful Arrival of the Hero with the Orange-brown Suntan and Amazingly White Teeth; Revelation of the Two Rivers Political Theory

> "... it can be said with a fair amount of certainty that the essence of his political attractiveness is his extraordinary political intelligence. He has a mind quite unlike that of any other Democrat of this century. It is not literary, metaphysical and moral, as Adlai Stevenson's is. Kennedy is articulate and often witty, but he does not seek verbal polish. No one can doubt the seriousness of his concern with the most serious political matters, but one feels that whereas Mr. Stevenson's political views derive from a view of life that holds politics to be a mere fraction of existence, Senator Kennedy's primary interest is in politics. The easy way in which he disposes of the question of Church and State—as if he felt that any reasonable man could quite easily resolve any possible conflict of loyalties—suggests that the organization of society is the one thing that really engages his interest."
>
> — RICHARD ROVERE, *The New Yorker,* July 23, 1960

The afternoon he arrived at the convention from the airport, there was of course a large crowd on the street outside the Biltmore, and the best way to get a view was to get up on an outdoor balcony of the Biltmore, two flights above the street, and look down on the event. One waited thirty minutes, and then a honking of horns as wild as the getaway after an Italian wedding sounded around the corner, and the Kennedy cortege came into sight, circled Pershing Square, the men in the open and leading convertibles sitting backwards to look at their leader, and finally came to a halt in a space cleared for them by the police in the crowd. The television cameras were out, and a Kennedy band was playing some circus music. One saw him immediately. He had the deep orange-brown suntan of a ski instructor, and when he smiled at the crowd his teeth were amazingly white and clearly visi-

A Picture of Health

The Travell records reveal that during the first six months of his term, Kennedy suffered stomach, colon, and prostate problems, high fevers, occasional dehydration, abscesses, sleeplessness, and high cholesterol, in addition to his ongoing back and adrenal ailments. His physicians administered large doses of so many drugs that Dr. Travell kept a "medicine Administration Record," cataloguing injected and ingested corticosteroids for his adrenal insufficiency; procaine shots and ultrasound treatments and hot packs for his back; Lomotil, Metamucil, paregoric, phenobarbital, testosterone, and trasentine to control diarrhea, abdominal discomfort, and weight loss; penicillin and other antibiotics for his urinary tract infections and an abscess; and Tuinal to help him sleep. Before press conferences and nationally televised speeches his doctors increased his cortisone dose to deal with tensions harmful to someone unable to produce his own corticosteroids in response to stress. Though the medications occasionally made Kennedy groggy and tired, he did not see them as a problem. He dismissed questions about Dr. Max Jacobson's injections [of amphetamines], saying, "I don't care if it's horse piss. It works."

Excerpted from Robert Dallek, "The Medical Ordeals of JFK," *Atlantic Monthly,* December 2002.

ble at a distance of fifty yards. For one moment he saluted Pershing Square, and Pershing Square saluted him back, the prince and the beggars of glamour staring at one another across a city street, one of those very special moments in the underground history of the world, and then with a quick move he was out of the car and by choice headed into the crowd instead of the lane cleared for him into the hotel by the police, so that he made his way inside surrounded by a mob, and one expected at any moment to see him lifted to its shoulders like a matador being carried back to the city after a triumph in the plaza.

All the while the band kept playing the campaign tunes, sashaying circus music, and one had a moment of clarity, intense as a *déjà vu,* for the scene which had taken place had been glimpsed before in a dozen musical comedies; it was the scene where the hero, the matinee idol, the movie star comes to the palace to claim the princess, or what is the same, and more to our soil, the football hero, the campus king, arrives at the dean's home surrounded by a court of open-singing students to plead with the dean for his daughter's kiss and permission to put on the big musical that night. And suddenly I saw the convention, it came into focus for me, and I understood the mood of depression which had lain over the convention, because finally it was simple: the Democrats were going to nominate a man who, no matter how serious his political dedication might be, was indisputably and willy-nilly going to be seen as a great box-office actor, and the consequences of that were staggering and not at all easy to calculate.

Since the First World War Americans have been leading a double life, and our history has moved on two rivers, one visible, the other underground; there has been the history of politics, which is concrete, factual, practical, and unbelievably dull if not for the consequences of the actions of some of these men; and there is a subterranean river of untapped, ferocious, lonely, and romantic desires, that concentration of ecstasy and violence which is the dream life of the nation.

The twentieth century may yet be seen as that era when civilized man and underprivileged man were melted together into mass man, the iron and steel of the nineteenth century giving way to electronic circuits which communicated their messages into men, the unmistakable tendency of the new century seeming to be the creation of men as interchangeable as commodities, their extremes of personality singed out of existence by the psychic fields of force the communicators would impose. This loss of personality was a catastrophe to the future of the imagination, but billions of people might first benefit from it by having enough to eat—one did not know—and there remained citadels of resistance in Europe where the culture was deep and roots were visible in the architecture of the past.

Nowhere, as in America, however, was this fall from individual man to mass man felt so acutely, for America was at once the first and most prolific creator of mass communications, and the most rootless of countries, since almost no American could lay claim to the line of a family which had not once at least severed its roots by migrating here. But, if rootless, it was then the most vulnerable of countries to its own homogenization. Yet America was also the country in which the dynamic myth of the Renaissance—that every man was potentially extraordinary—knew its most passionate persistence. Simply, America was the land where people still believed in heroes: George Washington; Billy the Kid; Lincoln, Jefferson; Mark Twain, Jack London, Hemingway; Joe Louis, Dempsey, Gentleman Jim; America believed in athletes, rum-runners, aviators; even lovers, by the time Valentino died. It was a country which had grown by the leap of one hero past another—is there a county in all of our ground which does not have its legendary figure? And when the West was filled, the expansion turned inward, became part of an agitated, overexcited, superheated dream life. The film studios threw up their searchlights as the frontier was finally sealed, and the romantic possibilities of the old conquest of land turned into a vertical myth, trapped within the skull, of a new kind of heroic life, each choosing his own archetype of a neo-renaissance man, be it Barrymore, Cagney, Flynn, Bogart, Brando, or Sinatra, but it was almost as if there were no peace unless one could fight well, kill well (if always with honor), love well and love many, be cool, be daring, be dashing, be wild, be wily, be resourceful, be a brave gun. And this myth, that each of us was born to be free, to wander, to have adventure and to grow on the waves of the violent, the perfumed, and the unexpected, had a force which could not be tamed no matter how the nation's regulators—politicians, medicos, policemen, professors, priests, rabbis, ministers, *idéologues,* psychoanalysts, builders, executives, and endless communicators—would brick-in the modern life with hygiene upon sanity, and middlebrow homily over platitude; the myth would not die. Indeed a quarter of the nation's business must have depended upon its existence. But it stayed alive for more than that—it was as if the message in the labyrinth of the genes would insist that violence was locked with creativity, and adventure was the secret of love.

Once, in the Second World War and in the year or two which followed, the underground river returned to earth, and the life of the nation was intense, of the present, electric; as a lady said, "That was the time when we gave parties which changed people's lives." The forties was a decade when the speed with which one's own events occurred seemed as rapid as the history of the battlefields, and for the mass of people in America a forced march into a new jungle of emotion was the result. The surprises, the failures, and the dangers of that life must have terrified some nerve of awareness in the power and the mass, for, as if stricken by the orgiastic vistas the myth had carried up from underground, the retreat to a more conservative existence was disorderly, the fear of communism spread like an irrational hail of boils. To anyone who could see, the excessive hysteria of the Red wave was no preparation to face an enemy, but rather a terror of the national self: free-loving, lust-looting, atheistic, implacable—absurdity beyond absurdity to label communism so, for the moral products of Stalinism had been Victorian sex and a ponderous machine of material theology.

Forced underground again, deep beneath all *Reader's Digest* hospital dressings of Mental Health in Your Community, the myth continued to flow, fed by television and the film. The fissure in the national psyche widened to the danger point. The last large appearance of the myth was the vote which tricked the polls and gave Harry Truman his victory in '48. That was the last. Came the Korean War, the shadow of the H-bomb, and we were ready for the General. Uncle Harry gave way to Father, and security, regularity, order, and the life of no imagination were the command of the day. If one had any doubt of this, there was Joe McCarthy with his built-in treason detector, furnished by God, and the damage was done. In the totalitarian wind of those days, anyone who worked in government formed the habit of being not too original, and many a mind atrophied from disuse and private shame. At the summit there was benevolence without leadership, regularity without vision, security without safety, rhetoric without life. The ship drifted on, that enormous warship of the United States, led by a secretary of state whose cells were seceding to cancer, and as the world became more fantastic—Africa turning itself upside down, while some new kind of machine man was being made in

China—two events occurred which stunned the confidence of America into a new night: the Russians put up their Sputnik, and civil rights—that reluctant gift to the American Negro, granted for its effect on foreign affairs—spewed into real life at Little Rock. The national Ego was in shock: the Russians were now in some ways our technological superiors, and we had an internal problem of subject populations equal conceivably in its difficulty to the Soviet and its satellites. The fatherly calm of the General began to seem like the uxorious mellifluences of the undertaker.

Underneath it all was a larger problem. The life of politics and the life of myth had diverged too far, and the energies of the people one knew everywhere had slowed down. Twenty years ago a post-depression generation had gone to war and formed a lively, grousing, by times inefficient, carousing, pleasure-seeking, not altogether inadequate army. It did part of what it was supposed to do, and many, out of combat, picked up a kind of private life on the fly, and had their good time despite the yaws of the military system. But today in America the generation which respected the code of the myth was Beat, a horde of half-begotten Christs with scraggly beards, heroes none, saints all, weak before the strong, empty conformisms of the authority. The sanction for finding one's growth was no longer one's flag, one's career, one's sex, one's adventure, not even one's booze. Among the best in this newest of the generations, the myth had found its voice in marijuana, and the joke of the underground was that when the Russians came over they could never dare to occupy us for long because America was too hip. Gallows humor. The poorer truth might be that America was too Beat, the instinct of the nation so separated from its public mind that apathy, schizophrenia, and private beatitudes might be the pride of the welcoming committee any underground could offer.

Yes, the life of politics and the life of the myth had diverged too far. There was nothing to return them to one another, no common danger, no cause, no desire, and, most essentially, no hero. It was a hero America needed, a hero central to his time, a man whose personality might suggest contradictions and mysteries which could reach into the alienated circuits of the underground, because only a hero can capture the secret imagination of a people, and so be good for the vitality of his nation; a hero embodies the fantasy and so allows each private mind the liberty to consider its fantasy and find a way to grow. Each mind can become more conscious of its desire and waste less strength in hiding from itself. Roosevelt was such a hero, and Churchill, Lenin, and De Gaulle; even Hitler, to take the most odious example of this thesis, was a hero, the hero-as-monster, embodying what had become the monstrous fantasy of a people, but the horror upon which the radical mind and liberal temperament foundered was that he gave outlet to the energies of the Germans and so presented the twentieth century with an index of how horrible had become the secret heart of its desire. Roosevelt is of course a happier example of the hero; from his paralytic leg to the royal elegance of his geniality he seemed to contain the country within himself; everyone from the meanest starving cripple to an ambitious young man could expand into the optimism of an improving future because the man offered an unspoken promise of a future which would be rich. The sexual and the sex-starved, the poor, the hard-working and the imaginative well-to-do could see themselves in the president, could believe him to be like themselves. So a large part of the country was able to discover its energies because not as much was wasted in feeling that the country was a poisonous nutrient which stifled the day.

Too simple? No doubt. One tries to construct a simple model. The thesis is after all not so mysterious; it would merely nudge the notion that a hero embodies his time and is not so very much better than his time, but he is larger than life and so is capable of giving direction to the time, able to encourage a nation to discover the deepest colors of its character. At bottom the concept of the hero is antagonistic to impersonal social progress, to the belief that social ills can be solved by social legislating, for it sees a country as all-but-trapped in its character until it has a hero who reveals the character of the country to itself. The implication is that without such a hero the nation turns sluggish. Truman for example was not such a hero, he was not sufficiently larger than life, he inspired familiarity without excitement, he was a character but his proportions came from soap opera: Uncle Harry, full of salty common sense and small-minded certainty, a storekeeping uncle.

Whereas Eisenhower has been the anti-hero, the regulator. Nations do not necessarily and inevitably seek for heroes. In periods of dull anxiety, one is more likely to look for security than a dramatic confrontation, and Eisenhower could stand as a hero only for that large number of Americans who were most proud of their lack of imagination. In American life, the unspoken war of the century has taken place between the city and the small town: the city which is dynamic, orgiastic, unsettling, explosive, and accelerating to the psyche; the small town which is rooted, narrow, cautious, and planted in the life-logic of the family. The need of the city is to accelerate growth; the pride of the small town is to retard it. But since America has been passing through a period of enormous expansion since the war, the double-four years of Dwight Eisenhower could not retard the expansion, it could only denude it of color, character, and the development of novelty. The small-town mind is rooted—it is rooted in the small town—and when it attempts to direct history the results are disastrously colorless because the instrument of world power which is used by the small-town mind is the committee. Committees do not create, they merely proliferate, and the incredible dullness wreaked upon the American landscape in Eisenhower's eight years has been the triumph of the corporation. A tasteless, sexless, odorless sanctity in architecture, manners, modes, styles has been the result. Eisenhower embodied half the needs of the nation, the needs of the timid, the petrified, the sanctimonious, and the sluggish. What was even worse, he did not divide the nation as a hero might (with a dramatic dialogue as the result); he merely excluded one part of the nation from the other. The result was an alienation of the best minds and bravest impulses from the faltering history which was made. America's need in those years was to take an existential turn, to walk into the nightmare, to face into that terrible logic of history which demanded that the country and its people must become more extraordinary and more adventurous, or else perish, since the only alternative was to offer a false security in the power and the panacea of organized religion, family, and the FBI, a totalitarianization of the psyche by the stultifying techniques of the mass media which would seep into everyone's most private associations and so leave the country powerless against the

Russians even if the denouement were to take fifty years, for in a competition between totalitarianisms the first maxim of the prize-fight manager would doubtless apply: "Hungry fighters win fights."

The Hipster as Presidential Candidate: Thoughts on a Public Man's Eighteenth-Century Wife; Face-to-Face with the Hero; Significance of a Personal Note, or the Meaning of His Having Read an Author's Novel

Some part of these thoughts must have been in one's mind at the moment there was that first glimpse of Kennedy entering the Biltmore Hotel; and in the days which followed, the first mystery—the profound air of depression which hung over the convention—gave way to a second mystery which can be answered only by history. The depression of the delegates was understandable: no one had too much doubt that Kennedy would be nominated, but if elected he would be not only the youngest president ever to be chosen by voters, he would be the most conventionally attractive young man ever to sit in the White House, and his wife—some would claim it—might be the most beautiful first lady in our history. Of necessity the myth would emerge once more, because America's politics would now be also America's favorite movie, America's first soap opera, America's best-seller. One thinks of the talents of writers like Taylor Caldwell or Frank Yerby, or is it rather *The Fountainhead* which would contain such a fleshing of the romantic prescription? Or is it indeed one's own work which is called into question? "Well, there's your first hipster," says a writer one knows at the convention, "Sergius O'Shaugnessy born rich," and the temptation is to nod, for it could be true, a war hero, and the heroism is bona-fide, even exceptional, a man who has lived with death, who, crippled in the back, took on an operation which would kill him or restore him to power, who chose to marry a lady whose face might be too imaginative for the taste of a democracy which likes its first ladies to be executives of home-management, a man who courts political suicide by choosing to go all out for a nomination four, eight, or twelve years before his political elders think he is ready, a man who announces a week prior to the convention that the young are better fitted to direct history than the old. Yes, it captures the attention. This is no routine candidate calling every shot by safety's routine book. ("Yes," Nixon said, naturally but terribly tired an hour after his nomination, the TV cameras and lights and microphones bringing out a sweat of fatigue on his face, the words coming very slowly from the tired brain, somber, modest, sober, slow, slow enough so that one could touch emphatically the cautions behind each word, "Yes, I want to say," said Nixon, "that whatever abilities I have, I got from my mother." A tired pause . . . dull moment of warning, ". . . and my father." The connection now made, the rest comes easy, ". . . and my school and my church." Such men are capable of anything.)

One had the opportunity to study Kennedy a bit in the days that followed. His style in the press conferences was interesting. Not terribly popular with the reporters (too much a contemporary, and yet too difficult to understand, he received nothing like the rounds of applause given to Eleanor Roosevelt, Stevenson, Humphrey, or even Johnson), he carried himself nonetheless with a cool grace which seemed indifferent to applause, his manner somehow similar to the poise of a fine boxer, quick with his hands, neat in his timing, and two feet away from his corner when the bell ended the round. There was a good lithe wit to his responses, a dry Harvard wit, a keen sense of proportion in disposing of difficult questions—invariably he gave enough of an answer to be formally satisfactory without ever opening himself to a new question which might go further than the first. Asked by a reporter, "Are you for Adlai as vice president?" the grin came forth and the voice turned very dry, "No, I cannot say we have considered *Adlai* as a vice president." Yet there was an elusive detachment to everything he did. One did not have the feeling of a man present in the room with all his weight and all his mind. Johnson gave you all of himself, he was a political animal, he breathed like an animal, sweated like one, you knew his mind was entirely absorbed with the compendium of political fact and maneuver; Kennedy seemed at times like a young professor whose manner was adequate for the classroom, but whose mind was off in some intricacy of the Ph.D. thesis he was writing. Perhaps one can give a sense of the discrepancy by saying that he was like an actor who had been cast as the candidate, a good actor, but not a great one—you were aware all the time that the role was one thing and the man another—they did not coincide, the actor seemed a touch too aloof (as, let us say, Gregory Peck is usually too aloof) to become the part. Yet one had little sense of whether to value this elusiveness, or to beware of it. One could be witnessing the fortitude of a superior sensitivity or the detachment of a man who was not quite real to himself. And his voice gave no clue. When Johnson spoke, one could separate what was fraudulent from what was felt, he would have been satisfying as an actor the way Broderick Crawford or Paul Douglas are satisfying; one saw into his emotions, or at least had the illusion that one did. Kennedy's voice, however, was only a fair voice, too reedy, near to strident, it had the metallic snap of a cricket in it somewhere, it was more impersonal than the man, and so became the least-impressive quality in a face, a body, a selection of language, and a style of movement which made up a better-than-decent presentation, better than one had expected.

With all of that, it would not do to pass over the quality in Kennedy which is most difficult to describe. And in fact some touches should be added to this hint of a portrait, for later (after the convention), one had a short session alone with him, and the next day, another. As one had suspected in advance the interviews were not altogether satisfactory, they hardly could have been. A man running for president is altogether different from a man elected president: the hazards of the campaign make it impossible for a candidate to be as interesting as he might like to be (assuming he has such a desire). One kept advancing the argument that this campaign would be a contest of personalities, and Kennedy kept returning the discussion to politics. After a while one recognized this was an inevitable caution for him. So there would be not too much point to reconstructing the dialogue since Kennedy is hardly inarticulate about his political attitudes and there will be a library vault of text devoted to it in the newspapers. What struck me most about the interview was a passing remark whose importance was invisible on the scale of politics, but was altogether meaningful to my particular competence. As we sat down for the first time, Kennedy smiled nicely and said that he had read my books. One muttered one's pleasure. "Yes," he said, "I've read . . ."

and then there was a short pause which did not last long enough to be embarrassing in which it was yet obvious no title came instantly to his mind, an omission one was not ready to mind altogether since a man in such a position must be obliged to carry a hundred thousand facts and names in his head, but the hesitation lasted no longer than three seconds or four, and then he said, "I've read *The Deer Park* and . . . the others," which startled me for it was the first time in a hundred similar situations, talking to someone whose knowledge of my work was casual, that the sentence did not come out, "I've read *The Naked and the Dead* . . . and the others." If one is to take the worst and assume that Kennedy was briefed for this interview (which is most doubtful), it still speaks well for the striking instincts of his advisers.

What was retained later is an impression of Kennedy's manners, which were excellent, even artful, better than the formal good manners of Choate and Harvard, almost as if what was creative in the man had been given to the manners. In a room with one or two people, his voice improved, became low-pitched, even pleasant—it seemed obvious that in all these years he had never become a natural public speaker and so his voice was constricted in public, the symptom of all orators who are ambitious, throttled, and determined.

His personal quality had a subtle, not quite describable intensity, a suggestion of dry pent heat perhaps, his eyes large, the pupils grey, the whites prominent, almost shocking, his most forceful feature: he had the eyes of a mountaineer. His appearance changed with his mood, strikingly so, and this made him always more interesting than what he was saying. He would seem at one moment older than his age, forty-eight or fifty, a tall, slim, sunburned professor with a pleasant weathered face, not even particularly handsome; five minutes later, talking to a press conference on his lawn, three microphones before him, a television camera turning, his appearance would have gone through a metamorphosis, he would look again like a movie star, his coloring vivid, his manner rich, his gestures strong and quick, alive with that concentration of vitality a successful actor always seems to radiate. Kennedy had a dozen faces. Although they were not at all similar as people, the quality was reminiscent of someone like Brando whose expression rarely changes, but whose appearance seems to shift from one person into another as the minutes go by, and one bothers with this comparison because, like Brando, Kennedy's most characteristic quality is the remote and private air of a man who has traversed some lonely terrain of experience, of loss and gain, of nearness to death, which leaves him isolated from the mass of others.

> The next day while they waited in vain for rescuers, the wrecked half of the boat turned over in the water and they saw that it would soon sink. The group decided to swim to a small island three miles away. There were other islands bigger and nearer, but the Navy officers knew that they were occupied by the Japanese. On one island, only one mile to the south, they could see a Japanese camp. McMahon, the engineer whose legs were disabled by burns, was unable to swim. Despite his own painfully crippled back, Kennedy swam the three miles with a breast stroke, towing behind him by a life-belt strap that he held between his teeth the helpless McMahon . . . it took Kennedy and the suffering engineer five hours to reach the island.

The quotation is from a book which has for its dedicated unilateral title *The Remarkable Kennedys,* but the prose is by one of the best of the war reporters, the former *Yank* editor, Joe McCarthy, and so presumably may be trusted in such details as this. Physical bravery does not of course guarantee a man's abilities in the White House—all too often men with physical courage are disappointing in their moral imagination—but the heroism here is remarkable for its tenacity. The above is merely one episode in a continuing saga which went on for five days in and out of the water, and left Kennedy at one point "miraculously saved from drowning (in a storm) by a group of Solomon Island natives who suddenly came up beside him in a large dugout canoe." Afterward, his back still injured (that precise back injury which was to put him on crutches eleven years later, and have him search for "spinal-fusion surgery" despite a warning that his chances of living through the operation were "extremely limited"), he asked to go back on duty and became so bold in the attacks he made with his PT boat "that the crew didn't like to go out with him because he took so many chances."

It is the wisdom of a man who senses death within him and gambles that he can cure it by risking his life. It is the therapy of the instinct, and who is so wise as to call it irrational? Before he went into the Navy, Kennedy had been ailing. Washed out of freshman year at Princeton by a prolonged trough of yellow jaundice, sick for a year at Harvard, weak already in the back from an injury at football, his trials suggest the self-hatred of a man whose resentment and ambition are too large for his body. Not everyone can discharge their furies on an analyst's couch, for some angers can be relaxed only by winning power, some rages are sufficiently monumental to demand that one try to become a hero or else fall back into that death which is already within the cells. But if one succeeds, the energy aroused can be exceptional. Talking to a man who had been with Kennedy in Hyannis Port the week before the convention, I heard that he was in a state of deep fatigue.

"Well, he didn't look tired at the convention," one commented.

"Oh, he had three days of rest. Three days of rest for him is like six months for us."

One thinks of that three-mile swim with the belt in his mouth and McMahon holding it behind him. There are pestilences which sit in the mouth and rot the teeth—in those five hours how much of the psyche must have been remade, for to give vent to the bite in one's jaws and yet use that rage to save a life: it is not so very many men who have the apocalyptic sense that heroism is the First Doctor.

If one had a profound criticism of Kennedy it was that his public mind was too conventional, but that seemed to matter less than the fact of such a man in office because the law of political life had become so dreary that only a conventional mind could win an election. Indeed there could be no politics which gave warmth to one's body until the country had recovered its imagination, its pioneer lust for the unexpected and incalculable. It was the changes that might come afterward on which one could put one's hope. With such a man in office the myth of the nation would again be engaged, and the fact that he was Catholic would shiver a first existential vibration of consciousness into the mind of the White Protestant. For the first time in our history, the Protestant would have the pain and creative luxury of feeling himself in some tiny degree part of a minority, and that was an experience which might be incommensurable in its value to the best of them.

A Sketch of the Republicans Gathered in Convention:
The Choice Between the Venturesome and the Safe; What May Happen
at Three o'Clock in the Morning on a Long Dark Night

One did not go to the other convention. It was seen on television, and so too much cannot be said of that. It did however confirm one's earlier bias that the Republican Party was still a party of church ushers, undertakers, choirboys, prison wardens, bank presidents, small-town police chiefs, state troopers, psychiatrists, beauty-parlor operators, corporation executives, Boy Scout leaders, fraternity presidents, tax-board assessors, community leaders, surgeons, Pullman porters, head nurses, and the fat sons of rich fathers. Its candidate would be given the manufactured image of an ordinary man, and his campaign, so far as it was a psychological campaign (and this would be far indeed), would present him as a simple, honest, dependable, hard-working, ready-to-learn, modest, humble, decent, sober young man whose greatest qualification for president was his profound abasement before the glories of the Republic, the stability of the mediocre, and his own unworthiness. The apocalyptic hour of Uriah Heep.

It would then be a campaign unlike the ones which had preceded it. Counting by the full spectrum of complete Right to absolute Left, the political differences would be minor, but what would be not at all minor was the power of each man to radiate his appeal into some fundamental depths of the American character. One would have an inkling at last if the desire of America was for drama or stability, for adventure or monotony. And this, this appeal to the psychic direction America would now choose for itself, was the element most promising about this election, for it gave the possibility that the country might be able finally to rise above the deadening verbiage of its issues, its politics, its jargon, and live again by an image of itself. For in some part of themselves the people might know (since these candidates were not old enough to be revered) that they had chosen one young man for his mystery, for his promise that the country would grow or disintegrate by the unwilling charge he gave to the intensity of the myth, or had chosen another young man for his unstated oath that he would do all in his power to keep the myth buried and so convert the remains of Renaissance man as rapidly as possible into mass man. One might expect them to choose the enigma in preference to the deadening certainty. Yet one must doubt America's bravery. This lurching, unhappy, pompous, and most corrupt nation—could it have the courage finally to take on a new image for itself, was it brave enough to put into office not only one of its ablest men, its most efficient, its most conquistadorial (for Kennedy's capture of the Democratic Party deserves the word), but also one of its more mysterious men (the national psyche must shiver in its sleep at the image of Mickey Mantle-cum-Lindbergh in office, and a First Lady with an eighteenth-century face). Yes, America was at last engaging the fate of its myth, its consciousness about to be accelerated or cruelly depressed in its choice between two young men in their forties who, no matter how close, dull, or indifferent their stated politics might be, were radical poles apart, for one was sober, the apotheosis of opportunistic lead, all radium spent, the other handsome as a prince in the unstated aristocracy of the American dream. So, finally, would come a choice which history had never presented to a nation before—one could vote for glamour or for ugliness, a staggering and most stunning choice—would the nation be brave enough to enlist the romantic dream of itself, would it vote for the image in the mirror of its unconscious, were the people indeed brave enough to hope for an acceleration of Time, for that new life of drama which would come from choosing a son to lead them who was heir apparent to the psychic loins? One could pause: it might be more difficult to be a president than it ever had before. Nothing less than greatness would do.

Yet if the nation voted to improve its face, what an impetus might come to the arts, to the practices, to the lives and to the imagination of the American. If the nation so voted. But one knew the unadmitted specter in the minds of the Democratic delegates: that America would go to sleep on election eve with the polls promising Kennedy a victory on the day to come, yet in its sleep some millions of Democrats and

independents would suffer a nightmare before the mystery of un-
charted possibilities their man would suggest, and in a terror of all the
creativities (and some violences) that mass man might now have to
dare again, the undetermined would go out in the morning to vote
for the psychic security of Nixon the way a middle-aged man past adventure holds to the stale bread of his marriage. Yes, this election
might be fearful enough to betray the polls and no one in America
could plan the new direction until the last vote was counted by the
last heeler in the last ambivalent ward, no one indeed could know until then what had happened the night before, what had happened at
three o'clock in the morning on that long dark night of America's
search for a security cheaper than her soul.

Taken from Norman Mailer, *The Presidential Papers* (New York: Putnam's,
1963), pgs. 37–49 and 58–60.

Would John F. Kennedy have done what Lyndon Johnson did
in the spring and summer of 1965—commit U.S. ground troops
to Vietnam? Robert S. McNamara, secretary of defense through
the Kennedy and Johnson years, says Kennedy planned to withdraw the 16,000 "advisors" in Vietnam in 1963 after the 1964
elections. Yet faced with a possible Communist victory in South
Vietnam in early 1965, Kennedy's own men, McNamara chief
among them, recommended escalation to Johnson. How could
Kennedy have stood against them? One answer is that Kennedy
had done it before, in 1961, when the Pentagon (and Mc-
Namara) urged him to introduce ground troops "on a substantial
scale" to avert a communist takeover of the South. Why did he
send advisors instead, knowing they would not be enough to
stave off a Communist victory? Was he prepared to accept defeat
in Vietnam rather than escalate? Why? And were the reasons he
refused to Americanize the war in 1961 likely to lead him to a

similar decision four years later? In 1967, while preparing the Pentagon Papers, the secret history of the Vietnam War commissioned by McNamara, Daniel Ellsberg put these questions to Robert F. Kennedy, then a New York senator critical of the war. In *Secrets: A Memoir of Vietnam and the Pentagon Papers* Ellsberg recreates a dramatic scene in Kennedy's Capitol Hill office.

I told him briefly why I had picked that year to study and how I was now more puzzled than ever by the combination of decisions I found the president had made. In rejecting ground troops and a formal commitment to victory, he had been rejecting the urgent advice of every one of his top military and civilian officials. With hindsight, that didn't look foolish; it was the advice that looked bad. Yet he did proceed to deepen our involvement, in the face of a total consensus among his advisers that without the measures he was rejecting, in fact without adopting them immediately, our efforts were bound to fail.

He thought about what I put to him for a moment and then said: "We didn't want to lose in Vietnam or get out. We wanted to win if we could. But my brother was determined never to send ground combat units to Vietnam." His brother was convinced, Bobby said, that if he did that, we'd be in the same spot as the French. The Vietnamese on our side would leave the fighting to the United States, and it would become our war against nationalism and self-determination, whites against Asians. That was a fight we couldn't win, any more than the French.

I pressed him for more. In late 1964 and early 1965 it looked to the same advisers as if U.S. ground combat involvement were now essential to avoid defeat *in the short run*. Yet at that point it would have been even harder politically to get out or to accept defeat than in 1961. What would Kennedy have done then if he had lived?

Bobby answered carefully, in a way that made what he said more credible: "Nobody can say for sure what my brother would actually have done, in the actual circumstances of 1964 or '65. I can't say that, and even he couldn't have said that in '61. Maybe things would have gone just the same as they did. But I do know what he *intended*. All I can say is that he was absolutely determined not to send ground units."

I went on to the hard question. Would JFK really have been willing to accept defeat, to see Saigon go Communist, as the alternative to sending troops? Again Bobby answered in an even tone. "We would have fuzzed it up. We would have gotten a government in that asked us out or that would have negotiated with the other side. We would have handled it like Laos."

In Laos, Kennedy had rejected military urging to put in ground troops and instead had entered into negotiations that led to a coalition government, including Communists. Most of his officials, and Kennedy himself in official discussions, had always ruled out the acceptability of treating Vietnam like Laos. Bobby's comment to me was the first and only time I ever heard that JFK had even entertained the possibility of a "Laotian solution" for South Vietnam. Obviously none of Kennedy's most senior advisers shared this view. I also hadn't thought of JFK as having idiosyncratic opinions, let alone a conviction like that, about Indochina. I asked, a little impudently, "What made him so smart?"

Whap! His hand slapped down on the desk. I jumped in my chair. "Because *we were there!*" He slammed the desktop again. His face contorted in anger and pain. "We were there, in 1951. We saw what was happening to the French. *We saw it.* My brother was determined, determined, never to let that happen to us."

Excerpted from Daniel Ellsberg, *Secrets: Memoirs of Vietnam and the Pentagon Papers* (New York: Viking, 2002), pgs. 195–197.

Lyndon B. Johnson

COMPETING WITH FDR

William E. Leuchtenburg's theme is the shadow cast on LBJ by FDR, what the literary critic Harold Bloom calls "the anxiety of influence." Presidents after Roosevelt are like writers after Shakespeare—forever, in John Keats's lament, staring over their shoulders at a figure who grows larger every year. FDR's most recent biographer calls him "the most important person of the twentieth century." FDR's achievements humble theirs. His political skills, his hundred days, his fireside chat intimacy with the American people, the rhythms and phrases of his speeches, the brilliance of his advisers, the symbolic weight of his wife, his immortal dog— no politician can match him, including the real Franklin D. Roosevelt, who, from secretly taping conversations in the Oval Office to using the IRS to harass political opponents to violating civil liberties in the name of national security, pioneered the practices of the "Imperial Presidency," casting them in a perniciously heroic glow.

Although he knew the real Roosevelt, LBJ competed with the legend. He meant to exceed it, and would brook no invidious comparisons of his record with Roosevelt's—or any other president's. When Leuchtenburg interviewed him about the Great Society, in September 1965, he got a taste of Johnson's competitive fervor.

"Mr. President," Leuchtenburg began, "this has been a remarkable Congress. It is even arguable whether this is the most significant Congress ever." "Before I could add one more sentence to frame a question," Leuchtenburg writes, "Johnson interjected. 'No, it isn't. It's not arguable.' I grinned, then realized he was dead serious, even angry. It was my first indication that he believed his accomplishments were the most important in all our history. 'Not if you can read,' he snapped. 'You can perform a great service,' the President continued, 'if you say that never before have the three independent branches of government been so productive. Never has the American system worked so effectively in producing quality legislation—and at a time when our system is under attack all over the world.'" It took such grandiosity to put FDR in the shadow of LBJ.

LYNDON B. JOHNSON
In FDR's Shadow
William E. Leuchtenburg

On the evening of April 12, 1945, "in a gloomy Capitol corridor," a Washington correspondent came upon Congressman Lyndon Johnson, tears in his eyes, altogether disconsolate about the dreadful news he had just heard. At the end of that day's session, shortly after Harry Truman had left Sam Rayburn's office, Johnson had wandered in. The phone had rung, and Johnson had seen the Speaker pick up the receiver, listen silently, swallow, then look over at him and relay what he had just been told: Franklin D. Roosevelt was dead. Johnson was devastated. Though some minutes passed before the newspaperman encountered him, the thirty-six-year-old Texan still had difficulty putting words together as he sought to explain what FDR meant to him. For, as the correspondent observed, this "leading member of the Roosevelt 'Young Guard'" typified "a hundred formerly obscure young men whose leap into national prominence had been immeasurably aided by President Roosevelt's paternal coaching."

Johnson "clamped a shaking jaw over a white cigarette holder," then said of FDR:

He was just like a daddy to me always; he always talked to me just that way. He was the one person I ever knew—anywhere—who was never afraid. Whatever you talked to him about, whatever you asked him for, like projects for your district, there was just one way to figure it with him. I know some of them called it demagoguery; they can call it anything they want, but you can be damn sure that the only test he had was this: Was it good for the folks?

Johnson went on: "I don't know that I'd ever have come to Congress if it hadn't been for him. But I do know I got my first great desire for public office because of him—and so did thousands of other young men all over the country." He skimmed a eulogy Rayburn had scrawled for the press, then added, "God, God, how he could take it for us all."

Johnson acquired surrogate fathers so often that some writers have been skeptical of how profoundly he felt about this particular daddy, but there is no mistaking his anguish on learning that Roosevelt was gone. "His grief was just unreal," a secretary has recalled. "He just literally wasn't taking telephone calls and he just literally shut himself up. His grief was vast and deep and he was crying tears. Manly tears, but he actually felt like and expressed this in these terms, that it was just like losing his father." Nor was the sorrow short-lived. Johnson's brother has written, "We all knew that Roosevelt's death had deeply affected him. He lost some of his drive, periodically pausing in the middle of his still-crowded work day to stare out the window with a troubled look in his eyes. He might spend a half hour that way."

FDR had greater meaning for Johnson than for any other of his successors. If Roosevelt cast a darker shadow over Truman, it was only because Truman took office immediately after the great man died, and memories were still green. FDR never served as a model for Truman to anywhere near the same extent that he did for Johnson. Nor did any other chief executive associate himself so intimately with Roosevelt's point of view.

Yet praise and grief were not the only feelings Johnson revealed on learning of FDR's death. Even at that special moment, he said defensively:

They called the President a dictator and some of us they called "yes men." Sure, I yessed him plenty of times—because I thought he was right—and I'm not sorry for a single "yes" I ever gave. I have seen the

President in all kinds of moods—at breakfast, at lunch, at dinner—
and never once in my five terms here did he ever ask me to vote a certain way, or even suggest it. And when I voted against him—as I have
plenty of times—he never said a word.

This declaration indicated the attitudes that were to characterize
Johnson's behavior for the rest of his days—fealty to FDR's memory
combined with a determination to get out from under Roosevelt's
shadow. To the very last he remained a Roosevelt man, committed to
social reform and a bold foreign policy. Yet he also wanted to put his
own brand on the history of his times, indeed to achieve so much that
he would outrank even FDR. In the end his ambition not merely to
match his master but to surpass him had fateful consequences, for the
nation and for his own place in history.

★   ★   ★

Lyndon Johnson had first come to FDR's attention in a significant
way at a critical moment in Roosevelt's life. On February 5, 1937, the
president had announced a daring scheme to add as many as six jus-
tices to the United States Supreme Court, ostensibly to improve the
efficiency of the judiciary but in fact, critics charged, in order to pack
the Court with judges of the New Deal persuasion. Opponents
claimed that the country was overwhelmingly against the plan, while
the Roosevelt circle insisted that the nation was with him, as it had
been a few months earlier when he had swept all but two of the forty-
eight states. No one knew for sure. But in late February a Texas congressman died, and the ensuing election provided the first
meaningful test at the polls of how the people felt.

Even before the campaign began, Texas had become one of the
main battlefields of the Court fight. On February 9 the Texas Senate
had astounded the country by voting 22–3 to instruct the Texas congressional delegation to reject the proposal. In no other state did so
large a bloc of Democratic legislators turn against the president. The
opposition in Texas stirred up a hornet's nest. In New York, Republicans in both houses of the legislature introduced a measure adopted

word for word from the Texas resolution, and in Washington an irate congressman accused the head of the American Bar Association of prompting the resolution and called for a House investigation of that "band of rapacious corporation-controlled lawyers." As the candidates in the special election took to the field, the civil war among the Democrats became more acrimonious. On March 2 Senator Tom Connally, long counted an administration regular, spoke out against the bill in an address to the Texas legislature and received a standing ovation; even the pro-Roosevelt governor, it was said, had been spied clapping his hands under the table. Roosevelt in turn sent first Harold Ickes, then Jim Farley, to Austin to deliver rousing addresses to the Texas legislature. With so much national attention focused on Texas, the White House followed with lively interest developments in the Tenth Congressional District, where two of the nine candidates were outspoken opponents of Court-packing.

Almost no one thought much of the chances in that contest of a twenty-eight-year-old outsider who owed what little claim to recognition he had almost wholly to FDR. An admirer of Roosevelt from the day that he saw him nominate Al Smith at the 1928 Democratic convention in Houston, he had made himself over in his hero's image. When he was chosen Speaker of the Little Congress of congressional aides, he pledged a "New Deal" for his constituents and promised to watch out for the "forgotten man" on Capitol Hill. The president loomed still larger in Johnson's life when in 1935 Roosevelt appointed him to head the National Youth Administration in Texas, the biggest state in the union. Not yet twenty-seven, Johnson was the youngest state director of the NYA.

In a manner that would soon be legendary, Johnson seized upon this opportunity. Driving himself and those around him mercilessly, he put thousands of destitute young men to work on a number of imaginative projects, notably a series of roadside parks that attracted the attention of the White House. On a trip to Texas in 1936, Eleanor Roosevelt made a point of stopping at the NYA office in Austin, explaining to reporters that she wanted to see this young administrator about whom she had heard so much, and a generation later the NYA director for the state of Washington reminded Johnson of a June day in 1936 at Hyde Park: "You were called up to sit near the President and Mrs. Roosevelt and to tell them and the group about your projects in Texas, particularly the roadside parks. I have wondered whether that may have been the time when you were marked for greater things." When the president visited the Texas Centennial exposition in 1936, he was delighted by the tribute Johnson arranged for him: a battalion of NYA workers standing at attention along the highway between Dallas and Fort Worth, their shovels at present arms, Johnson at their head, his hand raised in a military salute. No less important, the NYA provided the nucleus of the political organization that would have its first test under fire in the 1937 primary.

In a race against much better-known candidates, that organization would not have begun to be enough had Johnson not shrewdly exploited FDR's popularity in the Tenth District as his route to a seat in Congress. To the consternation of some of his opponents, Johnson managed to create the impression that he was the only one of the nine candidates who supported FDR's Court-packing plan, a claim that was palpably false. Sure, some others might say they backed Roosevelt, Johnson asserted, but he alone did so unreservedly. "I didn't have to hang back like a steer on the way to the dipping vat," he said. "I'm for the President. When he calls on me for help I'll be where I can give him a quick lift, not out in the woodshed practicing a quick way to duck." If you want to aid the president, he told voters, then cast your ballot for me. "A vote for me will show the President's enemies that the people are behind him," Johnson declared. "Mr. Roosevelt is in trouble now. When we needed help, he helped us. Now *he* needs help. Are we going to give it to him? Are *you* going to give it to him? Are you going to help Mr. Roosevelt? That's what this election is all about."

Johnson reminded the voters that the eyes not only of Texas but of the country were upon them, for they were making a choice that could determine the whole future of the Roosevelt presidency. He leafleted the district with fliers carrying an excerpt from Ray Tucker's "National Whirligig" column: "Major plebiscite on the supreme court will take place in Texas April 10.... Young Lyndon Johnson, former national youth administrator, carries FDR's judicial colors...."

Several senators now lukewarm towards the White House scheme may suddenly shift if Mr. Roosevelt wins out there by proxy."

It did not take long for Roosevelt's circle to buy the idea that Johnson was FDR's "proxy." Elliott Roosevelt announced publicly for Johnson because, as he explained in a telegram to Jim Farley, "Congressional race to pick successor is coming to a head down here as straight out fight between Lyndon Johnson who is backing father wholeheartedly on his whole program including the court issue and two other candidates who have refused to support father on that question." Farley himself deviated from his usual posture of strict neutrality in primary bouts. On a tour of Texas, ostensibly to dedicate some post offices, the Democratic national chairman referred to Johnson as FDR's "champion."

By identifying himself with FDR, Johnson won a stunning victory that was widely interpreted as a vote of confidence for Roosevelt and Court-packing. The Associated Press ticker announced: "Youthful Lyndon B. Johnson, who shouted his advocacy of President Roosevelt's court reorganization all over the Tenth Texas District, was elected today," while a Texas newspaper headlined the results:

JOHNSON ELECTED TO
CONGRESS BY BIG VOTE
FDR'S COURT PROPOSAL
OKAYED BY 10TH
DISTRICT

That was just the way Johnson wanted his success to be perceived. "This is not a personal triumph," he maintained. "This is but approval of the president's program.... The people of the 10th district are sending to Washington the message that they are ... as strong as horse radish for Roosevelt."

The president, gratified by Johnson's victory at a time when the Court struggle was not going at all well, saw to it that his supporter's role was properly acknowledged. When Roosevelt's yacht docked in Galveston at the end of a fishing cruise in the Gulf of Mexico, the newly elected congressman was invited to take part in wharfside ceremonies, where, sporting a huge, garish oleander blossom, he was photographed with FDR and the governor of Texas. (Johnson subsequently had the governor effaced from the photograph to make it appear that he was alone with the president.) Johnson had the further honor of riding in the Roosevelt motorcade through the streets of Galveston, lined with thousands upon thousands of cheering Texans, and of accompanying FDR on the presidential train all the way to Fort Worth.

Johnson did not let this good fortune slip away from him. Though still in pain from an appendectomy and looking so gaunt that a reporter thought he was near death, Johnson overwhelmed the president with questions about how the tarpon were biting and how his family was doing and expressed a keen interest in the welfare of the U.S. Navy, a matter close to Roosevelt's heart. "I can always use a good man to help out with naval matters in Congress," the president responded. As the train pulled into Fort Worth, he scrawled a telephone number on a piece of paper and told Johnson that as soon as he got to Washington he should dial that number and ask to speak to Tom. It was in such fashion, as FDR's protégé, with instant access to Tommy Corcoran, one of Roosevelt's chief White House aides, that Johnson began his congressional career.

Lyndon Johnson became Franklin Roosevelt's pet congressman. Not until 1940 would he go in and out of the White House almost at will, but from the very beginning there were indications that he was the president's favorite. "By the time Lyndon arrived in Washington the word had gone out: 'Be nice to this boy,'" Tommy Corcoran has recalled. Roosevelt saw to it that the new congressman got a coveted spot on the House Naval Affairs Committee. Beyond that, intimates could discern that he was fond of Johnson; he "was kind of tickled to get a liberal from Texas and liked his sort of gung ho qualities," Roosevelt's associates remembered. The president became his tutor, "interested in say, educating him but interesting him in oh, things like water power and forestry; housing; oh, just everything." Roosevelt told one junior cabinet officer, "Keep an eye on that young Texan. He's going places." He even predicted that Johnson would one day be president. Roosevelt was heard to remark, "That's the kind of man I could have been if I hadn't had a Harvard education."

Johnson made use of his standing with FDR and the New Dealers to obtain millions of dollars in WPA and PWA construction, Federal Housing Project Number One in Austin, and, above all, the Pedernales River Electric Cooperative, which Johnson boasted was "the biggest co-op in the world both in area and power."

Johnson gave the president full value for what he and his constituents received. He became such a committed agent of FDR both on the Hill and in Texas that in 1940 the president insisted that he be treated as Sam Rayburn's equal in negotiations over the division of the Texas delegation to the Democratic convention. That same year Johnson performed an even more valuable service in running the national campaign to elect Democrats to the House. His astuteness, his energy, and his talent for fundraising impressed everyone, not least Franklin Roosevelt, for Johnson was not shy about keeping him informed about all he was accomplishing. After the election, in which Democratic candidates for the House did better than expected, Johnson wrote the president: "I know some of our Democratic brethren would have been utterly out in the cold except for your good offices. You made it possible for me to get down where I could whiff a bit of the powder, and this note is to say 'Thank you.' It was grand. The victory is perfect." He ended "with assurances of my very great esteem, my pride in your leadership, my confidence in the future under that leadership, and my affection."

. . .

Just three days after Pearl Harbor, Johnson became the first member of Congress to go into uniform. He waited only long enough to vote to declare war against Germany. Not content with desk duty, Johnson persuaded the president to send him to the Southwest Pacific, where he flew one mission that won him a Silver Star. On July 1, 1942, Roosevelt ordered all members of Congress in the armed services to return to Washington, and on the day that the president announced that Dr. New Deal had given way to Dr. Win the War, his luncheon guest was the young Texas representative. There was no other Texan Roosevelt relied on with such confidence. In December 1943 Johnson even sided with the president against his own state's oil interests in opposing a bill to raise petroleum prices, the kind of proof of devotion that Roosevelt appreciated. When in 1944 Johnson's first daughter was born, a White House car rolled up to the congressman's residence with a gift, a book about FDR's Scottie, Fala, inscribed "From the master—to the pup." A year later, the master was dead, leaving Johnson bereaved but comforted by the thought that he had been from first to last what one of FDR's closest aides called him, "a perfect Roosevelt man."

With Roosevelt gone, Johnson felt freer to accommodate himself to the increasing conservatism of his Texan constituents, though never to the point of repudiating FDR directly. Even while Roosevelt was alive, Johnson had deprecated "these old domestic museum pieces, the PWA, FHA and WPA," which "have now outlived their usefulness," and Roosevelt, who understood that Johnson could not go along with him on every question and hope to rise in Texas politics, had tolerated his deviations. Nonetheless, FDR's death made it easier for Johnson to distance himself from the New Deal. When he won election to the Senate in 1948, he insisted that no one should mistake him for a liberal, and after taking over as majority leader in 1955, he behaved not as a latter-day New Dealer but as a man of the center. Still, he continued to think of himself as an FDR follower, one who was adapting Roosevelt's ideas to the age of the Cold War.

In 1956 Texas Democrats distributed a column lauding Johnson as "the tall traveler [who] came to Congress as a follower of Franklin Roosevelt but a number of years later . . . was riding in the first-class coach of arch-Republicanism," and the following year Johnson said, "I have to admit, I am perhaps more conservative than I once was."

Johnson's transformation created considerable friction between the majority leader and FDR loyalists. In 1956 Sam Rosenman warned that "Lyndon Johnson and the conservatives of the South will try to capture the Party and change its character for the next decade, unless the New Deal–Fair Deal elements of the Party can overcome this effort." Roosevelt, the FDR faithful told the majority leader, would be heartsick if he knew that his favorite congressman had deserted his liberal colleagues. Richard Rovere has written:

> Once, at a small stag dinner of men who had worked with Roosevelt, this proposition was put in the form of a toast, and Johnson was reduced to tears and to replying that it was all too true but that his old friends simply could not know his loneliness and the difficulties of his position as a majority leader trying to hold the party together against the day when Eisenhower could no longer cast his magic spells over the country. A day would come, he said, when they would see that he was loyal to his past.

On another occasion, though, when Abe Fortas and others from the Roosevelt era were trying to get Johnson to advance their legislation, Johnson said angrily, "You New Dealers make me sick, because where would you be if you could not get people like me elected to Congress?"

Eleanor Roosevelt constituted a particularly thorny problem for Johnson. As majority leader, he did all he could to win her favor. He gave a party for her, and in the midst of a struggle over civil rights legislation, he talked to her about his tribulations. "I'm here every night all night, day and night, but where are all the liberals?" he asked. His entreaties got him nowhere. In August 1957, after the Senate approved a civil rights measure that liberals found inadequate, Johnson wrote Mrs. Roosevelt, "I was very much disappointed by your column last Saturday. I had always thought of you as a fair-minded person who would always insist on knowing all the facts before coming to a conclusion on the motives of men." He added, "If I am 'trying to fool the people,' I have a large company with me," and he named such co-workers as Ben Cohen and Jim Rowe, who had served under FDR.

As these comments indicated, Johnson still wanted to be regarded as one of the Roosevelt circle, and he took particular pains to associate himself with Roosevelt as the 1960 election drew nearer. At the end of a stormy night session of the Senate in August 1958, he corraled Hubert Humphrey and Anthony Lewis of the *New York Times,* gave a bravura performance in instructing Humphrey on how to behave on the Senate floor, then wheeled abruptly and, pointing to FDR's portrait behind his desk, cried, "Look. Look at that chin!" The big Democratic victory in the 1958 midterm elections led him to remind a columnist of "back in Roosevelt's day," when "we used to have Tom Corcoran and Ben Cohen charting policy," and in his campaign for the Democratic presidential nomination in 1960, he let out all the stops. If elected, he told a group of New Yorkers, he would be "more liberal than Eleanor Roosevelt."

His identification with FDR did not suffice to win Johnson the nomination, and he had to be content with the second spot on the ticket. John Kennedy chose him as his running mate though Johnson had derided him as the son of the man who had undercut Roosevelt's foreign policy. "I never thought Hitler was right," he cried. "I was never any Chamberlain umbrella man." In the ensuing campaign Johnson's association with FDR helped to attract voters in closely contested southern states, and some people credited the majority leader with an indispensable contribution to Kennedy's narrow victory.

When Lyndon Johnson succeeded to the presidency in November 1963, he declared openly that FDR was his model. "In both pride and humility," Johnson said on the occasion of the eighty-second anniversary of the birth of Franklin Roosevelt, "I readily admit that my own course in life has been influenced by none so much as this great man." Johnson relied upon advisers who had been FDR's counsellors—Abe Fortas, Jim Rowe, Anna Rosenberg, Tommy Corcoran, Ben Cohen—and he borrowed freely from the New Deal experience. A White House secretary recalled, "The first winter that he was President,

January, it seemed to me that every time I turned around, every time I took a breath, the President was having some kind of a ceremony with relation to FDR." If as president Lyndon Johnson was in Roosevelt's shadow, he gave every indication of purposefully stepping into the shade.

Johnson presented himself to the world as the designated heir of Franklin Roosevelt. He was forever reminding people of the laying on of hands in his own version of apostolic succession and Petrine supremacy. In the spring of 1964 he told a White House audience, "FDR brought me into this house and this room when I was only 27." He boasted of how often in the war years he had partaken of Sunday lunches with Roosevelt, and again and again he would announce that FDR was his beau ideal. He behaved toward him as one should toward paragons. It has been said that "every time he met a young person, Johnson lectured him on the greatness of Roosevelt."

From the outset Johnson surrounded himself with icons of FDR. On his very first day in the White House, he moved into his office a desk that Roosevelt had used. A year later, he said, "Whenever I feel I've done a good day's work, whenever I feel I've really accomplished something, I look at that desk. And then I go back to work, because I know I've only begun." As soon as he took over, he began a search for an appropriate portrait of his idol, and he insisted that it be the very best. At the end of a party on December 23, the day that the black crepe of mourning gave way to Christmas decorations, he led four women reporters to the Cabinet Room to show them where he would mount the painting of Roosevelt, "the ablest man we ever had in this town." It took him longer than he anticipated to find a suitable picture, but when he finally did, he hung it on a wall directly across from where he sat, so that FDR's face looked at him through every cabinet meeting of his tenure.

Washington observers soon discerned resemblances to Franklin Roosevelt in almost everything Johnson did. It was noted that the LBJ rubric copied the FDR insignia; that Johnson's cabinet sat around a table given to Roosevelt by Jesse Jones; even that the president favored the same kind of soft felt hat that his mentor had worn. The State of the Union message of January 1964 gave Johnson his first opportunity to make a distinctive mark, but correspondents viewed the address as an awkward effort to imitate FDR's style. "Johnson was very much influenced by Roosevelt in every kind of way, even in his manner of speaking when he became President," said an associate who had first met him in the 1930s. "It was very clear to people who had known him over a period of time. I don't think he was consciously mimicking. I think he just had absorbed so much of Roosevelt." So close did the identification become that by the spring of 1964, Eric Goldman has written, "curiously enough, the face of the rough-and-ready Texas President was taking on some of the lines of his hero, the New York patrician FDR."

. . .

Much of the time Johnson appeared to dwell not in the 1960s but in the 1930s. "Not even the Presidency is more stirring to him" than the age of FDR, observed the correspondent William S. White, who knew him well. He added, "The old years, the New Deal, the Depression, the War, made ineradicable marks upon him at a more impressionable age. And, as with many men of his generation, these old battles stir up the greatest nostalgia of all."

Johnson had a huge storehouse of tales about the glory days when FDR ruled the land, and he used these anecdotes not just to entertain but as parables to instruct his subordinates. He was particularly fond of telling about the swell-headed congressman who boasted to his colleagues one day in the thirties of how he had marched into the White House and chewed out the president; Speaker Rayburn is said to have replied, "I am not interested in what you told Roosevelt, but I am damn sure interested in what Roosevelt told you!" A quarter of a century later, whenever a bureaucrat or a member of the White House staff ran on about how he had pressed his ideas on some notable, Johnson would interrupt him with "Now, that's all very good, but I sure am interested in what Roosevelt told you."

Quite apart from the lasting influence Roosevelt exerted, Johnson found it politically advantageous to link himself to FDR. Many liberals had deep misgivings about a man they remembered as a southern conservative of the Eisenhower era, and Johnson made full use of his association with the age of Roosevelt to reassure them.

At a time of anxiety about what policies the new president would pursue, Johnson emphasized his fidelity to the FDR legacy. On the day after the assassination, he told Walter Heller that he wanted to go full speed ahead on the poverty program. As Heller started out of the office at the end of their conference, the president beckoned him back and added:

> Now I wanted to say something about all this talk that I'm a conservative who is likely to go back to the Eisenhower ways or give in to the economy bloc in Congress. It's not so, and I want you to tell your friends—Arthur Schlesinger, Galbraith and other liberals—that it is not so. I'm no budget slasher. . . . If you looked at my record, you would know that I am a Roosevelt New Dealer. As a matter of fact, to tell the truth, John F. Kennedy was a little too conservative to suit my taste.

Johnson's last sentence is suggestive, for one of the most important benefits he derived from identification with Roosevelt was help in eluding the never-ceasing comparisons to his immediate predecessor. There was no way to come out ahead in a contest with an immortal, and the Roosevelt association diverted attention from that matchup and placed Johnson in a different frame of reference.

Johnson also found the Roosevelt heritage useful in devising a program distinguishable from Kennedy's New Frontier, for FDR's New Deal served as midwife at the birth of Johnson's Great Society. The phrase "Great Society" first appeared in the draft of a speech prepared by Richard Goodwin for the president to deliver at an Eleanor Roosevelt Memorial meeting. Johnson decided not to use the talk on that occasion but to save it for later. He liked the draft and became increasingly fond of the phrase, for he was seeking a slogan like "New Deal," and "the Great Society" improved upon the expression he had been toying with, "the Better Deal." When he did unveil his program, commentators had no doubt about its pedigree. One called it a "Second New Deal," a continuation of the later New Deal that had been interrupted by the Court-packing defeat and World War II. Another wrote flatly, "The Great Society is an attempt to codify the New Deal's vision of a good society."

No feature of the Great Society attracted more attention than the War on Poverty, and that, too, was a direct descendant of the New Deal. In January 1964 Johnson declared: "The meek and the humble and the lowly share this life and this earth with us all. We must never forget them. President Roosevelt never did." When Johnson and his aides put together the poverty legislation, they were acutely aware of the experience of the 1930s. The Job Corps provision drew its inspiration from the Civilian Conservation Corps, and the college work-study program owed even more to the National Youth Administration.

★   ★   ★

If Johnson made much of Roosevelt in his first months in office, he became all but obsessed with him in the 1964 campaign. During the summer of 1964, he asked Eric Goldman to put together a series of memos on the history of Democratic conventions. Goldman has recalled: "As always, the LBJ eye was fixed on FDR. Typically, the memo on acceptance speeches came back with a notation instructing, 'Give me more on R in '32.'" At the president's request Goldman prepared a painstaking dissection of FDR's 1932 presentation, which gave vogue to the phrase "the New Deal." Johnson studied it assiduously in the hope of producing the same kind of effect, and he wound up modeling his own acceptance address on FDR's speech.

.   .   .

Johnson had the good fortune to be opposed in 1964 by a man who appeared to place in jeopardy many of the gains of the Roosevelt years and who harbored grievances against FDR more than three decades old. "If I hadn't been a registered Republican, my dissatisfaction with President Roosevelt would have caused me to change my registration," Barry Goldwater later commented. "As a merchant I deeply resented the provisions in the National Recovery Act which gave the federal government the power to impose its will on private business. I think the foundations of my political philosophy were rooted in my resentment against the New Deal."

Johnson's landslide victory in 1964 owed much to the determination of voters to preserve benefits won in the 1930s from Goldwater's assault and to the strength of the Roosevelt coalition. In Florida, a retired auto worker from Detroit interrupted his fishing long enough to tell a reporter: "First, the Democrats gave us the Wagner Act, then Social Security, then they guaranteed deposits in the bank. Lots of people were saved from starvation by the W.P.A. I'm voting for Johnson." An elderly man sunning himself in a waterfront park explained why he, too, would pull down the Johnson lever: "Everything I got, I got under a Democratic administration. You name it—unemployment compensation, Social Security. Goldwater seems to want to tear down a lot of these laws that were made 25 years ago." Blessed by a challenger who permitted him to draw political lines precisely as he wanted to—between those who were faithful to FDR and those who were hostile—Johnson easily won election to a second term.

Returned to office with the biggest Democratic margin in Congress since the 1930s, when he had entered the House as FDR's protégé, Johnson moved quickly to drive through Congress a series of bills that he frankly acknowledged were in the Roosevelt tradition. "The Johnson program was his own, but its roots were in the Roosevelt Administration; in the Roosevelt second term," a writer commented on one Johnson message. "Clearly, the President was picking up where the New Deal left off in 1938." In submitting a report of the Housing and Home Finance Agency in 1965, Johnson observed, "The great Franklin D. Roosevelt first pleaded with Congress to approve housing measures for the good of all Americans." After Congress enacted one of his own housing bills, he remarked, "I have waited for this moment for 35 years." Even when he broke new ground, he looked back toward FDR. On signing the bill appropriating money for the Elementary and Secondary Education Act, Johnson stated, "Twenty-one years ago, President Franklin Roosevelt issued an urgent call to Congress for Federal assistance to education

in this country. . . . Today we are helping to write the answer to that
historic challenge."

When Lyndon Johnson, with former president Truman by his side,
signed the Medicare bill into law in a ceremony at Independence,
Missouri, in the summer of 1965, he said:

> In 1935 when the man that both of us loved so much, Franklin Delano
> Roosevelt, signed the Social Security Act, he said it was, and I quote
> him, "a cornerstone in a structure which is being built but . . . is by no
> means complete."
>
> Well, perhaps no single act in the entire administration of the
> beloved Franklin D. Roosevelt really did more to win him the illustri-
> ous place in history that he has as did the laying of that cornerstone.

In the spring of 1965, at a time when the 89th Congress was swiftly
advancing his own claim to a place in history, Johnson summed up his
public attitude toward FDR. On April 12, 1965, on the twentieth anniversary of FDR's death, Johnson released a statement declaring:

> Twenty years ago—wearied by war, strained by the cares and tri-
> umphs of many years—the great heart of Franklin Roosevelt came to
> a stop.
>
> Most of us here shared the darkness of that day, as we had shared
> the difficult and shining days which had gone before. And wherever
> we were, when the unbelievable word came, for a moment the light
> seemed to waver and dim.
>
> But we were wrong about that. For he had worked too well. What
> he had set aflame was far beyond the poor and futile power of death to
> put out. . . .
>
> Therefore, I come here to perform a task which is already done.
> This entire Nation is at once his grave and monument. Millions of
> men at work and healthy children are his monument. Freedom here,
> and in many distant lands, is his monument. And we—his friends, his
> colleagues, and his followers—are also his monument. . . .
>
> Truly today's America is his America more than it is the work of
> any man.

Such was the message that Lyndon Johnson conveyed to the world—that he revered Franklin Roosevelt; hoped, as best he could, to carry on his ideas; and was fully content to remain in his shadow.

In fact, Johnson wanted a great deal more than that. He was not satisfied to go down in the history books merely as a successful president in the Roosevelt tradition. He aimed instead to be "the greatest of them all, the whole bunch of them." And to be the greatest president in history, he needed not just to match Roosevelt's performance but to surpass it. As two Washington writers observed, "He didn't want to equal his mentor, Franklin Roosevelt; he wanted to eclipse him."

Johnson had gargantuan aspirations. "Down there inside of Johnson somewhere was an image of a great popular leader something like Franklin Roosevelt, except more so, striding over the land and cupping the people in his hands and molding a national unity that every President dreams about but none is ever able to achieve," a White House correspondent has written. "Johnson's ambitions, of course, were bigger than any other President's." And FDR stood, like a huge thermometer in the town square at the start of a community chest drive, as the gauge of whether Johnson would go over the top. By the summer of 1965, Johnson said later, "I could see and almost touch my youthful dream of improving life for more people and in more ways than any other political leader, including FDR." At the same moment he was expanding the war in Vietnam, for he was determined, in the words of one of his biographers, to "out-Roosevelt Roosevelt" by imposing an American solution overseas at the same time that he achieved unprecedented social reforms in the United States. In the end, he anticipated, the American people, dazzled by his achievement in "pulling off both that war in Vietnam and the Great Society at home," would acclaim him the greatest president of all time.

Though Johnson's desire to go down in history as a greater president than FDR derived in large part from early experiences that shaped his outsized personality, it owed something, too, to resentments built up in the years when he was so much in Roosevelt's shadow. For if there were advantages to being FDR's pet congressman, there was also a price to pay. In the 1941 senatorial contest, Representative Martin Dies dismissed Johnson as a "water carrier," a taunt that led Johnson to write an exceptionally obsequious letter to President Roosevelt:

> In the heat of Texas the last week, I said I was glad to be called a water-carrier—that I would be glad to carry a bucket of water to the Commander-in-Chief any time his thirsty throat or his thirsty soul needed support, for you certainly gave me support nonpareil.
>
> One who cannot arise to your leadership shall find the fault in himself and not in you!

When Johnson turned up at the Texas Democratic convention in 1944, conservatives cried, "Throw Roosevelt's pin-up boy out of there." In sum, the role diminished him. As the authors of one account have observed, the early Johnson "is but a dim memory to many of the congressmen he served with then. He was known as Roosevelt's man, a man who ran private political errands for the President. . . . His own powerful personality was sublimated to that of his powerful 'chief.' The LBJ of colorful Washington legend would come later; then in the Roosevelt era, Lyndon lived more in the shadows than on the center stage." If history would accord him a higher place than FDR, he would gain a measure of revenge for the humiliation of being Roosevelt's errand boy.

Eleanor Roosevelt's attitude also grated. When he was majority leader, she thought of him as a clever tactician without strong convictions. Told by a friend that Johnson was a "secret liberal," she replied, "You're crazy." In 1959 he agreed to speak at a Memorial Day service in the Rose Garden at Hyde Park. "Mrs. Roosevelt, there's no suggestion that could ever be made to me by any Roosevelt that I wouldn't want to comply with," he told her. In fact, he resented having been asked as a substitute only after Truman could not come, and not until he had left repeated phone messages from Mrs. Roosevelt unanswered did he accept the invitation, just forty-eight hours before the event. When he did appear, Mrs. Roosevelt was conspicuously absent. Nothing daunted, Johnson busied himself saying things that would impress her when his words got back to her. By early 1960 she was beginning to speak publicly of his good points, but she never took him into her fold.

. . .

Johnson's rivalry with Roosevelt, though, cannot be accounted for simply by recourse to rational explanations. One senses an obsessive quality that is altogether missing in the attitude of a Truman or a Kennedy. Alone of Roosevelt's successors Johnson was disposed to relate FDR to members of his own family and perhaps to confuse Roosevelt with his own "daddy." Asked in 1964 to comment on presidents he had known, he replied, according to one of his assistants, that "Roosevelt had a heart as compassionate as that of his own mother, and a mind as strategic as that of his father. He recalled that Roosevelt, like his father, 'had a touch of the populist.'"

This comment suggests that Johnson held his father and FDR in very high esteem, but in fact his sentiments were more ambivalent. Toward each man he appears to have felt both affection and resentment. Johnson's lifelong quest for surrogate fathers may have indicated nothing more than a desire to find patrons who would ease his advancement, but it is likely that it also reflected some dissatisfaction with a father he thought to be an unsuitable role model. Furthermore, Johnson's "inner need to both emulate and surpass his father," in Doris Kearns's words, resonated later in his determination to acknowledge the Roosevelt legend but also to outperform the man he called "daddy." Throughout his career, Johnson had cannibalized the fathers he had adopted. As Kearns has written, "he became the invaluable helper, the deferential subordinate willing and able to perform a dazzling range of services for his master, until, step by step, the apprentice accumulated the resources that enabled him to secure the master's role." It would be extravagant to say that in determining to outdo Roosevelt, Johnson was committing a form of symbolic patricide, for in a number of ways he continued to be an admiring son, but at the very least he sought to show that he was a stronger man than his "daddy."

Johnson revealed his feelings nakedly on election night 1964, when the television screen in his hotel suite in Austin showed him rolling up a huge victory over Goldwater. The happy tidings might have been expected to create an enormous sense of contentment, but when he left his suite at 10 P.M., a reporter was startled to have the president snap at him when he asked a question. Johnson was cranky because he did not yet have the answer to the only question that interested him: How was he doing compared to Roosevelt in 1936? For Johnson was not running against Goldwater; he was running against FDR. He phoned Eric Goldman in Washington to ask him whether he was outpointing Roosevelt, and when Goldman warned him against making any premature claims to all-time records, he became peevish. Not until the next day was it fully clear that Johnson's percentage of the popular vote had, in fact, exceeded FDR's in 1936, and that his plurality had broken Roosevelt's record, though his proportion of the two-party vote was not so great, nor was his tally in the Electoral College so impressive.

President Johnson continued to vie with FDR when the new Congress convened. Conscious of Roosevelt's achievement in the Hundred Days of 1933, Johnson harried his congressional leaders to enact as much legislation as possible before the hundredth day of the 1965 session, as though he were in a race with FDR; and when the hundredth day came, he stated that in this period he had compiled "a record of major accomplishments without equal or close parallel in the present era." A week earlier he had told newsmen, "The Senate has already passed 15 substantial measures in this program. I think you will find that they have passed more measures already than were passed the first 100 days of the Roosevelt administration, about which you have been writing for 30-odd years."

These comments indicate that Johnson believed that less than two years after he took office he already overshadowed FDR, and his remarks at the end of the first session of "the fabulous Eighty-ninth Congress" confirm this inference. He called the session "the greatest in American history," and in a White House interview he said of Roosevelt: "He did get things done. There was regulation of business, but that was unimportant. Social security and the Wagner act were all that really amounted to much, and none of it compares to my education act of 1965."

Many of those around him shared that view. "This Congress is a lot more impressive than the Hundred Days Congress," said Johnson's legislative liaison officer for the House of Representatives in 1965. "It's not meeting in a crisis."

. . .

Others besides the White House staff gave Johnson and the 89th Congress the same high marks. In midsummer, at a time when the first session still had more than two months left, Tom Wicker wrote in the *New York Times,* "The list of achievements is so long that it reads better than the legislative achievements of most two-term Presidents, and some of the bills—on medical care, education, voting rights, and Presidential disability, to pick a handful—are of such weight as to cause one to go all the way back to Woodrow Wilson's first year to find a congressional session of equal importance." On Capitol Hill leaders of both parties were prepared to go even further. The Republican Charles Halleck, who had entered the House in 1935, said, when asked about relative political effectiveness, "I thought Roosevelt was pretty good," but Johnson was "the best I ever saw." Even more forthright was the Senate majority leader, Mike Mansfield of Montana. "Johnson has outstripped Roosevelt, no doubt about that," he declared in the fall of 1965. "He has done more than FDR ever did, or ever thought of doing."

★   ★   ★

Johnson refused to remain in Roosevelt's shadow not only because of his vaulting ambition but because in more than one respect he regarded FDR not as a model but as a bad example. If Johnson sought to emulate Roosevelt, he also attempted to avoid his predecessor's mistakes. "I never wanted to demagogue against business, Wall

Street, or the power companies," he once said. "I thought FDR was wrong." In the fall of 1965 Johnson stated:

> If you have great power, you mustn't use it; that was one of the troubles with FDR. The President has terrible power. People are fearful of the President's power. That fear brought this republic into being. When people did not like what Roosevelt was doing, he called them economic royalists and moneychangers. He said they had met their match and would meet their master. It was like people fighting and spitting at one another.

Johnson, who fancied himself the magistrate of a consensus presidency, made a point of claiming in 1965, perhaps the last time he could still do so, "We have cut down the fear that destroyed Roosevelt."

Once the first session of the 89th Congress had concluded its labors, Johnson turned his thoughts less to new programs than to administering what had already been enacted, in part because of lessons he drew from the FDR experience. The outbreak of World War II had prevented Roosevelt from making the final New Deal laws work satisfactorily, Johnson believed, and he did not want that to be said of the Great Society. In a White House interview Bill Moyers declared: "Johnson's approach is to attack and consolidate. The consolidation period may take longer than the advance. Roosevelt advanced too far without consolidation." Moreover, Johnson was determined that the laws would be enforced in a spirit different from that of the New Dealers. Moyers explained: "This administration has been relatively free of the Ickes-Hopkins kind of feuding. Johnson learned from watching Roosevelt that this did not work. Roosevelt seemed to find enjoyment in watching his own gladiators fighting. Johnson does not like this."

All of the Roosevelt errors that Johnson brought to mind paled beside one vivid episode: the Court-packing fracas of 1937. "I was the only Member of Congress to be elected on President Roosevelt's Supreme Court plan," he pointed out in 1964, and that remained the single most important memory of his earlier years. He had seen a president win an awesome victory at the polls, and then have his expectations for the New Deal explode only a few months later when the Court-packing bill was interred. Johnson, too, had just won overwhelmingly. He was determined that he would not repeat FDR's mistake in judgment.

Again and again, Johnson referred to this ordeal of a president which he had witnessed when he first entered Congress. "Johnson cites the Roosevelt experience all the time," one of the president's White House aides reported in September 1965. "As congressman, he saw what could go wrong with as big a mandate as that of 1936. He is deeply aware that one major miscalculation and a president has had it. He knows that in the ferocious environment in which a president lives, he may never be careless." On that same day, Johnson himself went out of his way to say, "In 1936, Roosevelt won by a landslide. But he was like the fellow who cut cordwood and sold it all at Christmas, and then spent it all on firecrackers. It all went up with a bang." Two months later at the White House, Bill Moyers recounted a sentence Johnson had once delivered to him: "When Roosevelt reached the summit of his power, he took on the gods of Olympus and got rolled back, and he never reached those heights again."

In the immediate aftermath of his enormous victory in 1964, Johnson let everyone know that his recollection of 1937 led him to be cautious. He remembered that when he took his seat in the House in April 1937 he found his new colleagues up in arms against the president; FDR, he concluded, had moved too quickly, with too little forethought. He told both White House aides and newspapermen that he planned to "avoid another 1937," that he would not overdraw his account by asking Congress to enact all of the Great Society at once. So rife were these reports that Robert Kennedy said, "It worries me a little when I read these stories about how much the President is thinking about Roosevelt and how he lost his popularity in 1936, because he did too much. But you can lose popularity by doing something, or you lose it by doing nothing. You lose it anyway. It's there to be spent."

Kennedy need not have fretted, for Johnson soon reached precisely the same conclusion. It was imperative, Johnson decided, to seize the hour, not to waste the advantage of his great triumph as he thought

FDR had done after his impressive win in 1936. . . . Johnson compared that situation to the one he now confronted:

> I was just elected President by the biggest popular margin in the history of the country, fifteen million votes. Just by the natural way people think and because Barry Goldwater scared hell out of them, I have already lost about two of these fifteen and am probably getting down to thirteen. If I get in any fight with Congress, I will lose another couple of million, and if I have to send any more of our boys into Vietnam, I may be down to eight million by the end of the summer.

Consequently, he had to ram the Great Society program through immediately, while there was still time, by compelling Congress to perform as it had done in FDR's First Hundred Days.

Johnson spoke more prophetically than he knew. For at the very moment when he was carrying out a domestic program that might earn him a higher place in history than Franklin Roosevelt's, he was setting out to send "more of our boys into Vietnam," a course that would gravely imperil his ambition to be regarded as the greatest of American presidents. A correspondent who observed this chain of events later recalled that over lunch in 1964 Johnson told reporters that he would not squander success as Roosevelt had done after 1936 on a single policy error. Tom Wicker wrote:

> Lyndon Johnson would not forget the limits of power; he would not carelessly throw away the fruits of his great victory for some unattainable goal, as Roosevelt had done in trying to pack the Supreme Court.
>   But he did.
>   . . . He had gone a long way, from the dust of the hill country to the loneliest peak of American political power and opportunity. And then, like Roosevelt before him, he . . . reached too far, believed too much, scaled the heights, only—in the blindness of his pride—to stumble and fall.

★   ★   ★

The stumble and fall came in foreign affairs where, at least as much as in domestic policy, Franklin Roosevelt served as Johnson's model. If Johnson sought to outdo FDR, it would not be by departing from his program but by doing more of it, as well as by avoiding the single big error. Though he competed with Roosevelt, he did not reject FDR's ideas. Indeed, it was in the age of Roosevelt that he had absorbed a lesson in foreign policy that he never forgot. World War II, he discerned, had resulted from the appeasement of the fascist powers, which had been emboldened by America's disregard of FDR's warnings. In the Cold War era, Johnson bore Roosevelt's experience constantly in mind. Mechanically substituting Soviet Russia for Nazi Germany, he summed up what he believed to be the appropriate response to Communist aggression in a single phrase: "No more Munichs."

In an interview with the historian Henry Graff in 1965, the president returned frequently to memories of the 1930s and 1940s. Johnson emphasized that his first serious thinking about diplomatic questions had begun as Hitler was rising to power, and he claimed that Roosevelt had wanted him on the Naval Affairs Committee because the Navy had been permitted to deteriorate and the president counted on Johnson to help see to it that the country had adequate force. He took pride in the fact that in 1941 he had persuaded Secretary of State Cordell Hull to write a letter that he liked to think had provided the margin of difference when the House approved by only one vote an extension of the draft less than four months before Pearl Harbor. As Johnson spoke, Graff noted, "he mentioned 'the Nyes, the Borahs, and La Follettes and Chamberlain'—as if the whole panorama of the isolationist years had come alive for him again."

It had been not just Roosevelt the New Dealer but Roosevelt the Big Navy Man who had first attracted Lyndon Johnson. It was as champion of FDR's rearmament program that Johnson had ingratiated himself with the White House circle, and when in World War II he toned down his enthusiasm for social measures to appease right-wingers in Texas, he retained his value to the administration by clamoring for increased arms spending. The portrait of Roosevelt that Johnson hung in the White House was not that of the champion of the New Deal but that of the World War II commander in chief. And when he stepped up American involvement in Southeast Asia in 1965, he was sure that he was being faithful to FDR's precepts.

Johnson looked at the situation in Vietnam through spectacles ground in the 1930s. He frequently analogized the challenge in Southeast Asia to that posed by Hitler at Munich. When Kennedy sent him to Saigon in 1961, Johnson had likened Ngo Dinh Diem to Roosevelt, and as president he said cheerily that Premier Ky "sounded like Rex Tugwell." He even proposed to establish a TVA in a Vietnamese river basin. "I want to leave the footprints of America in Vietnam," he declared in 1966. "I want them to say when the Americans come, this is what they leave—schools, not long cigars. We're going to turn the Mekong into a Tennessee valley."

. . .

In the spring of 1967, the columnist Roscoe Drummond compared Johnson's situation in Vietnam with FDR's on the eve of World War II. Just as bitter words were directed at Johnson from college campuses, so had Roosevelt been required to endure intellectual gadflies who told him to ignore the Axis threat. "President Roosevelt did not take their advice when he concluded that America had to join in resisting aggression in Europe and President Johnson is not following their advice today in his conviction that America must arrest the tide of aggression in Southeast Asia," Drummond stated. "FDR had his critics on resisting aggression but he proved to be right. Mr. Johnson has his critics on resisting aggression but, I believe, he, too, will prove to be right."

That was a line of argument Johnson frequently employed himself. When at a press conference in November 1967 Johnson was asked why there was "so much confusion, frustration and difference of opinion about the war in Vietnam," he replied, "You know what President Roosevelt went through," and others had endured a similar response. "Now, when you look back upon it, there are very few people who would think that Wilson, Roosevelt, or Truman were in error." Such, too, he implied, would be the judgment of history on his own actions.

Some observers agreed that the president had much in common

with FDR, but not in the way Johnson intended. When Johnson, having won election on a peace appeal in 1964, soon afterward expanded the Vietnam struggle, it was remembered that Franklin Roosevelt had pledged in 1940 that he would send no boys into foreign wars and then had led the nation step by step toward involvement in World War II. Similarly, Roosevelt's guile and deceit during 1941 suggested Johnson's misrepresentation of such episodes as the Tonkin Gulf affair. One writer later stated: "Roosevelt could be said to have taught his successors, the most worshipful of whom was Lyndon Johnson, that lying succeeded and could be for the 'public good.'"

In Johnson's second term, critics likened his government to the welfare-warfare state that had flourished under Franklin Roosevelt. "For Johnson, as for Wilson and the two Roosevelts before him, as for Bismarck, who created the welfare state, and Lloyd George, who adapted it for assimilation into Anglo-Saxon society, the welfare state evolved as a compound of militarism and reform," one commentator noted. Another charged that Johnson had deliberately chosen war as "the best way to pay off campaign backers" and "to keep a nation working and prosperous and content with his administration."

. . .

Such a view, though far from uncommon, commanded the support of only a minority. The majority rejected it not primarily because the analysis was so simplistic, ignoring as it did that Johnson heated up the Vietnam intervention precisely when the economy was flourishing and when the spectacular success of the tax cut had given every reason to suppose that the nation could prosper without war. More significantly, the conflict in Southeast Asia, however much it owed to such earlier presidents as FDR, had by 1968 unmistakably become "Johnson's war." In particular, there was a quality of grandiosity to the conflict, as there was to the Great Society, which had become LBJ's hallmark. As Doris Kearns has written:

Lyndon Johnson had wanted to surpass Franklin Roosevelt; and Roosevelt, after all, had not only won the reforms Johnson envied; he had also waged a war. But there was a critical difference: Roosevelt did not attempt the New Deal and World War II at the same time. Only Johnson among the Presidents sought to be simultaneously first in peace and first in war; and even Johnson was bound to fail.

With each passing month, critics drummed home the same message: that Johnson had, after all, made the one big mistake; and when it came time to decide what course he should follow in 1968, his most vivid memory of the Roosevelt years returned to him. "He recalled coming in as a Congressman and seeing FDR immobilized domestically over the Supreme Court issue," Walt Rostow has said. "He felt that he could beat Nixon, but wouldn't be able to accomplish anything in his second term. He had too many 'tin cans' tied to him. He had used up his capital on civil rights and on the war." Like Roosevelt, he had miscalculated, and the consequences would be far more costly for him than they had been for FDR. Roosevelt could claim that the Court-packing gamble had ended in victory, for the Supreme Court never again struck down a New Deal law. Moreover, he was returned to office for an unprecedented third term and then elected for a fourth term. For Johnson, though, the string had run out. On March 31, 1968, no longer able to sustain the burdens of an unpopular war and domestic disorder, he shocked the nation by announcing that he would not be a candidate for another term. His strenuous effort to win recognition as "the greatest of them all, the whole bunch of them," had come to an end.

In the aftermath of Johnson's March 31 announcement, which appeared to signal the demise of the age of Roosevelt, such commentators as Eric Goldman, who had served on the White House staff, offered a compelling explanation for the president's difficulties: he had remained an FDR man in an era altogether different from the Great Depression. "America had been rampaging between the 1930s and the 1960s," Goldman wrote. "The alterations were so swift and so deep that the country was changing right out from under President

Lyndon Johnson." Goldman went on to say that "like a good 1930's man, he expressed his authentic thinking during the campaign of 1964 when he would shout, 'Remember Molly and the children,' or 'We Americans don't want much. We want decent food, housing and clothing.'" But in the 1960s, though "there were still plenty of Mollys with plenty of troubles," the main problem had shifted from subsistence to "how to live with a weirdly uneasy general affluence—one that was marked by a maldistribution no longer accepted by a significant section of the population and by a race revolt that was only in part economic." Johnson continued to address himself to the needs and aspirations of the FDR coalition, but "now much of labor sounded like threatened burghers"; white workers had less concern about social reform than status trauma; black militants were distrustful even of such well-intentioned whites as Johnson; and the young, with no memory of the Roosevelt era, "were inclined to think of bread-and-butter liberalism as quaint if not downright camp." Throughout all of society, the values that had sustained America in the age of Roosevelt and for generations before were being questioned. In such a situation, Goldman concluded, "President Johnson, acting upon the kind of consensus domestic policy that would merely codify and expand the 1930s, was about as contemporary as padded shoulders, a night at the radio and Clark Gable."

Theodore White has made a similar point about the political situation in 1968. "In an age of affluence and education the blind urges that had once created atavistic Democratic votes in slums, factories, ghettos, universities were no longer blind," he has observed. The Roosevelt coalition had been based on the assumption that the working class would be satisfied by the activities of the government in doling out federal benefits. But by 1968 white workers no longer depended on Washington as they had done in the 1930s, and Johnson was asking them to do something Roosevelt had not demanded of them—to accede to the aspirations of blacks for a fair share of power and perquisites that they were reluctant to surrender. "All through 1968," White noted, "the working-class base of the Democratic coalition was to be torn almost as if by civil war, as white workingmen questioned the risk and the pace imposed on them in the adventure."

. . .

Though these observations contain important insights, they fall short of fully explaining Johnson's troubles, especially in the realm of foreign affairs. Clearly, there are resemblances between FDR's foreign policy and Johnson's. But there are also critical differences. As Goldman acknowledges, Johnson had "laid hold of an attic doctrine which included even apostrophes to the flag and international deeds of derring-do," an approach that suggests not Roosevelt's measured attitude but an earlier era of forays against banana republics. Johnson's behavior toward the Dominican Republic, in particular, contravened the spirit of FDR's Good Neighbor Policy. Nor is Johnson's persistence in the Southeast Asian disaster readily traceable to Roosevelt. So sympathetic was FDR to the aspirations of the Vietnamese that one student of the Vietnam disaster has concluded, "If Roosevelt had lived, the history of Southeast Asia might have been different." That is probably an overstatement, for by the time of his death FDR had been compelled to beat a retreat in the face of French and British resistance and Chinese weakness. Nonetheless, when Ho Chi Minh appealed to American correspondents for understanding after World War II, he cited the outlook of Franklin Roosevelt as testimony to the rightness of his cause.

It has not been convincingly demonstrated, either, that Johnson came to grief with the Great Society because the FDR legacy was outmoded in the 1960s. In many respects the Roosevelt tradition was a source of strength for Johnson. It provided him with an identity, the core of an electoral coalition, a cadre of advisers, and a storehouse of ideas, especially those for the War on Poverty. To be sure, the problems of the sixties differed from those of the thirties, and Johnson needed to adapt to the imperatives of a new age. But he ran into trouble not so much because he adhered to Roosevelt's programs as because he grafted onto them feckless innovations.

Johnson foundered less because the FDR legacy was faulty than because of his own misconceptions of it and, even more, because of his egregious behavior. When he imitated Roosevelt, he did so with such frenzy that the Johnson White House, one of his aides has written, emerged as a "caricature" of FDR's, "a grotesque and very unattractive scene which, at best, resembled the dances in the Hall of the Mountain King in *Peer Gynt*." In his determination to outdo Roosevelt, he carried everything to excess—the overladen apparatus of the Great Society; the insistence on having both guns and butter, which had calamitous inflationary repercussions; and, most of all, the body counts and the napalm and the saturation bombing.

Johnson had high hopes of history, but those hopes were to be blighted. He would tell visitors to the LBJ Ranch: "This is the tree I expect to be buried under and when my grandchildren see this tree I want them to think of me as the man who saved Asia and . . . who did something for the Negroes in this country." He had thought, too, that his child, the Great Society, would "grow into a beautiful woman" and that the American people would "want to keep her around forever, making her a permanent part of American life, more permanent even than the New Deal." But he lived long enough to see that at the 1972 Democratic National Convention, FDR's picture was displayed along with those of other party leaders but his own portrait was nowhere to be seen. Not many months later, Senator Vance Hartke, peering at his coffin, reflected, "On balance, Lyndon Johnson will be remembered as a sincere humanitarian in the Franklin Roosevelt mold, but with this caveat: the Vietnam War will be hanging over that judgment. Some of the living will forgive him—the dead, never."

Yet if Johnson failed in his effort to put FDR in his shadow, he did not leave the Roosevelt tradition unaltered. A month before Johnson died, the Harris poll released findings that may have been one of the last things he ever read. Asked which recent president "most inspired confidence," respondents chose FDR 393 to 28 over Johnson. (By February 1976 the ratio had risen to 508–14.) The results suggested that the FDR appeal had not faded away in 1968. But, as a result of Johnson's behavior, the Roosevelt emphases were more than ever perceived to contain ingredients of evil as well as good. Johnson's successors would eye the Roosevelt legacy warily, conscious of the malign consequences that could follow from it. It was in this unintended and perverse fashion that Lyndon Johnson, who claimed to want nothing more than to exalt the hero of his youth, did in the end achieve his covert ambition—to cast a shadow on FDR.

_____

Excerpted from William E. Leuchtenburg, *In the Shadow of FDR: From Harry Truman to Bill Clinton*, Second Edition, Revised and Newly Updated (Ithaca: Cornell University Press, 1983), pgs. 121–160.

Richard Nixon

TRICKY

"Political satire isn't writing that lasts," Philip Roth said in a 1971 interview about *Our Gang,* his satire on the Nixon administration. Few who remember Nixon will agree. Set against the convention-gelded reporting of the time, or the work of subsequent historians, Roth's distorted Nixon seems the abiding Nixon. Straight writing straightens Nixon. By normalizing him, *it* distorts him. Television revealed what the political writers and talking heads ignored: THIS MAN IS WEIRD. But revealed to whom? Millions voted for Nixon. Television also showed: THIS MAN IS TOUGH. That's what majorities wanted, and got, from Nixon. Of all our presidents, he owed the most to *resentment.* The country was going to hell: losing a war for the first time ever, its cities burning, its culture of restraint breaking up. A vote for Nixon was a vote against the sixties.

What "triggered—that's the word for it, too"—Roth's satire was Nixon's announcement that Lt. William Calley, convicted for the massacre of "four times as many unarmed civilians as Charles Manson" at My Lai, would not be confined in the post stockade ("alongside those who go AWOL and the Benedict Arnolds who get caught snoozing on guard duty") while awaiting the results of his appeal; he could remain in his quarters until Nixon reviewed the verdict himself. "I thought: Tricky, I knew you were a moral ignoramus, I knew you were a scheming opportunist, I knew you were fraudulent right down to your shoelaces, but truly, I did not think that even you would sink to something like this." But, Roth says, this reaction was naïve. "Why shouldn't he sink to it?... If

50.1% of the voters wanted to make a hero out of a convicted multiple murderer, then maybe there was something in it—for him."

Roth played off Nixon's abject proclivity for electoral pandering. *It would be easy to do the popular thing,* Nixon would say before doing the popular thing. In the first chapter of *Our Gang,* President Trick E. Dixon proclaims his belief in the rights of the unborn, as President Nixon did in the statement reprinted below, and engages in a dialogue with a "Troubled Citizen" who agrees with him about the unborn. In killing Vietnamese women, the Troubled Citizen asks, might Lt. Calley have violated the rights of an unborn Vietnamese carried by a possibly pregnant woman? No, Tricky—speaking "as a trained lawyer"—replies: "[I]f she was not 'showing,' Lt. Calley could not be said to have engaged in an unacceptable form of population control." As he gains the Troubled Citizen's moral admiration for his solicitude towards the unborn, the electoral strategy Tricky announces in "Tricky Holds a Press Conference" takes shape in the amniotic fluid of his mind: What if the unborn could vote?

> ... *And I remember frequent Discourses with my Master concerning the Nature of Manhood, in other Parts of the World; having Occasion to talk of* Lying, *and* false Representation, *it was with much Difficulty that he comprehended what I meant; although he had otherwise a most acute Judgment. For he argued thus; That the Use of Speech was to make us understand one another, and to receive Information of Facts; now if anyone said the Thing which was not, these Ends were defeated; because I cannot properly be said to understand him; and I am so far from receiving Information, that he leaves me worse than in Ignorance; for I am led to believe a Thing* Black *when it is* White, *and* Short *when it is* Long. *And these were all the Notions he had concerning that Faculty of Lying, so perfectly well understood, and so universally practised among human Creatures.*
>
> —JONATHAN SWIFT, *A Voyage to the Houyhnhnms,* 1726

> ... *one ought to recognize that the present political chaos is connected with the decay of language, and that one can probably*

*bring about some improvement by starting at the verbal end. . . .
Political language—and with variations this is true of all political
parties, from Conservatives to Anarchists—is designed to make lies
sound truthful and murder respectable, and to give an appearance of
solidity to pure wind.*
— GEORGE ORWELL, "Politics and the English Language," 1946

*From personal and religious beliefs I consider abortions an
unacceptable form of population control. Furthermore, unrestricted
abortion policies, or abortion on demand, I cannot square with my
personal belief in the sanctity of human life—including the life of the
yet unborn. For, surely, the unborn have rights also, recognized in
law, recognized even in principles expounded by the United Nations.*
— RICHARD NIXON, San Clemente, April 3, 1971

TRICKY COMFORTS A TROUBLED CITIZEN
Philip Roth

CITIZEN: Sir, I want to congratulate you for coming out on April 3
for the sanctity of human life, including the life of the yet unborn.
That required a lot of courage, especially in light of the November
election results.

TRICKY: Well, thank you. I know I could have done the popular
thing, of course, and come out *against* the sanctity of human life.
But frankly I'd rather be a one-term president and do what I believe is right than be a two-term president by taking an easy position like that. After all, I have got my conscience to deal with, as
well as the electorate.

CITIZEN: Your conscience, sir, is a marvel to us all.

TRICKY: Thank you.

CITIZEN: I wonder if I may ask you a question having to do with
Lieutenant Calley and his conviction for killing twenty-two Vietnamese civilians at My Lai.

TRICKY: Certainly. I suppose you are bringing that up as another example of my refusal to do the popular thing.

CITIZEN: How's that, sir?

TRICKY: Well, in the wake of the public outcry against that conviction, the popular thing—the most popular thing by far—would have been for me, as commander-in-chief, to have convicted the twenty-two unarmed civilians of conspiracy to murder Lieutenant Calley. But if you read your papers, you'll see I refused to do that, and chose only to review the question of his guilt, and not theirs. As I said, I'd rather be a one-term president. And may I make one thing more perfectly clear, while we're on the subject of Vietnam? I am not going to interfere in the internal affairs of another country. If President Thieu has sufficient evidence and wishes to try those twenty-two My Lai villagers posthumously, according to some Vietnamese law having to do with ancestor worship, that is his business. But I assure you, I in no way intend to interfere with the workings of the Vietnamese system of justice. I think President Thieu, and the duly elected Saigon officials, can "hack" it alone in the law and order department.

CITIZEN: Sir, the question that's been troubling me is this. Inasmuch as I share your belief in the sanctity of human life—

TRICKY: Good for you. I'll bet you're quite a football fan, too.

CITIZEN: I am, sir. Thank you, sir . . . But inasmuch as I feel as you do about the unborn, I am seriously troubled by the possibility that Lieutenant Calley may have committed an abortion. I hate to say this, Mr. President, but I am seriously troubled when I think that one of those twenty-two Vietnamese civilians Lieutenant Calley killed may have been a pregnant woman.

TRICKY: Now just one minute. We have a tradition in the courts of this land that a man is innocent until he is proven guilty. There were babies in that ditch at My Lai, and we know there were women of all *ages,* but I have not seen a single document that suggests the ditch at My Lai contained a *pregnant* woman.

CITIZEN: But what *if,* sir—what *if* one of the twenty-two was a pregnant woman? Suppose that were to come to light in your judicial review of the lieutenant's conviction. In that you personally believe in the sanctity of human life, including the life of the yet unborn, couldn't such a fact seriously prejudice you against Lieutenant Calley's appeal? I have to admit that as an opponent of abortion, it would have a profound effect upon me.

Nixon Compassionate

The president clearly pressed on welfare matters from the beginning. Whether it "absorbed more of his interest than any other domestic issue," as Moynihan claimed, is debatable, and the direction he was heading remained unclear for months. "I wanted to be an activist president in domestic policy," Nixon said in his *Memoirs,* "but I wanted to be certain that the things we did had a chance of working." He warned members of his cabinet: "Don't promise more than we can do, but do more than we can promise." The most effective evidence of Nixon's personal interest in welfare as a "compassionate conservative" was found in a memorandum to a speechwriter, Raymond Price, suggesting he put the idea in "human" terms for a future presidential address:

Paint a picture of what a terrible mark [welfare] leaves on the child's life. Point out that [Nixon's proposed reform] takes away the degradation of social workers snooping around, of making some children seem to be a class apart. . . .

Point out that the greatest [problem] of the present welfare program is the effect it has on children, and that the greatest benefit of all families in America is to stand proud with dignity without being singled out as those who are getting food stamps, welfare, or what have you.

[I]n the depression years I remember when my brother had tuberculosis for five years and we had to keep him in a hospital, my mother didn't buy a new dress for five years. We were really quite desperately poor, but as Eisenhower said it much more eloquently at Abilene in his opening campaign statement in 1952, the glory of it was that we didn't know it.

The problem today is that the children growing up in welfare families receiving food stamps and government largess with social workers poking around are poor and they do know it. . . .

[T]his is our chance now to see that every child, at least, will grow up in a family where he will not have the fact constantly thrown in his face that his father never married his mother and doesn't live at home, and that therefore in common parlance he is a bastard and further that he is on welfare, while his school mates can point with some degree of pride to the fact that their fathers at least are taking care of the family and have a little pride. The need for dignity, pride, character to be instilled in those first five years of life is something that could well be [included].

Despite his sensitivity to poor and disadvantaged Americans, Nixon and his speechwriters never did succeed in projecting this image to the public.

Excerpted from Joan Hoff, *Nixon Reconsidered* (New York: Basic Books, 1994), pgs. 118–119.

TRICKY: Well, it's very honest of you to admit it. But as a trained lawyer, I think I might be able to go at the matter in a somewhat less emotional manner. First off, I would have to ask whether Lieutenant Calley was *aware* of the fact that the woman in question was pregnant *before* he killed her. Clearly, if she was not yet "showing," I think you would in all fairness have to conclude that the lieutenant could have had no knowledge of her pregnancy, and thus, in no sense of the word would he have committed an abortion.

CITIZEN: What if she *told* him she was pregnant?

TRICKY: Good question. She might indeed have tried to tell him. But in that Lieutenant Calley is an American who speaks only English, and the My Lai villager is a Vietnamese who speaks only Vietnamese, there could have been no possible means of verbal communication. And as for sign language, I don't believe we can hang a man for failing to understand what must surely have been the gestures of a hysterical, if not deranged, woman.

CITIZEN: No, that wouldn't be fair, would it.

TRICKY: In short then, if the woman was not "showing," Lieutenant Calley could *not* be said to have engaged in an unacceptable form of population control, and it would be possible for me to square what he did with my personal belief in the sanctity of human life, including the life of the yet unborn.

CITIZEN: But, sir, what if she *was* "showing"?

TRICKY: Well then, as good lawyers we would have to ask another question. Namely: did Lieutenant Calley believe the woman to be pregnant, or did he, mistakenly, in the heat of the moment, assume that she was just stout? It's all well and good for us to be Monday Morning My Lai Quarterbacks, you know, but there's a war going on out there, and you cannot always expect an officer rounding up unarmed civilians to be able to distinguish between an ordinary fat Vietnamese woman and one who is in the middle, or even the late, stages of pregnancy. Now if the pregnant ones would wear maternity clothes, of course, that would be a great help to our boys. But in that they don't, in that all of them seem to go around all day in their pajamas, it is almost impossible to tell the men from the women, let alone the pregnant from the nonpregnant. Inevitably then—and this is just one of those unfortunate things about a war of this kind—there is going to be confusion on this whole score of who is who out there. I understand that we are doing all we can to get into the hamlets with American-style maternity clothes for the pregnant women to wear so as to make them more distinguishable to the troops at the massacres, but, as you know, these people have their own ways and will not always consent to do even what is clearly in their own interest. And, of course, we have no intention of forcing them. That, after all, is why we are in Vietnam in the first place—to give these people the right to choose their own way of life, in accordance with *their* own beliefs and customs.

CITIZEN: In other words, sir, if Lieutenant Calley assumed the woman was simply fat, and killed her under that assumption, that would still square with your personal belief in the sanctity of human life, including the life of the yet unborn.

TRICKY: Absolutely. If I find that he assumed she was simply overweight, I give you my utmost assurance, I will in no way be prejudiced against his appeal.

CITIZEN: But, sir, suppose, just *suppose,* that he *did* know she was pregnant.

TRICKY: Well, we are down to the heart of the matter now, aren't we?

CITIZEN: I'm afraid so, sir.

TRICKY: Yes, we are down to this issue of "abortion on demand," which, admittedly, is totally unacceptable to me, on the basis of my personal and religious beliefs.

CITIZEN: Abortion on *demand*?

TRICKY: If this Vietnamese woman presented herself to Lieutenant Calley for abortion . . . let's assume, for the sake of argument, she was one of those girls who goes out and has a good time and then won't own up to the consequences; unfortunately, we have them here just as they have them over there—the misfits, the bums, the tramps, the few who give the many a bad name . . . but if this woman presented herself to Lieutenant Calley for abortion, with some kind of note, say, that somebody had written for her in English, and Lieutenant Calley, let's say, in the heat and pressure of the moment, performed the abortion, during the course of which the woman died . . .

CITIZEN: Yes. I think I follow you so far.

TRICKY: Well, I just have to wonder if the woman isn't herself equally as guilty as the lieutenant—if she is not more so. I just have to wonder if this isn't a case for the Saigon courts, after all. Let's be perfectly frank: you cannot die of an abortion, if you don't go looking for the abortion to begin with. If you have not gotten yourself in an abortion *predicament* to begin with. Surely that's perfectly clear.

CITIZEN: It is, sir.

TRICKY: Consequently, even if Lieutenant Calley did participate in a case of "abortion on demand," it would seem to me, speaking strictly as a lawyer, mind you, that there are numerous extenuating factors to consider, not the least of which is the attempt to perform a surgical operation under battlefield conditions. I would think that more than one medic has been cited for doing less.

CITIZEN: Cited for what?

TRICKY: Bravery, of course.

CITIZEN: But . . . but, Mr. President, what if it wasn't "abortion on demand"? What if Lieutenant Calley gave her an abortion without her demanding one, or even asking for one—or even wanting one?

TRICKY: As an outright form of population control, you mean?

CITIZEN: Well, I was thinking more along the lines of an outright form of murder.

TRICKY (*reflecting*): Well, of course, that is a very iffy question, isn't it? What we lawyers call a hypothetical instance—isn't it? If you will remember, we are only *supposing* there to have been a pregnant woman in that ditch at My Lai to begin with. Suppose there *wasn't* a pregnant woman in that ditch—which, in fact, seems from all evidence to have been the case. We are then involved in a totally academic discussion.

CITIZEN: Yes, sir. If so, we are.

TRICKY: Which doesn't mean it hasn't been of great value to me, nonetheless. In my review of Lieutenant Calley's case, I will now be particularly careful to inquire whether there is so much as a single shred of evidence that one of those twenty-two in that ditch at My Lai was a pregnant woman. And if there is—if I should find in the evidence against the lieutenant anything whatsoever that I cannot square with my personal belief in the sanctity of human life, including the life of the yet unborn, I will disqualify myself as a judge and pass the entire matter on to the vice president.

CITIZEN: Thank you, Mr. President. I think we can all sleep better at night knowing that.

TRICKY HOLDS A PRESS CONFERENCE

MR. ASSLICK: Sir, as regards your San Dementia statement of April 3, the discussion it provoked seems now to have centered on your unequivocal declaration that you are a firm believer in the rights of the unborn. Many seem to believe that you are destined to be to the unborn what Martin Luther King was to the black people of America, and the late Robert F. Charisma to the disadvantaged chicanos and Puerto Ricans of the country. There are those who say that your San Dementia statement will go down in the history books alongside Dr. King's famous "I have a dream" address. Do you find these comparisons apt?

TRICKY: Well, of course, Mr. Asslick, Martin Luther King was a very great man, as we all must surely recognize now that he is dead. He was a great leader in the struggle for equal rights for his people, and yes, I do believe he'll find a place in history. But of course we must not forget he was not the president of the United States, as I am, empowered by the Constitution, as I am; and this is an important distinction to bear in mind. Working *within* the Constitution I think I will be able to accomplish far more for the unborn of this *entire* nation than did Dr. King working *outside* the Constitution for the born of *a single race.* This is meant to be no criticism of Dr. King, but just a simple statement of fact.

Now, of course I am well aware that Dr. King died a martyr's tragic death—so let me then make one thing very clear to my enemies and the enemies of the unborn: let there be no mistake about it, what they did to Martin Luther King, what they did to Robert F. Charisma and to John F. Charisma before him, great Americans all, is not for a moment going to deter me from engaging in the struggle that lies ahead. I will not be intimidated by extremists or militants or violent fanatics from bringing justice and equality to those who live in the womb. And let me make one thing more perfectly clear: I am not just talking about the rights of the fetus. I am talking about the microscopic embryos as well. If ever there was a group in this country that was "disadvantaged," in the sense that they are utterly without representation or a voice in our national government, it is not the blacks or the Puerto Ricans or the hippies or what-have-you, all of whom have their spokesmen, but these infinitesimal creatures up there on the placenta.

You know, we all watch our TV and we see the demonstrators and we see the violence, because, unfortunately, that is the kind of thing that makes the news. But how many of us realize that throughout this great land of ours, there are millions upon millions of embryos going through the most complex and difficult changes in form and structure, and all this they accomplish without waving signs for the camera and disrupting traffic and throwing paint and using foul language and dressing in outlandish clothes. Yes, Mr. Daring.

MR. DARING: But what about those fetuses, sir, that the vice president has labeled "troublemakers"? I believe he was referring specifically to those who start in kicking around the fifth month.

Do you agree that they are "malcontents" and "ingrates"? And if so, what measures do you intend to take to control them?

TRICKY: Well, first off, Mr. Daring, I believe we are dealing here with some very fine distinctions of a legal kind. Now, fortunately (*impish endearing smile*) I happen to be a lawyer and have the kind of training that enables me to make these fine distinctions. (*Back to serious business.*) I think we have to be very very careful here—and I am sure the vice president would agree with me—to distinguish between two kinds of activity: *kicking* in the womb, to which the vice president was specifically referring, and *moving* in the womb. You see, the vice president did not say, despite what you may have heard on television, that *all* fetuses who are active in the womb are troublemakers. Nobody in this administration believes that. In fact, I have just today spoken with both Attorney General Malicious and with Mr. Heehaw at the FBI, and we are all in agreement that a certain amount of movement in the womb, after the fifth month, is not only inevitable but *desirable* in a normal pregnancy.

But as for this other matter, I assure you, this administration does not intend to sit idly by and do nothing while American women are being kicked in the stomach by a bunch of violent five-month-olds. Now by and large, and I cannot emphasize this enough, our American unborn are as wonderful a group of unborn as you can find anywhere. But there are these violent few that the vice president has characterized, and I don't think unjustly, in his own impassioned rhetoric, as "troublemakers" and "malcontents"—and the attorney general has been instructed by me to take the appropriate action against them.

MR. DARING: If I may, sir, what sort of action will that be? Will there be arrests made of violent fetuses? And if so, how exactly will this be carried out?

TRICKY: I think I can safely say, Mr. Daring, that we have the finest law enforcement agencies in the world. I am quite sure that Attorney General Malicious can solve whatever procedural problems may arise. Mr. Respectful.

MR. RESPECTFUL: Mr. President, with all the grave national and international problems that press continually upon you, can you tell us why you have decided to devote yourself to this previously

Nixon Tough

Oval Office, April 25, 1972

PRESIDENT NIXON: We've got to quit thinking in terms of a three-day strike [in the Hanoi-Haiphong area]. We've got to be thinking in terms of an all-out bombing attack—which will continue until they—Now by all-out bombing attack, I am thinking about things that go far beyond ... I'm thinking of the dikes, I'm thinking of the railroad, I'm thinking, of course, the docks. . . .

KISSINGER: . . . I agree with you.

PRESIDENT NIXON: . . . we've got to use massive force. . . .

Two hours later, at noon, H. R. Haldeman and Ron Ziegler joined Kissinger and Nixon:

PRESIDENT: How many did we kill in Laos?

ZIEGLER: Maybe ten thousand—fifteen?

KISSINGER: In the Laotian thing, we killed about ten, fifteen. . . .

PRESIDENT: See, the attack in the North that we have in mind ... power plants, whatever's left—POL [petroleum], the docks ... And, I still think we ought to take the dikes out now. Will that drown people?

KISSINGER: About two hundred thousand people.

PRESIDENT: No, no, no ... I'd rather use the nuclear bomb. Have you got that, Henry?

KISSINGER: That, I think, would just be too much.

PRESIDENT: The nuclear bomb, does that bother you? ... I just want you to think big, Henry, for Christsakes.

One week later, on May 2, after hearing from Kissinger and Al Haig the merits of combining bombing and blockade, the president agreed to do both. As he concluded, "[B]lockade plus surgical bombing will inevitably achieve our objective—bring the North Vietnamese to their knees." Thus, even "if the South Vietnamese collapse" in the meantime, a possibility according to Kissinger, the

North, under the dual pressure, had "got to give us back our prisoners; *America* is not defeated. We must not lose in Vietnam. . . . So—we must draw the sword. So—the blockade is on. And I must say . . . that I like it. . . . And I want this clearly understood. The surgical operation theory is all right, but I want that place bombed to *smithereens.* If we draw the sword, we're gonna bomb those bastards all over the place. Let it fly, *let it fly.*"

On May 4, discussing his decision with Kissinger, Al Haig, and John Connally, Nixon put the confrontation with Vietnam in perspective. Heard on the Oval Office tape, he thumped his desk as he pointed to an imaginary or perhaps a real map on it:

> Vietnam: Here's those little cocksuckers right in there, here they are. (Thump.) Here's the United States. (Thump.) Here's Western (thump) Europe, that *cocky* little place that's caused so much devastation. . . . Here's the Soviet Union (thump), here's the (thump) Mid-East. . . . Here's the (thump) silly Africans. . . . And (thump) the not-quite-so-silly Latin Americans. Here *we* are. They're taking on the United States. Now, goddamit, we're gonna *do* it. We're going to *cream* them. This is not in anger or anything. This old business, that I'm "petulant," that's all bullshit. I should have done it long ago, I just didn't follow my instincts.
>
> . . . I'll see that the United States does not lose. I'm putting it quite bluntly. I'll be quite precise. South Vietnam may lose. But the United States *cannot* lose. Which means, basically, I have made the decision. Whatever happens to South Vietnam, we are going to *cream* North Vietnam.
>
> . . . For once, we've got to use the maximum power of this country . . . against this *shit-ass* little country: to win the war. We can't use the word, "win." But others can.

Excerpted from Daniel Ellsberg, *Secrets: A Memoir of Vietnam and the Pentagon Papers* (New York: Viking, 2002), pgs. 418–419.

neglected issue of fetal rights? You seem pretty fired up on this issue, sir—why is that?

TRICKY: Because, Mr. Respectful, I will not tolerate injustice in any area of our national life. Because ours is a just society, not merely for the rich and the privileged, but for the most powerless among us as well. You know, you hear a lot these days about Black Power and Female Power, Power this and Power that. But what about Prenatal Power? Don't they have rights too, membranes though they may be? I for one think they do, and I intend to fight for them. Mr. Shrewd.

MR. SHREWD: As you must know, Mr. President, there are those who contend that you are guided in this matter solely by political considerations. Can you comment on that?

TRICKY: Well, Mr. Shrewd, I suppose that is their cynical way of describing my plan to introduce a proposed constitutional amendment that would extend the vote to the unborn in time for the '72 elections.

MR. SHREWD: I believe that is what they have in mind, sir. They contend that by extending the vote to the unborn you will neutralize the gains that may accrue to the Democratic Party by the voting age having been lowered to eighteen. They say your strategists have concluded that even if you should lose the eighteen-to-twenty-one-year-old vote, you can still win a second term if you are able to carry the South, the state of California, and the embryos and fetuses from coast to coast. Is there any truth to this "political" analysis of your sudden interest in Prenatal Power?

TRICKY: Mr. Shrewd, I'd like to leave that to you—and to our television viewers—to judge, by answering your question in a somewhat personal manner. I assure you I am conversant with the opinions of the experts. Many of them are men whom I respect, and surely they have the right to say whatever they like, though of course one always hopes it will be in the national interest. . . . But let me remind you, and all Americans, because this is a fact that seems somehow to have been overlooked in this whole debate: I am no Johnny-come-lately to the problem of the rights of the unborn. The simple fact of the matter, and it is in the record for all to see, is that I myself was once unborn, in the great state of California. Of course, you wouldn't always know this from what you see on television or read in the papers (*impish endearing smile*) that some of you gentlemen write for, but it happens nonetheless to be the truth. (*Back to serious business.*) I was an unborn Quaker, as a matter of fact.

And let me remind you—since it seems necessary to do so, in the face of the vicious and mindless attacks upon him—vice president What's-his-name was also unborn once, an unborn Greek-American, and proud to have been one. We were just talking about that this morning, how he was once an unborn Greek-American, and all that has meant to him. And so too was Secretary Lard unborn and so was Secretary Codger unborn, and the attorney general— why, I could go right on down through my cabinet and point out to you one fine man after another who was once unborn. Even Secretary Fickle, with whom as you know I had my differences of opinion, was unborn when he was here with us on the team.

And if you look among the leadership of the Republican Party in the House and the Senate, you will find men who long before their election to public office were unborn in just about every region of this country, on farms, in industrial cities, in small towns the length and breadth of this great republic. My own wife was once unborn. As you may recall, my children were both unborn.

So when they say that Dixon has turned to the issue of the unborn just for the sake of the votes . . . well, I ask only that you consider this list of the previously unborn with whom I am associated in both public and private life, and decide for yourself. In fact, I think you are going to find, Mr. Shrewd, with each passing day, people around this country coming to realize that in this administration the fetuses and embryos of America have at last found their voice. Miss Charmin', I believe you had your eyebrows raised.

MISS CHARMIN': I was just going to say, sir, that of course President Lyin' B. Johnson was unborn, too, before he came to the White House—and he was a Democrat. Could you comment on that?

TRICKY: Miss Charmin', I would be the first to applaud my predecessor in this high office for having been unborn. I have no doubt that he was an outstanding fetus down there in Texas before he came into public life. I am not claiming that my administration is the first in history to be cognizant of the issue of fetal rights. I am saying that we intend to do something about them. Mr. Practical.

MR. PRACTICAL: Mr. President, I'd like to ask you to comment upon the scientific problems entailed in bringing the vote to the unborn.

TRICKY: Well, of course, Mr. Practical, you have hit the nail right on the head with the word "scientific." This is a scientific problem of staggering proportions—let's make no mistake about it. Moreover, I fully expect there are those who are going to say in tomorrow's papers that it is impossible, unfeasible, a utopian dream, and so on. But as you remember, when President Charisma came before the Congress in 1961, and announced that this country would put a man on the moon before the end of the decade, there were many who were ready to label him an impossible dreamer, too. But we did it. With American know-how and American teamwork, we did it. And so too do I have every confidence that our scientific and technological people are going to dedicate themselves to bringing the vote to the unborn—and not before the decade is out either, but before November of 1972.

MR. PRACTICAL: Can you give us some idea, sir, how much a crash program like this will cost?

TRICKY: Mr. Practical, I will be submitting a proposed budget to the Congress within the next ten days, but let me say this: you cannot achieve greatness without sacrifice. The program of research and development such as my scientific advisers have outlined cannot be bought "cheap." After all, what we are talking about here is nothing less than the fundamental principle of democracy: the vote. I cannot believe that the members of the Congress of the United States are going to play party politics when it comes to taking a step like this, which will be an advance not only for our nation, but for all mankind.

You just cannot imagine, for instance, the impact that this is going to have on the people in the underdeveloped countries. There are the Russians and the Chinese, who don't even allow adults to vote, and here we are in America, investing billions and billions of the taxpayers' dollars in a scientific project designed to extend the franchise to people who cannot see or talk or hear or even think, in the ordinary sense of the word. It would be a tragic irony indeed, and as telling a sign as I can imagine of national confusion and even hypocrisy, if we were willing to send our boys to fight and die in far-off lands so that defenseless peoples might have the right to choose the kinds of government they want in free elections, and then we were to turn around here at home and continue to deny that very same right to an entire segment of our population, just because they happen to live on the placenta or in the uterus, instead of New York City. Mr. Catch-Me-in-a-Contradiction.

MR. CATCH-ME-IN-A-CONTRADICTION: Mr. President, what startles me is that up until today you have been characterized, and not unwillingly, I think, as someone who, if he is not completely out of touch with the styles and ideas of the young, has certainly been skeptical of their wisdom. Doesn't this constitute, if I may use the word, a radical about-face, coming out now for the rights of those who are not simply "young" but actually in the gestation period?

TRICKY: Well, I am glad you raised that point, because I think it shows once and for all just how flexible I am, and how I am always willing to listen and respond to an appeal from *any* minority group, no matter how powerless, just so long as it is reasonable, and is not accompanied by violence and foul language and throwing paint. If ever there was proof that you don't have to camp on the White House lawn to get the president's attention away from a football game, I think it is in the example of these little organisms. I tell you, they have really impressed me with their silent dignity and politeness. I only hope that all Americans will come to be as proud of our unborn as I am.

MR. FASCINATED: Mr. President, I am fascinated by the technological aspect. Can you give us just an inkling of how exactly the unborn will go about casting their ballots? I'm particularly fascinated by these embryos on the placenta, who haven't even developed nervous systems yet, let alone limbs such as we use in an ordinary voting machine.

TRICKY: Well, first off, let me remind you that nothing in our Constitution denies a man the right to vote just because he is physically handicapped. That isn't the kind of country we have here. We have many wonderful handicapped people in this country, but of course, they're not "news" the way the demonstrators are.

MR. FASCINATED: I wasn't suggesting, sir, that just because these embryos don't have central nervous systems they should be denied the right to vote—I was thinking again of the fantastic *mechanics* of it. How, for instance, will the embryos be able to weigh the issues and make intelligent choices from among the candidates, if they are not able to read the newspapers or watch the news on television?

TRICKY: Well, it seems to me that you have actually touched upon the very strongest claim that the unborn have for enfranchisement, and why it is such a crime they have been denied the vote for so long. Here, at long last, we have a great bloc of voters who simply are not going to be taken in by the lopsided and distorted versions of the truth that are presented to the American public through the various media. Mr. Reasonable.

MR. REASONABLE: But how then will they make up their minds, or their yolks, or their nuclei, or whatever it is they have in there, Mr. President? It might seem to some that they are going to be absolutely innocent of whatever may be at stake in the election.

TRICKY: Innocent they will be, Mr. Reasonable—but now let me ask you, and all our television viewers, too, a question: what's *wrong* with a little innocence? We've had the foul language, we've had the cynicism, we've had the masochism and the breast-beating— maybe a big dose of innocence is just what this country needs to be great again.

MR. REASONABLE: *More* innocence, Mr. President?

TRICKY: Mr. Reasonable, if I have to choose between the rioting and the upheaval and the strife and the discontent on the one hand, and more innocence on the other, I think I will choose the innocence. Mr. Hardnose.

MR. HARDNOSE: In the event, Mr. President, that all this does come to pass by the '72 elections, what gives you reason to believe that the enfranchised embryos and fetuses will vote for you over your Democratic opponent? And what about Governor Wallow? Do you think that if he should run again, he would significantly cut into your share of the fetuses, particularly in the South?

TRICKY: Let me put it this way, Mr. Hardnose: I have the utmost respect for Governor George Wallow of Alabama, as I do for Senator Hubert Hollow of Minnesota. They are both able men, and they speak with great conviction, I am sure, in behalf of the extreme right and the extreme left. But the fact is that I have never heard either of these gentlemen, for all their extremism, raise their voices in behalf of America's most disadvantaged group of all, the unborn.

Consequently, I would be less than candid if I didn't say that when election time rolls around, of course the embryos and fetuses of this country are likely to remember just who it was that struggled in their behalf, while others were addressing themselves to the more popular and fashionable issues of the day. I think they will remember who it was that devoted himself, in the midst of a war abroad and racial crisis at home, to making this country a fit place for the unborn to dwell in pride.

My only hope is that whatever I am able to accomplish in their behalf while I hold this office will someday contribute to a world in which *everybody,* regardless of race, creed, or color, will be unborn. I guess if *I* have a dream, that is it. Thank you, ladies and gentlemen.

MR. ASSLICK: Thank you, Mr. President.

Excerpted from Philip Roth, *Our Gang* (New York: Random House, 1971), pgs. 13–26.

Richard J. Daley

BOSS

"If ever a man reflected a city, it was Richard J. Daley of Chicago," Mike Royko wrote in the *Chicago Sun-Times* after Daley's death in 1976, in the twenty-first year of his reign as mayor. Daley embodied the "best" and "worst" of Chicago: "[S]trong, hard-driving, working feverishly, pushing, building," yet also "arrogant, crude, conniving, ruthless, suspicious, intolerant."

Chicago is a city of neighborhoods: Daley was born and raised, and died, in blue-collar Bridgeport—like others in his Chicago, a neighborhood for white neighbors only.

Daley talked like a cement mixer. "Well, Chicago is not an articulate town, Saul Bellow notwithstanding," Royko writes. "Maybe it's because so many of us aren't that far removed from parents and grandparents who knew only bits and pieces of the language."

In Carl Sandburg's "Hog Butcher to the World" clean government can seem an affectation: Daley made Chicago "work." Its 3,400 precinct captains dispensing 40,000 patronage jobs, the Daley machine delivered basic city services to the neighborhoods while the mayor watered the downtown businesses. Chicago held elections, but Daley won them by Albanian margins. With the Democratic Party an arm of his machine, the Republicans long dormant, and the city establishment, including much of the press, accepting of the "Chicago works" rationale for Daley's power, Chicago sacrificed the substance of democracy for efficiency—and, according to Royko, did not miss it one bit: "The niceties of the democratic process weren't part of the immigrant experience."

Graft greased the machine. But Daley, who began every day with a Mass, "made sure our carnal vices were kept to a public minimum." At the 1968 Democratic National Convention in Chicago, where Daley's police beat up scores of anti-war demonstrators, Daley's aides wanted the world to know that the Mayor had *not* shouted "Fuck you" at Senator Abraham Ribicoff of Connecticut, who had departed from his speech nominating Senator George McGovern to denounce "the Gestapo in the streets of Chicago." The mayor said "faker," not "fuck you." He was a family man; he would never use dirty language. Meanwhile, chanting "kill the motherfuckers," Daley's cops were sweeping through Lincoln Park clubbing kids, clergymen, reporters, and bystanders, some of them blocks away from the park. The violence surging around the convention took down the man it nominated for president, Vice President Hubert H. Humphrey, and, though Daley won re-election to his fifth term in 1971 with 70 percent of the vote and to a sixth term in 1975, beyond Chicago "Chicago" sealed the mayor's reputation as a political thuggist.

In this excerpt from his unsparing biography *Boss: Richard J. Daley of Chicago,* Mike Royko presents a day in the life of his city-containing subject. Published in 1970, *Boss* quickly became a national bestseller, but in Chicago two hundred bookstores refused to sell it until overwhelmed by a public that included many in the working-class neighborhoods Daley had kept white. If Daley was its intolerant ruler, Royko, who died in 1997, was the compassionate voice of Chicago.

MAYOR DALEY'S DAY

Mike Royko

The workday begins early. Sometime after seven o'clock a black limousine glides out of the garage of the police station on the corner, moves less than a block, and stops in front of a weathered pink bungalow at 3536 South Lowe Avenue. Policeman Alphonsus Gilhooly, walking in front of the house, nods to the detective at the wheel of the limousine.

It's an unlikely house for such a car. A passing stranger might think that a rich man had come back to visit his people in the old neighborhood. It's the kind of sturdy brick house, common to Chicago, that a fireman or printer would buy. Thousands like it were put up by contractors in the 1920s and 1930s from standard blueprints in an architectural style fondly dubbed "carpenter's delight."

The outside of that pink house is deceiving. The inside is furnished in expensive, Colonial-style furniture, the basement paneled in fine wood, and two days a week a woman comes in to help with the cleaning. The shelves hold religious figurines and bric-a-brac. There are only a few volumes—the Baltimore Catechism, the Bible, a leather-bound *Profiles in Courage,* and several self-improvement books. All of the art is religious, most of it bloody with crucifixion and crosses of thorns.

Outside, another car has arrived. It moves slowly, the two detectives peering down the walkways between the houses, glancing at the drivers of the cars that travel the street, then parks somewhere behind the limousine.

At the other end of the block, a blue squad car has stopped near the corner tavern, and the policemen are watching Thirty-sixth Street, which crosses Lowe.

In the alley behind the house, a policeman sits in a car. Like Gilhooly, he has been there all night, protecting the back entrance, behind the high wooden fence that encloses the small yard.

Down the street, in another brick bungalow, Matt Danaher is getting ready for work. He runs the two thousand clerical employees in the Cook County court system, and he knows the morning routine of his neighbor. As a young protégé he once drove the car, opened the door, held the coat, got the papers. Now he is part of the ruling circle, and one of the few people in the world who can walk past the policeman and into the house, one of the people who are invited to spend an evening, sit in the basement, eat, sing, dance the Irish jig. The blue-blooded bankers from downtown aren't invited, although they would like to be, and neither are men who have been governors, senators, and ambassadors. The people who come in the evening or on Sunday are old friends from the neighborhood, the relatives, people who take their coats off when they walk in the door, and loosen their ties.

Danaher is one of them, and his relationship to the owner of the house is so close that he has served as an emotional whipping boy, so close that he can yell back and slam the door when he leaves.

They're getting up for work in the little houses and flats all across the old neighborhood known as Bridgeport, and thanks to the man for whom the limousine waits, about two thousand of the forty thousand Bridgeport people are going to jobs in City Hall, the County Building, the courts, ward offices, police and fire stations. It's a political neighborhood, with political jobs, and the people can use them. It ranks very low among the city and suburban communities in education. Those who don't have government jobs work hard for their money, and it isn't much. Bridgeport ranks low in income, too.

It's a suspicious neighborhood, a blend of Irish, Lithuanian, Italian, Polish, German, and all white. In the bars, heads turn when a stranger comes in. Blacks pass through in cars, but are unwise to travel by on foot. When a black college student moved into a flat on Lowe Avenue in 1964, only a block north of the pink bungalow, there was a riot and he had to leave.

Well before eight o'clock, the door of the pink bungalow opens and a short, stout man steps out. His walk is brisk and bouncy. A nod and smile to Patrolman Gilhooly and he's in the limousine. It pulls out from the curb and the "tail car" with the two detectives trails it, hanging back to prevent the limousine from being followed.

It's a short drive to work. The house is about four miles southwest of the Loop, the downtown business district, within the problem area known as the "inner city." If the limousine went east, to Lake Shore Drive, it would go through part of the black ghetto. If it went straight north, it would enter a decaying neighborhood in transition from white to Latin and black. It turns toward an expressway entrance only a few blocks away.

The two cars take the Dan Ryan Expressway, twelve lanes at its widest point, with a rapid-transit train track down the center. It stretches from the Loop, past the old South Side ghetto, past the giant beehive public housing with its swarming children, furious street gangs, and weary welfare mothers.

He built that expressway, and he named it after Dan Ryan, another big South Side politician, who was named after his father, a big South Side politician.

The limousine crosses another expressway, this one cutting through the big, smokey, industrial belt, southwest toward white backlash country, where five years ago Dr. Martin Luther King was hit in the head with a brick when he led marchers into the neighborhood for the cause of open housing—which exists only on a few pages of the city's ordinance.

He built that expressway, too, and named it after Adlai Stevenson, whom he helped build into a presidential candidate, and whom he dropped when it was time.

The limousine passes an exit that leads to the Circle Campus, the city's branch of the University of Illinois, acres of modern concrete buildings that comprise one of the biggest city campuses in the country. It wasn't easy to build because thousands of families in the city's oldest Italian neighborhood had to be uprooted and their homes and churches torn down. They cried that they were betrayed because they had been promised they would stay. But he built it.

Another mile or so and the limousine crosses another expressway that goes straight west, through the worst of the ghetto slums, where the biggest riots and fires were ignited, for which the outraged and outrageous "shoot to kill" order was issued. Straight west, past the house where the Black Panthers were killed, some in their beds, by the predawn police raiders.

He opened that expressway and named it after Dwight D. Eisenhower, making it the city's only Republican expressway.

As the limousine nears the Loop, the Dan Ryan blends into still another expressway. This one goes through the Puerto Rican ghetto and the remnants of the old Polish neighborhood, where the old people remain while their children move away, then into the middle class far Northwest Side, where Dr. King's marchers walked through a shower of bottles, bricks, and spit. It ends at O'Hare Airport, the nation's busiest jet handler.

He built that expressway, too, and he named it after John F. Kennedy, whom he helped elect president, and he built most of the airport and opened it, although he still calls it "O'Hara."

During the ride he reads the two morning papers, the *Chicago Sun-Times* and the *Chicago Tribune,* always waiting on the back seat. He's a fast but thorough reader and he concentrates on news about the city. He is in the papers somewhere every day, if not by name—and the omission is rare—at least by deed. The papers like him. If something has gone well, he'll be praised in an editorial. If something has gone badly, one of his subordinates will be criticized in an editorial. During the 1968 Democratic Convention, when their reporters were being bloodied, one of the more scathing newspaper editorials was directed at a lowly Police Department public relations man.

He, too, was criticized, but a week after the convention ended, his official version of what had happened on Chicago's streets was printed, its distortions and flat lies unchallenged. He dislikes reporters and writers, but gets on well with editors and publishers, a trait usually found in Republicans rather than Democrats. If he feels that he has been criticized unfairly, and he considers most criticism unfair, he doesn't hesitate to pick up a phone and complain to an editor. All four papers endorsed him for his fourth term—even the *Tribune,* the voice of Middle West Republicanism—but in general, he views the papers as his enemy. The reporters, specifically. They want to know things that are none of their business, because they are little men. Editors, at least, have power, but he doesn't understand why they let reporters exercise it.

The limousine leaves the expressway and enters the Loop, stopping in front of St. Peter's, a downtown church. When the bodyguards have parked and walked to his car, he gets out and enters the church. This is an important part of his day. Since childhood he has attended daily mass, as his mother did before him. On Sundays and some work days, he'll go to his own church, the Church of the Nativity, just around the corner from his home. That's where he was baptized, married, and the place from which his parents were buried. Before Easter, his wife will join the other neighborhood ladies for the traditional scrubbing of the church floors. Regardless of what he may do in the afternoon, and to whom, he will always pray in the morning.

After mass, it's a few steps to the side door of Maxim's, a glass and plastic coffee shop, where, in the event he comes in, a table is set up in the privacy of the rear. It is not to be confused with Chicago's other Maxim's, which serves haute cuisine, has a discotheque, and enjoys a social-register clientele. He won't go to those kinds of places. He doesn't like them and people might think he was putting on airs. He eats at home most of the time, and for dinner out there are sedate private clubs with a table in a quiet corner.

He leaves a dollar for his coffee and roll and marches with his bodyguards toward City Hall—"the Hall" as it is called locally, as in "I got a job in the Hall," or "See my brother in the Hall and he'll fix it for you," or "Do you know anybody in the Hall who can take care of this?"

He glances at the new Civic Center, a tower of russet steel and glass, fronted by a gracious plaza with a fountain and a genuine Picasso-designed metalwork sculpture almost fifty feet high.

He put it all there, the Civic Center, the plaza, the Picasso. And the judges and county officials who work in the Civic Center, he put most of them there, too.

Wherever he looks as he marches, there are new skyscrapers up or going up. The city has become an architect's delight, except when the architects see the great Louis Sullivan's landmark buildings being ripped down for parking garages or allowed to degenerate into slums.

None of the new buildings were there before. His leadership put them there, his confidence, his energy. Everybody says so. If he kept walking north a couple more blocks, he'd see the twin towers of Marina City, the striking tubular downtown apartment buildings, a self-contained city with bars and restaurants, ice rinks, shops and clubs, and balconies on every apartment for sitting out in the smog.

His good friend Charlie Swibel built it, with financing from the Janitors' Union, run by his good friend William McFetridge. For Charlie Swibel, building the apartment towers was coming a long way from being a flophouse and slum operator. Now some of his friend Charlie's flophouses are going to be torn down, and the area west of the Loop redeveloped for office buildings and such. And his friend Charlie will do that, too. Let people wonder why out-of-town investors let Charlie in for a big piece of the new project, without Charlie having to put up any money or take any risk. Let people ask why the city, after acquiring the land under urban renewal powers, rushed through approval of Charlie's bid. Let them ask if there's a conflict of interest because Charlie is also the head of the city's public housing agency, which makes him a city official. Let them ask. What trees do they plant? What buildings do they put up?

Head high, shoulders back, he strides with his bodyguards at the pace of an infantry forced march. The morning walk used to be much longer than two blocks. In the quiet of the 1950s, the limousine dropped him near the Art Institute on Michigan Avenue, and he'd walk a mile and a half on Michigan Avenue, the city's jeweled thoroughfare, grinning at the morning crowds that bustled past the shops and hotels, along the edge of Grant Park. That ritual ended in the sixties, when people began walking and marching for something more than pleasure, and a man couldn't be sure who he'd meet on the street.

He rounds the corner and a bodyguard moves ahead to hold open the door. An elderly man is walking slowly and painfully close to the wall, using it as support. His name is Al, and he is a lawyer. Years ago he was just a ward boss's nod away from becoming a judge. He had worked hard for the party and had earned the black robe, and he was even a pretty good lawyer. But the ward boss died on him, and judgeships can't be left in wills. Now his health was bad and Al had an undemanding job in county government.

He spots Al, calls out his name, and rushes over and gives him a two-handed handshake, the maximum in City Hall affection. He has seen Al twice in ten years, but he quickly recalls all of his problems, his work, and a memory they shared. He likes old people and keeps them in key jobs and reslates them for office when they can barely walk, or even when they can't. Like the marriage vows, the pact between jobholder and party ends only in either's death, so long as the jobholder loves, honors, and obeys the party. Later that day, Al will write an eloquent letter in praise of his old friend to a paper, which will print it.

The bodyguard is still holding the door and he goes in at full stride. He never enters a room tentatively—always explosively and with a sense of purpose and direction, especially when the building is City Hall.

Actually, there are two identical buildings—City Hall and the Cook County Building. At the turn of the century, the County Building was erected on half a city block, and shortly thereafter City Hall was put up. Although identical, City Hall cost substantially more. Chicago history is full of such oddities. Flip open any page and somebody is making a buck.

Although the main lobby and upstairs corridors extend through both buildings, he never goes through the County Building. That's a political courtesy, because the County Building is the domain of another politician, the president of the Cook County Board, known as "the mayor of Cook County," and, in theory, second only to him in power. But later in the day, the president of Cook County will call and ask how his domain should be run.

The elevator operators know his habits and are holding back the door of a car. The elevators are automated, but many operators remain on the job, standing in the lobby pointing at open cars and saying, "Next." Automation is fine, but how many votes can an automatic elevator deliver?

He gets off at the fifth floor, where his offices are. That's why he's known as "the Man on Five." He is also known as "duh mare" and "hizzoner" and "duh leader."

He marches past the main entrance to his outer offices, where people are already waiting, hoping to see him. They must be cleared first by policemen, then by three secretaries. He doesn't use the main entrance because the people would jump up, clutch at his hands, and overexcite themselves. He was striding through the building one day when a little man sprung past the bodyguards and kissed his hand.

Down the corridor, a bodyguard has opened a private door, leading directly to his three-room office complex. He almost always uses the side door.

The bodyguards quickly check his office, then file into a smaller adjoining room, filled with keepsakes from presidents and his trip to

Ireland. They use the room as a lounge, while studying his schedule, planning the routes and waiting. Another room is where he takes important phone calls when he has someone with him. Calls from President Kennedy and President Johnson were put through to that room.

Somewhere in the building, phone experts have checked his lines for taps. The limousine has been parked on LaSalle Street, outside the Hall's main entrance, and the tail car has moved into place. His key people are already in their offices, always on time or early, because he may call as soon as he arrives. And at 9 A.M. he, Richard Joseph Daley, is in his office and behind the big gleaming mahogany desk, in a high-backed dark green leather chair, ready to start another day of doing what the experts say is no longer possible—running a big American city. But as he, Daley, has often said to confidantes, "What in hell do the experts know?" He's been running a big American city for fifteen of the toughest years American cities have ever seen. He, Daley, has been running it as long or longer than any of the other famous mayors—Curley of Boston, LaGuardia of New York, Kelly of Chicago—ran theirs, and unless his health goes, or his wife says no, he, Daley, will be running it for another four years. Twenty is a nice, round figure. They give soldiers pensions after twenty years, and some companies give wristwatches. He'll settle for something simple, like maybe another jet airport built on a man-made island in the lake, and named after him, and maybe a statue outside the Civic Center, with a simple inscription, "The greatest mayor in the history of the world." And they might seal off his office as a shrine.

It's a business office. Like the man, the surroundings have no distracting frills. He wears excellently tailored business suits, buying six a year from the best shop on Michigan Avenue. The shirt is always radiant white, the tie conservative. Because his shoulders are narrow, he never works in his shirt sleeves, and is seldom seen publicly in casual clothes. The businesslike appearance carries through the office. The carpets, furniture, and walls are in muted shades of tan and green. The only color is provided by the flags of the United States and the city of Chicago, and a color photograph of his family. When a prominent cultural leader offered to donate some paintings for the office, an aide said, "Please, no, he can't accept them. People would think he's going high-hat."

The desk, with a green leather inset, is always clear of papers. He is an orderly man. Besides, he doesn't like to put things on paper, preferring the telephone. Historians will look in vain for a revealing memo, an angry note. He stores his information in his brain and has an amazing recall of detail.

The office is a place to work. And the work begins immediately. The first call will be to his secretary, checking the waiting visitors and asking that his press secretary be summoned, so he can let him know if he wants to talk to the press that morning. He holds more press conferences than any major public official in the country—at least two, and usually three, a week. In the beginning, they were often relaxed, casual, friendly and easy, with the reporters coming into his office, getting the q's and a's out of the way, and swapping fish stories and a few jokes, but always clean jokes because he walks away from the dirty ones. But with television, the press conferences became formal. They moved to a conference room, and became less friendly as the times became less friendly. He works at self-control, but it is impossible not to blow up and begin ranting. Reporters are like experts. What do they know?

If he is going to see them, Earl Bush, the press aide, will brief him on likely questions. The veteran City Hall reporters are not hostile, since they have to live with him, but the TV personalities sometimes ask questions that are calculated to cause a purple face and a fit of shouting rather than evoke information. He knows it, but sometimes it is hard not to get purple and shout.

If he doesn't feel like bothering, he'll just tell Bush, "To hell with them," and go on to other work. Bush never argues. He's been there since the beginning, a hungry journalist, operating a struggling neighborhood newspaper news service, who had a hunch that the quiet man running the county clerk's office was going to go somewhere. On the day after the first mayoralty election, Daley threw three hundred-dollar bills in his rumpled lap and said, "Get yourself some decent-looking clothes." Bush has since slept a night in the White House.

After Bush will come someone like Deputy Mayor David Stahl, one of the young administrators the old politicians call "the whiz kids." Like the other "whiz kids," Stahl is serious, well educated, obedient, ambitious, and keeps his sense of humor out of sight. He was hired for these qualities and also because his father-in-law is a real estate expert and a close friend.

On a day when the City Council is meeting, Ald. Thomas Keane will slip in the side door to brief him on the agenda. Keane is considered to be second in party power, but it is a distant second. Keane wanted to be in front, but he was distracted by a craving for personal wealth. You can't do both if the man you're chasing is concentrating only on power. Now Keane is rich, but too old to ever be the successor.

If there is a council meeting, everybody marches downstairs at a few minutes before ten. Bush and the department heads and personal aides form a proud parade. The meeting begins when the seat of the mayor's pants touches the council president's chair, placed beneath the great seal of the city of Chicago and above the heads of the aldermen, who sit in a semi-bowl auditorium.

It is his council, and in all the years it has never once defied him as a body. Keane manages it for him, and most of its members do what they are told. In other eras, the aldermen ran the city and plundered it. In his boyhood they were so constantly on the prowl that they were known as "the Gray Wolves." His council is known as "the Rubber Stamp."

He looks down at them, bestowing a nod or a benign smile on a few favorites, and they smile back gratefully. He seldom nods or smiles at the small minority of white and black independents. The independents anger him more than the Republicans do, because they accuse him of racism, fascism, and of being a dictator. The Republicans bluster about loafing payrollers, crumbling gutters, inflated budgets—traditional, comfortable accusations that don't stir the blood.

That is what Keane is for. When the minority goes on the attack, Keane himself, or one of the administration aldermen he had groomed for the purpose, will rise and answer the criticism by shouting that the critic is a fool, a hypocrite, ignorant, and misguided. Until his death, one alderman could be expected to leap to his feet at every meeting and cry, "God bless our mayor, the greatest mayor in the world."

But sometimes Keane and his trained orators can't shout down the minority, so Daley has to do it himself. If provoked, he'll break into a rambling, ranting speech, waving his arms, shaking his fists, defending his judgment, defending his administration, always with the familiar "It is easy to criticize . . . to find fault . . . but where are your programs . . . where are your ideas . . . "

If that doesn't shut off the critics, he will declare them to be out of order, threaten to have the sergeant at arms force them into their seats, and invoke *Robert's Rules of Order,* which, in the heat of debate, he once described as "the greatest book ever written."

All else failing, he will look toward a glass booth above the spectator's balcony and make a gesture known only to the man in the booth who operates the sound system that controls the microphones on each alderman's desk. The man in the booth will touch a switch and the offending critic's microphone will go dead and stay dead until he sinks into his chair and closes his mouth.

The meetings are seldom peaceful and orderly. The slightest criticism touches off shrill rebuttal, leading to louder criticism and finally an embarrassingly wild and vicious free-for-all. It can't be true, because Daley is a man who speaks highly of law and order, but sometimes it appears that he enjoys the chaos, and he seldom moves to end it until it has raged out of control.

Every word of criticism must be answered, every complaint must be disproved, every insult must be returned in kind. He doesn't take anything from anybody. While Daley was mediating negotiations between white trade unions and black groups who wanted the unions to accept blacks, a young militant angrily rejected one of his suggestions and concluded, "Up your ass!" Daley leaped to his feet and answered, "And up yours too." Would John Lindsay have become so involved?

Independent aldermen have been known to come up with a good idea, such as providing food for the city's hungry, or starting day-care centers for children of ghetto women who want to work; Daley will acknowledge it, but in his own way. He'll let Keane appropriate the idea and rewrite and resubmit it as an administration measure. That way, the independent has the satisfaction of seeing his idea reach fruition and the administration has more glory. But most of the independents' proposals are sent to a special subcommittee that exists solely to allow their unwelcome ideas to die.

The council meetings seldom last beyond the lunch hour. Aldermen have much to do. Many are lawyers and have thriving practices, because Chicagoans know that a dumb lawyer who is an alderman can often perform greater legal miracles than a smart lawyer who isn't.

Keane will go to a hotel dining room near City Hall, where at a large round table in a corner, he lunches each day with a clique of high-rise real estate developers, financiers, and political cronies. The things they plan and share will shape the future of the city, as well as the future of their heirs.

Daley has no such luncheon circle, and he eats only with old and close friends or one of his sons. Most afternoons, he darts across the street to the Sherman House hotel and his office in the Democratic headquarters, where as party chairman he will work on purely political business: somebody pleading to be slated for an office or advanced to a judgeship, a dispute between ward bosses over patronage jobs. He tries to separate political work from his duties as mayor, but nobody has ever been able to see where one ends and the other begins.

Lunch will be sent up and he might be joined by someone like Raymond Simon, the Bridgeport-born son of an old friend. Daley put him in the city legal department when he was fresh out of law school, and in a few years he was placed in charge, one of the highest legal jobs in the country. Now Simon has taken on an even bigger job: he resigned and went into private practice with Daley's oldest son, Richard Michael, not long out of law school. The name Daley and Simon on the office door possesses magic that has the big clients almost waiting in line. Daley's next oldest son, Michael, has gone into practice with a former law partner of the mayor, and has a surprisingly prosperous practice for so young and inexperienced an attorney. Daley filled Simon's place in his cabinet with another bright young lawyer, the mayor's first cousin.

When there is time, Daley is driven to the private Lake Shore Club for lunch, a swim, or a steam bath. Like most of the better private clubs in the fine buildings along the lake front, the Lake Shore Club accepts Jews and blacks. But you have to sit there all day to be sure of seeing one.

It's a pleasant drive to the club. Going north on Michigan Avenue, he passes the John Hancock Building, second in size only to the Empire State, and twice as high as anything near it. It was built during Daley's fourth term, despite cries of those who said it would bring intolerable traffic congestion to the gracious streets that can't handle it and lead to other oversized buildings that would destroy the unique flavor of the North Michigan Avenue district. It's happening, too, but the Hancock is another tall monument to his leadership.

From Michigan Avenue, he goes onto Lake Shore Drive, with the lake and beaches on the right, which were there when he started, and ahead the great wall of high-rise buildings beginning on the left, which wasn't. Dozens of them, hundreds, stretching mile after mile, all the way to the city limits, and almost all constructed during his administration, providing city living for the upper middle class, and billions in profits for the real estate developers. They are his administration's solution to keeping people in the city.

Behind the high-rises are the crumbling, crowded buildings where the lower-income people live. No answer has been found to their housing problems because the real estate people say there's not enough profit in building homes for them. And beyond them are the middle-income people, who can't make it to the high-rises and can't stay where they are because the schools are inadequate, the poor are pushing toward them, and nothing is being done about their problems, so they move to the suburbs. When their children grow up and they retire, maybe then they can move to a lake front high-rise.

By two o'clock he's back behind his desk and working. One of his visitors will be a city official unique to Chicago city government: the director of patronage. He brings a list of all new city employees for the day. The list isn't limited to the key employees, the professional people. All new employees are there—down to the window washer, the ditch digger, the garbage collector. After each person's name will be an extract of his background, the job, and most important, his political sponsor. Nobody goes to work for the city, and that includes governmental bodies that are not directly under the mayor, without Daley's knowing about it. He must see every name because the person becomes more than an employee: he joins the political Machine, part of the army numbering in the thousands who will help win elections. They damn well better, or they won't keep their jobs.

He scans the list for anything unusual. A new employee might be related to somebody special, an important businessman, an old political family. That will be noted. He might have been fired by another city office in a scandal. That won't keep him from being put to work somewhere else. Some bad ones have worked for half the governmental offices in the city. There might be a police record, which prompts a call to the political sponsor for an explanation. "He's clean now." "Are you sure?" "Of course, it was just a youthful mistake." "Three times?" "Give him a break, his uncle is my best precinct captain." "Okay, a break, but keep your eye on him." As he has said so often, when the subject of ex-cons on the city payroll comes up, "Are we to deny these men honest employment in a free society . . . are we to deprive them of the right to work . . . to become rehabilitated . . ." He will forgive anything short of Republicanism.

The afternoon work moves with never a minute wasted. The engineers and planners come with their reports on public works projects. Something is always being built, concrete being poured, steel being riveted, contractors being enriched.

"When will it be completed?" he asks.

"Early February."

"It would be a good thing for the people if it could be completed by the end of October."

The engineers say it can be done, but it will mean putting on extra shifts, night work, overtime pay, a much higher cost than was planned.

"It would be a good thing for the people if it could be completed by the end of October."

Of course it would be a good thing for the people. It would also be a good thing for the Democratic candidates who are seeking election in early November to go out and cut a ribbon for a new expressway or a water filtration plant or, if nothing else is handy, another wing at the O'Hare terminal. What ribbons do their opponents cut?

The engineers and planners understand, and they set about getting it finished by October.

On a good afternoon, there will be no neighborhood organizations to see him, because if they get to Daley, it means they have been up the ladder of government and nobody has been able to solve their problem. And that usually means a conflict between the people and somebody else, such as a politician or a business, whom his aides don't want to ruffle. There are many things his department heads can't do. They can't cross swords with ward bosses or politically heavy businessmen. They can't make important decisions. Some can't even make petty decisions. He runs City Hall like a small family business and keeps everybody on a short rein. They do only that which they know is safe and that which he tells them to do. So many things that should logically be solved several rungs below finally come to him.

Because of this, he has many requests from neighborhood people. And when a group is admitted to his office, most of them nervous and wide-eyed, he knows who they are, their leaders, their strength in the community. They have already been checked out by somebody. He must know everything. He doesn't like to be surprised. Just as he knows the name of every new worker, he must know what is going on in the various city offices. If the head of the office doesn't tell him, he has somebody there who will. In the office of other elected officials, he has trusted persons who will keep him informed. Out in the neighborhoods his precinct captains are reporting to the ward committeemen, and they in turn are reporting to him.

His police department's intelligence-gathering division gets bigger and bigger, its network of infiltrators, informers, and spies creating massive files on dissenters, street gangs, political enemies, newsmen, radicals, liberals, and anybody else who might be working against him. If one of his aides or handpicked officeholders is shacking up with a woman, he will know it. And if that man is married and a Catholic, his political career will wither and die. That is the greatest sin of all. You can make money under the table and move ahead, but you are forbidden to make secretaries under the sheets. He has dumped several party members for violating his personal moral standards. If something is leaked to the press, the bigmouth will be tracked down and punished. Scandals aren't public scandals if you get there before your enemies do.

So when the people come in, he knows what they want and whether it is possible. Not that it means they will get it. That often depends on how they act.

He will come out from behind his desk all smiles and handshakes and charm. Then he returns to his chair and sits very straight, hands folded on his immaculate desk, serious and attentive. To one side will be somebody from the appropriate city department.

Now it's up to the group. If they are respectful, he will express sympathy, ask encouraging questions, and finally tell them that everything possible will be done. And after they leave, he may say, "Take care of it." With that command, the royal seal, anything is possible, anybody's toes can be stepped on.

But if they are pushy, antagonistic, demanding instead of imploring, or bold enough to be critical of him, to tell him how he should do his job, to blame him for their problem, he will rub his hands together, harder and harder. In a long, difficult meeting, his hands will get raw. His voice gets lower, softer, and the corners of his mouth will turn down. At this point, those who know him will back off. They know what's next. But the unfamiliar, the militant, will mistake his lowered voice and nervousness for weakness. Then he'll blow, and it comes in a frantic roar:

"I want *you* to tell *me* what to do. *You* come up with the answers. *You* come up with the program. Are we perfect? Are *you* perfect? We all make mistakes. We all have faults. It's easy to criticize. It's easy to find fault. But *you* tell me what to do. This problem is all over the city. We didn't create these problems. We don't want them. But we are doing what we can. *You* tell me how to solve them. *You* give me a program." All of which leaves the petitioners dumb, since most people don't walk around with urban programs in their pockets. It can also leave them right back where they started.

They leave and the favor seekers come in. Half of the people he sees want a favor. They plead for promotions, something for their sons, a chance to do some business with the city, to get somebody in City Hall off their backs, a chance to return from political exile, a boon. They won't get an answer right there and then. It will be considered and he'll let them know. Later, sometimes much later, when he has considered the alternatives and the benefits, word will get back to them. Yes or no. Success or failure. Life or death.

Some jobseekers come directly to him. Complete outsiders, meaning those with no family or political connections, will be sent to see their ward committeemen. That is protocol, and that is what he did to the tall young black man who came to see him a few years ago, bearing a letter from the governor of North Carolina, who wrote that the young black man was a rising political prospect in his state. Daley told him to see his ward committeeman, and if he did some precinct work, rang doorbells, hustled up some votes, there might be a government job for him. Maybe something like taking coins in a tollway booth. The Rev. Jesse Jackson, now the city's leading black civil rights leader, still hasn't stopped smarting over that.

Others come asking him to resolve a problem. He is the city's leading labor mediator and has prevented the kind of strikes that have crippled New York. His father was a union man, and he comes from a union neighborhood, and many of the union leaders were his boyhood friends. He knows what they want. And if it is in the city's treasury, they will get it. If it isn't there, he'll promise to find it. He has ended a teachers' strike by promising that the state legislature would find funds for them, which surprised the Republicans in Springfield, as well as put them on the spot. He is an effective mediator with the management side of labor disputes, because they respect his judgment, and because there are few industries that do not need some favors from City Hall.

There are disputes he won't bother with, such as that between two ranking party members, both lawyers, each retained by a rival business interest in a zoning dispute. That was the kind of situation that can drive judges, city agencies, and functionaries berserk. He angrily wiped his hands of the matter, bawled the lawyers out for creating the mess, and let them take their chances on a fair decision. There are so many clients, peace should exist among friends.

The afternoon is almost gone, but they still keep coming in the front door and those he summons through the side. The phone keeps ringing, bringing reports from his legislators in Springfield, his congressmen in Washington, and prominent businessmen, some of whom may waste a minute of his time for the status of telling dinner guests, "I mentioned that to Dick and he likes the idea . . ."

Finally the scheduled appointments have been cleared, the unscheduled hopefuls told to come back again, and a few late calls made to his closest aides. It's six o'clock, but he is still going, as if reluctant to stop. The workdays have grown longer over the years, the vacations shorter. There is less visible joy in it all, but he works harder now than ever before. Some of his friends say he isn't comfortable anywhere but in the office on five.

The bodyguards check the corridor and he heads downstairs to the limousine. Most of the people in the Hall have left, and the mop crews are going to work, but always on the sidewalk outside will be the old hangers-on, waiting to shout a greeting, to get a nod or a smile in return.

On the way out, Bush hands him a speech. That's for the next stop, a banquet of civic leaders, or a professional group, or an important convention. The hotel grand ballroom is a couple of minutes away and he'll speed-read the speech just once on the way, a habit that contributes to his strange style of public speaking, with the emphasis often on the wrong words, the sentences overlapping, and the words tumbling over each other. Regardless of where he goes, the speech will be heavy in boosterism, full of optimism for the future, pride in the city, a reminder of what he has done. Even in the most important of gatherings, people will seek out his handshake, his recognition. A long time ago, when they opposed him, he put out the hand and moved the few steps to them. Now they come to him. He arrives after dinner, in time to be introduced, speak, and get back to the car.

The afternoon papers are on the back seat and he reads them until the limousine stops in front of a funeral home. Wakes are still part of political courtesy and his culture. Since he started in politics, he's been to a thousand of them. On the way up, the slightest connection with the deceased or his family was enough reason to attend a wake. Now he goes to fewer, and only to those involving friends, neighbors. His sons fill in for him at others. Most likely, he'll go to a wake on the South Side, because that's where most of his old friends are from. The funeral home might be McInerney's, which has matchbooks that bear a poem beginning, "Bring out the lace curtains and call McInerney, I'm nearing the end of life's pleasant journey." Or John Egan's, one of the biggest, owned by his high school pal and one of the last of the successful undertaker-politicians. The undertaker-politicians and the saloon keeper-politicians have given way to lawyer-politicians, who are no better, and they don't even buy you a drink or offer a prayer.

He knows how to act at a wake, greeting the immediate family, saying the proper things, offering his regrets, somberly and with dignity. His arrival is as big an event as the other fellow's departure. Before leaving, he will kneel at the casket, an honor afforded few of the living, and sign the visitor's book. A flurry of handshakes and he is back in the car.

It's late when the limousine turns toward Bridgeport. His neighbors are already home watching TV or at the Pump Tavern having a beer, talking baseball, race, or politics. His wife Eleanor, "Sis" as he calls her, knows his schedule and will be making supper. Something boiled, meat and potatoes, home-baked bread. She makes six loaves a week. His mother always made bread. And maybe ice cream for dessert. He likes ice cream. There's an old ice cream parlor in the neighborhood, and sometimes he goes there for a sundae, as he did when he was a boy.

The limousine passes Comiskey Park, where his beloved Sox play ball. He goes to Wrigley Field, too, but only to be seen. The Sox are his team. He can walk to the ball park from the house. At least he used to be able to walk there. Today it's not the same. A person can't walk anywhere. Maybe someday he'll build a big superstadium for all the teams, better than any other city's. Maybe on the Lake Front. Let the conservationists moan. It will be good for business, drawing conventioneers from hotels, and near an expressway so people in the suburbs can drive in. With lots of parking space for them, and bright lights so they can walk. Some day, if there's time, he might just build it.

Across Halsted Street, then a turn down Lowe Avenue, into the glow of the brightest street lights of any city in the country. The streets were so dark before, a person couldn't see who was there. Now all the streets have lights so bright that some people have to lower their shades at night. He turned on all those lights, he built them. Now he can see a block ahead from his car, to where the policeman is guarding the front of his home.

He tells the driver that tomorrow will require an even earlier start. He must catch a flight to Washington to tell a committee that the cities need more money. There are so many things that must be built, so many more people to be hired. But he'll be back the same day, in the afternoon, with enough time to maybe stop at the Hall. There's always something to do there. Things have to be done. If he doesn't do them, who will?

Excerpted from Mike Royko, *Boss: Richard J. Daley of Chicago* (New York: Dutton, 1970), pgs. 3–23.

Ronald Reagan

THE USES OF HUMOR

"The drama's laws, the drama's patrons give and we who live to please must please to live."
— ALEXANDER POPE

"Hang a lantern on your troubles," Tip O'Neill advised politicians. Disarm criticism by arming it yourself. Ronald Reagan was the oldest president in U.S. history and a former actor. So he joked about his age, "I'm one of the few persons old enough to remember that"—the emperor Diocletian's wage and price controls; and his movie career, "*Bedtime for Bonzo* made more sense than what they were doing in Washington." Lazy, he joked about his industry, "It's true hard work never killed anybody, but I figure why take the chance?" He even joked to doctors poised to remove a bullet from his chest, "Please tell me you're all Republicans." A one-liner in his second debate with Walter Mondale, "I am not going to exploit, for political purposes, my opponent's youth and inexperience" effaced the impression left by the first debate, when he got lost in his anecdotage, that he was too old for the job. Reagan's jocose self-deprecation spread an avuncular fog over how much there was to deprecate.

Blacks found little to laugh about in an administration more hostile to civil rights than any since Woodrow Wilson's. Through eight years Reagan refused to raise the minimum wage. The troglodytes Reagan appointed to the Interior Department, OSHA, and the EPA gave him the worst record on the environment of any president before George W. Bush. Reagan violated interna-

372

tional law in Central America, mining Nicaragua's harbors, and broke domestic law in re-supplying the contra rebels against Nicaragua and in trading arms with Iran. With John Poindexter, Reagan's national security advisor, Oliver North betrayed the public trust in the Iran-Contra scandal, yet Reagan called North "a national hero." Reagan left the government's finances in disarray, and bequeathed a fragile economy to his successor. The laughter faded; the record remains.

Lou Cannon offers a more dappled view of that record in his justly lauded political biography *President Reagan, The Role of a Lifetime.* As a reporter for the *San Jose Mercury-News* and the *Washington Post,* Cannon covered Reagan from his years as governor of California through his presidency. No president could wish for a fairer witness: Cannon's fifty-page analysis of the Iran-Contra scandal is heroic in its commitment to rounded truth. This excerpt from *President Reagan, The Role of a Lifetime* provides comic relief from those dark pages. Cannon asks us to laugh with Reagan, and one is surprised, now, at how easy that is. Reader advisory: Italian-Americans and Polish-Americans may be offended by some of Reagan's jokes.

KIDDING ON THE SQUARE
Lou Cannon

Ronald Reagan's sense of humor was a key to his character. He was the resident humorist and gag writer in a White House where nearly everything else was done for him while he engaged in governance by anecdote. While adversaries interpreted his heavy reliance on anecdotes as a telltale reflection of a deficient intellect, Reagan treasured humorous stories and knew that his willingness to poke fun at himself was a vital component of his popularity. A sense of humor was essential to the role Reagan had created for himself in Hollywood and politics and, in humorist Bob Orben's phrase, the basis for the "balance of goodwill" upon which he drew in time of trouble.

Reagan came to this role quite naturally. His father, Jack Reagan, had a gift for storytelling, common among Irish-Americans and useful for any salesman. And his mother, Nelle, nurtured Reagan's interest in dramatics, for which he had a natural flair. Reagan's appreciation for anecdotes was further honed in Hollywood, where the self-deprecating jokes that form an essential characteristic of Jewish humor were deeply embedded in the film culture. One of Hollywood's most valued ceremonies is the "roast," an entertainment at which celebrities are feted with an exchange of personal insults that concludes in sentimental tribute to the guest of honor. Reagan was an adept participant in such events, and he was pleased to learn in Sacramento that the roast also prospers in politics, perhaps because of the respite such events provide from the ferocity of daily political combat. As president, Reagan exploited his mastery of this art form, fully matching Washington reporter Owen Ullmann's description of him as "the Johnny Carson of national politics, the Joker-in-Chief of the United States." Reagan quipped, kidded, and bantered in nearly every White House meeting, charming visitors and aides alike. Early in his presidency Reagan met in the Oval Office with his wife, Mike Deaver, and John F. W. Rogers, the young White House administrative officer. Rogers had been brought into the Oval Office this particular morning to discuss the decorations and the furniture, a subject in which Reagan had no interest. When Deaver and Nancy Reagan went into a side room to continue the discussion, Rogers was left alone with the president for the first time in his life. He was nervous, not knowing what to say, and Reagan picked up the slack. "I guess they're going to go and figure out what we're supposed to do," said Reagan, as if Rogers shared with him the predicament of having others decide his affairs. Rogers still did not know what to say, and Reagan tried again. Glancing at the Oval Office wall, he pointed to a famous portrait of George Washington in which the father of our country has a hand thrust inside his coat in Napoleonic pose. "What do you think he's doing with his hand?" Reagan asked. Rogers had no idea. "I bet he's in there scratching himself," Reagan said. Rogers, disarmed, laughed heartily with the president.

This was Reagan's way. During his eight years in the White House he won the allegiance of subordinates and secretaries with endless banter and little jokes that reassured them and made them feel part of a great enterprise. The quips and patter enabled Reagan to keep his emotional distance from his entourage while also giving the White House rank and file a sense of belonging. Anecdotes were Reagan's fundamental form of communication. He used his stock stories and improvised one-liners to break the ice, entertain aides, pass the time, practice for performances, amuse audiences, deflate adversaries, and fill awkward gaps at meetings when the discussion bored him or drifted beyond his depth. Reagan needed the approval conveyed by laughter and engaged in a constant quest for stories that would enhance his repertoire. Members of the inner circle who in other administrations might have contested over policy responded to Reagan's need for stories by competing among themselves to find anecdotes that pleased the president. This competition was even more intense among cabinet members who wanted to become part of the inner circle. Some cabinet members, notably Treasury Secretary Donald Regan, quickly learned that they stood a better chance of gaining Reagan's attention with an anecdote than with an argument and used Reaganesque stories to ingratiate themselves. Others, notably Secretary of State Alexander Haig, never understood this and failed to form the easy relationship with Reagan that was necessary for political survival.

Though Reagan liked stories for their own sake, there was usually a purpose to his patter. In his years on the banquet circuit he had learned that stories tend to soften up audiences and make them more receptive to the speaker's message. "He often used humor as a bonding device to put an audience at ease," says Bob Orben. "The essence of presidential humor is to eliminate the huge psychological gap of awe that exists between a president and his audience. Reagan used humor to put his audiences on the same level." E. B. White once wrote that Americans "cherish the ideal of the 'sense' of humor and at the same time are highly suspicious of anything that is non-serious." It is doubtful if Reagan had read E. B. White, but he shared the understanding that humor was too important to be strictly a laughing matter. He insisted on anecdotes in his speeches and provided them himself when speechwriters failed to do so. If he did not like the anecdotes that were sent to him, he substituted his own. Economist Alan Greenspan formed the view that Reagan was "psychologically a professional comedian, a professional raconteur" who had accumulated a vast store of anecdotes that he used to express his fundamental ideas and his attitude toward life. Greenspan considered Reagan's grasp of economic issues to be unsophisticated and often superficial, but he also recognized that Reagan could convey the import of an idea through an anecdote and that he possessed a comic talent for puncturing economic portentousness with deft one-liners. ("You know economists; they're the sort of people who see something works in practice and wonder if it would work in theory." And, "If all the economists in the world were laid end to end, they still wouldn't reach a conclusion.") While it was Greenspan and Martin Anderson who had in 1980 constructed the budget plan that gave Reagan's economic proposal a semblance of credibility, it was Reagan who had devised the formulation that roused the public: "A recession is when your neighbor loses his job. A depression is when you lose yours. And recovery is when Jimmy Carter loses his."

Reagan occasionally yielded to puns to make a point. When, as governor, he acceded to the appeal of a tiny Indian tribe and blocked construction of a high dam that would have violated an ancient treaty by flooding sacred burial grounds, Reagan said, "We've broken too damn many treaties." He liked jokes that made fun of government, Communists, ministers, movie producers, and himself. He also liked trick answers. (Attempting to cheer up a downcast aide on a helicopter flight over Washington's monuments, Reagan asked her, "How many are dead in Arlington Cemetery?" She was baffled, and he said, "They all are.") Reagan also favored long-remembered one-liners of such vintage that younger people who heard them wrongly assumed them to be original. ("Honey, I forgot to duck," he said to Nancy Reagan after he was shot, recycling a quip attributed to Jack Dempsey when he lost the heavyweight boxing title to Gene Tunney in 1926.) Many of the one-liners in Reagan's mental card file were scraps of film dialogue that popped out at unexpected but often appropriate occasions. (The most famous of these, or at least the most effective, was Reagan's line when he seized the microphone and routed George Bush in their celebrated 1980 debate in Nashua, New Hampshire. "I paid for this microphone, Mr. Green," said Reagan, winning the audience while he mangled the name of the moderator, Jon Breen. But Spencer Tracy had said it first, in the 1948 film *State of the Union:* "Don't you shut me off! I'm paying for this broadcast.")

Reagan related the story of his life in anecdotes. As Lyn Nofziger once put it, Reagan was always nostalgic for "the job he did before the job he was in." When Reagan was an actor he told stories about his days as a sports announcer. When he became governor, he told acting stories. And when he became president, he told stories, both real and invented, about his days in Sacramento. Reagan also told dialect jokes in stage-Irish to evoke his father's Irish Catholic heritage, populist jokes to emphasize his humble origins ("I was born in a small town in the Midwest, and I was in poverty before the rich folks got hold of it"), and Russian jokes to remind conservatives of his anticommunist credentials at a time he was promoting a fundamental change in U.S.-Soviet relationships. Often, his stories were tailored to specific audiences. Recognizing that people laugh readily at good-humored jokes about their vocations, he relished telling anti-economist jokes to economists, anti-lawyer jokes to attorneys, and anti-clerical jokes to ministers. These stories were so carefully chosen that some of Reagan's listeners adopted them as their own, as Greenspan did with a joke that became a standard anecdote in his own speeches. (Brezhnev is watching the annual May Day parade of Soviet military might from the Kremlin wall. Amid the tanks and nuclear missiles and rows of soldiers is a truck containing a collection of unkempt civilians. An aide apologizes to Brezhnev for their presence, saying he doesn't know what they are doing in the parade. "Calm down, comrade," Brezhnev says. "Those are my economists, an integral part of the military might of the Soviet Union. I put them in the parade. You have no idea how much damage they can do.") White House Counsel A. B. Culvahouse similarly appreciated Reagan's stories about lawyers. (A pope and a lawyer arrive at St. Peter's gate simultaneously. The pope is assigned a modest condominium in a courtyard while the lawyer is given a splendid Tudor mansion overlooking a golf course. "How can this be?" the lawyer asks St. Peter. "The father of Christendom merits only a nice condominium and I have been given this magnificent mansion." St. Peter replies, "Well, we have thirty-nine popes here, but you're the first lawyer.") Reagan used variations of this story, depending on the audience. Sometimes it was politicians who were the rarity in heaven.

Reagan's most frequent target was Reagan. No president since Lincoln was as self-effacing, and no president in the history of the republic was as effective at self-ridicule. In public and in private Reagan regularly poked fun at his age, his work habits, his movies, his ideology, his vanities, his memory lapses, his supposed domination by his wife, and even the widely held view that he was unintelligent. Reagan was aware that many of his critics thought him a modest man with much to be modest about. But he also realized that he could upstage his adversaries by beating them to the punch. When he was informed during the 1980 campaign that some of his opponents intended to make a point of his age by sending him greetings on his sixty-ninth birthday, Reagan started using Jack Benny jokes about his birthday, which he called "the thirtieth anniversary of his thirty-ninth birthday."

This tactic diffused the age issue so effectively that such jokes became a permanent part of the Reagan repertoire, sometimes combined with references to other presumed disabilities. ("You know, that brings me to a story—almost everything does. Maybe I've told this story to you before, but then you'll just have to hear it again, because life not only begins at forty but so does lumbago and the tendency to tell the same story over and over again.") Reagan could do this because he was personally secure enough to make himself the butt of his humor. He once explained to me in some detail how his friend Jack Benny had used self-ridicule as the foundation of his comedy, emphasizing that it was Benny's self-security that made his art possible. In Reagan's view this freed him to portray a character (stingy, self-centered) that was the opposite of the real Jack Benny. Reagan most often played himself, but it seemed to me that he was saying something about himself as well as Benny. Reagan could poke fun at his ignorance because he considered himself abundantly blessed with common sense. He could laugh at himself because he knew he had a serious purpose. He was not afraid to say what came into his head. When a wire service reporter asked him to autograph an old studio picture showing Reagan with the chimpanzee Bonzo, he happily obliged. The inscription read "I'm the one with the watch."

Poet Marianne Moore might have had Reagan in mind when she penned her famous observation that "humor saves a few steps, it saves years." Not even the most devout of Reagan admirers considered him a hard worker, and even aides who thought he put in enough hours in the Oval Office regarded him as intellectually lazy. Reagan believed that he worked quite diligently at those things that mattered most to him. He thought that the Hollywood pattern of working intensively in spurts was quite sensible. Reagan wasn't kidding in the slightest when he told television interviewer Charlie Rose during the 1980 campaign, "Show me an executive who works long, overtime hours, and I'll show you a bad executive." But Reagan recognized the comic value of his reputation as a nine-to-five president who napped the day away, and he deflated his critics by outdoing them in jokes about his work habits. (Autographing a photo of a sleeping Marlin Fitzwater that had been taken on Air Force One, Reagan wrote, "Hey, Marlin, we're only supposed to do this in cabinet meetings.") Reagan knew that humor must touch the heart, and that it must not spare the humorist or his frailties in the process. In this sense, humor was Reagan's ultimate self-defense and his ultimate weapon. It was also a way of reaching him. His more attentive advisers knew that Reagan found it extremely difficult to acknowledge mistakes, inconsistencies, or policy failures in formal discussions, but could be made to face them if he needed an anecdote to impress an audience. ("I'm not worried about the deficit; it's big enough to take care of itself," he said at the 1984 Gridiron Dinner.) This ability would prove a saving grace late in his presidency when Reagan's public credibility was shattered by the Iran-contra affair, and those who cared most deeply about him were trying to make him face the unpleasant truth that he had traded U.S. arms for American hostages.

Red Hen

On November 16, 1976, Reagan's essay for his radio address included a parable he had written about a little red hen:

Once upon a time there was a little red hen who scratched about the barnyard until she uncovered some grains of wheat. She called her neighbors and said, "If we plant this wheat, we shall have bread to eat. Who will help me plant it?"

"Not I," said the cow.

"Not I," said the duck.

"Not I," said the pig.

"Not I," said the goose.

"Then I will," said the little red hen. And she did. The wheat grew tall and ripened into golden grain. "Who will help me reap my wheat?" asked the little red hen.

"Not I," said the duck.

"Out of my classification," said the pig.

"I'd lose my seniority," said the cow.

"I'd lose my unemployment compensation," said the goose.

"Then I will," said the little red hen, and she did.

At last it came time to bake the bread. "Who will help me bake the bread?" asked the little red hen.

"That would be overtime for me," said the cow.

"I'd lose my welfare benefits," said the duck.

"I'm a dropout and never learned how," said the pig.

"If I'm to be the only helper, that's discrimination," said the goose.

"Then I will," said the little red hen.

She baked five loaves and held them up for her neighbors to see.

They all wanted some and, in fact, demanded a share. But the little red hen said, "No, I can eat the five loaves myself."

"Excess profits," cried the cow.

"Capitalist leech," screamed the duck.

"I demand equal rights," yelled the goose.

And the pig just grunted.

And they painted "unfair" picket signs and marched round and round the little red hen, shouting obscenities.

When the government agent came, he said to the little red hen, "You must not be greedy."

"But I earned the bread," said the little red hen.

"Exactly," said the agent. "That is the wonderful free enterprise system. Anyone in the barnyard can earn as much as he wants. But under our modern government regulations, the productive workers must divide their product with the idle."

And they lived happily ever after, including the little red hen, who smiled and clucked, "I am grateful, I am grateful."

But her neighbors wondered why she never again baked any more bread.

Excerpted from Peter J. Wallison, *Ronald Reagan: The Power of Conviction and the Success of His Presidency* (New York: Westview, 2003), p 63.

Reagan's skill at self-deprecation also reassured Americans that his head had not been turned by the presidency. By telling jokes about himself, said columnist Mark Shields, Reagan conveyed an "egalitarian message" that was appreciated by the public. "He's saying, 'Even though I'm up here, I'm not so important. I still want your approval and acceptance.'" Reagan accomplished this by kidding on the square, with stories that cut close to the bone. ("Let me tell you a story," he would say, if someone complimented him on the way he looked or the relaxed manner in which he bore the burdens of the presidency. "There were two psychiatrists, one young and one old, with offices across the hall from each other. Every morning they'd meet in the elevator, fresh and dapper, but by day's end, when they met leaving the building, the young psychiatrist was disheveled and exhausted while the older man looked as neat and rested as he had when he arrived. One evening the young psychiatrist could stand it no longer. He said to the older man, 'I don't understand it. You look so fresh all the time. I hear these terrible stories from my patients every day. How do you put up with it? What's your secret?' The older man looked at the young psychiatrist and said, 'I don't listen.'")

Reagan's joke file included many off-color stories that he shared with his closest aides at morning staff meetings or the old members of his California kitchen cabinet at their increasingly infrequent gatherings. His generation eschewed such jokes in mixed company, an etiquette Reagan violated only in times of unusual stress. He also told a range of stories for private consumption that were less politically palatable than his public witticisms, although not necessarily less humorous. When an aide asked him during his first term what he would do if Senator Edward M. Kennedy became a presidential candidate again, Reagan winked and said, "I guess I'd just have to point out that I used to be a lifeguard." In 1988, he told the annual Alfalfa Club Dinner, "The other night I had a dream that Gary Hart was president, and he was meeting with Margaret Thatcher. Mrs. Thatcher told him, 'I want your hands off Nicaragua, your hands off Afghanistan, and your hands off my knee.'" The joke was a hit with the good old boys of the Alfalfa Club, a Washington organization of the important and self-important that holds an annual dinner without the perceived impediments of women guests or reporters of either gender. And Reagan also won a hearty laugh from his Irish-American rival, House Speaker Tip O'Neill, during hard bargaining with him over the budget in 1982. (A doctor asked a simple Irish washerwoman for a specimen to conduct a laboratory test. The washerwoman, not wishing to confess her ignorance, returned home and went next door to ask a neighbor the meaning of the doctor's request. She came back bruised and disheveled. When her husband asked what had happened, she said, "I asked her what a specimen was, and she told me to go pee in a bottle. So I said, 'Go shit in your hat' and the fight was on.")

Reagan often told elaborate jokes in an exaggerated dialect that he fondly believed to be Irish, one of them a long-winded story about an Irishman who collects a large insurance settlement after an auto accident by pretending that his injuries have put him in a wheelchair for life. When representatives of the insurance company warn him that he will be pursued by them the rest of his life until they establish the fallacy of his claims, he responds by telling them that they will be following him to the Catholic religious shrine of Lourdes and "there you're going to see the greatest miracle you've ever seen in your life." Reporters groaned after they had heard this story for the umpteenth time, but most of Reagan's audiences seemed to like the tale, fake dialect and all.

Reagan did less well during the 1980 New Hampshire primary when he unwisely told a different sort of ethnic joke to aides within the earshot of national reporters who were covering the campaign. ("How do you tell who the Polish fellow is at a cock fight? He's the one with the duck. How do you tell who the Italian is at the cock fight? He's the one who bets on the duck. How do you know the Mafia was there? The duck wins.") When the account of this joke was published, it caused consternation in the Reagan camp and prompted Ed Meese to make a Reaganesque quip: "There goes Connecticut," in reference to the prominent political participation of Italian-Americans in that state. But Reagan realized, then and always until the Iran-contra affair, that he could best the media in a contest of credibility. When the supporter of another candidate asked Reagan about this joke following a Republican debate in Manchester, Reagan said he had been "stiffed" by the press and calmly lied on national television, claiming he had told the story as an example of jokes that politicians shouldn't tell. Reagan got away with it, in part because the joke was relatively innocuous and in part because the national press is unpopular with conservative New Hampshire voters. These voters, especially Italian-American voters, might have been less amused by some of the ethnic stories Reagan told his kitchen cabinet and others whom he trusted to keep their mouths shut. One of these jokes, which Reagan began telling in his days as governor of California, concerned a fellow who was prejudiced against Italians. Walking down the street with a friend one day, he encountered an Italian organ-grinder with a monkey and threw five dollars in the monkey's hat. The friend was aghast. "You've been telling me for years how much you hated Italians, and here you do that," he said. Replied the man who was prejudiced against Italians, "Well, they're so cute when they're little."

Reagan was the butt of jokes as well as a master raconteur. Long before he became president, he was notorious for gaffes and oddball statistics. The most outlandish of these tended to be flights of fancy that were loosely based on stories or statistics he had taken from *Human Events, Reader's Digest,* or the local newspaper and lodged in his mental card file. Reagan was sort of an equal opportunity reader, who tended to believe that anything he saw in print was true, particularly if it reinforced his point of view. He had a powerful but indiscriminate memory that rarely distinguished between the actual and the apocryphal. He also had an eye for topical stories and startling statistics that could be used to spruce up his basic speech and make it more relevant to his audiences. All of this had worked well for him in the General Electric days when he was of necessity his own researcher, but his methodology proved insufficient for the more exacting standards applied to presidential candidates. During the six-year interregnum between the end of his governorship and the beginning of his presidency, Reagan often stirred up a storm by drawing upon information in his mental card file that turned out to be unverifiable or demonstrably inaccurate. In the 1980 campaign he claimed that "the finest oil geologists" had told him that the United States had more oil reserves than Saudi Arabia, an absurdity that Mark Shields spoofed as reflective of Reagan's belief that there is "more oil under second base at Yankee Stadium" than in the Middle East. Reagan attracted even more attention with his discovery that trees and other vegetation were primarily responsible for air pollution and with his wildly incorrect "suspicion" that the Mount St. Helens volcano had released more sulfur dioxide into the atmosphere "than has been released in the last ten years of automobile driving." Mount St. Helens at the peak of activity produced 2,000 tons of sulfur dioxide daily, compared to 81,000 tons of sulfur dioxide then produced each day by automobiles. As for the trees, Reagan apparently confused nitrous oxide, emitted by plants, with nitrogen dioxide, which is emitted by smokestacks. No other mistaken belief of Reagan's in the 1980 campaign was as widely ridiculed. When he spoke at Claremont College in California, students tacked a sign to a tree: "Chop Me Down Before I Kill Again."

Reagan's campaign aides despaired at his misstatements but found it difficult to keep up with them because they often had no clue to Reagan's sources. As Martin Anderson blithely explained to a *New York Times* reporter, one problem was that Reagan used "hundreds of stories for examples" in his campaign speeches. "Ninety-nine times out of a hundred, things checked out, but sometimes the source was wrong." And sometimes Reagan was wrong, too. Experienced damage-control experts on the Reagan team, of whom Anderson was one of the best, recognized that the candidate's mind sometimes wandered during briefings, particularly those that bordered on the technical. The talent most valued in a briefer by the Reagan inner circle was the ability to explain complicated issues in everyday language. The best briefers were those who could make their points through anecdotes.

After Reagan became shielded by the presidency, the problem of protecting him from unwanted questions became marginally easier, while the consequences of potential misstatements increased. It was a constant worry for the aides, particularly Deaver, who knew that Reagan's natural friendliness prompted him to answer questions even when he didn't know the answers. Deaver was inventive at devising rules to protect Reagan from random questioning, but reporters quickly learned that the president would often respond to shouted questions even when his aides would have preferred him to keep silent. And Reagan liked to make news. When Ed Meese urged him during a preparatory session for an early news conference to "be dull, Mr. President," Reagan responded honestly, "Being dull is very hard for me."

Being dull was rarely Reagan's problem. He was consistently colorful even when his comprehension failed, and he was unable to resist playing to whatever audience he had at hand. When his cabinet members were wrangling in 1981 over the best way to dispose of a prodigious government store of surplus butter, Reagan brought the meeting to a tumultuous conclusion by declaring, "Four hundred and seventy-eight million pounds of butter! Does anyone know where we can find 478 million pounds of popcorn?" But when everyone had stopped laughing they realized they were no closer to finding a politically acceptable solution to the butter disposal problem than when the meeting began.

And this was typically the case when a decision required Reagan's participation. Reagan sometimes used humor to avoid facing issues he ought to have faced, particularly the reality that it was impossible to increase military spending, reduce taxes, and balance the budget simultaneously. His biggest problem was that he didn't know enough about public policy to participate fully in his presidency—and often didn't realize how much he didn't know. Reagan's legal advisers learned that he knew little about the law, his national security advisers found that he was devoid of knowledge on the capabilities of most U.S. and Soviet weapons systems, and his economists discovered that he was poorly informed on economics, even though he sometimes reminded them that he had majored in economics and sociology at Eureka College. Sometimes his ignorance became evident in public. At a December 17, 1981, news conference, Reagan was asked his view of an affirmative action agreement between an aerospace company and a labor union to train minorities and move them up in the work force. "I can't see any fault with that," Reagan said. "I'm for that." But his administration wasn't in favor of affirmative action, then or ever, even when management and labor agreed on its desirability. At the insistence of Attorney General William French Smith, the White House press office several days later issued a statement saying that the Justice Department was seeking to overturn in court the very agreement with which Reagan found no fault.

The gaps in Reagan's knowledge were compounded by gaps in his memory. Reagan remembered stories, statistics, movies, and dramatic events. He could memorize almost anything that was given to him on paper, even though he often mentally erased the material immediately after delivering it. But he had an exceptionally faulty memory for names, possibly the consequence of living so long in an actor's world where casts, scripts, and scenes changed constantly. Reagan called Environmental Protection Agency administrator William D. Ruckelshaus "Don" at one important meeting. He shocked National Security Adviser Robert (Bud) McFarlane months after his appointment by entirely forgetting his name. Such private lapses were injurious to the egos of some administration officials but did no larger damage. In contrast, Housing and Urban Development Secretary

Sam Pierce, the only Reagan cabinet member to serve a full two terms, never quite recovered from the embarrassment of being addressed by the president as "Mr. Mayor" at a June 12, 1981, visit of a dozen mayors to the White House. This was a revealing lapse. Reagan's failure to recognize his HUD secretary after both of them had been six months on the job accurately reflected the president's almost total lack of interest in HUD, which he never visited during his eight years in office. Some of Reagan's other lapses appeared simply to have been the product of absentmindedness. During a picture-taking session with Liberian leader Samuel K. Doe, Reagan referred to this military ruler as "Chairman Moe." Doe's views of the incident were not recorded. Neither was the reaction of Singapore's Lee Kuan Yew when Reagan greeted him at the White House south portico by saying, "It gives me great pleasure to welcome Prime Minister Lee Kuan Yew and Mrs. Lee to Singapore."

All politicians and performers make fluffs, of course, and Reagan was better than most of them at shrugging off his gaffes and goofs and proceeding with the business at hand. He often had much to shrug away. White House transcripts of presidential speeches were dotted with asterisks informing reporters that Reagan had meant to say "Mayor Bradley" instead of "Mayor Bartlett" or "1981" instead of "1941." Some of these mistakes were simple reading errors. Reagan, who has been badly nearsighted since childhood, often misread his texts unless he was wearing glasses or using a TelePrompTer. But he also often did not pay attention to what he was saying. At a Republican fundraiser he said, "Now we're trying to get unemployment to go up, and I think we are going to succeed." Launching a campaign for welfare reform he declared, "Even though there may be some misguided critics of what we're trying to do, I think we're on the wrong path." He told the Washington bureau of the *Dallas Morning News* that he had not read even the summary of his Treasury Department's tax reform proposal "because my mind is too filled with the budget." He told a group of business leaders that "nuclear war would be the greatest tragedy, I think, ever experienced by mankind in the history of mankind." He sent a group of high-school student ambassadors off to Europe after telling them, "And yes, it's all right to have an affinity for what was the mother country for all of us, because if a man takes a wife unto himself, he doesn't stop loving his mother because of that. But at the same time, we're all Americans."

These locutions and an array of dubious assertions ("There has never been a war between two free countries") tended to ratify the widely held Washington view that Reagan's intellect fell considerably below rocket-scientist standards. The conventional estimate of Reagan's intellectual capabilities was summed up by Clark Clifford at a fashionable Georgetown party, where he described the president as "an amiable dunce." The phrase stuck, and the opinion it expressed was not limited to Democrats or Reagan's critics in the media.

The portrait of Reagan that most often emerges from the memoirs written by departed and often disaffected members of his administration is of a president who was long on decency and determination and short on intellect. David Stockman's portrayal of Reagan in action is particularly searing. When the budget director explained to Reagan that members of his cabinet were planning payroll reductions that would save only a half-billion dollars at a time when the projected budget deficit ranged between $111 billion and $185 billion, Reagan treated this bad news as if Stockman had delivered a glowing progress report. "That's just what's going to happen when the management efforts of our people take hold," Reagan said, appearing to miss the point entirely. "Somehow, he had drawn the exact opposite conclusion from what I had just told him about how little the cabinet was willing to cut from the payroll," recalled Stockman despairingly. Similar difficulties were encountered by Dick Cheney and other members of the Republican congressional leadership when they tried to engage Reagan in substantive discussion of weapons systems or arms control. Reagan would listen, but respond to the congressmen from the "talking points" written on his cards. Eventually, the congressional leaders gave up and conducted their policy discussions with Reagan's ever-changing cast of national security advisers or other members of the White House staff.

Even some of Reagan's friends and supporters on the right had their doubts about his intellectual candlepower. Richard Perle, the brainy resident nemesis of arms control at the Pentagon, thought that

Reagan consistently engaged in "intellectual delegation of authority." Columnist George Will, who probably saw more of Reagan at close quarters during his presidency than any other conservative intellectual outside the administration, wondered how anyone so uninformed could reach the top of the American political system. Reagan's substitution of anecdotes for analysis particularly annoyed Will, who is highly analytical. At a reception preceding a White House dinner just before he left the presidency, Reagan startled Will and William F. Buckley by saying, "Well, you know, Bill, is it possible that we conservatives are the real liberals and the liberals are the real conservatives?" Will thought the remark a "terribly banal ... Durango, Colorado, Rotary thought." Buckley, also unimpressed but more inclined to accept Reagan on his own terms, murmured something affable. Will, offended by what seemed to him an empty comment, did not. "I knew you were a liberal all along," he said to the president, and walked off.

Nonetheless, Will and others who knew Reagan personally or who dealt with him over a long period of time usually concluded that he was smarter, maybe much smarter, than he seemed on the surface. While Reagan was sometimes stunningly ignorant about matters on which he was expected to be well informed, those with the most exposure to him reject out of hand the view that he was a "dunce." Some of them also believe that Reagan's amiability was overstated. Martin Anderson, an intellectual economist and writer, decided that Reagan was bright, decisive, and tough-minded—but basically uncaring about the human feelings of those around him, "a warmly ruthless man." His wife, Annelise Anderson, also an economist and writer, served as one of Stockman's principal deputies and attended numerous meetings with Reagan in the early days of the presidency. She was impressed with Reagan's decisiveness and intellectual grasp and reached the conclusion that Reagan was underrated intellectually because he always dealt in "specific concrete experience" rather than the abstractions preferred by academics. Pollster Richard Wirthlin, who also has an academic background, thought Reagan "extremely gifted and extremely bright in picking up oral briefings." Wirthlin was convinced that Reagan was so highly focused on the three or four things he wanted to accomplish—"relations with the Soviets, the economy, federalism"—that he deliberately excluded almost everything else except his performances from his mental radar screen.

While a number of those closest to Reagan were put off, at least initially, by his extreme passivity, they also were impressed by his ability to focus on his core objectives. George Shultz, often considered the most accomplished member of the Reagan cabinet, thought that the "substantive achievements" of the administration, in particular the improvement in U.S.-Soviet relations, were in large part a product of Reagan's highly focused approach to governance. "I think he manages to get the essence of the problems pretty well," Shultz said. "And oftentimes the people who are immersed in the detail sort of lose the essence." It was in the essences that Reagan excelled. "He understood the ambient circumstances, which required a high degree of intelligence and knowledge," said Buckley, who was a friend to Reagan and took him seriously. "He knew, for instance, that people were afraid of inflation. He had an innate capacity to know what things people were worried about." Buckley's observation is an elegant version of what Stu Spencer saw as the "Joe Sixpack" in Reagan. This was the quality that set Reagan apart from other politicians and refutes the description of "amiable dunce."

But the nature of Reagan's intellect remains a puzzlement. Annelise Anderson came to the conclusion that he was "super bright," and observed that in discussions he often rejected the conventional wisdom, "a characteristic of extremely intelligent and creative people." Robert Kaiser of the *Washington Post,* a liberal journalist with expertise in Soviet affairs and the arcane discipline of arms control, notes that Reagan particularly scorned the conventional wisdom of "the nuclear priesthood." He was not terrified at holding in his hands the power to unleash thousands of nuclear weapons because he understood better than his predecessors that the superpowers would never use these weapons, Kaiser believes.

Reagan's ideas and ideology had been forged in the crucible of experience. He had, in Annelise Anderson's phrase, "fought very hard for the knowledge and understanding" he had acquired, and he did not surrender his positions easily. The mask of amiability concealed a stubbornness that was at once the wonder and despair of those who worked for him. Stockman, Howard Baker, Richard Darman, and Commerce Secretary Malcolm Baldrige ran into a stone wall when they tried at different times to make the deficit-reduction case for higher taxes. So, later on, did Buckley, Will, and other conservatives when they opposed the Intermediate Nuclear Forces (INF) treaty and tried to convince Reagan that Soviet leader Mikhail Gorbachev was not to be trusted. On things that mattered to him, the passive president could also be unyielding.

He could also be curious, despite his widespread reputation as the least curious of men. Again, the question is more complicated than it seems at first glance. Reagan was certainly uncurious about most aspects of public policy. He never peeked to find out what was going on below the surface of the government of which he was the chief executive. While he often fumed over "leaks" about the feuds and policy struggles within his official family, he rarely sought to locate the sources of these stories, even when they were obvious to almost everyone else in Washington. And he was so quiet at White House briefings that his aides sometimes wondered if he had been paying attention. But Reagan sometimes expressed curiosity about subjects far from the beaten track of the presidency. During a luncheon at the *Washington Star* in August 1981, when the discussion had turned to mistranslations of the dialogue in Hollywood westerns when the subtitles were in French or Italian, Reagan suddenly asked, "Where did we get the English language? Where did English come from?" There was an awkward pause while the editors attempted to calculate the intent of the question. Finally, an answer came from Ed Yoder, a Rhodes scholar and Pulitzer Prize-winning editorial page writer, who explained to Reagan that English was "a blend of Anglo-Saxon and Norman French that began to develop in the eleventh century . . . and reached a recognizable modern form in Chaucer's time." Reagan thanked Yoder, who was struck by Reagan's lack of embarrassment at asking a question that it would have been inconceivable for other presidents to ask.

On another occasion Reagan turned to George Will and asked, "What makes the Blue Ridge Mountains blue?" Will didn't have the foggiest notion of the answer, but he never forgot the question. He, too, was struck by Reagan's lack of concern about displaying ignorance and he became convinced over time that Reagan possessed an "eclectic curiosity" about matters that lay outside the boundaries of his settled views. "On the first nine levels Reagan is the least interesting of men," Will said. "But if you postulate a tenth level, then he's suddenly fascinating."

I share that fascination. I interviewed Reagan at least forty times over a period of twenty years. I watched him give hundreds of speeches and perform at scores of news conferences and other question-and-answer sessions. (News conferences became a rarity during the Reagan presidency but were held on a near-weekly basis during much of Reagan's first term as governor.) The overall impression of this experience is contradictory. Reagan was usually highly effective with a script and often ineffective without one. But the most passionate and effective political speeches of his life came in the 1976 North Carolina primary when he discarded his script and spoke from the heart about the issues that mattered most to him. In many of his presidential news conferences he groped for words and sometimes lost his train of thought. But when he was challenged sharply by a reporter or a political opponent in a debate he could display the same fire and eloquence he had shown in Nashua. Most of Reagan's formal interviews were disappointments, at least from a journalist's point of view, because he so frequently resorted to familiar formulas or oft-told anecdotes when asked to analyze an issue or explain the details of his position. This did not necessarily bespeak a lack of intelligence; on the contrary, Reagan often demonstrated considerable skill in evading politically troublesome questions he did not wish to answer. When speaking informally or off the record, he was less evasive but not always more comprehensible. He was apt to lapse into incoherence when even slightly tired, almost as if the mental cassettes in his mind could not be pushed into a "play" position. At other times he was insightful, particularly when explaining the craft of performance or offering consolation to someone who had suffered a personal loss. It was clear to me that he was not a dunce, amiable or otherwise. But it was difficult to understand how his mind worked.

What fascinated me most were the lengths Reagan would go to demonstrate that his present opinions were consistent with past views, even when they obviously were not, and his tenacity at defending policy positions with whatever argument came to mind. For instance, Reagan had long used Lenin as the measure of Marxist morality and often quoted some of the more cold-blooded declarations by the founder of the Soviet state to show that Communists would stop at nothing to achieve their goal of world domination. Answering a question from Sam Donaldson about the Kremlin's motives at the first news conference of his presidency, Reagan said about the Soviets that "the only morality they recognize is what will further their cause, meaning they reserve unto themselves the right to commit any crime, to lie, to cheat." The answer ratified the worst fears of the Soviet leadership about Reagan and prompted a furious denunciation of the new president in the Soviet press, which compared him to Hitler. When I asked Reagan about his answer at a subsequent interview, he replied blandly that he was only quoting Lenin. But by the end of his presidency, when Reagan was defending his view that Mikhail Gorbachev was "a different kind of Soviet leader" against conservative criticism, he had another Lenin in mind. One difference in Gorbachev, the president told me without any sense of irony, was that "he is the first leader that has come along who has gone back before Stalin and that he is trying to do what Lenin was teaching." Reagan went on in this vein, praising Lenin and Gorbachev as if they were new-age capitalists. He seemed to have no memory whatsoever of the lying, cheating Lenin whose quotations had been a staple of his speeches on the conservative banquet circuit.

The riddle of Reagan's intelligence for a long time seemed insoluble. When I asked people who knew Reagan well and were willing to honestly discuss the issue of his intelligence, I found they were often equally frustrated in trying to understand what made him tick. "People say he is a simpleton, which isn't right, and when they realize he isn't they're apt to go to the other end of the spectrum and compare him to Socrates, which doesn't work either," said William Buckley.

For the more thoughtful members of the inner circle, Reagan's intelligence was an enigma. If offered the protection of anonymity, friends and family members could cite contradictory examples of Reagan's "brilliance" or "ignorance" but found it difficult to construct a theory that would account for his varying modes of intellectual behavior. Then I came across the work of Howard Gardner, a Harvard psychologist who has pioneered in developing a theory of "multiple intelligences." Gardner's work, which has gained grudging acceptance in the scientific community, challenges the conventional belief that "intelligence" is a general capacity possessed to greater or lesser extent by every human being. In place of a single intelligence that can be measured by a standardized "intelligence test," Gardner postulates seven specific intelligences with distinctive characteristics. In Gardner's categorization Reagan ranks high in a form of intelligence he calls "interpersonal," high in "bodily-kinesthetic intelligence," high in an aspect of "language intelligence" and low in the "logical-mathematical intelligence" at which lawyers and professors usually excel. Reagan is not the least lawyerlike. "Reagan's good with language, but not logically," Gardner observes. "He makes sense of the world narratively. Scientists can be deductive and understand logic but often can't tell stories. Stories are not necessarily logical." Gardner believes that the combination of intelligences exhibited by Reagan is unusual for a president, but not necessarily for an actor. "Actors find it easier to mimic than to understand," says Gardner. "They are kids who often have difficulty with the usual school stuff, but they can parrot things back and get reinforcement from others. Many people in acting are not happy with who they are. What sets Reagan apart is that he is extraordinarily happy with himself—and with the role of Reagan."

Gardner's analysis of the way Reagan functioned intellectually produced in me the sense of discovery that a scientist or a detective must feel when a gigantic mystery abruptly becomes comprehensible. Others who have struggled even longer to explain Reagan think this theory of his intelligence makes sense. "That's exactly right," said Stuart Spencer, who understands Reagan as well as anyone I know. "Exactly. I'm always asked to explain him, and I talk about him as intelligent but not intelligent in the way politicians are intelligent. This explains him." Spencer had been telling me for more than two decades that the ability Gardner describes as "interpersonal intelligence" was Reagan's strong suit. It was what Spencer had in mind when he warned me, many years ago, never to underestimate Reagan's abilities. Former White House chief of staff Ken Duberstein also believes that Gardner's analysis is valid. Duberstein had often told me that Reagan was more intelligent than he seemed to the politicians who watched him read from four-by-six cards.

If Reagan is viewed as an intelligent person whose combination of intelligences is unusual in a president, a number of apparent mysteries of his behavior become soluble. Take the mimicry and the memory, for instance. When I interviewed Neil Reagan, then sixty, while writing my first book about his brother in 1968, he told me that the young Ronald Reagan had "a photographic mind." Neil recalled that one of Ronald Reagan's professors at Eureka College (probably economics professor Archibald Gray) had complained that he "never opened a book" but always knew the answers at examination time. He then explained the way that his brother did his studying: "He would take a book the night before the test and in about a quick hour he would thumb through it and [mentally] photograph those pages and write a good test." This ability freed Ronald Reagan for activities he enjoyed more than studying, and it stood him in good stead in Hollywood, where he earned the reputation as a quick study who rapidly memorized his lines.

But Reagan's ability to mentally "photograph" and store textual material proved a mixed blessing in public life. As Gardner puts it, people lacking Reagan's phenomenal skill of memorization learn to translate or "recode" the information they receive into a language of their own in order to remember it. "A good linguistic memory can collide with analytic facility because if you remember something perfectly, there is no need to re-code it, thereby making it your own," Gardner observed. Over time, the advantage of Reagan's superior memory gave way to the disadvantage of his deficient analytic skills.

. . .

Ed Meese has observed that Reagan's mistakes at news conferences often were the result of an unsuccessful attempt at literal repetition of technical material from a meeting or briefing paper. When Reagan groped for words, as he frequently did, he was actually trying to reconstruct visually what he had read or heard, much as he had done when taking tests at Eureka. Sometimes he misremembered vital details of the information he had tried to memorize, in effect producing an out-of-focus picture from his photographic mind. At other times he recalled exactly what had been said to him and repeated it in answer to a question on a related but slightly different subject, producing an answer that was off the point.

Greenspan's remark that Reagan was "psychologically a professional comedian" is also a valuable key to understanding him. What first made me think that Reagan was intelligent was his sense of humor, readily evident in his early political career when he wrote his own material and obscured in the White House by the armada of speechwriters that surrounds any president. In the old days Reagan wrote his own one-liners ("Their signs said, make love, not war, but they didn't look like they could do either"), and he could also be spontaneously humorous. At one tense situation on the University of California's Santa Cruz campus during his governorship, when Reagan's limousine was slowly proceeding through a group of hostile demonstrators, a bearded youth stuck his face up to the car, yelling, "We are the future." Reagan borrowed a piece of paper from an aide and scribbled a message that he held up to the car window. It said, "I'll sell my bonds."

Reagan also understood, both consciously and intuitively, that humor was a wonderful tool for deflating political opponents and sidetracking their most significant assertions. During the rehearsal for Reagan's 1980 debate with independent candidate John B. Anderson, Stockman imitated Anderson's grim assessment of Reagan's environmental policies. "Well, John, sounds like I better get a gas mask," Reagan responded. This remark never made it off the cutting-room floor, but Reagan's most famous line in his 1980 campaign debate with Carter was the product of a similar process. By this time, Stockman was impersonating Carter. During one rehearsal he hammered away at Reagan on the nuclear proliferation issue. Reagan was ineffective in response. In a critique afterward, aides pressed Reagan to sharpen the content of his answer while Reagan mused about his rhetorical ineffectiveness. Commenting on the reply he had delivered in rehearsal, Reagan said, "I was about ready to say, 'There you go again.' I may save it for the debate." And he did, rescuing an otherwise deficient reply to Carter's claim that Reagan "began his political career campaigning against Medicare" by saying, "There you go again." The response was funny, irrelevant—and thoroughly authentic. It did not answer Carter's point, but it revealed a functioning intellect. What was on display that October night in Cleveland, as in the Carter and Reagan presidencies, were different types of intelligence.

Ultimately, Reagan's sense of humor provided a measure of the man. The people recognized this quickly, and his wiser adversaries learned it over time. Paying tribute to Reagan at the 1988 Gridiron Dinner, New York governor Mario Cuomo quoted John F. Kennedy's observation that "there are only three things in life that are real—God, human folly, and laughter—and since the first two are beyond our comprehension, we must do what we can with the third." Cuomo went on to compare the two presidents, saying that Kennedy's gift of laughter was one of the reasons that Americans loved him and "it's one of the reasons that we Americans love and respect another man of gentle humor, our president, Ronald Reagan."

Reagan treasured that tribute. When he was riding high, his stories and one-liners delighted audiences and heartened all who heard the sound of his voice. When he was down, his self-deprecating stories helped him overcome his own fears and uncertainties and sent a message to the nation that all would ultimately be well. "Please tell me you're all Republicans," he said to the doctors who were preparing him for surgery after he was shot on March 30, 1981. Reagan was deeply frightened at the time and doing his best to laugh in the face of the Great Fear. That night, in the recovery room at George Washington Hospital, with tubes in his throat that prevented him from speaking, Reagan signaled for a notepad. "All in all, I'd rather be in Philadelphia," he wrote, paraphrasing comedian W. C. Fields. In his greatest personal crisis, and all others, Reagan's sense of humor proved his saving grace.

Taken from Lou Cannon, *President Reagan, The Role of a Lifetime* (New York: PublicAffairs, 2000), pgs. 95–114.

Jesse Jackson

SOMEBODY

Jesse Jackson is among the most interesting men ever to run for president. We don't judge candidates on their complexity, but if we did Jackson not only would have defeated Michael Dukakis, the spark-less governor of Massachusetts, and won the Democratic nomination for president, but also would have defeated the Republican nominee, George H. W. Bush—and in a landslide. Ambition shrinks the man inside the politician. Ambition filled out Jackson—made him more and more himself. Jackson's religious commitments lent balancing depth to his swollen persona, but often tripped him up politically. For Jackson justice was the overriding moral issue, and he judged American society harshly for scorning the poor. But this moralism about economics deserted Jackson when it came to people. He could not bring himself to indulge the ordinary politician's ritualistic bashing of foreign bad guys. Partly, of course, because, from Castro to Arafat, he had physically *embraced* many of them. But partly, too, because his faith would not let him write off even the worst of sinners. If a debate moderator had asked Jackson to name his favorite political philosopher, he might, with George W. Bush, have answered, "Jesus."

Though Jackson got more votes than any candidate running for any office other than president in 1988, he felt unwelcome in the Democratic Party. Jackson saw the Democrats' embarrassment with him as revelatory of their embarrassment with black voters. The Democrats, in Jackson's view, treated blacks as "the party concubines—they get the fun with us, then they marry other people. We want to be full partners." To be accepted as full partners:

respect and rejection, Garry Wills shows, are the master themes of Jackson's life and politics.

MARGINAL MAN
Garry Wills

In a Christmas sermon delivered during World War II, a black preacher said:

> You see, there's some question about *all* our ancestry. Jesus knows how we feel. When he was born, there was some question about *his* ancestry. He shares with the lowest men and races in our society the stigma of questionable parentage!

In James Baldwin's novel of black life *Go Tell It on the Mountain,* the young hero is living with his mother's husband, who himself had sons by two different women. The confused relationship of black young men with their fathers gives special meaning to Scripture passages on Isaac's sons by different women: "Only the son of the bondman stood where the rightful heir should stand," Baldwin writes.

"Sometimes I feel like a motherless child," goes one of the more forlorn spirituals. But even in later verses of that song, which ring changes on the sad theme ("Sometimes I feel like I'm almos' gone"), one does not hear the singer feel like "a fatherless child"—that is too common a situation to be treated as an extremity of suffering.

Jesse Jackson would in time use his illegitimacy as a credential, a sign that he can sympathize with social outsiders. He has even compared his plight to that of Jesus—shocking some, though the identification is common in black churches. His situation was not unusual in a world that has done so much to batter the black family. As Joe Mathis, his high school football coach in Greenville, South Carolina, told me: "I was brought up like Jesse, no daddy, momma working, back door or no door to anything better. I knew that if I left Benedict College, the mill where I had been working would defeat me, the way it did others, who ended up dead or addicted to alcohol." Mathis had just completed a term on the Greenville city council when I interviewed him.

In some respects, Jackson was better off than he might have been. He knew who his father was—Noah Robinson, who gave him his father's name, Jesse, and his own middle name, Louis. Robinson wanted a son and thought his wife could not give him one (though later she did). He had his son by a neighbor girl, who later married Charles Henry Jackson. Jesse was adopted by Jackson, and grew up calling him father. But the fascinating side of his family was represented by his natural father. Noah Robinson's father had been a preacher, part of a famous team of twin brother evangelists. Robinson told me, in 1983, the family legend of the twins' preaching debut at age fourteen. One led off: "I *am* the *way*." The other responded, "*And* the truth *and* the *life*." The jazzy responsorial rhythms are those of Jackson's own trademark chant: "I *am* some*body*." He had heard the story of his grandfather and great-uncle from childhood on. Soon Jackson was saying that he would be a preacher too. Robinson did not take him seriously at first. But when he went to visit him in college, "He told me again. I didn't believe it. But he told me he had a dream that he was called. 'I can do it. I dreamed I was a preacher, leading people through the rivers of the waters.'" Noah Robinson was impressed by that. Dreams are an important matter in his family. After his own father died, he was tending the sickbed of his uncle, the other twin, who told him: "Tonight I'm going to see blessed Buddy [his brother]. Blessed Buddy came to me in a dream and told me I would be seeing him tonight." He died that night.

I asked Jackson if he could remember any intense prayer experience. He thought a moment and said it was when he arrived at Chicago Theological Seminary to begin his studies for the ministry. He had just moved his own and his wife's few things into their rented room. "I sat on the bed and just cried." Why? "I knew I was where I was meant to be."

He had moved partway in from the margin. Good as his real father and his adopted father were to him, Jackson moved enviously around the periphery of the Robinson house, outside looking in, watching his half-brother Noah live in a home he could only visit. When he ran for president, people said he was seeking "recognition." He claimed that he wanted recognition for blacks in general, who have been treated as "the party concubines—they [the Democrats] get the fun with us, then they marry other people. We want to be full partners." The imagery is revealing. It is also, as we have seen, biblical, the claim of a whole people whose marriage has been sealed by covenant.

Jackson's path to the seminary (which he entered in 1964) involved the normal tests of manhood for one growing up in the pre-civil-rights black South. He was a football star on a team that instilled pride under Joe Mathis, one that specialized in surprise and psychological warfare. "They called us a cocky team, but I wanted them to feel they could handle anybody. We would just ease onto the field, no rah-rah, and do our calisthenics without a word. Then we'd *explode* on the first play." Even more than physical quickness, one needed deft verbal powers to be a leader in the black ghetto. "Dozening," the ritual insult game, was a daily test of one's survival skills. Dick Gregory described the daily obstacle course: "Before they could get going, I'd knock it out first, *fast, knock* out those jokes so they wouldn't have time to set and climb all over me." Black militants would dozen "whiteys" in the sixties, Rap Brown boasting, "I'm peeter jeeter the womb beater, the baby maker, the cradle shaker."

In Greenville, dozening was called "signifying," and Jackson was a master at it. A friend from that time, LeRoy Greggs, remembers: "He would stick that needle in." Did Greggs ever feel the needle? "No, we had a neighborhood concept. We stuck by each other and signified against rivals." Jackson's rhyme-responses would be mocked in later years, and could get him in trouble. When accused of not following up on projects he had launched, he replied, "I'm a tree shaker, not a jelly maker." That would come back to haunt him when he asked for positions of responsibility, including the presidency. So would his boast to fellow Greenville outsiders that he and other waiters at Greenville's Poinsetta Hotel spit in the white folks' food before serving it to them. He tried to shrug that off by saying, "They lynched us, we played tricks on them."

On his graduation from high school, Jackson was offered a contract to play professional baseball, but he knew he would need an education to reach the ministry, to have the kind of influence he wanted. A football scholarship took him, briefly, to the University of Illinois, but he found his path to stardom blocked by another black quarterback already on the scene. (Later he would say he left because blacks were discriminated against.) He went where he *could* star—near home, at North Carolina Agricultural and Technical College. Lunch counter sit-ins had begun in the South, and in 1963 he led some students in one. He was arrested for organizing this protest ("inciting to riot" in the quaint language of the region) and spent a night in jail.

In 1964 he won a Rockefeller scholarship to Chicago Theological Seminary, one of the respected cluster of divinity schools on the campus of the University of Chicago. There he studied the basic curriculum of Old Testament, New Testament, modern theology. "He was serious about what he wanted to learn," says Perry Lefevre, a former dean of the school who taught him the basic theology course. Jackson talked his way through classes that did not interest him, avoiding written assignments whenever possible. His natural gift is entirely oral. He is vigorous and eloquent when he can speak his mind. When his grammar gets bent, it gains by the experience. At debate after debate in the 1988 campaign, Jackson asked those in the audience who had a television set or stereo to raise their hands; then he asked those who owned their own intercontinental missile to hold up *their* hands. When none were raised, he said, "We makin' what ain't nobody buyin'." That is the pretense-shattering language of the spirituals: "Ever'body talkin' 'bout heaven ain't going there." Reduced to print, such a passage loses the ease of Jackson's perfectly placed "ain't." In fact, most of those who quoted the comment tried to tidy it up, and just destroyed its rhythm.

But the colloquial mode should not mislead people. Jackson's mind is creative, and creativity involves the extraordinary ingestion of material to be remade. He is a quick learner and shrewd analyst. At Chicago Theological Seminary, he was drawn to activist teachers in an academic setting—it was the sixties, and all of higher education had to cope with a world wrenched free of its moorings. In Jackson's case, that made two of his teachers special mentors, the kind who like a student with the curiosity and drive Jackson showed. One of these, Ross Snyder, had established an exchange program with South African theologians and their students. This gave an international basis to Jackson's thinking, at a time when the African heritage of blacks was being recaptured. Jackson would wear a mushroom-cloud Afro in the years ahead, and a stylish range of dashikis; but he was fortunate in making his first acquaintance with the continent in terms of common *Christian* efforts against oppression at home and abroad. Jackson never thought that re-Africanization meant de-Christianization. The religion of the slaves in America was not, of necessity, a slave religion in his eyes. He stayed on the side of Dr. King in this respect.

The other teacher who influenced Jackson, and gave him influence, taught at the University of Chicago Divinity School, but attracted activist students from all the affiliated theological schools. Alvin Pitcher was a white participant in the community organizing that gave many blacks their voice in Chicago, where the black establishment had been indebted to the machine. Pitcher introduced Jackson to fellow members of Al Raby's Coordinating Council of Community Organizations and to black pastors like Clay Evans (who would later ordain Jackson).

By his second year at the seminary, when he led a group of fellow students down to the 1965 Selma march, Jackson could tell Dr. King that he might prove useful if King heeded the people asking him to go north into Chicago's different world of segregation. The Selma situation was tense, following as it did on the murder of Jimmie Lee Jackson and the march to Montgomery aborted at Edmund Pettus Bridge on "bloody Sunday," March 7, 1965. Organizing a new march was proving difficult. Dr. King's Southern Christian Leadership Conference was being criticized as not radical enough by the leaders of the Student Nonviolent Coordinating Committee. SNCC's attempts to create a new policy were "marked by repeated shouting matches with SCLC's Jim Bevel."

Jesse Jackson intruded on this scene with typical assurance, giving out speeches and advice. King's advisers, young in absolute terms (King was only thirty-six himself), had lived through beatings, hoses, dogs, and jails—whole generations, as it were, of white weapons systems—and they did not want to listen to a latecoming loudmouthed kid. Yet Jackson found one ally in the King circle, and at its very center. Ralph Abernathy, King's contemporary and friend, had trouble keeping the leader's ear in the press of younger men around him. Perhaps another young voice, added to the clamor, would dilute the influence of the aging "kids" who pushed at each other and at Abernathy. In this way, the man who would later have most to resent in Jackson's rise helped gain him entry.

Jackson went back to Chicago after the Selma march, ready to beat the drum for King's intercession in that city. When King arrived in Chicago the next year, Jackson dropped out of the seminary to be helpful to him—he was driving the car that picked him up at O'Hare Airport. Though Jackson was himself a newcomer to Chicago, his marginal status could be put to use. Since he was not ordained, he did not look like a rival to the established preachers of the area, each of whom had his own church. When Jackson began services for his own SCLC activity (Operation Breadbasket), he held them on Saturday morning, avoiding any conflict with the Sunday-morning sermons of his elders.

Operation Breadbasket, which SCLC had developed in Philadelphia, involved "covenants" between black buyers and businesses that would commit themselves to black hiring, especially at management levels. The opposite of covenant favors to any business was a withdrawal from buying—boycott. Jackson would be accused of blackmailing businessmen by his critics on the right, and of capitalist deal-making by his critics on the left. Meanwhile, Jackson marched around Chicago with Dr. King, part of King's ineffectual search for a confrontation with Mayor Daley. Daley could blur the talk about schools, housing, and police behavior with double-talk about administrative difficulties. He eluded King's attempts at a moral showdown. With a sense, almost, of relief, King turned back south to the Memphis garbage strike.

Jackson was not involved in the garbage strike, but he was carping at King's other plan for shifting the focus from Chicago—a poor people's march on Washington. When militants broke up one march in Memphis, King called in his organizers from Atlanta, Chicago, and elsewhere to keep the peace at a new march. Jackson was still arguing

Celebrity

Few people beyond political junkies actually know what the "Rainbow Coalition" is, and many assume from its name that it has something to do with, maybe, after-school programs for at-risk children of various races (I did for many years). But it is no such thing, nor has Jackson ever run such a thing. The "Rainbow Coalition" is, today, one of several labels for an operation whose main purpose has become to line the pockets of Jesse Jackson's rich friends, period. For all of his populist rhetoric, Jackson has left behind not a single sustained and successful project designed to improve black lives beyond the boardroom.

He is sure to pop up before the news cameras at any race-based fracas lending itself to an indignant speech. But stories are legion of Jackson's meanwhile turning down local, cash-strapped black organizations who call on him to appear on the behalf of causes just as urgent but less sensational, because such groups cannot afford his fat fees for speeches—imagine King having his aides blow off Mississippi Delta churches unless they could cough up thousands of dollars. And seeking international scope, he has forged relations with the likes of Yasser Arafat, Hafez Assad, Slobodan Milosevic, and African dictator thugs Sani Abacha, Charles Taylor, and Foday Sankoh. Jackson also ran for president a couple of times, but these were largely symbolic gestures of no meaning to black lives on the ground. And with friends abroad like his, we should be thankful that he has gotten no further in elected public office.

Celebrity is shallow, and Jackson will remain a rock star on sheer recognizability, combined with his oratorical knack. He has no effect on the lives of most black Americans, and as such he is nothing to worry about. But thirty-five years of his self-aggrandizing machinations confirm that one thing black Americans cannot expect from this man is leadership.

Excerpted from John McWhorter, *Authentically Black: Essays for the Black Silent Majority* (New York: Gotham Books, 2003), pgs. 240–242.

with a harassed King about the wisdom of going to Washington. At an afternoon meeting at the Lorraine Motel, where all the aides were shouting at each other, King told Jackson to go start his own movement if the SCLC's did not satisfy him.

Later, when King went out onto the balcony to talk with those driving him to dinner, he patched things up with Jackson, who stood in the parking area under the balcony with Rev. Samuel (Billy) Kyles, at whose house the SCLC group meant to eat. King's last words were spoken to the two men, since the assassin's bullet shot away his jaw on one side and part of his neck. Jackson, whose area of responsibility was in Chicago, with Operation Breadbasket, flew back there and went on television to plead for peace as riots broke out and Mayor Daley ordered police to shoot looters. Jackson also, to the disgust of other SCLC leaders, went on national television the next morning from Chicago. His colleagues later claimed that he left Memphis only to grab the limelight—which would have shown an odd sense of self-promotion. I know, from my own luck in getting a last seat out of Baltimore, that there was a rush of journalists and cameras toward Memphis, where the very people later critical of Jackson were aggressively courting attention. When these people left Memphis, it was to the even better-covered funeral in Atlanta, and then they left so abruptly that the garbage strikers had to find their own buses. The story, at the outset, was in Memphis, and anyone concerned exclusively with exposure would have done better to stay there.

But what most offended the younger echelon of SCLC leaders—an offense relayed in Barbara Reynolds's influential first biography of Jackson—was his claim when he appeared in Chicago to be wearing a turtleneck shirt stained with Dr. King's blood. People like Hosea Williams swear he never got near Dr. King's body. He was standing below the balcony when his conversation with King was cut off. Like the others, he crouched down, waiting for more shots. But Billy Kyles, beside him, had rushed up to the body. The body was pumping blood from its neck artery, not stanched by the towel put on it. "There was blood everywhere," Kyles says. When he put a motel bedspread over King's body, he got blood on his hands, and wiped it off on a handkerchief—he still had the handkerchief when I talked to him in

1983. It is a natural instinct to save the blood of martyrs. When Jesuit priests were hanged, drawn, and quartered in Elizabethan England, Catholics used to press around the scaffold to dip handkerchiefs in the spattered blood (the actual butchered limbs were kept from them by the authorities, to deny them "first-class relics"). Shakespeare recalls that scene when Decius, in *Julius Caesar* (2.2.90), predicts that great men shall push each other around the "fountain" of Caesar's blood to acquire "tinctures, stains, relics, and cognizance [emblem]." Responsive to that instinct, Jacqueline Kennedy would not remove the suit stained with her husband's blood while she was returning from Dallas to Washington.

Billy Kyles does not doubt what was on Jackson's turtleneck: "Of course he got blood on him—we all did." It was inevitable that Jackson would go up the stairs to get a last glimpse of his fallen leader. Even car accidents draw the curious to look, and Jackson is not shy about such things. And if he got anywhere near the body, he got near the blood. It is odd that those who accuse Jackson of shouldering his way too close to King at his first meeting in Selma think he would keep an unnatural distance that night in Memphis. Even if we take the most unfavorable view of Jackson, as a calculating fellow who wanted to have something that looked like King's blood on his shirt, the most readily available thing that would *look* like the blood *was* the blood. The charge that he would go away from the obvious source and contrive some substitute for the tragically available original stuff is a measure of the anger Jackson inspired in other followers of King when this latecomer got so much attention. He will always be, in some measure, illegitimate in his claims—of ambiguous paternity where King is concerned, just as with his first two fathers.

But there can be no doubt that Jackson planned to *make* himself King's heir, in the most conscious way. He schemed with Chicago political manager Don Rose to do just that in the aftermath of King's death. By using Chicago as his base, rather than Atlanta, he put himself outside King's last orbit, where "legitimate" successors would scramble with each other, over the years, united only in their conviction that whoever wore the mantle in the long run, Jesse Jackson should not even make a *bid* to assume it.

There were special problems, having nothing to do with internal SCLC tensions, in the choice of Chicago as a base. This was the city that had defeated King. It was Mayor Daley's fiefdom, a place where even black politicians rose only with the help of Daley's machine. Later in the year of Dr. King's death, Daley became infamous for beating white middle-class youths who came to his city for the Democratic convention. But one of the most interesting (if least noticed) aspects of that August riot in the streets is that resident blacks took no part in it. Daley had given Lyndon Johnson his word that black neighborhoods would be sedated by the end of the summer—all of them set afloat in the gush of new swimming facilities and loose cash that washed around black precinct workers' circles. In Chicago, succeeding to Dr. King's position was putting oneself in line for humiliation.

Jackson tried to fight back in symbolic ways, as Dr. King had done, putting himself up for ridicule when he tried to mount an independent race against Daley for mayor. Jackson tried to enter the Democratic party as he had the civil rights movement, in a slanting arrival through a side door, ignoring the long flight of steps one had to climb toward the front door. He watched in 1971 as another outsider in the civil rights "family"—Shirley Chisholm—mounted a maverick campaign for president from her independent New York base. The black "elders" tried to head her off, then had to give her grudging support as a matter of black solidarity, in a first small version of what would happen with Jackson twelve years later.

The full measure of Jackson's illegitimacy in the Democratic party came out in 1972. That was the year he helped William Singer run a slate of delegates to supplant Mayor Daley's at the Miami Democratic convention—but under withering questions from the Illinois credentials committee it emerged that Jackson had not even voted in the primary he was challenging, or in any other Illinois election. As Mike Royko put it, in a mocking column: "Jesse the Jetstream didn't make it to his local polling place. He's being hailed as a new political powerhouse, and he couldn't deliver his own vote." Jackson's dubiously assembled slate prevailed over Daley's in Miami—more from Larry O'Brien's autocratic rulings, and from Daley's refusal to bargain with the reformers, than from any skills at party maneuver on Jackson's part. His prominence in Miami would become another count against him back in Chicago, where he had earned more enemies than friends among Democrats of all degree. Even his successes at achieving "covenants" with local corporations hurt him with the wider audience in Chicago, where he was seen as hustling for black interests rather than creating community ideals. When his annual "Black Expo" became successful, he detached it from the SCLC, which was foundering under Ralph Abernathy's uncertain leadership. Abernathy suspended Jackson, and Jackson resigned from the SCLC. He was on his own for the first time.

The reform Democrats Jackson had worked with in 1971 helped him during the Carter years. Joseph Califano, Carter's secretary of Health, Education, and Welfare, proposed a grant to Jackson's Operation PUSH (People United to Save Humanity, later amended to *Serve* Humanity) after hearing how Jackson preached discipline and study to black students. The federal moneys that went to the resulting PUSH/Excel program were poorly accounted for, and Jackson's program was never very good apart from Jackson's own performances in the schools. Ernest R. House, who was given a federal contract to evaluate the government's own evaluation of PUSH/Excel, concluded that the program was run like "the Baptist church, historically the strongest institution in the black social order." That was also the way SCLC's finances had been managed—to Andrew Young's continuing exasperation. But the PUSH/Excel program did keep Jackson on the road, forming a national constituency among the young at a time when other civil rights leaders disappeared into local politics or private misery. During the 1970s Jackson was the only black spokesman still addressing a national audience. He kept up his ties to Africa and—through the Black Muslims—with Arab countries. These latter ties were useful when Jackson negotiated with Syria for the release of the downed American flyer Robert Goodman in 1984. They would become a hindrance when Black Muslim Louis Farrakhan's anti-Semitism became an issue.

When Jackson decided to run for president, he used a typical preacher's device to include others in the decision-making process. Pat Robertson would do the same thing four years later—asking supportive congregations if they wanted this to happen and were willing to back it. That is the way televangelists raise money for ambitious new churches, broadcast facilities, or universities. Jackson varied the formula by making the "Run, Jesse, Run" rallies an appeal for *many* minority candidates to run—blacks, women, Asian Americans, and others. The "Rainbow Coalition" would unite all the dispossessed or underrepresented in another "covenant"—Noah's rainbow sign was a covenant with humanity.

The civil rights "family" was even unhappier with Jackson's bid than with Shirley Chisholm's in the seventies. They had not yet come to terms with his leverage in the black generation that had come of age since Dr. King's death. An ABC poll in 1983 showed that Jackson was considered by 51 percent of blacks as their most important leader. The runner-up, Andrew Young, got only 8 percent. The rest went down, toward invisibility, from there.

Jackson hoped for liberal support of his coalition, definitely including Jewish support. Black militants had forsworn white contributions to their cause by the end of the sixties, arguing that Jews, in particular, spoke more for service providers than service receivers. This was the source of conflict in the Ocean Hill-Brownsville school dispute in New York and the affirmative-action debates around the *Bakke* case. But Jackson, whose "covenanting" strategy was always negotiatory and inclusive, tried to keep the Jewish-black alliance alive. He had formed the anti-Daley delegation in 1972 with William Singer, a Jewish liberal Democrat. He and his family marched with Jews protesting a Ku Klux Klan rally in Skokie, and he sent a letter of protest when General George Brown, chairman of the Joint Chiefs of Staff, said that Jews control America's banks and newspapers.

But Jackson was suspect among Jews for his support of Palestinian rights, a support given vivid expression when he was photographed in his travels embracing Yasir Arafat. Thus when it became known that he had referred to Jews as "Hymies" in private conversation, and that his Black Muslim supporters called the Jewish religion "dirty,"

Jackson was accused of anti-Semitism. For a week he tried to deny or shrug off the "Hymie" issue—a bad mistake, since it gave time for emotions to become indurated on either side. Some Jews were ready to admit that *schvartzes* was used as readily in their circles as *Hymies* had been in Greenville when Jackson was growing up. But the man who had rebuked General Brown for insensitivity should have acknowledged his own lapse the minute it was drawn to his attention. By the time he brought himself to apologize, the firestorm of criticism around him was taken by many blacks as a form of Jewish racism. Adolph Reed, in an otherwise scholarly book, denounces it as "caterwauling." Some made it a point of principle, by then, that Jackson *not* apologize. (His wife was in their number.) When Jackson apologized a *second* time, there was anger among his followers—and even more when he apologized still again in his speech at the Democratic convention. But his own rhetoric of reconciliation among the afflicted made apology mandatory.

The same dynamic was observable when Louis Farrakhan became an issue. The Black Muslims were widely respected in black communities for their success against drugs, their discipline, their restoration of proud black manhood in convicts and reformed criminals. I first heard of Farrakhan when I called Barbara Reynolds in 1983 to ask if she had altered any of the harsh views she expressed about Jackson in her 1975 book. She said no, that she found more representative leadership, now, in the sermons of Minister Farrakhan.

Farrakhan had gone to Syria with Jackson, providing him bodyguards for that and other trips. He considered all white religions, and white people, "dirty"—he had a biblical/physiological explanation of the racial degeneration of whites. Farrakhan, an ally of Malcolm X, had supplanted the Muslim leaders responsible for Malcolm X's death; but he had not taken part in politics until Jackson enrolled him in Harold Washington's campaign to become mayor of Chicago. The ethos of black solidarity forbids any renunciation of a "brother" who has come under white criticism—but Jackson professed to be speaking, now, for a larger coalition. Though the closed code of one strand in the "rainbow" was incompatible with other strands in it, Jackson was driven by the "Hymie" controversy back on his narrower base in the black churches, to restore his own confidence and the larger campaign's finances. The rainbow that was to be brown, yellow, red, white, and black was restricted to the original black by the time Jackson distanced himself (too late) from Farrakhan.

Even his contracted band of followers went to the 1984 convention bitterly divided among themselves and hostile to the party's organizers. His own followers said Jackson was making insufficient demands on the platform committee—and even those reforms were being rejected. When the Mondale forces chose Andrew Young to present the platform committee's rejection of Jackson's plank against runoff elections, they thought they would placate Jackson supporters. Instead, the use of Young was considered a further provocation. Even a moderate Jackson delegate, who later published his journal of the campaign, said he was "shocked and surprised that Andrew Young would choose to oppose Jackson's key plank openly on national TV." This, too, broke the code of black solidarity. When Young appeared on Tuesday, he was booed by black delegates.

Jackson's troops were seething that Tuesday, when Jackson was scheduled to address the convention. The delegate's diary continues:

> Believe that Mondale had made critical misjudgment as to impact of defeat of Jackson's minority planks—not necessarily in defeat of specific planks but in the way in which Mondale people wanted to show their control of the convention, particularly to show how badly he could beat Jackson and generally how he could show other interests that he was not giving in to yet another interest. Along with many other Jackson delegates, I personally resented deeply this kind of treatment. Wounds deep and won't heal easily.

It was against this background that Jackson rose to speak. He had kept his message secret from the Mondale people (who were asking for his support) and his own delegates (who were encouraging him to defiance). The apology he offered in the speech came as an unpleasant surprise to his own wife—and it infuriated people like Victor McTeer, who had worked on his platform proposals: "When he said to the Jewish community, forgive me—my reaction was: for what? . . .

There were a lot of supporters who'd been upset with a conciliatory speech at that moment." But after saying that to a friend, McTeer began to notice the response of others in his own Mississippi delegation: "White people around me are crying. I mean the men. I'm not talking about no light-weight little white girls. I'm talking about we're-going-to-fight-you-nigger-till-you're-gone white folks. . . . I'm standing there next to this white lady from Mississippi who's there in tears on my shoulder. I realized, 'My God, I'm part of something important.'" Jackson had asked forgiveness for any "error of temper, taste, or tone" in his campaign, and he went on to plead:

> We must turn from finger-pointing to clasped hands. We must share our burdens and our joys with each other once again. We must turn to each other and not on each other and choose higher ground. . . . All of us count and all of us fit somewhere. We have proven that we can survive without each other. But we have not proven that we can win and progress without each other. We must come together.

Jackson, driven back to the margin of politics, was only legitimate as the voice of the dispossessed. And it was religion that, in his case as in King's, let him reach people with an authentic voice for common suffering. As Victor McTeer said, with wonder: "Jesse Jackson held church in the Democratic National Convention."

Standing over my seat in his own chartered airplane, Jackson shadowboxes with the empty aisle just darkened for takeoff. It is February, deep into the primary campaigns of 1988, and he is explaining the Cold War. "It's like a fighter who's got his guard up high, looking over at the Bear"—his head periscopes around his hands—"and you expose yourself to these terrible body blows. Drugs!" His midsection hardens at the imagined blow, but the hands stay up. "Debt!" He buckles. "The purchasing of America!" A grunt. "Energy!" Another. "I start my policy toward Russia from here, from the hurt"—he spreads his fingers on his ribs—"and move on out to others. We've been leading with our left, with our left"—he jabs automatically. "Always military first, not economic, not diplomatic."

Still standing up during takeoff, Jackson says, above the engines' roar: "Reagan said something that should have got more attention from the press. He said the last forty years have not been good for the West. These last forty years have been the most exciting and liberating for the world. Whole empires have fallen, new nations been created, people taking charge of their own lives. What Reagan meant is that all those little shits in the UN have been beating up on us for forty years—*us,* Somoza; *us,* Batista; *us,* Marcos. We've got to redefine *us.*"

One of Jackson's skills as a preacher is his ability to put complex ideas in vivid form, or to give them concrete applications. I went with him, once, on one of his high school tours. He was teaching constantly. Standing with students in an airport, he continued his lesson on the need to learn. "Go get a ticket. If you can't count, you get the wrong change. If you can't read, you go to the wrong gate. If you can't handle numbers, you get the wrong flight at the wrong time." Arguing about the arms race, the drive for ever bigger weapons, he says—as five of us crowd into a little car—"We make elephant weapons for Toyota wars." Sitting next to the driver, he makes the same point by stabbing repeatedly at the dashboard: "Since we can't find the right place and put the key in, we just keep making bigger keys."

In the string of 1988 debates among Democratic candidates, Jackson's vivid formulations of the problems—problems of corporate responsibility, of drug interdiction, of trade imbalance—were echoed, sometimes verbatim, by other candidates as the series progressed, prompting Michael Dukakis to say, "That's Jesse's line!" Columnist George Will, who seemed to think Jackson became vivid only by oversimplifying, undertook the role of intellectual disqualifier on the ABC Sunday-morning show *This Week with David Brinkley.* Like an old Southern cracker giving a literacy test at the polls, he asked: "As president, would you support measures such as the G–7 measures [*sic*] and the Louvre Accords [*sic*]?" Like the redneck quizzers, Will got the trick question slightly wrong—the Louvre Accord *was* a G-7 measure for the international market.

What was surprising about Jackson's debating was his ability to explain himself *without* falling into the usual oversimplifications. While Richard Gephardt was Japan-bashing, Jackson criticized American firms for seeking cheap labor abroad. He argued that tax incentives as well as penalties should keep those jobs home. Jackson's populism did not feed on the hatreds that are populism's ordinary and disheartening fuel. His plea that all the outsiders should unite to confront their problems went counter to the claim that Jackson was acting only for black interests. He said that corporate barracudas "swim very deep, where it's very dark; they can't even tell whether they are swallowing white fish or black fish."

Jackson's didactic flair drew on the preacher's use of parable and Scripture tales. No other candidate was so open in his religiosity. When discussing homelessness, he said that Jesus was homeless, born in a stable. When discussing health insurance, he said Jesus did not ask the woman with a hemorrhage if she could pay before he healed her. This religious note embarrassed some secular blacks almost as much as if he had reverted to minstrel-show stereotypes. Yale political scientist Adolph L. Reed, Jr., found it debilitating that blacks should still depend on "the principle of clerical political spokesmanship." He points out that church activism on civil rights must be measured against church acquiescence in the power arrangements of the past. Reliance on preachers revealed, in the early stages of black activism, "several factors that retarded political development." When genuine (i.e., secular) political organization takes place, it renders the church matrix "a politically redundant entity." And in the process the authoritarian, nonaccountable model of leadership by preachers is submitted to democratic pressures. Politics and religion are at enmity by their very nature, since "the realm of politics by definition is temporal intervention."

Reed admits that some preachers—Andrew Young, Walter Fauntroy, William Gray—have entered electoral politics. But that gives them an entirely new kind of validation. Electoral discrimination replaces the emotional acclamation of the preacher's audience. By entering local races, these valid spokespersons for their constituents "meet the requirements of more formally articulated legitimating rules."

They move from symbolic politics to real politics. By election they are cleansed of their suspect clerical antecedents:

> Elected officials are the only claimants to black political leadership status who are held accountable for their actions by the presence of unambiguous mechanisms for popular ratification within the Afro-American community. . . . The rise of elected officialdom has regularized black political participation, and provided a set of concrete, systematic avenues for expression and realization of *black* interests . . . [so that] elected officials should be seen as the principal bearers of *black* political interests.

I italicize *black* in that last quote because, in Reed's model of pluralism an authentic voice must speak for *particular* interests in the push and shove of the total society. Jackson, by pretending to embody a "rainbow" of varying interests, did not attend to the one and only interest he might have represented. Claiming to promote everyone, he ends up nobody's real champion, as one could see by the grab bag of proposals he made to the 1984 platform committee. His opposition to nuclear "first strike," for instance, "cannot be considered a distinctively black concern." Reed thinks elected black officials were right to oppose Jackson's intrusion on their turf, and he finds it a sign of maturing in the black political community that Jackson was treated as an outsider when he tried to mediate for blacks in Miami after a civil disturbance there.

That Miami incident brings to mind what was in some ways the most dramatic episode of Jackson's 1984 campaign. Reed does not mention it—neither, surprisingly, do Bob Faw and Nancy Skelton in their book on that campaign. After Andrew Young had been booed by black delegates for proposing the Mondale platform, a black caucus was called for the next day. It was a very emotional session, with angry cries at Young when he appeared. Coretta Scott King, as the widow of the sainted leader, rose to bring back peace—and *she* was booed. When she tried to mention Young's services in the civil rights cause, Jackson delegates shouted, "That was yesterday!" and "What have you done recently?" Dr. Reed would, presumably, answer that Young had got elected, first to Congress, then to the mayor's office in Atlanta. That did not seem to satisfy the delegates. Young skipped out a door behind the congregation. Finally, when the emotions seemed to be reaching a crescendo, Jackson arrived, went onto the platform, hugged Mrs. King, and rebuked those who had booed her: "When I think about the roads I've walked with Andy, and the leadership of Mrs. King—her home bombed, her husband assassinated, her children raised by a widow—she deserves to be heard." Jackson soon had all the leaders present up on the stage, linked hand to hand, swaying back and forth as they sang "We Shall Overcome." The angers turned to emotional reconciliation and tears. It was a more virtuoso performance than Jackson's speech to the convention the day before; and he was the only one in America who could have brought it off.

Admittedly, these were Jackson delegates, activated and brought into the political process by his campaign. But by Reed's norms they were illegitimate voices of their community. They had been interested and sophisticated enough to get themselves elected to their party's national convention, but they had done so in response to a symbolic preacher, not a real power broker, according to Reed's analysis.

Still, here at the heart of the national convention of a major party, even Andrew Young, an elected mayor, had to rely on memories of church leadership past—on Dr. King's widow—to reconcile him with a new generation of black politicians; and even that had not worked until the most "retardative" leader stepped in. That is a sequence that should give Dr. Reed pause.

For one thing Reed seems to do, in his attack on Jackson, is validate Jackson's claim to be the heir of Martin Luther King. Everything Reed criticizes—symbolic leadership, lack of electoral validation, concern for larger issues than black welfare, moral appeals to a broad spectrum of clashing interests—marked King's life and work. And if Jackson continued along the course marked out by King, it was not by any conscious *defiance* of King's values, as some have claimed. Nor was there anything wrong, on the face of it, in aspiring to continue that legacy. Others certainly attempted it—Ralph Abernathy, for instance, and Hosea Williams, and James Bevel (all later critics of Jackson).

James Bevel, who delivered the greatest speech I have ever heard in my life, was expelled from the SCLC, like Jackson; his demagogic bent was at least as great as Jackson's, but less disciplined. Bevel set up Making a Nation (MAN) in Baltimore, and tried to recruit me as a celebrant of his one-man march on the UN, where he would demand separate representation for the black nation in America. Williams, less erratic than Bevel but also undisciplined, ended up with similar promotional efforts in Atlanta. Abernathy, jealous of King while King lived, was prickly in wanting the same kind of adulation after King's death. Abernathy's need for attention would finally make him support even Ronald Reagan, when Republicans were among the few still courting him.

The strains within the civil rights movement are glossed over by those who take testimony from its veterans against Jesse Jackson. Danger, persecutions, exhilarating victories, and soul-draining defeats took a devastating toll on those who bought our freedoms with their pain. If Jackson kept up a national vision of black pride throughout the seventies, it was by a *refusal* to succumb to the temptations that faced so many activists when the heady times of suffering and witnessing seemed to have faded entirely. The seventies was a period of hangover for many former leaders. Jackson's campaign against drugs and alcohol in the high schools was a witness that—like the Muslims'—had a special appeal for blacks in that "decompressing" aftermath to the movement.

Some, of course, did go into electoral politics, with success. But they were not all free from the excesses of the church structure that Reed thinks electoral politics must supplant. Authoritarian rule was still possible, *especially* when based on the kind of sheer *black* interest Reed calls for. Jackson ran PUSH/Excel as a church organization; but Marion Barry and Coleman Young also ran their respective city halls that way. Their critics found they were as immune from blame among their "congregations" as any black preacher of the old days. Even Andrew Young, a man of entirely different disciplines, was seen by Atlantans—especially by blacks—as "too much the preacher" rather than an ordinary politician.

.   .   .

Many people in the 1960s claimed that Dr. King had no right to speak out on the war. They wanted to confine him to "his" concerns—to put limits around his citizen activity. Others, in the South, had earlier denied that he could speak legitimately even on civil rights: As a clergyman, they said, he should have confined himself to matters of private morality, not issues of public policy. Ironically, Adolph Reed is updating this kind of restriction in the critique he makes of Jackson.

Jackson's clerical background was not something that resonated only in the depths of blacks who heard him. Many whites gave him a readier hearing because he is a preacher. This was one of the least-noticed aspects of the campaign. In Iowa, when Jackson, the urban black activist, first talked to white farmers, he was somehow less menacing, less alien, because he shared their language on Sundays. Staying overnight in voters' homes, he said prayers before meals. He appeared in local pulpits. Was this taking unfair advantage of people? Only if one thinks political issues can be debated in a kind of isolation from personal values and historical ties. It is hard to invent an entirely new moral language for each situation, as the 1988 campaign of Gary Hart demonstrated.

But even if the Democrats could, in the name of "value-free" discussion of public policy, divorce their politics from religious values, they could not enforce a similar self-denying ordinance on the Republicans, who profit from appeals to the evangelical Right. Democrats of the Dukakis persuasion will themselves into a tongue-tied state. No wonder Jackson seemed so comparatively free, grounded, and eloquent in the debates. He was reaching toward a larger audience, using traditional appeals, just as Ronald Reagan had in his 1980 debates.

Jackson's religious references did not seem to disturb his secular supporters, any more than Father Drinan's clerical collar bothered *his* allies in the opposition to Vietnam. Many of those allies had been at civil rights and peace demonstrations where Roman collars were frequently in evidence. But white evangelicals like Bert Lance did have a special affinity with Jackson, who did not yield any tactical advantage to the president in his 1984 convention speech: as Jackson had taken the hand of the security man at the Citadel and joined with him in prayer, so he answered Ronald Reagan's calls for prayer.

Mr. Reagan will ask us to pray, and I believe in prayer. I have come this way by the power of prayer. But then, we must watch false prophecy. He cuts energy assistance to the poor, cuts breakfast programs from children, cuts lunch programs from children, cuts job training from children, and then says to an empty table, "Let us pray." Apparently he is not familiar with the structure of prayer. You thank the Lord for the food that you are about to receive, not the food that just left. I think we should pray, but don't pray for the food that left. Pray for the man that took the food—to leave.

Jackson not only preached and campaigned in churches white and black, he also raised campaign funds in (mainly) black church gatherings. That does seem to violate the separation of church and state—though even so ardent a proponent of separation as Nat Hentoff sees nothing wrong with it. He argues, in fact, that it is the right of any group of citizens to support the views and people they want in a democracy. Some churches have partially surrendered that right to protect their tax-exempt status. That presents no problem to Hentoff, who does not believe that churches should be tax-exempt. In terms of actual political support, what Jackson was taking from the churches did not essentially differ from the support sought by Ronald Reagan, George Bush, and Dan Quayle at the annual meetings of the National Religious Broadcasters or the national prayer breakfasts.

In the past, a candidate's religion clearly was taken into account in voters' assessment of his representative character. That is why it took so long to put a Catholic into the White House. And even when John Kennedy was elected, it was not on the grounds that his religion was irrelevant. He surely profited as much from the importance of Catholic city machines in the Democratic party as he was hurt by Protestant misgivings. Anyone who saw nuns turn out to cheer Kennedy could not really believe his Catholicism was electorally irrelevant.

I saw the equivalent of those nuns in Atlanta, on the day when Jackson's campaign bus pulled into Piedmont Park for the 1988 convention, after a barnstorming tour down from Chicago. Asked why he took the bus to town, Jackson told the cheering crowd: "We took the bus north. We just came back on the other side of the highway."

Jackson was coming to town on the vehicle blacks have traveled in for years. He reminded the crowd that he is a part of them. "Weren't no cameras at the door when I was born. My momma could not serve us turkey dinner at three o'clock on Thanksgiving Day. She was busy making another family's turkey. That's my testimony [the church term for public witnessing]. But when my name goes in nomination for president, my momma's prayers are confirmed." The young black woman standing next to me was almost in tears at this point. She was well attired in a professional-looking suit, but she had sung and clapped along with the hymn to the Holy Spirit that the crowd bellowed just before Jackson's bus arrived.

Excerpted from Garry Wills, *Under God* (New York: Simon & Schuster, 1990), pgs. 222–239, 242–244.

Tip O'Neill

LIBERAL

I interviewed Tip O'Neill in 1982, in the midst of the struggle between him, the Democratic Speaker of the House, and President Ronald Reagan that John Aloysius Farrell chronicles below. I was profiling O'Neill for the *New Republic*. While I sat in his office waiting to begin our conversation, O'Neill talked on the telephone to Reagan's chief of staff, James A. Baker. He was hectoring Baker to include in the administration's budget some public works projects to mitigate the then-severe recession. I did not have a tape recorder but remember his saying something like this: *Jim, we need the jobs in the bill. Good construction jobs. Yeah, yeah; I understand that. But you've got to understand something too. We're talking about men feeding their families here. About kids needing to go to the dentist. Jesus, what it costs today! We're talking about taking the wife out to a movie; maybe dinner. Good wages get spread around. Follow me? Sure, sure; but listen. I want those jobs in the bill.* The conversation took another turn, but just as he was signing off O'Neill came back to the jobs. *Remember, Jim, put those jobs in the bill.* He hung up the phone, then pivoted in his chair to face me. "Who the hell are you?"

I was a goner, that's who. That the Speaker of the House thought government should provide work and wages to the unemployed, that he stayed true to his working-class North Cambridge roots, that he stood up for real family values in Reagan's Washington, and that he was a big red-faced Irishman who reminded me of my uncle Mike, a former O'Neill constituent— all this made me a goner. I became his Peggy Noonan, writing a paean to a giant of common decency. But even in full gush I did not imagine what O'Farrell's book, *Tip O'Neill and the Democratic Century,* reveals: that Tip O'Neill ranks among the great public men of his time. Certainly he was its greatest Democrat. In 1981 he squared off against its greatest Republican, Ronald Reagan.

"At least on the surface," O'Neill wrote in his 1987 memoir, *Man of the House,* "President Reagan and I have a lot in common." Both Irish-Americans from "modest backgrounds," O'Neill and Reagan "had FDR as our hero as we came of age in the 1930s." How then did they "come to have such different visions of America?" O'Neill asked. "Maybe it all boils down to the fact that one of us lost track of his roots while the other guy didn't." Tip stuck with North Cambridge. Reagan went Hollywood. "As a man of wealth, he doesn't really understand the past thirty years," O'Neill wrote. "God gave him a handsome face and a beautiful voice, but he wasn't that generous to everyone. With Ronald Reagan in the White House, somebody had to look out for those who were not so fortunate.

"That's where I came in."

CLASH OF TITANS

John Aloysius Farrell

The *Christian Science Monitor* breakfast was a Washington institution. A half-dozen times a month, generally when Congress was in session, some ten to twenty reporters from the capital's press corps would join a "man in the news" for bacon and eggs in the dining room of a stately downtown hotel. On April 7, 1981, O'Neill was the featured guest. The Speaker was taking the plunge into the type of media politics at which Reagan excelled; O'Neill, Dan Rostenkowski, and Jim Jones had scheduled public events in an orchestrated attempt to sell the Democratic alternative to the president's economic plan. His staff had prepared a six-page briefing packet with a suggested theme: "Democrats in the House have their act together. They have adjusted to the new economic—and political—realities." But for O'Neill, the morning did not go well. He was too much himself. As the reporters snickered, he defended, in most memorable terms, the big-spending days of the Great Society.

"I've been one of the big spenders of all time," O'Neill confessed. "Ah, I've been a big spender.

"I remember when a doctor came in and told us the average dwarf was twenty-six inches high. He said he could increase that to fifty-two inches. He brought in six dwarfs," O'Neill said. "Over the years I sneaked into the budget $45 million." There was the money for sickle-cell anemia. And $12 million for turned-in ankles. "I remember putting in $18 million for knock knees. I put in $160 million for research on cancer of the breast. I put in money for research on spinal injuries . . . whales can fuse their spines, China and the Soviet Union were doing research, and the greatest nation on earth wasn't. There are thousands of veterans who need it.

"We used to be able to sneak these in. Nobody knew. But nobody is going to be able to do that anymore," O'Neill lamented. "There are 150,000 dwarfs in America. Does anyone have an obligation? Is it the obligation of the federal government? I think it is.

"I'm just giving my philosophy," O'Neill said. He spoke with reverence of the days of Roosevelt. "That day is gone now. The people are more interested in a second home, better recreation, more education . . . with affluence, people change." As the meeting broke up, and the reporters rushed to their bureaus to write about Tip O'Neill and the dwarfs, he looked ruefully at his cold, hardly touched plate and said: "I want to thank you for that one piece of bacon."

As an initial foray into media politics, O'Neill's performance at the Sperling breakfast was "off-message" at best. "One of the things that made him remarkable was that this was a person driven in large measure by his sense of compassion—his sense of trying to help people who were suffering for one reason or another," his aide Ari Weiss recalled. "And he started to make this speech which reflected his deepest commitments and emotions. Of how this was something that the families of those children could not provide, and wasn't it the role of government. And as he began to talk about it, straight from the

heart, the reporters started to guffaw." Back on the Hill, the boll weevils groaned, thinking what sport the Republicans would make in
their one-minute speeches and televised ads of big Tip O'Neill and
his federal funding for the dwarfs and the knock-kneed. "He was
quite serious," the *Washington Star* felt the need to inform its readers.

Yet lost in the jokes about Tip and the dwarfs was an important
development. The old dog was trying new tricks. The Speaker was
fighting back, and on Reagan's turf, in a battle for popular opinion.
The decision had been made: it was Tip O'Neill who would step out
of the cloakroom to challenge Ronald Reagan, not some telegenic
young stand-in of a congressman. O'Neill would not lead the Democratic Party from the confines of the Speaker's lobby. He would serve
as its public spokesman and symbol. He would make the Speakership
the forum from where the Democrats issued their response to Reagan. It was an audacious idea. No twentieth-century Speaker had attempted such a thing: to challenge a presidency so.

★   ★   ★

"The pendulum swings," O'Neill kept telling his staff and colleagues.
He and the Democrats were flailing about, searching for a political
opening when, in May, the Reagan administration made its first political blunder. It was an issue that was custom-made for O'Neill: the
Republicans were scheming to cut back Social Security. The president's problems could be traced to Reagan budget director David
Stockman's rosy scenarios. If the defense budget was untouchable,
and the tax cut sacrosanct, the Reagan administration would face
massive budget deficits unless it reduced the soaring costs of Social
Security and other so-called entitlements, like Medicare, unemployment insurance, and veterans' pensions, where double-digit inflation
had led to mammoth cost-of-living hikes. The Social Security program alone cost some $200 billion a year, about a third of the nonde-
fense budget. Stockman thought it "a giant Ponzi scheme," and once
the first round of budget and tax cuts were enacted, the entitlements
became the administration's next target. Could the Reagan era truly
be revolutionary if it gave a free pass to such social insurance pro-

grams—failed even to take a swipe at the heart of Franklin Roosevelt's legacy? "If not us, who? If not now, when?" Reagan asked.

Republicans in the House and Senate were game for the campaign, which Stockman described as "a frontal assault on the very inner fortress of the American welfare state." But an attack of that magnitude demanded time, planning, preparation, and unanimity—qualities that, during the frantic and frenetic days of spring, the White House found in short supply. Instead, the GOP launched its assault in a wavering, piecemeal fashion. Within his early rounds of budget cuts, Stockman had proposed that Congress chip away at some extraneous Social Security benefits, like the minimum monthly payment, and was lulled by his initial success. Indeed, a Ways and Means subcommittee led by Democratic Representative J.J. "Jake" Pickle of Texas had introduced its own Social Security reform bill, with several billion dollars in savings, as a first step toward meeting an anticipated shortfall of $75 billion over the next four or five years. Pickle even invited the administration to join him in the search for a bipartisan solution.

In early May, Stockman made his move, proposing to cut back Social Security benefits for beneficiaries who chose early retirement. It was a logical step, to cut first among those who left the workforce voluntarily. The system had been created to guarantee dignity and security, not an extra decade on the golf course in Florida. To his credit, Reagan signed on. But chief of staff Jim Baker and his aide Richard Darman, quaking when they heard the news, insisted that Health and Human Services secretary Richard Schweiker, not the White House, announce the cuts. The president got the worst of both worlds: as the White House switchboard was jammed with calls from panicky retirees, Democrats caught the whiff of Republican hesitancy. "Someone planning to retire in nine months who thought he was going to be getting $650 per month would now be getting $450. The cut was tough—but the lack of warning was devastating," Stockman admitted. "I just hadn't thought through the impact of making it effective immediately." As the news spread on Capitol Hill, the press revealed that the administration was also planning to delay that summer's cost-of-living increase.

It was a critical turning point, Kirk O'Donnell, one of the Speaker's top aides, recalled. "This was right from O'Neill, right from his gut. He was on his way to work, reading the paper, and he read about Stockman's cuts and he came in to the morning conference we had and asked, 'What do you know about these proposals?' And nobody knew anything about them," he remembered.

"Call Danny," O'Neill said.

O'Donnell spoke to the Ways and Means staff, and discovered that the chairman, Dan Rostenkowski, and Pickle were playing down the controversy because they felt a fiduciary responsibility, as good Democrats, to work with the White House to make Social Security solvent. "Danny doesn't want to play politics with it," O'Donnell told the Speaker. Though O'Neill generally let his committee chairmen make such calls, this time the knife was too close to bone. "Danny wanted to deal with it in a responsible, nonpolitical way. But O'Neill saw the Reagan administration overreaching and at that point he just jumped on it. And that was him. All him. Totally him. And he never let it go," O'Donnell recalled.

"I have a statement on the Social Security," O'Neill said at his May 13 press conference, reading from a typed page. "A lot of people approaching that age have either already retired on pensions or have made irreversible plans to retire very soon. These people have been promised substantial Social Security benefits at age sixty-two. I consider it a breach of faith to renege on that promise. For the first time since 1935 people would suffer because they trusted in the Social Security system."

"Are you saying that is a serious political mistake?" a reporter asked.

"I'm not talking about politics. I'm talking about decency. It is a rotten thing to do," O'Neill said. "It is a despicable thing."

The Speaker stunned the Capitol press corps by arriving in the House radio and television gallery a few days later to announce the results of that morning's Democratic caucus. To no one's surprise, the caucus had condemned Reagan's plans for Social Security. To everyone's surprise, here was the Speaker looking to get on television. He also invited crews from CBS and NBC to interview him in his office.

He made all three network news shows that night, and clips from the interviews were used throughout the following week. "I will be fighting this every inch of the way," the Speaker promised. It was the first time he had drawn a line at Reagan's feet.

"Reagan finally has made a wretched mistake," House Majority Leader Jim Wright told his diary. "The administration is badly stung by the wrath of millions of aging Americans." The Republican-controlled Senate voted 96 to 0 on May 20 to repudiate any solution that would "precipitously and unfairly penalize early retirees." In a letter to the Speaker, Reagan sued for peace, saying he was "not wedded to any single solution," and calling for a bipartisan approach.

★   ★   ★

The next clash came in June. Departing the White House after a meeting with Reagan, O'Neill told Rostenkowski he was ready to "beat the bejesus" out of the president, and then informed the scrum of reporters that the Reagan tax plan was a "windfall for the rich." The following weekend, after getting the producers of ABC's *Issues and Answers* show to tape his appearance from the Speaker's office, O'Neill broke a three-year drought and appeared on a Sunday talk show. The first question was a softball about the president's tax bill. "I'm opposed to the Reagan tax bill, number one, because it's geared for the wealthy of the nation instead of being spread out among the working class of America and the poor people. Number two, it's going to send inflation through the roof. The deficits are going to be so high that I fear for America," O'Neill said.

He stumbled a bit when trying to explain the technical differences between the White House tax bill and the Democratic alternative, but then went for Reagan's throat. "He has no concern, no regard, no care for the little man of America. And I understand that. Because of his lifestyle, he never meets those people. And so consequently, he doesn't understand their problems. He's only been able to meet the wealthy," O'Neill said.

"You're saying he's callous," said ABC's Charles Gibson.

"I think that he has very, very selfish people around him, very selfish people around him, people only of the upper echelon of the wealth

Reagan's Toast to Tip

"Tip was an old-fashioned pol: He could be sincere and friendly when he wanted to be, but when it came to the things he believed in, he could turn off his charm and friendship like a light switch and become as bloodthirsty as a piranha," Reagan wrote in his memoirs. "Until six o'clock, I was the enemy and he never let me forget it."

"Tip has joined that chorus back here that's bent on a lynching, with me in the noose," Reagan wrote to Frank Sinatra when, toward the end of the president's term, Sinatra suggested that O'Neill be appointed ambassador to Ireland.

And yet, despite their differences, O'Neill and Reagan had a begrudging regard for each other, and were not averse to some mutual political back-scratching. "Kenny Duberstein and I were the only two guys who were there when Reagan had Tip upstairs, in the family dining room, for his seventieth birthday," said Reagan aide Mike Deaver. "And God it was just amazing. Kenny and I sat there with these two old Irishmen, and they told Irish jokes back and forth, and about 1 P.M. Reagan, who really didn't drink—I mean he would have a screwdriver occasionally or a glass of wine—rings the buzzer for the butler and orders a bottle of champagne."

The butler poured the champagne and the president said, "Tip, if I had a ticket to heaven and you didn't have one too, I would give mine away and go to hell with you."

Said Deaver: "It was an old Irish toast he had heard somewhere. Well, Tip's eyes were all filled up, you know, it was just incredible. And they left the dining room with their arms around each other's waist and Reagan took him down to the elevator and Tip went out on the South Lawn and beat the shit out of Reagan with the press.

"Reagan thought Tip was absolutely wrong, and pigheaded. And Tip thought Reagan didn't understand anything about this country except the rich," said Deaver. "But there was a lot of respect that both of them had for each other." O'Neill later wrote Reagan, thanking him for "a birthday I will never forget."

Excerpted from John Aloysius Farrell, *Tip O'Neill and the Democratic Century* (New York: Little, Brown and Company, 2001), pgs. 620–621.

of this nation, and they are his advisers," O'Neill said. "I think he'd do much better if he had brought in some people close to him who are from the working force of America, who have suffered along the line, not those who have made it along the line and forgotten from where they've come."

Forgotten from where they've come. Breach of faith. Windfall for the rich. These were the ultimate epithets in the O'Neill canon, not freshly minted sound bites. What made the Speaker's performance so effective was that his rhetoric so reflected his personal beliefs. The viewers at home could taste the authenticity. So could Reagan, who went into a slow burn. "Ronnie," his wife, Nancy, recalled, "was very hurt by the harsh criticism that Tip had leveled."

After ending a nationally televised news conference on June 16, Reagan retook the podium when ABC's Sam Donaldson shouted a final challenge: "Tip O'Neill says you don't understand about the working people, that you have just a bunch of wealthy and selfish advisers."

Reagan growled, "One more," and returned to the microphone. "Tip O'Neill has said that I don't know anything about the working man. I'm trying to find out about his boyhood, because we didn't live on the wrong side of the railroad tracks, but we lived so close to them we could hear the whistle real loud," he said.

"And I know very much about the working group. I grew up in poverty and got what education I got all by myself and so forth, and I think it is sheer demagoguery to pretend that this economic program which we've submitted is not aimed at helping the great cross-section of people in this country that have been burdened for too long by big government and high taxes."

Sheer demagoguery. The ball was back in O'Neill's court. Taking an occasional shot at Reagan was all part of playing the loyal opposition. But staging a public, man-to-man quarrel with an American president was something else. It was time to fight or flee. He could cement his new claim of being Reagan's foil, or retreat to the cloakroom. In the Speaker's office, as the press clamored for a response, his staff was divided. The older hands urged O'Neill to duck it—that it was unseemly to make it personal. "Let it pass, Tom," said Leo Diehl. The younger guys told O'Neill he had to respond. In fact, they relished the opportunity.

"I'm going up to the gallery," O'Neill decided.

"He went into the bathroom, combed his hair, straightened his tie, left the sanctuary of the Speaker's rooms behind," Chris Matthews, then an O'Neill adviser, recalled.

Upstairs, as the camera lights blinked red, O'Neill took the high road, but didn't back down.

"I would never accuse a president, whoever he was, of being a demagogue," O'Neill said. He had "too much respect for the president, for the institution . . . [and] I assume that in the future he would have the same feeling for the Speakership."

But what about Reagan's tax bill? he was asked. "The Reagan program speaks for itself," O'Neill said. "It is geared toward the wealthy."

Reagan phoned the next day to make peace. "Ronnie called him to clear the air, and Tip told him right then, 'Old buddy, that's politics—after six o'clock we can be friends; but before six it's politics.'"

★   ★   ★

The battle raged all summer. "Tip took him on," said Dick Bolling. "Rostenkowski didn't take him on. The rest of them wouldn't take him on. Jim Wright was scared to death of Reagan in 1981. Everybody was running. Tip was getting no support from Democratic chairmen, except the black ones." In late June, O'Neill stirred a United Steelworkers of America meeting, saying Reagan's program was "for the selfish, the greedy, and the affluent." On July 7, O'Neill told another union convention, "Let's face it. This is a callous, right-wing administration committed to repealing the Great Society, the New Frontier, the Fair Deal and the New Deal. It has made a target of the politically weak, the poor, the working people."

He called Reagan "a tightwad" and "a real Ebenezer Scrooge." But "when it comes to giving tax breaks to the wealthy of this country, this president has a heart of gold," O'Neill said.

Two days after the "Scrooge" speech, the Democrats were cheered by a minor miracle—a Democrat beat a Reagan Republican in an offterm congressional election in a GOP district in Mississippi. The party as a whole was doing a little better. An economic "truth squad" was named, with Dick Gephardt as its leader. Gillis Long led the caucus "Committee on Party Effectiveness." Weekly leadership packets were sent to every Democratic member. Democratic administrative assistants and press secretaries met to coordinate their efforts. The whips set up a schedule of one-minute speeches for the floor. O'Neill began to stop for interviews with the TV crews that gathered to catch him as he arrived at the Capitol each day. At the steering committee, Ari Weiss and Jack Lew pioneered the tactic of drawing up "distributional analyses" that measured the effects of each of Reagan's proposals on the middle class, blue-collar Americans, the poor, and other income groups. The Democratic Congressional Campaign Committee began to target the districts of moderate Republicans, especially those whose constituencies had low median family incomes. The Speaker himself sat down with Ways and Means aides and helped draw up the tax tables for a Democratic alternative to the Kemp-Roth tax cut, targeting relief to those who earn/ed $50,000 or less a year.

"They would trot out the wheelchairs, as they always do, and trot out the women with aid to dependent children and all that sort of thing—the poor and the old," Deaver said dismissively. But it was a far different Tip O'Neill who stood on the House floor on July 29, to close debate on the Reagan tax plan. Wright and Rostenkowski had wanted to compromise with the president—perhaps trade some Social Security cutbacks for reductions in Reagan's tax bill. But "in all this, Tip [was] the hardest boulder to budge," Wright told his diary. "He instinctively mistrusts Reagan and his whole crew, wants instead to offer House members a clear choice." O'Neill was trim, well coiffed, and armed with a succinct set of remarks, printed in large type on 4-by-6 index cards. It was the day of Princess Diana's wedding, O'Neill noted. "If the president has his way, this could be a big day for the aristocracy of the world," O'Neill began. "This morning there was quite a royal wedding. This afternoon President Reagan is proposing a royal tax cut."

The Republicans laughed aloud at O'Neill, taunting him with calls of "Vote! Vote!"

"You can snicker. . . . I recognize the breeding," he said, staring them down across the aisle.

"This proposition has no precedent. It is a terrible gamble. If it fails, the consequences for the nation will be horrible. Deficits will soar, inflation will persist, budgets will be cut. Amongst the casualties will be the Social Security program, health care and education programs, and possibly a reduced defense program," he said.

★   ★   ★

"If—as they think likely—our economic policies fail, they could become the ultimate winners," Darman privately warned Reagan. It was a prospect that, amid all the celebrations that summer, was increasingly worrying David Stockman.

The problem was in the math, for the White House was losing its riverboat gamble. As the Washington press corps hailed the victorious "revolution," the nation's financial community was scrutinizing Stockman's balance sheet. Wall Street traders don't believe in rosy scenarios, and wanted to know what cuts would be made to replace the magic asterisk Stockman had inserted to signal "cuts to come." The political victories of the Reagan revolution had not set off the bull market that Stockman had predicted when making his economic assumptions, while over at the Federal Reserve, Chairman Paul Volcker had embarked on a tight-money course to wring inflation from the economy. The bidding wars on the tax and budget bills further fed the tide of red ink. There was no way around it: Stockman needed more cuts. He turned once again to Social Security, where a relatively obscure section of the budget bill did away with Social Security's monthly minimum payment. Stockman thought the benefit was wasteful because it primarily benefited "double-dippers," who could get by quite nicely with their income from other pension plans. And, in truth, the truly impoverished elderly were still fully protected. But in a neat bit of demagoguery, O'Neill and his lieutenants used the abolition of the monthly minimum to fan the glowing embers of that spring's firestorm over early retirement. In a letter to Reagan, the

Speaker attacked the president for promoting "ill-advised, unacceptable . . . unconscionable" cuts in benefits.

"The eighty-two-year-old woman sitting by her television set doesn't hear all the details—what comes through is they're cutting Social Security," Senator Pat Moynihan acknowledged. National seniors' groups staged a rally of 5,000 people at the Capitol. Moynihan and Wright introduced resolutions promising to restore the minimum monthly payment and charging the White House with a "breach of faith." The House passed it by a 405 to 13 vote.

"At the time, I dismissed the vote as a gesture, a symbolic sense-of-the-House resolution. I believed, incredibly, that the 405 stampeding congressmen could be corralled," Stockman wrote later. "Now I see it in a different light. The vote was historically significant: it was the *coup de grace*. If the politicians could not bring themselves to make even that adjustment to Social Security, then the $44 billion magic asterisk was just that: magic."

On August 3, fresh from their summer of legislative triumphs, Reagan and his aides gathered in the cabinet room at the White House for a working lunch, and Stockman showed Reagan the consequence of that summer's victories: they would need from $250 billion to $500 billion in further spending cuts over the next four years, or face triple-digit budget deficits. "Dave, if what you are saying is true," said Reagan, "then Tip O'Neill was right all along."

"Oh, no," said Stockman quickly. Why, he had plans for a "September offensive." But in the Speaker's office, they were planning an offensive of their own.

★   ★   ★

On August 4, as the press continued to sing of Reagan's victories and Stockman and his colleagues paged through their black budget books, earmarking proposed cuts in Social Security, veterans' pensions, food stamps, farm subsidies, mass-transit grants, and other popular federal programs, Kirk O'Donnell delivered an eleven-page memo to his boss. O'Neill would come to call it "The Plan."

"Out of the triumph of the Republican Economic Program, Democrats have some consolation," O'Donnell wrote. "The economy is no longer our burden; it is a Republican economy. The economic program is uniquely Reagan's and his party's. By not choosing to compromise with House Democrats, Reagan has assumed total responsibility." Democratic pollster Peter Hart had identified a soft spot in Reagan's popularity, O'Donnell noted: stagflation persisted, and the voters were getting impatient. The wounded Reagan's heroics of the spring were fading in memory; people wanted results and "solutions, not heroes," said Hart. The Federal Reserve's effort to wring inflation from the economy would only increase the pain of working families. "Republican congressmen have tied their fortunes to Reagan's policies almost without exception," O'Donnell wrote. "It is time to take the offensive."

The first issue that O'Neill confronted was Social Security. Jake Pickle's subcommittee had worked long and hard at being good stewards of the New Deal's brightest jewel. And there was no doubt about it, Pickle was right: Social Security was in trouble. O'Neill's own steering committee analysts had been privately warning him for two years that the main trust fund was in "truly alarming" and "critical" shape and likely to run out of money in 1982. Reagan had shown his willingness to hold hands with the Democrats and make the painful changes that were required to restore the system's solvency. But to save the House, O'Neill needed an issue, and Social Security promised to be one.

"The motives of the administration must remain suspect and their entreaties for bipartisanship rejected," O'Donnell wrote O'Neill. "Democrats need not be defensive or accommodating in our defense of the system. This debate offers a real opportunity to demonstrate the genuine differences between the two parties." Representative Claude Pepper of Florida, champion of senior citizens, also urged O'Neill to exploit the Social Security issue. In a private note, Pepper asked the Speaker to "restrain Jake Pickle's efforts" to strike a deal with the White House. The government could postpone the fiscal reckoning by giving the old-age trust fund a transfusion of money from the system's other accounts, he said. "Opposition to the President's efforts to cut Social Security benefits is rising enormously," Pepper said happily.

And so O'Neill made a far-reaching decision to politicize Social Security, ordering his Democrats to withdraw from the bipartisan alliance with Republican moderates that had guarded the social insurance programs from conservative attacks in the postwar era. For the next twenty years, whenever Reagan or his heirs would mount a fresh offensive on the American welfare state, Democrats would follow O'Neill's lead and cry, "Save Social Security!" or "They want to cut Medicare!"

"O'Neill took Social Security and just drove it home ruthlessly and in some respects dishonestly, but with great effectiveness," Newt Gingrich recalled. From a political standpoint, it was a brilliant short-term tactic. "The Republicans, to this day, haven't gotten over it," O'Donnell said in 1998. "O'Neill and his actions had made an entitlement, probably the most significant New Deal entitlement that exists, untouchable."

Yet Pickle had a point. Social Security was then on an iconic shelf—removed from partisan give-and-take. By folding Social Security and the other social insurance programs into the political mix, O'Neill was exposing them to assault—indeed, daring Republicans to make the attack. The Democratic scare tactics upset senior citizens, exposed the party to the charge of demagoguery, and fed the growing cynicism about politics and government. It all began to look like a game, and Social Security and Medicare became but pieces on the board. "The Republicans will never trust the Democrats again on Social Security," said Lud Ashley. "It was made clear to them, indelibly and lastingly, that this is the third rail and if you touch it you get burned. It will never be anything other now, because nobody will ever trust each other again, and that was almost totally Tip's doing."

★   ★   ★

O'Neill brought the curtain down on Pickle's efforts in typically sly fashion. On September 17, after the House had returned from its five-week summer recess, Pickle was summoned to a conference of war in O'Neill's office. The Speaker "had a cigar and he put it in his mouth and he let Pickle make his appeal," said Jim Shannon, who served on Pickle's subcommittee. "Pickle made a very impassioned speech, saying this is a bedrock issue ... the Democratic Party ... we have to solve this. And Tip didn't say a word. He didn't take the cigar out of his mouth. Twirling it. Puffing it. Pickle finished his pitch and Tip still didn't say anything."

Bolling cleared his throat. "Mr. Speaker, can I say something?" the Rules Committee chairman asked.

"Sure, Dick," said O'Neill.

"Jake, we are all proud of your work," Bolling told Pickle. "But I want to say one thing. As long as I am chairman of the Rules Committee there won't be any Social Security legislation in this Congress."

There was silence for a moment. Pickle looked at Bolling, then to an implacable O'Neill.

"I know when I'm licked," Pickle said.

The Reagan administration was out to "wreck the system," O'Neill told the press when the doors were opened. The Democrats would not cooperate with Reagan's efforts to pare back Social Security. Pickle's subcommittee "does not intend to go forward at the present time," O'Neill said, as its muzzled chairman stood by his side.

For insurance, the Speaker ordered Shannon to serve as a saboteur. "You don't let him move a bill," O'Neill told his young protégé.

"Pickle wants to write the bill. Danny agrees. We're Democrats. We're responsible," Shannon recalled. "But Kirk's view is that Social Security is all we got. I had to spend a year throwing sand in the gears."

Reagan had no hand to hold. The House Republicans lost their stomach for the fight, and sent a message to the president via conservative representative Trent Lott of Mississippi. Without political cover from the Democrats, Lott told Reagan, "not a corporal's guard" would vote for further cuts in Social Security. The Senate caved in next. "Tip O'Neill has blown the prospect of any major Social Security legislation out of the water. We were having quite a lot of success working towards a bipartisan coalition, but after what he said this week, there's just no way to do it," said Republican senator William Armstrong of Colorado, chairman of the Senate's Social Security subcommittee. On September 24, Reagan capitulated. In a letter to O'Neill, the president renounced the assortment of cutbacks he had proposed and called for the establishment of a bipartisan commission to seek a permanent solution. A month later the Senate, following the House's lead, restored the minimum monthly benefit that had been cut in the budget bill.

Stockman's "September offensive" had failed. As the economy slowed under Volcker's tight rein, unemployment rose to 8 percent and interest rates hit 20 percent. The president chose an option from Stockman's briefing papers that was called "Muddle Through." Finally, in mid-October, Reagan admitted the truth. There would be no robust supply side dividend, no 5 percent or better annual growth. The economy was in recession. "The new consensus economic forecast resulted in a budget which showed cumulative red ink over five years of more than *$700 billion*," Stockman said. "That was nearly as much national debt as it had taken America two hundred years to accumulate. It just took your breath away."

. . .

The Speaker's "Plan" now called for Democratic unity and O'Neill's invisibility. At a closed-door caucus in September, the Democratic leadership announced an amnesty for the Southerners who had voted with the Republicans. Then, as committee chairmen fanned out across America to document the effects of Stockman's budget cuts, O'Neill let the recession do his work for him. "Republicans are fighting with Wall Street; Republicans are fighting with themselves—I think I'll sit on the sidelines for a while," he said.

The recession of 1982 was the worst economic downturn since the Great Depression, and the jobless rate rose to 10.8 percent, putting millions of Americans out of work, before it ended in 1983. Many of those jobs never came back. Unlike previous cyclical slowdowns, the soaring interest rates and the ravages of recession gave a final, fatal shove to many American companies and industries, already in deep trouble from Japanese and European competition. In the industrial East and Midwest, a whole way of life ended. No longer could a young man graduate from his hometown high school and confidently follow his father to a $17-an-hour union job, plus overtime, at the local steel mill or auto plant in Allentown, Baltimore, or Youngstown. The new factory jobs were in nonunion plants in the South. The computer boom was still a decade away, and the newly created jobs up North were in the lower-paying service sector. And small businesses were failing at a rate unmatched since 1933.

The press, which O'Neill had repeatedly chided as Reagan apologists in 1981, began to roast the administration with months of headlines and TV news reports about plant closings and layoffs as more than 60 House committee hearings were scheduled, most in major media markets across the nation, in the last three months of 1981. In April, CBS aired a much-imitated Bill Moyers documentary that showed how the cutbacks in federal programs affected the poor, the crippled, and the hungry. The return of a Depression-era phenomenon—homelessness—made an appearance on the network news. Hundreds of local editors sent reporters out in their communities to chronicle the effects of Reaganomics.

"The trouble with this TV story ... was that it bore little resemblance to the real world of budget cuts. For all the furor and anguish in Congress over paring social spending for 1982 by $35 billion, the cuts were hardly apocalyptic," wrote conservative columnist Fred Barnes. "One reason was the cuts were often not cuts *per se;* rather they were cuts from the 'baseline' level of spending for a program. In other words, the program got less than was projected if it had been allowed normal growth."

Reports of a $180 billion budget deficit led to negotiations by leaders of both parties after Jim Baker broke the ice in a secret visit to O'Neill's home on March 20. The negotiators called themselves "the Gang of 17," and their peace talks ultimately led to a face-to-face session between O'Neill and Reagan. The Speaker was willing to negotiate, but under one condition: that the White House be the first to propose any changes in Social Security. "He has to go first. . . . They're trying to set me up," O'Neill warned. The president traveled to the Hill on April 28 and sat down for three hours with O'Neill, Howard Baker, and other leaders in the President's Room, off the Senate floor. The squabbling started immediately, as O'Neill objected to the seating chart, which put him next to Reagan instead of across the mahogany table with the other Democrats. He also demanded that Weiss be allowed into the room, since the president had Jim Baker. The White House then added Stockman and Treasury Secretary Donald Regan to the group; it was quite a compliment to Weiss.

O'Neill was persuaded that the White House just wanted a photo opportunity so that the blame for the resultant deadlock would fall on both parties, and his instincts were correct. Richard Darman's game plan was for Reagan to make a "thoroughly reasonable offer—that O'Neill will nonetheless reject." Indeed, the White House speech-writers had already drafted the president's subsequent speech, blaming the Speaker for slamming "the gate . . . on all those hours and weeks of effort to work out an official, bipartisan settlement."

O'Neill gave Reagan a lecture about tax cuts for the rich, massive deficits, and the historic achievements of the New Deal. "I know you people don't like to hear it, but you're just advocating trickle-down economics," the Speaker said. Nevertheless, the Democrats would accept another $35 billion in domestic spending cuts, O'Neill said.

Reagan responded by blaming the Democrats for waste and taxes and inflation. "Our defense spending as a percentage of the budget is much lower than in John F. Kennedy's day," said Reagan. He cited the Kennedy tax cut as well. "I'm just advocating President Kennedy's program," Reagan said. "We haven't thrown anybody out in the street to die." He wanted $60 billion in cutbacks.

Each side tried to maneuver the other into offering cutbacks in Social Security.

"Mr. President, are you putting Social Security on the table or not?" O'Neill asked.

"You're not going to trap me on that," said Reagan. "I didn't put this proposal on the table."

"It's not coming from us," O'Neill said. Jim Wright offered an alternative deal: the Democrats would accept more domestic spending cuts if Reagan would cut the third year of his tax cut by half, from 10 to 5 percent.

"You can get me to crap a pineapple," Reagan said, "but you can't get me to crap a cactus."

The efforts at reaching a compromise ended. At the end of the meeting the participants shifted uneasily in their seats, wanting to leave but worried that the other side would accuse them of breaking off the talks.

"I think we're all waiting for you to get up, Mr. President," said O'Neill.

"Let's all stand up together," Baker suggested. And so they did.

Reagan addressed the nation on television the following night, claiming that the Democrats wanted "more and more spending and more and more taxes." O'Neill passed out bumper stickers that said, "Vote Democratic—Save Social Security." Bolling was chosen to make the Democratic response to Reagan on television. "The key issue is fairness," he said. "If we are going to have an enormous increase in defense, everybody in the country should help do it—the rich and the poor alike."

. . .

The economy continued to be O'Neill's great ally. In January, an administration analysis of Reagan's tax plan had concluded, "The job creation push of the tax cuts is actually far less than thought and will cause a serious shortfall in new jobs created. Tens of billions of dollars in tax benefits now flow to firms who will make only minor contributions to our jobs goals." Volcker, meanwhile, had succeeded where Nixon and Ford and Carter had failed: by April 1982, the recession brought the consumer price index down to 2.4 percent, and the years of the Great Inflation were over. But after so many years of battling so formidable a foe, the economic policymakers at the Fed decided it was better to be safe than sorry, and the huge budget deficits gave Volcker whatever excuse he needed to keep wringing the economy. He relented only when a series of U.S. bank failures threatened the international monetary system that summer. Reagan had wanted to whip inflation, and get the resultant recession out of the way by the time he ran for reelection in 1984. He would achieve both goals. But for Republican congressional candidates in 1982, the first sign of recovery—that fall's surge in the stock market—came too late.

The recession would not end until 1983, and it savaged Republicans in the fall election season. The downturn brought 20 percent unemployment rates to construction, steel, and other manufacturing industries, and led blue-collar workers to put aside their reservations about abortion, school prayer, or busing and come home to the Democratic party. "Social conservatives are the part of the Reagan coalition which is wavering," one anxious White House memo reported. "Its core is the blue-collar ethnic voter." The Democratic base—labor unions, liberals, environmentalists, minorities, and women—were energized as they recognized the threat Reagan posed.

★   ★   ★

As the 1982 balloting neared, the White House predicted that the Republicans would lose just 8 to 15 seats—about average for the midterm election of a new president's first term. The Democrats needed to pick up 20 seats to regain ideological control of the House chamber. Then a Republican mistake allowed O'Neill to revive the Social Security issue on the eve of the election.

From a reporter, Matthews heard about a Republican Party fundraising letter that asked donors if they wouldn't like to make Social Security a voluntary pension system. O'Donnell urged Matthews to push the story, *hard,* and Matthews wrote and released a statement by O'Neill, calling on Reagan to "repudiate" the idea. The GOP had labored mightily to inoculate its candidates on the issue, with a TV ad campaign that showed a happy mailman delivering Social Security checks "with the 7.4 percent cost-of-living raise that President Reagan promised." Now the Democrats, who had alleged all summer and fall that the Republicans were scheming to cut Social Security benefits, had a fresh hook. Reporters confronted Reagan at a campaign appearance, where he denounced the Democratic charges as a "dishonest canard." The media seized on the controversy, and the story led all three network news shows that night. "They used it against us and killed us with it. Absolutely killed us," Jim Baker recalled. O'Neill campaigned among seniors with a blown-up copy of the GOP fundraising letter, and Democrats across the nation bought TV time that weekend to drive the issue home. The voters went to the polls on November 2 and gave O'Neill an impressive victory. The Democrats picked up 26 seats in the House of Representatives—a total that exceeded both expectations and historical precedents.

O'Neill received the news in his office in the Capitol. "Hi, Mom," he told his wife, Millie, on the telephone. "Everything is going great." He kept track of the won and lost seats on a yellow legal pad, breaking away from the phone at his desk for a plate of beef stew and a Canadian Club and water. "God bless ya," he told Representative Phil Sharp, of Indiana. "You had us scared. It was the old Hail Marys that did it. I guess they work."

"You know," the Speaker told a *Newsweek* reporter, "the good Lord said to Solomon, 'You have great power and beautiful wisdom, what can I do for you?' And Solomon said, 'Give me a heart that hears.' That is what the president doesn't have. I think it's because of the company he keeps. This man is unbelievable. He has forgotten where he comes from."

O'Neill had won elections before. Knowing what to do with such a victory was as important a test. He was determined to use his mandate well. Until the economy fully emerged from its tailspin in late 1983 and the increasing preoccupation with the presidential election year of 1984 closed off most avenues of compromise in Washington, the Speaker had a brief window in which hard times and a chastened Republican Party would give him some freedom to maneuver. In his first honeymoon, in 1977, O'Neill had spent his political capital on jobs, ethics, and energy—important short-term goals, but with little historic importance. The Speaker would use his second honeymoon on a more lasting mission: protecting the legacy of the New Deal and the Great Society.

Reagan feared the worst. "It will be a brand new ballgame; one in which we are not now prepared to play . . . going on bended knee to Tip O'Neill for his support on issue after issue," a White House analysis decided. "Given the previous situation, it would surprise no one if O'Neill told us all to get lost." But O'Neill recognized the limited mandate of the 1982 election. Peter Hart and his other advisers had warned the Speaker that the voters had opted for a "mid-course correction," not a counterrevolution. And though the balloting had brought him a militant group of freshmen, most of whom had run against the excesses of Reaganomics, and many of whom admired his Horatio-at-the-bridge act, they were, by style and philosophy, more akin to Gephardt, Tony Coelho, and the other young Democratic chieftains than to the old-fashioned liberalism of Tip O'Neill. Nor did the Speaker have any illusions that Reagan's postelection offers of accommodation were more than a temporary phenomenon, brought on by the politics of the moment.

So as he assembled his priorities for 1983, O'Neill followed the advice he had given to Jimmy Carter, and kept the list short. First up, the Speaker knew, was relief for the victims of the recession, especially the hard-hit blue-collar families that had returned to the Democratic fold. He promised to "take the offensive for jobs, jobs, and more jobs." With unemployment at 10.8 percent, Howard Baker made the walk from the Senate to the House, cut a deal with O'Neill, and (after Bob Byrd spent some time fuming) joined the Democrats in passing a nickel hike in the federal gasoline tax to pay for a job-generating highway and transit construction bill. The president grimaced but signed the $27 billion gas-tax hike and by March, with Reagan's support, Congress passed a $4.9 billion public works bill as well. A turning point in that debate occurred when Reagan and O'Neill had another verbal brawl in the Oval Office in January. White House aides and congressional leaders watched mutely as O'Neill and Reagan wrangled for forty minutes.

It was "the toughest going-over I've ever heard a president subjected to," Wright told his diary. "The Speaker, asked by Reagan to support the budget request, told the President very plainly that Democrats could not acquiesce in good conscience to this passive acceptance of high unemployment and its attendent evils without making every effort to amend such a budget. Reagan's face grew red and he swore, 'God damn it, Tip, we do care about those people.' But the Speaker was not assuaged. 'It's easy to say that you care but you aren't willing to do anything about it,' he said."

Reagan ultimately turned the meeting over to Regan and Stockman, but before leaving he calmed down, and walked up to O'Neill and said, "Dave tells me we're really not that far apart."

"Clearly the Speaker had scored," Wright wrote.

Next up was the budget, and here the Democrats had several goals: to demonstrate to the voters that they could handle the responsibility; to reduce the size of the budget deficit (which many of the freshmen had used as a campaign issue); to chip away at the Reagan defense buildup; and to sap the administration's ongoing attack on domestic programs. This was no time for liberal self-indulgence, O'Neill told his troops: "We're going to be moderate. We couldn't pass a bill if we go the liberal route."

. . .

After cutting a little bit more from defense and a little bit less from domestic programs than the Republican Senate, the House passed a budget resolution on March 23. O'Neill lost only 36 Southern Democrats and got 4 Republican crossovers in a 229 to 196 victory. The budget called for $30 billion in higher tax revenues, and restored funds to food stamps, Medicaid, welfare, and other social programs. O'Neill won more kudos from the press, and announced that he would run for another term in 1984.

. . .

He had won on jobs and the budget, but the real cornerstone of O'Neill's second honeymoon—and one of his lasting achievements as Speaker—was the deal he struck with Reagan to preserve Social Security. In 1981, when O'Neill had taken the calculated risk to politicize the Social Security debate, his staff and colleagues warned him that the system teetered on the brink of insolvency. Reagan proposed to let a commission led by his economic adviser Alan Greenspan come up with necessary "reforms." O'Neill was wary of a trap, but the quality of the appointees—who included Bob Dole, Pat Moynihan, Claude Pepper, and AFL-CIO president Lane Kirkland—eased his concerns. The Speaker's most important appointee was former Social Security commissioner Robert Ball, O'Neill's personal guru on the issue. For most of 1982, the commissioners struck public poses while their staff researched the problems and drafted possible solutions. "We weren't going to put our head back in that noose, and the Speaker wasn't going to come forward unless the president came forward, and so we just danced around and danced around," Ken Duberstein recalled.

Then, over the course of several weeks following the 1982 election, Greenspan convened a series of secret meetings with Dole, Moynihan, and Ball—and White House staffers Baker, Duberstein, Darman, and Stockman. "Are we going to let this commission die without giving it one more try?" Moynihan asked Dole on the Senate floor, when stalemate seemed all but certain.

Meeting at Baker's house on Foxhall Road in Washington and in other out-of-the-way locations, the small group of negotiators arrived at a formula: any bailout plan would consist of both benefit cuts and tax hikes, on a 50–50 basis. Ball and Baker were the two essential players, for they represented O'Neill and Reagan. From the first days of May 1981, when O'Neill had bludgeoned the GOP over early-retirement benefits, Baker had been determined to neutralize Social Security as a political issue before the president's 1984 reelection campaign. The chief of staff, as Stockman put it, prowled the White House corridors as if armed with a bazooka, ready to blow up any budget proposal that had cuts in Social Security. The major conceptual breakthrough was a trial balloon that Ball proposed: to apply the federal income tax to the Social Security benefits of wealthier recipients. To this the commission added a postponement of COLA raises, acceleration of previously scheduled payroll taxes, and other cost-saving measures. Reagan's victory over inflation had eased the pressure on the trust funds, and Pickle and Rostenkowski—getting revenge for the way O'Neill had taken the issue from Ways and Means—engineered a gradual increase in the retirement age, despite O'Neill's objections. (Physically worn blue-collar workers, the Speaker argued in vain, could not extend their working years as easily as their higher-income white-collar counterparts.) The friction with Rostenkowski was to be expected: the Speaker was spreading the word in the cloakroom that Jim Wright, not Rosty, was his preferred choice as a successor.

The final negotiations on Social Security were held at Blair House, from where the president's aides would shuttle across Pennsylvania Avenue in the frigid cold to brief Reagan, and Ball or O'Donnell would telephone O'Neill—who was playing golf at the Bob Hope Tournament in Palm Springs, California. With Reagan, O'Neill, and Pepper on board, even the powerful senior citizen interest groups

couldn't derail the train. The Speaker rarely attended such ceremonies, but he was there at the White House on a cold April day
when Reagan signed the bill into law. O'Neill had shown a remarkable sense of the moment. Roosevelt's jewel had been saved, for at
least another two decades.

★   ★   ★

With the signing of the Social Security bill the Reagan Revolution
came, with the scratch of souvenir pens, to an end. For the true conservative revolutionaries, those who wanted Reagan to dismantle the
core of the welfare state, the president might just as well have signed
a treaty of surrender. Indeed, Stockman would argue that a brief historic window for radical change had been slammed shut by O'Neill's
ruthless use of the Social Security issue as early as the spring and summer of 1981.

The real Reagan "revolution" was attitudinal. For students of politics and public policy, the Reagan era is a remarkably creative and liberating time—an explosive episode in U.S. history when a
half-century's assumptions and theory were ripped raw and opened
to reexamination. When it ended, Reagan could justly claim to have
ended the nation's drift toward a Western European-style social
democracy. Americans had reaffirmed their love of risk and freedom,
of markets and entrepreneurs. In the twenty years after Reagan's election there would be no new federal agencies or departments; the U.S.
government workforce would shrink; Reagan-Bush appointees to the
Supreme Court would dismantle chunks of the Warren Court's
legacy; and the one Democratic effort to create a new federal entitlement—the doomed push for national health care in 1993—would
lead to a Republican takeover of the House of Representatives. To
win reelection in 1996, Democrat Bill Clinton would promise that
"the era of big government is over." Reagan couldn't have said it better himself.

"If you define the 'revolution' to mean that you are going to eliminate the departments of Commerce and Energy and Education, get
rid of Legal Services and all that, then you can say, I suppose, that

part hasn't gone over," said Jim Baker, in a 1998 interview. "But given his druthers, Tip would never have wanted to see that 70 percent tax rate go down, and we did it. Tax reductions, the impetus to the economy, free trade, the elimination of a lot of regulations, downsizing of government—that is all still working today, and you don't hear anybody out there arguing to go back."

. . .

In no small part because of Tip O'Neill, who staggered against the ropes in the summer of 1981 and bled for the dwarfs and the knock-kneed and the elderly and the rest of those millions of Americans whose voices were stilled by lack of talent or money or education or health or by the color of their skin or their accents or ancestry, the Reagan "revolution" remained attitudinal. Slowly, but largely because this bleeding, pained old man kept hollering "fairness" and "justice" as Reagan pounded him around the ring, the American people stopped to consider those principles, began the long dialogue of democracy, considered what was too costly and what was unfair, and put the revolution on hold.

"There should be no doubt about what experience has demonstrated: The specific ideas necessary to make radical cuts in modern American government consistently fail the test of public acceptability," Dick Darman concluded, after Newt Gingrich's attempt to reprise the "revolution" failed in 1995. "The reality is that the American government is as big as it is, acting in the areas that it does, primarily because a substantial majority of Americans wants it roughly so."

O'Neill may have sensed it, as he huddled in his overcoat on the White House lawn, watching Reagan sign the Social Security bill on a raw April day. It was exactly fifty years since Roosevelt's 100 days. The Democrats' biggest loss during the Reagan revolution was the gravy of the welfare state—the supplements and hikes in benefits that O'Neill and his colleagues had spooned out, with presidential help, during the Nixon, Ford, and Carter years.

Of the $110 billion that Reagan and Stockman had chopped from the baseline budget of the Carter years in their first thirty months in office, about $26 billion was from retirement programs like Social Security and veterans' benefits; $25 billion from public works jobs programs like CETA; $27 billion in welfare payments, food stamps, unemployment insurance, and other income security programs; $18.5 million from Medicare and other health care programs; and $13.7 billion in education and social services. Projected domestic spending had been cut from $1.63 trillion to $1.52 trillion over four years—about 7 percent. Real people had been affected—325,000 families lost their welfare payments, 3 million students lost school lunches, 1 million people lost their food stamps, and 700,000 college students lost guaranteed federal loans. But because the war had been fought over *tightening eligibility* for such things as college scholarships, food stamps, and school lunches, the authorizing legislation remained on the books.

"The budget cuts brought about a halt in the growth of spending on programs for the near-poor and poor," Fred Barnes reported. "They were achieved largely by trimming around the edges. Requirements were tightened and rules were made more stringent. Except for public service jobs (and, eventually, revenue sharing and urban development grants) no major program was eliminated."

It was the near-poor who suffered: the working folk whose incomes were just enough to push them past the federal poverty level or state welfare standard. About 850,000 people, for example, were dropped from the food stamp program in 1981, leaving 22 million recipients, as the food stamp budget dropped from $11.4 billion in 1981 to $11.3 billion the following year. Reagan's budget cuts may have been debatable public policy, in that cutting benefits like food stamps and Medicaid for the working poor may have removed the incentive for staying off welfare, but they were hardly cataclysmic.

The Reagan tax cuts, on the other hand, were indeed revolutionary. They benefited the very wealthy, held the middle class harmless, and penalized the poor. Yet taxes can be raised and adjusted, and were—seven times under Reagan and by congressional Democrats acting in concert with George Bush in 1990 and Bill Clinton in 1993. In the meantime, the muscle and bone—and even some flab—of the New Deal and the Great Society survived.

"All the indications were that 1982 should have been a realignment year. But O'Neill led a strategic retreat that turned into a successful offensive," said O'Donnell. "In the process he probably saved the New Deal welfare state. In the final analysis it is the laws that make the difference. Reagan was able to de-fund some programs, but he wasn't able to de-authorize them. Head Start. Aid to Families with Dependent Children. They stayed and the environmental laws stayed and the Voting Rights Act stayed. Unless you get the laws off the books you do not dismantle the New Deal state."

Much of what Reagan claimed as victories—cutbacks in public works jobs, tax cuts, and increased defense spending—were already features, albeit more modestly, of Jimmy Carter's budgets. In 1980, Carter had promised a 25 percent hike in defense spending, over five years. Reagan was never to cut enough to match the low 20.6 percent spending-to-GNP ratio of Carter's FY 1979 budget, and by the time Reagan left office, and the Congress had finished adding a major tax increase and a host of smaller ones, the percentage of taxes to GNP was just about where Carter had left it.

The Great Society was bruised, yet breathing. And the New Deal? Franklin Roosevelt's legacy was untouched. The souvenir pen in O'Neill's hand was proof. "This is a happy day for America," the Speaker said. He had remembered where he came from. He had kept the faith.

Excerpted from John Aloysius Farrell, *Tip O'Neill and the Democratic Century* (New York: Little, Brown and Company, 2001), pgs. 563–606.

George H. W. Bush

WHAT IT TAKES

"Politics ain't beanbag."
— MR. DOOLEY

The attack ad measures the ruthlessness it takes to win in American politics. At any rate candidates who won't stoop to them usually lose. For most of us viewer/voters, these ads *are* politics. We hate them, and ads like the one run in South Dakota in 2002 showing the face of Tom Daschle, then the Senate Majority leader, morphing into Saddam Hussein make us hate politics. They deplete the morale of democracy. They poison faith as surely as corruption or government lying.

In comparison, what could be toxic about a photograph showing the entrance to New York's Holland Tunnel? Yet that image was the Willie Horton ad of 1928. Its target was Al Smith, the first Catholic to run for president. The photograph helped Herbert Hoover become the first GOP presidential candidate in history to win five states in the Bible Belt South, because it bore the legend, "Secret Tunnel to the Vatican." As many vote *against* as for, and nothing roils the *aginners* like religion and race.

The 1988 presidential campaign between Vice President George H. W. Bush and Massachusetts governor Michael S. Dukakis is memorable only for the "Willie Horton ad," a metaphor for wedge-issue politics at its worst. The ad depicts a line of convicts passing through the revolving doors of a prison while a narrator warns in transparent code: lock up your wives and daughters if Dukakis gets elected, because he will furlough rapists who will rape them—as one of his Massachusetts furloughs did to a Maryland woman. *That* was the soft ad; the hard ad showed a mug shot of the convict, Willie Horton, a black man, leaving the race of his victim to the imagination. With its *Birth of a Nation* iconography, the ad exploits the psychosexual core of American racism. Mounted on behalf of the campaign of George Herbert Walker Bush, it "defined" Michael Dukakis not as the white guy who'd just defeated Jesse Jackson in a string of primaries to capture the Democratic presidential nomination. *That* Dukakis, having whipped the most potent black man in America, stood 15 points ahead in the polls. No, Dukakis as the great white hope had to be replaced by a new image: Dukakis as a dangerously "liberal" governor. Never mind that a Republican governor began the Massachusetts furlough policy or that the federal prison system administered by Ronald Reagan and George Bush routinely granted furloughs. In this excerpt from *What It Takes,* his group biography of the politicians running to replace Ronald Reagan in 1988, Richard Ben Cramer recreates the meeting at the Bush summer home in Maine where George Bush decided to dig his tunnel to the White House.

SCIENCE AT KENNEBUNKPORT

Richard Ben Cramer

The negatives came from Jim Pinkerton, in research. Lee Atwater gave him a file card and told him: "You git me the stuff to beat this little bastard. Ah wancha put it on this card."

The card was three inches by five.

"Use both sides," Atwater said.

Pinkerton came up with seven entries: Dukakis's national defense positions, his record on taxes and spending, the pollution of Boston Harbor, his opposition to the death penalty and to mandatory sentences for drug offenders. . . . The longest entry on the card was Dukakis's policy on prison furloughs—including one case in which a murderer named Horton got a furlough from a Massachusetts pen and attacked a couple in Maryland, raping the woman, stabbing her fiancé.

Pinkerton found out about the case from the question Al Gore asked Dukakis at the New York debate. Pinkerton called up Andy Card, his best Massachusetts source—did he know about this? Card did, indeed. He pointed Pinkerton to the *Lawrence Eagle-Tribune,* which had won a Pulitzer Prize for its investigation of prison furloughs. What shocked Pinkerton was not the incident, but that Dukakis refused afterward to change the policy. Massachusetts was, at that time, the only state allowing furloughs for murderers who had no chance of parole.

"I don't get it," Pinkerton said. "When they find out this thing is all screwed up . . . why wouldn't he change it?"

"You don't know Dukakis," Card said. "You can't tell him anything." Card had served in the Massachusetts legislature. He told Pinkerton how they'd passed a bill to require recitation of the Pledge of Allegiance, ". . . so this guy vetoes the Pledge of Allegiance!"

Pinkerton tucked that onto the file card, too.

To Atwater, this did not require a lot of thought: Bush, Inc., had a candidate who was fifteen points behind—and falling. George Bush had "negative ratings" of forty percent with the voters. Dukakis's "negatives" were only twenty percent. There were two choices: they could work on building a more positive Bush-image . . . or they could stick so much shit on Dukakis's head that his "negatives" would shoot through the roof.

They'd tried for three years to show what a sterling fellow was George Bush.

To Atwater, there was only one choice now.

The day before the white men went up to Kennebunkport for the big Memorial Day sit-down with the Veep, they gathered in a shopping center in Paramus, New Jersey, for a focus group with the sort of voters that Bush, Inc., would have to turn around.

They were suburbanites, forty thousand a year, or better . . . they used to be Democrats . . . but they voted for Reagan . . . now they were for Dukakis.

Why?

Well, he seemed able, middle-of-the-road, nonthreatening. Seemed like a good man, a successful governor, and smart.

The Bush white men watched from behind a one-way mirror. There was a moderator—one of Bob Teeter's ops from Michigan—at a table with the voters.

The moderator told the story of Willie Horton and the prison furloughs. Then he said Dukakis was against the death penalty. Then he said Dukakis was against prayer in the schools. Then he said Dukakis vetoed the bill to require kids to say the Pledge . . .

Within ninety minutes, half the voters had switched to Bush.

★ ★ ★

As the family liked to tell it, George Bush was the calmest hand on deck. Friends were calling from all over the country, wringing their hands and moaning: Why couldn't he *do something?* The Gee-Six were in a lather . . . panicky about Dukakis's lead.

Junior knew that, of course, with his office on the Wing of Power. Hell, he was among them enough to worry, too. He knew all the bad news: the polls, the "internals," the "gender gap," the "negatives." He knew the schedule for the next two months held nothing to help Bush get back on the evening news. Dukakis looked like the centrist statesman in his week-to-week wins over Jesse Jackson. He would hold the spotlight through July, as the Democrats convened in Atlanta. George Bush couldn't even throw his own body around the country to get onto *local* TV. . . . GBFP had spent the legal limit; the travel budget was a hundred thousand *overspent* . . . no one wanted to tell the Veep.

Junior talked to his father, just before Memorial Day. He kept it casual—the normal stuff: Laura's fine . . . the kids . . .

Only at the end, Junior asked: "How are you, Dad? . . . Are you okay with this thing? You think it's all right?"

"Yeah," said George Bush. He sounded surprised by the question. "People don't know who this guy is . . ."

He meant Dukakis. There was no doubt in Bush's mind what the issue would be in this campaign. And also no doubt: Dukakis had no idea about life in the bubble.

That would make all the difference.

"I mean, who is this guy? . . . You've got to remember, Dukakis has never been here before."

★   ★   ★

As Atwater liked to tell it, the focus groups proved they had the silver bullet. Hell, they had enough ammo to perforate Dukakis. And Lee was just the man to make Bush pull the trigger. Lee brought video-tapes of the focus groups to Maine. If Bush could only *see* those voters . . . when they found out how liberal Dukakis was . . . well, he'd have to agree! He'd have to go negative.

Atwater meant to get the whole Gee-Six, present Bush with a blank white wall of consensus: he *had* to attack. Lee had to make sure of Rob Mosbacher. He was the only Gee-Six who had not seen the fo-cus groups. "Ah'm tellin' you, this is *it*," Lee said. "These people were, uh, *stunned* when they started hearin' this shit . . ."

Teeter had the numbers: by his count, Bush was seventeen points down—worse with women. Voters didn't know much about either candidate . . . but they knew what they liked. Bush was behind on the critical "internals," like "leadership" and "able to get things done." Worse, still, most voters described themselves as "conservative," or "somewhat conservative." And when asked which candidate was more "conservative," the majority answered . . . Dukakis!

Lee went to work on Teeter to convince him: Bush had to attack, *now*. They had to drive up the negatives on Dukakis—*now*—or risk falling so far behind that Bush would never catch up. Like Jerry Ford against Jimmy Carter, they could run a *perfect* campaign, and still fall one or two points short. "You gotta tell George Bush," Atwater said. (Lee knew, if Teeter would play ball, Nick Brady would fall into line.) "Ah'll tell 'im th' same thing," Lee said. "But don't you come in there an' fuck me, now!"

Roger Ailes maintained he didn't need the numbers, focus groups, or any high-tech bullshit to prove to *him* what Bush had to do: he had to paint Dukakis as an out-to-lunch-in-left-field *liberal* . . . from the *most liberal corner* (Brookline) . . . of the *most liberal state* . . . who'd never been anywhere, or done anything, that taught him *a single god-dam thing* about the rest of the country. Ailes and Atwater were in agreement on tactics: hit Dukakis, early and often. Atwater thought it was crucial for the race. Ailes thought it was crucial for Bush.

Ailes had divined a fact about the Veep—it came clear while Ailes interviewed Bush for a bio ad. They were talking about World War II, about the bombing run over Chichi Jima. Bush recounted how he saw flames shoot along the wing of his plane, and smoke fill his cockpit.

"Why didn't you bail out?" Ailes asked.

Bush didn't pause, didn't think, didn't blink. "I hadn't completed my mission," he said.

That's when Ailes knew: if you gave Bush that sense of mission . . . the only way you'd stop him, after that, was to kill him.

So Ailes was working on the Veep. "Two things voters have to know about you," Ailes said. "You can take a punch, and you can throw a punch. . . . You're gonna have to make the hit."

By the time they all arrived in Maine, the Gee-Six were collegially, collectively agreed: they would make the case for attack—*right now*. They would come at Bush from every angle, and convince him—or wear him down. Teeter would do the numbers. Atwater would show the ammo—he'd *make* Bush watch those tapes. Ailes would sketch out the language, the ads. Mosbacher would assure Bush that Party surrogates would sing the song. Craig Fuller (Fuller was in!) would make sure the White House hummed along.

All together, they would make George Bush go after Dukakis. It was their only hope! They had to do *something!* . . . They gathered at dinner—the night before their first sit-down with Bush at Walker's Point—and rehearsed their roles. They would not back down! They would all insist! They'd fight all week if they had to.

They didn't have to fight. From his terrace, Bush gazed out at the rocks and sea and said, mildly: "Well, you guys are the experts . . . "

Sure, he'd watch the focus-group tapes.

He didn't mind going after Dukakis.

He didn't need surrogates—he'd do the attack himself.

It was over in five minutes.

True, they sat around most of that day . . . but there was nothing more to decide. On the schedule, there were five more days of meetings in Maine . . . but that would be just blather with the issues groups. The real issues were settled over one cup of coffee.

Atwater was on a plane for D.C. the next day. Lee was triumphant . . . but mystified. He never even had to speak!

What none of the white men could quite concede was that the issue was settled before coffee was served . . . before any Gee-Sixes got to the big house, to tell George Bush what he had to do.

Bush knew what he had to do.

Bush would do what he had to, to win.

If that meant *mano a mano* with Dukakis—so much the better. There, at last, was a message that meant something to Bush:

That guy shouldn't be president!

★   ★   ★

It all went back to the view from that big house. (Maybe it was not entirely coincidence that the course was set at Walker's Point.) All the research, the focus groups, were just detail, to Bush—had nothing to do with the decision. *One look* told Bush all he had to know.

In the view from the Point, Dukakis was *obviously* a little outsider (Who *was* he? Where'd he ever *been?*) . . . who did not know the world, as it was to George Bush.

Dukakis was another one-worlder, blame-America-first, UN, World Court, human-rights *liberal* . . . who was going to *give away the store!*

Dukakis was another put-on-a-sweater, turn-down-the-thermostat, fifty-five-mile-an-hour, five-thousand-pages-of-Energy-Department-regs *governor* . . . who'd try to thin the mixture in the great economic engine.

Dukakis was another brainy tax-and-tinker-technocrat *Democrat* . . . who was going to . . . *screw* . . . *everything* . . . *up!*

Dukakis was . . . *Jimmy Carter.*

That solved a lot of problems for George Bush.

Bush could vow (in fact, he did, while he hosted the press that weekend) that he'd labor to define himself . . . he'd show the country what he believed in ... he'd work like the devil on that vision thing.... But he wouldn't have to. The Bush campaign would not be—could not be—about nothing ... as long as it was about Dukakis. *He* shouldn't be president!

From the moment Dukakis appeared in the bombsight, there would be no lack of mission. Bush would protect the heritance!

If the W-word at the Point was Winning ... if there was only one man to tend the big house ... if there was, in every *good* family, one in each generation who must be steward ... then there must be one to take his turn at the helm of the great ship, and steer it on, unharmed, to the shores of well-being. Bush lived his life to be that man.

There was a line that crept into his speeches, after that weekend. It never got famous, like the catchy bluster of "Read my lips!" ... but people in the crowds would look up when he said it ... there was such an (unusual) air of conviction in Bush's voice.... It came at the end of his praise for Ronald Reagan, how people felt differently about the U.S.A. now ... how different was the economy, the business climate, the tax code ... Bush would praise all these supposed achievements, and then say:

"And I'm not going to let them take it away."

There was the mission! (It wasn't just "me-me-me," after all.) There was the message of the campaign, in one line. And that line made perfect sense to Bush—once "them" became Michael Dukakis.

After that, Bush would do ... whatever it took.

By the time that started to show, the white men had told everybody—everybody who was in-the-know—how they got together (collegially) up in Maine, on Memorial Day, and set the course ... they convinced George Bush.

For the book writers and other keepers of the index entries of History, there were long, loving analyses of the focus groups, the people-meters, the attitude sampling, the ad testing ... the science behind the lightning bolts that leapt from trembling white fingers. There were accounts of the fateful dinner, where the Gee-Six hammered out the crucial consensus, *the attack on Dukakis* ... which they carried, thence, to Walker's Point.

It was all that loving, knowing science that let the newsmagazine savants declare this ... (ta dumm!) ... The Year of the Handler.

It was the handlers describing their dinner.

Of course, Bush had to eat, too ... but there wasn't the same level of science: just a motorcade to Mabel's Lobster Claw ... cheers on the porch ... Mabel made her usual fuss ... got everybody seated, got the Service squared away, and came over to shoot the shit with Bush.

"George, do you know how to potty-train a Greek boy?" She didn't wait for an answer. "Do ka-ka!"

Bush threw his head back and laughed at the ceiling. Then he motioned her close, and asked her, in a near whisper: "What's fourteen inches long, and hangs in front of an asshole?"

Mabel gave him a dirty look. He must have heard that one from her own cook!

"Oh, George, I heard that! ... Dukakis's tie!"

Excerpted from Richard Ben Cramer, *What It Takes* (New York: Vintage, 1993), pgs. 996–1001.

PERMISSIONS

Tom Watson: From *Tom Watson: Agrarian Rebel* by C. Vann Woodward; copyright © 1963 by Oxford University Press, Inc. Used by permission of Oxford University Press, Inc.

Theodore Roosevelt: From *U.S.A.: The 42nd Parallel* by John Dos Passos; copyright © 1930, renewed 1958 J. Dos Passos; reprinted with permission of Lucy Dos Passos Coggins.

James Michael Curley: From *The Rascal King* by Jack Beatty; copyright © 1992 by Jack Beatty; reprinted with permission of The Perseus Books Group.

Herbert Hoover: From *The American Political Tradition* by Richard Hofstadter, copyright © 1948, 1973 by Alfred A. Knopf, a division of Random House, Inc. and renewed 1976 by Beatrice Hofstadter. Used by permission of Alfred A. Knopf, a division of Random House, Inc.

Huey P. Long: Originally appeared in the *American Mercury* magazine in 1949, from Hodding Carter. Reprinted with permission of Hodding Carter III and the Carter family.

Sam Rayburn: From *The Years of Lyndon Johnson: The Path to Power,* by Robert A. Caro; copyright © 1982 by Robert A. Caro. Used by permission of Alfred A. Knopf, a division of Random House, Inc.

Franklin Delano Roosevelt: From *Franklin Delano Roosevelt: Champion of Freedom,* by Conrad Black; copyright © 2003 by Conrad Black. Reprinted by permission of PublicAffairs, a member of Perseus Books, L.L.C.

Eleanor Roosevelt: Excerpt pp. 338–380 (adapted); from *Eleanor Roosevelt, Vol. I: 1884–1933* by Blanche Weisen Cook; copyright © 1992 by Blanche Weisen Cook. Used by permission of Viking Penguin, a division of Penguin Group (USA) Inc.

461

right © 2003 by John McWhorter. Used by permission of Gotham Books, an imprint of Penguin Group (SA) Inc.

Tip O'Neill: From *Tip O'Neill and the Democratic Century* by John Farrell. Copyright © 2001 by John A. Farrell. By permission of Little, Brown and Company (Inc.).

George H. W. Bush: From *What It Takes* by Richard Ben Cramer, copyright © 1992 by Richard Ben Cramer. Used by permission of Random House, Inc.

Every effort has been made to trace or contact all copyright holders. The publishers will be pleased to make good any omissions, or rectify any mistakes brought to their attention, at the earliest opportunity.

PublicAffairs is a publishing house founded in 1997. It is
a tribute to the standards, values, and flair of three persons
who have served as mentors to countless reporters, writers,
editors, and book people of all kinds, i.ncluding me.

I. F. Stone, proprietor of *I. F. Stone's Weekly,* combined a
commitment to the First Amendment with entrepreneurial
zeal and reporting skill and became one of the great independent journalists in American history. At the age of
eighty, Izzy published *The Trial of Socrates,* which was a
national bestseller. He wrote the book after he taught himself ancient Greek.

Benjamin C. Bradlee was for nearly thirty years the
charismatic editorial leader of *The Washington Post*. It was Ben
who gave the *Post* the range and courage to pursue such historic issues as Watergate. He supported his reporters with a
tenacity that made them fearless, and it is no accident that so
many became authors of influential, best-selling books.

Robert L. Bernstein, the chief executive of Random
House for more than a quarter century, guided one of the
nation's premier publishing houses. Bob was personally responsible for many books of political dissent and argument
that challenged tyranny around the globe. He is also the
founder and was the longtime chair of Human Rights
Watch, one of the most respected human rights organizations in the world.

.   .   .

For fifty years, the banner of Public Affairs Press was carried
by its owner, Morris B. Schnapper, who published Gandhi,
Nasser, Toynbee, Truman, and about 1,500 other authors. In
1983 Schnapper was described by *The Washington Post* as
"a redoubtable gadfly." His legacy will endure in the books
to come.

Peter Osnos, *Publisher*